The Legacy of Northrop Frye

This collection of essays by scholars from a wide range of disciplines and institutions pays tribute to the richness, diversity, and significance of Northrop Frye's contributions to culture and society in Canada and around the world.

Alvin Lee and Robert Denham divide the papers into four cohesive sections: 'The Double Vision: Culture, Religion, and Society,' 'Imagined Community: Frye and Canada,' 'The Visioned Poet in His Dreams: Frye, Romanticism, and the Modern,' and 'Dunsinane, Birnam Wood, and Beyond: Frye's *Theoria* of Language and Literature.' The essays consider Frye in relation to Canadian culture, examine his understanding of Romanticism and modernism, and explore and evaluate his contributions to our understanding of literature, criticism, society, and religion. In their introductions, Alvin Lee presents an overview of the central issues, and Robert Denham provides an account of Frye's international presence. The volume also includes a list of Frye's books in their various editions and translations, the libretto of a masque, a poem by Margaret Atwood, and a tribute by Julia Kristeva.

As a text that celebrates the vitality and complexity of Northrop Frye as a cultural and literary critic, this book is ideal for classroom use. It is a valuable addition to the existing work on Frye, and will be of special interest to scholars of Canadian studies, literature, literary theory and criticism, and cultural and religious studies.

ALVIN A. LEE is Professor Emeritus, Department of English, McMaster University. He is the author and editor of numerous books and publications.

ROBERT D. DENHAM is Professor, Department of English, Roanoke College, Virginia. He has published numerous books on Northrop Frye.

The Legacy of
Northrop Frye

Edited by
Alvin A. Lee and
Robert D. Denham

UNIVERSITY OF TORONTO PRESS
Toronto Buffalo London

© University of Toronto Press Incorporated 1994
Toronto Buffalo London
Printed in Canada

ISBN 0-8020-0632-9 (cloth)
ISBN 0-8020-7588-6 (paper)

Printed on acid-free paper

Canadian Cataloguing in Publication Data

Main entry under title:

The Legacy of Northrop Frye

Based on a selection of papers prepared for a
conference held at Victoria University in the
University of Toronto, Oct. 29–31, 1992.
ISBN 0-8020-0632-9 (bound)
ISBN 0-8020-7588-6 (pbk.)

1. Frye, Northrop, 1912–1991 – Congresses.
2. Criticism – Canada – History – 20th century – Congresses.
3. Literature – History and criticism –
Theory, etc. – Congresses.
I. Lee, Alvin A., 1930–
II. Denham, Robert D.
PN75.F7L4 1995   801'.95'092   C94-932017-X

Cover photo: Steve Behal

University of Toronto Press acknowledges
the financial assistance to its publishing program of
the Canada Council and the Ontario Arts Council.

Contents

III. The Visioned Poet in His Dreams: Frye, Romanticism, and the Modern

IV. Dunsinane, Birnam Wood, and Beyond: Frye's *Theoria* of Language and Literature

Preface

The twenty-nine essays, the libretto of an auditory masque, and the poem by Margaret Atwood which comprise the four parts of this book originally were invited for presentation at an international conference, 'The Legacy of Northrop Frye,' held at Victoria University in the University of Toronto on 29–31 October 1992. The essay by Clara Thomas was published in *English Studies in Canada* in a special issue on Frye in June 1993. Several of the other twenty invited papers delivered at the conference, but not included here, have made, or are making, their way into print elsewhere. We are indebted to the fifty talented individuals who gave freely of their knowledge and time to make the three-day meeting in Toronto intellectually stimulating, and who provided rich resources for this book. To the selected papers, we have added a new essay on Frye's international presence, a chronology of Frye's life, and a list of his books.

For their intellectual liveliness, their knowledge of our subject, and their generous work as a planning committee, we thank Joseph Adamson, Margaret Burgess, Eleanor Cook, A.C. Hamilton, Linda Hutcheon, Lila Laakso, Peter Nesselroth, and Jane Widdicombe. For organizational, editorial, and word-processing assistance, all provided cheerfully and without complaint, we are grateful to Shawn Winsor at the Northrop Frye Centre of Victoria University. For preparation of the manuscript in camera-ready form, we thank Sarah Fick at the Humanities Computer Centre of McMaster University and Gwen Peroni of Acappella Business Services.

We are grateful for the alacrity and enthusiasm for this book shown by Ron Schoeffel, the editor-in-chief of the University of Toronto Press. We thank, too, Anne Forte of the Press and Linda Biesenthal for helping to ensure a thoroughly professional response to our efforts.

We record here our gratitude for generous financial assistance for the conference, and so also for the origins of the book, from the following: Victoria University, the University of Toronto, McMaster University, Queen's University, Acadia University, the Centre for Comparative Literature (University of Toronto), the Royal Society of Canada, Lilly Endowment Inc., the George R. Gardiner Foundation, Mary Jackman, the W. Garfield Weston Foundation, James McCutcheon, the Birks Family Foundation, and the Social Sciences and Humanities Research Council of Canada. We particularly thank the Department of the Secretary of State and Victoria University for enabling us to publish a truly new book. It is most fitting that this retrospective and prospective considera-tion of the work of Northrop Frye has attracted so many distinguished sponsors.

A.A.L. and R.D.D.
May 1994

Contributors

Joseph Adamson	*McMaster University, Canada*
Margaret Atwood	*Toronto, Canada*
John Beckwith	*University of Toronto, Canada*
G.E. Bentley, Jr	*University of Toronto, Canada*
Deanne Bogdan	*University of Toronto, Canada*
Margaret Burgess	*University of Toronto, Canada*
J. Edward Chamberlin	*University of Toronto, Canada*
Eleanor Cook	*University of Toronto, Canada*
Paul Cornea	*University of Bucharest, Romania*
Nella Cotrupi	*University of Toronto, Canada*
Robert D. Denham	*Roanoke College, USA*
Sandra Djwa	*Simon Fraser University, Canada*
Michael Dolzani	*Baldwin Wallace College, USA*
Michael Fischer	*University of New Mexico, USA*
Angus Fletcher	*City University of New York, USA*
Jan Gorak	*University of Denver, USA*
A.C. Hamilton	*Queen's University, Canada*
Linda Hutcheon	*University of Toronto, Canada*
Julia Kristeva	*University of Paris, France*
Wladimir Krysinski	*University of Montreal, Canada*
Eva Kushner	*University of Toronto, Canada*
Alvin A. Lee	*McMaster University, Canada*

Monika Lee	*Cornell University, USA*
James Reaney	*University of Western Ontario, Canada*
Imre Salusinszky	*University of Newcastle, Australia*
David Staines	*University of Ottawa, Canada*
Clara Thomas	*York University, Canada*
Helen Vendler	*Harvard University, USA*
Craig Stewart Walker	*University of Toronto, Canada*
Hayden White	*University of California, Santa Cruz, USA*
Thomas Willard	*University of Arizona, USA*
Milton Wilson	*University of Toronto, Canada*
Ross Woodman	*University of Western Ontario, Canada*

ALVIN A. LEE

Introduction

A decade ago in *Centre and Labyrinth* Paul Ricoeur examined what he called 'the order of paradigms' in *Anatomy of Criticism* with the intention of showing how Frye's account of literature takes its place 'on the level brought to light for the first time by Aristotle in his *Poetics*,' which is to say, on 'a higher level of rationality' than the one on which French structuralism proceeds. Ricoeur reasoned that Frye's multiple typologies are part of this first order of intelligibility and that they begin when Frye sets aside on principle every chronological, and therefore every narrative, feature of the structuralists' narratological rationality, in favour of the universals taught by poetry of which Aristotle spoke. To speak, in the second half of the twentieth century, 'of the universals taught by poetry' is to dare to do something beyond the intention or capacities of most educated men and women. But it is what Northrop Frye spent most of his lifetime doing. The rich gathering of essays in this book can be seen as a probing of the implications, validity, and successes or failures involved in that quest.

Although these essays were first brought together for the conference 'The Legacy of Northrop Frye,' held at Victoria University in the University of Toronto on 29–31 October 1992, this book is not a volume of conference proceedings. By design, the intellectual and imaginative program for the conference was both retrospective and prospective, and was intended to address two questions. What is the legacy left by Northrop Frye? And what might, or should, be done with this legacy? The meeting in Toronto was an exciting one, described by one participant as 'what an academic conference should be but almost never is.' It was attended by approximately three hundred people. From among the fifty formal presentations, we have selected for inclusion here twenty-nine essays, the libretto of a masque, and a poem by Margaret Atwood. Although the essays originally were prepared to be read at the conference, they also were written 'to be considered for publication' in a book. A number of them have been revised since, and we have also removed some of the more obvious occasional references. The selection has been considerably reordered and reshaped to encourage internal 'conversations' among the papers and to heighten what was already very evident at the conference, a sense of richly diverse perspectives and materials being brought to bear on the work of one of the great thinkers of our time. But the initial quaternary pattern, suited on more than one level to Northrop Frye as a subject, has remained.

Part I, entitled 'The Double Vision: Culture, Religion, and Society,' is a wide-ranging exploration of Frye's relation to what Ricoeur calls the 'first order of intelligibility.' A.C. Hamilton in 'The Legacy of Frye's Criticism in Culture, Religion, and Society' takes us to something at the centre of Frye's thought, which 'potentially contains everything he has ever said or tried to say.' Hamilton focuses on three recorded visionary moments of identity early in Frye's life, in which he had glimpses 'of a world that may not exist but completes existence, the world of the definitive experience that poetry urges us to have but which we never quite get' (CP, 174). These apocalyptic moments of insight led Frye to a sense of a far greater creative design than is ever found in literature and to a gradual realization of how metaphor and myth, directly experienced, are an extension into life of the ecstatic phase of their own creation. Hamilton suggests that because Frye always speaks through the best in Western culture, through its myths and metaphors, not its ideologies, his criticism will remain challenging and inexhaustible.

From a different perspective, Thomas Willard in 'Archetypes of the Imagination' also approaches the question of the basis or origin of Frye's double vision. Willard shows why at the time of The Great Code (1982) Frye abandoned the term 'archetype' after twenty-five years of defining, defending, and using it. By then he had come to see that too many of the ancient and medieval connotations (including an outdated cosmology) were still inextricably attached to the concept of the archetype for it to continue to be used effectively to inform modern literary criticism. There was another problem: Frye had not been able sufficiently to differentiate his use of the word from Jung's conception of innate, instinctual archetypes. Willard thinks, and there is an interesting question here for further exploration, that there is much more in common between Frye and Jung than Frye acknowledged. Willard suggests as well that, as each of the two thinkers relaxed his earlier scientific, even positivist anxieties, something close to convergence took place between what Frye called the imagination and what Jung meant by the collective unconscious.

Hayden White has called Frye the greatest natural cultural historian of our time. In his 'Frye's Place in Contemporary Cultural Studies' he explores and illustrates Frye's 'brilliance as a theorist of culture and renovator of humanistic studies in the second half of our century.' White likens Frye to Vico, Hegel, Marx, Nietzsche, Freud, and Weber as a thinker who learned to see dialectically. Because he was able to apprehend continuities and interanimations rather than oppositions, Frye was able to develop a theory of historical change, and of cultural/literary change, in which what is repeated or recollected from the past is re-created and awakened to new life.

Two of the other writers in Part I, Craig Stewart Walker and Margaret Burgess, probe in some depth the often enigmatic dimensions of Frye on the subject of religion. Walker, in 'Religious Experience in the Work of Frye,' sees him as one of a number of twentieth-century thinkers who address the problem of how to account for human identity in ways that make sense of spirituality but do not repudiate reason, so that human freedom and self-determination remain possible. Like Hamilton, Walker selects three crucial experiences early in Frye's life and shows both how they are 'religious' and how they lead to a general outlook that pervades all aspects of Frye's thought.

Burgess, in 'The Resistance to Religion,' addresses a question that has bedevilled numerous students and readers of Frye over the decades: Is he in fact religious at all and, if so, how? Part of the problem – as Frye himself shows in the introductions to *The Great Code* and *Words with Power* – is the anxieties in the contemporary academy about religion, including whether questions about it can even be taken seriously by educated, thoughtful people in the twentieth century. In addition, there are the worries of those who are defensive about orthodox beliefs or the authority of religious institutions. But as Burgess points out, to an extent not done before, there are three other, deeper reasons why on the matter of religion Frye has been a puzzle to many. One was his 'extreme reticence in the face of any direct discussion of his personal beliefs.' The second, connected no doubt to the first, was his mode of teaching, which was modelled on the dialogic method of Socrates, on the exercises in paradox of the Zen Buddhist koan master, and on the parables of Jesus. Finally, and here Burgess's account is filled with insight, there is the 'deeply ingrained cross-cultural taboo against the direct articulation and sharing of the most profound spiritual knowledge and experience.' Even with Frye's startling, almost naked exposure of himself as both natural and spiritual man in the posthumously published *The Double Vision*, a large part of the story of Frye and religion is only now beginning to be apprehended and told. One of the useful ways in which Burgess helps move this process forward is systematically to draw out for the first time the frequent analogies indicated by Frye himself between central insights in the mythological framework of Western culture and key conceptions in Zen Buddhism, Taoism, Vedanta, and Yoga. There is a rich area here for further study and thought. It is important that this work be done to ensure that Frye will not be absurdly and prematurely categorized and confined in minimally descriptive terms like 'Canadian Methodist' and 'clergyman' and that, more important, his most profound teachings can be put to work in identifying and illuminating real connections or interanimations among the cultures of the world. The main achievement of Burgess's paper may be that she has begun to show how Frye's legacy has as much to do with Lhasa, Benares, and Nara as with Jerusalem, Athens, Paris, and London, or with Moncton, Toronto, and New York.

Imre Salusinszky, Deanne Bogdan, and Michael Dolzani take us into the social dimension of Frye's thinking about culture and religion. In 'Frye and Ideology' Salusinszky concludes that it is because Frye places beside his 'myth of concern' a 'myth of freedom' that he is able to articulate a criticism capable of liberating literature from ideology. In this, he is unlike the practitioners of cultural materialism, cultural studies, and cultural poetics; he is able successfully to follow a middle way between social determinism, on the one hand, and aesthetic indeterminacy, on the other. He always recognizes the tension that exists between the social function of literature and its aesthetic integrity and is able to write successfully about both. In a complicated sense, Frye is a liberal humanist whose legacy 'is bound up inextricably with the destiny of the liberal mind.' Later in this book Jan Gorak 'reads' a different Frye, who is not a liberal (however complicatedly so) but a man like Kierkegaard living on 'the dangerous edge of things.'

In 'The (Re)Educated Imagination' Bogdan provides an autobiographical account of her initiation into, separation from, and return (with a difference) to Frye's conception of the educated imagination. From a postmodern feminist perspective, her response to what she calls Frye's 'quasi-mystical double vision of a perfectly integrated humanity' is that this vision is deficient, that 'the excluded initiative of the educated imagination,' as Frye has described it, 'is the silent Beatrice.' To fill this absence a 'reconfiguration' is needed, one that truly overcomes 'the gendered hierarchy between subject and object' by instating a (re)educated imagination capable of seeing 'from below.'

In 'Wrestling with Powers: The Social Thought of Frye' Dolzani argues that Frye's true legacy lies in his conception of the order of words, a completely noncanonical, democratizing idea capable of providing a model for a badly needed and greatly expanded social vision. For Frye literary theory and social perspective are two versions of the same thing; since language is the home of human life, a theory of society has to start with a theory of language and its various functions. It is this radical symbiosis (my term not Dolzani's) that underlies Frye's intense social concerns and impels him, near the end of his life, in Words with Power, to a very significant revision of his account of language.

Part II 'Imagined Community: Frye and Canada,' shows how Frye, whose sense of an audience was never provincial or nationalistic, did play a central shaping role as a major, direct participant in the development of Canadian culture. Linda Hutcheon, in 'Frye Recoded: Postmodernity and the Conclusions,' takes as her main texts Frye's Conclusion to each of the two editions of Literary History of Canada (1965; 1976), to which she brings a full array of postmodern perspectives. She points to a tension in Frye between what she sees as his dominantly modernist, humanist approach to literature and culture and his 'postmodern' willingness to study Canadian literature primarily as a part of Canadian life rather than as part of an autonomous world of literature.

James Reaney, in 'The Inheritors Read the Will,' initially steps back from more than four decades of working – as a poet, playwright, and teacher – with Frye's ideas and asks, 'what absolutely minimal group of words could be used to express what Northrop Frye has given us?' The words he comes up with – for the legacy of the critic who once described himself as thinking in metaphors, as poets do – are 'stories,' 'metaphor,' and 'Word.' From there, Reaney takes us through a metaphorical exploration of the idea that stories account for the different shapes of societies and that in our civilization we get the big problems wrong because we start out by getting the apparently little ones wrong, such as how to produce a great play like Macbeth or how to read the Bible in a visionary local way.

Sandra Djwa, in 'Forays in the Bush Garden: Frye and Canadian Poetry,' brings to light from her interviews with Frye biographical material about his early career at the University of Toronto. Her main interest is his relation with E.J. Pratt but she would reverse what has become the usual view of this friendship: that Frye honoured Pratt with his attention. She suggests instead that Pratt played a very significant role in the development of Frye's critical ideas, even that Pratt's poem 'The Truant' 'provides the argument' for chapter 1 of Fearful Symmetry. Milton Wilson, in 'Frye as Reviewer of Canadian Poetry,' probes into another little-discussed part of Frye's theory, what Wilson calls 'that pseudo-Aristotelian *melos-lexis-opsis* scheme which is the lead-in to Essay 4' of *Anatomy of Criticism*, and shows how basic it is to Frye's reviews of Canadian poetry, 'even if the terms themselves are not used.'

David Staines, in 'Frye: Canadian Critic/Writer,' approaches Frye's Canadian studies 'as a corpus of a writer' who consciously chose criticism as his creative mode and whose Canadian writings occupy a significant, unique place in his total work. The work on Canadian subjects produced a total of ninety essays, editorials, and reviews, which Staines divides into three periods: from 1939 to 1950; the 1950s; and the last decades. For more than fifty years Frye was continuously active 'giving a voice to his land' in a series of commentaries, addresses, and essays that embody a vision of Canada, its history and its culture, as well as his own hope for the future of a tolerant, cosmopolitan country which still needs, in part, to be imagined into existence. It should be noted that the three periods identified by Staines are those same ones in which Frye's main intellectual energies were going into the writing and re-peated rewriting of his three 'encyclopaedic' works – *Fearful Symmetry*, *Anatomy of Criticism*, and the Bible books. These two parallel writing careers, that of the Canadian and that of the critic of world literature or philosopher of culture, may be separable for discussion but they are one. It is this fusion that leads the distinguished senior scholar and Canadian-ist Clara Thomas, in 'Celebrations: Frye's *The Double Vision* and Margaret Laurence's *Dance on the Earth*,' to describe all Frye's work as 'an unbro-ken line of illumination,' in which the Canadian writings have an inte-gral place inside a splendid and 'ultimately unified literary enterprise.'

Part III has a bipolar subject: on the one hand, the profound, shaping influence on Frye of the literature and culture of the post-Renaissance period and, on the other, his own understanding and critical account of what that culture was and is. While reading this part, however, with its metaphorical title from Shelley's *Queen Mab* – 'The Visioned Poet in His Dreams: Frye, Romanticism, and the Modern' – it should be remembered that Frye wrote about many things beyond post-Renaissance culture. Al-though there is no prolonged study by him of any part of the philosophy and literature of the ancient and medieval worlds, he knew them and said many penetrating things about them. There is also a 'Renaissance' Frye, who did write extensively on sixteenth- and seventeenth-century texts, including four books on Shakespeare, one on Milton, and numer-ous articles on Renaissance topics, and whose *Anatomy of Criticism* con-tains 204 references to Shakespeare. Frye's was a mind that dared, in an age of ultra-specialisms, to embrace a wider range of cultural products, both Western and non-Western, than is normal among even the most learned of us late in the twentieth century. He was a polymath who began reading at the age of three, who read and thought constantly, and who seemed to retain in his astonishing personal memory theatre everything he had read. His mind processed whatever it encountered, from advertising slogans on a Toronto subway train to Dante's theory of the polysemous interpretation of texts. A book like this can go some distance in recognizing that extraordinary breadth of experience, and the intellectual, imaginative, and spiritual energy that drove it, but it is by no means possible to cover the whole achievement here, especially Frye's particular studies of individual authors and historical periods.

In 1983, thirty-six years after the publication of *Fearful Symmetry*, Frye told an audience at the Art Gallery of Ontario that his chief aim in writing the book 'was to remove the poet Blake from the mystical and occult quarantine that most commentators assigned him and put him in the middle of English literature, which is where he belongs and where he said he belonged' (*EAC*, 62). In 'Blake on Frye and Frye on Blake,' G.E. Bentley, Jr, uses bibliographical and biographical materials to delineate and dramatize this core part of Frye, giving special attention to the thirteen-year agonistic experience of writing *Fearful Symmetry*, and also to the book's extraordinary continuing impact on Blake studies and well beyond.

Monika Lee, in 'Shelley's *A Defence of Poetry* and Frye: A Theory of Synchronicity,' explores an important connection between Frye and English Romanticism, which for obvious reasons is much less well documented than the one with Blake. She does not set out to establish influences between Shelley and Frye, in either direction, though clearly she recognizes a literary historical relationship. Instead the focus is on the 'strikingly synchronous' way in which Shelley and Frye hold to the view, in Frye's terms, that 'literature is a human apocalypse, man's revelation to man, and criticism is not a body of adjudications, but the awareness of that revelation' or, in Shelley's words, that 'Poetry is indeed something divine.' Because Frye's account of the four narrative *mythoi* favours romance (the narrative of desire) as the foundation of myth, he credits the Romantic perspective with a reality rarely given it by critics, in Shelley's time or since. Both Shelley and Frye articulate theories of language 'that can be readily comprehended by those who understand metaphors to be more real than the assumptions they illustrate.'

Many of us with specialist knowledge of particular areas of literature are aware of the way Frye's synoptic, wide-ranging critical intelligence, often working at one or more removes from particular texts, can seem to

Alvin A. Lee

distort them or say things about passages in them that a more minute, close-up reading might repudiate. We know that even Homer nods, and so does Frye, according to Helen Vendler in 'Frye's *Endymion*: Myth, Ethics, and Literary Description.' She finds error and misreading in his commentary on Keats's *Endymion* but also shows how, because of his 'readerly experience' of Keats's greatness, he is led beyond the limitations of understanding that his own 'ethics' and critical disposition try to impose on the poem.

Joseph Adamson's essay, 'Frye's Structure of Imagery: The Case of Eros in the Poetry of William Carlos Williams,' illustrates how 'Frye's work provides the larger framework in which the imagery of an author's poetry, particular as it may be in its details, takes on the coherence of a total structure.' As probably Frye himself would have done had he written extensively about Williams's poetry, Adamson locates his subject in the global context of erotic imagery in Western culture, the one established in Genesis. This involves an archetypal cluster of garden-eros images described repeatedly by Frye throughout his career, but perhaps most fully in 'Second Variation: the Garden' in his late book *Words with Power*. With the help of Adamson's essay it is important to observe how Frye, among his perennial interests, stays with this archetype (it is also significant in the main argument of *The Great Code* and in the posthumously published *The Double Vision*); but as he does so, he develops a deeper understanding of it and a heightened sympathy for environmental and feminist imperatives.

Michael Fischer, in 'Frye and the Politics of English Romanticism,' finds it curious that English departments in American universities currently engaged in disputes about theory and 'the canon' so seldom cite Frye, who advocated many of the values that both theorists and antitheorists claim to be affirming, such as freedom, diversity, and democratic openness. Fischer reexamines what he calls Frye's 'residual anarchism,' his commitment to the individualizing of society inherited from the English Romantics, and sees in this commitment both kinship with recent theorists and distance from them. In Fischer's view, Frye is successful in achieving a 'pragmatic recuperation of objectivity,' which allows him – unlike those for whom all ideologies or beliefs can never be more than social constructions – critically to examine his beliefs (his myth of concern) even while holding them.

J. Edward Chamberlin, Paul Cornea, and Wladimir Krysinski all consider Frye in relation to the word 'modern' – either reading him as someone who articulates essential elements of the modern or as an astute describer and critic of it. In 'Mathematics and Modernism' Chamberlin focuses on the analogies drawn at different points in *Anatomy of Criticism*, especially in the closing pages, between the hypothetical languages of literature and mathematics. He sees in these relatively little discussed passages 'essential modernism, and quintessential Frye.' By this Chamberlin means that, in all these comments on mathematics and literature, the reader is drawn close to the central concerns of modernism: the autonomy of art; its self-reflexive language and self-contained logic; and its disinterested irrationalism, 'which gives it its power not just to change the way we see the world, but to change the world itself.'

Paul Cornea is an Eastern European scholar who first encountered the mind of Frye in the early 1970s. While on a trip to Montreal at a particularly dark time in Romania's history, he read *The Modern Century* and found it 'a great comfort' because it helped him realize 'that the fundamental landmarks of free thinking go on subsisting.' Since *The Modern Century* is arguably the darkest and least optimistic of all Frye's writings, there is food for thought in Cornea's contention, in 1992, 'that the great historical changes recently undergone' in Eastern Europe increase the book's diagnostic force.

For Wladimir Krysinski, Frye and Bakhtin are the two figures in the history of modern criticism who never relinquished wisdom in acquiring knowledge. In 'Frye and the Problems of Modern(ity)' Krysinski suggests that, so far as Frye is concerned, his irony and wisdom probably were weapons that protected him against the slogans of avant-garde modernity. Noting that Frye prefers the terms 'modern' or 'modern century,' Krysinski finds no systematic research into modernity in Frye's critical writings, but he sees *The Modern Century* as 'a discourse which paradoxically announces both the crisis of modernity and the coming of postmodernism.' In doing so, it anticipates Habermas's description of the malaise of modernity as an 'incomplete project.' As well, in its penetrating critique of the modern and its metanarratives, 'this highly political and critical book' anticipates Lyotard's *The Postmodern Condition*, which did not come until twelve years later. But even with these postmodern intuitions, Krysinski says, agreeing with Hutcheon, Frye cannot be called a postmodern thinker because, however darkly or ironically, he still holds to the hope of 'genuine human life.' This guarded optimism is in contrast to the postmoderns who, in Krysinski's view, 'have correctly understood the fact that after Auschwitz and after some other inhuman episodes in so-called human history the ideal of "genuine human life" cannot be realized.'

Part IV, entitled 'Dunsinane, Birnam Wood, and Beyond: Frye's *Theoria* of Language and Literature,' takes the metaphorical part of its title from the references to *Macbeth* in Reaney's essay in Part II ('Let every soldier hew him down a bough') and less directly from a statement about Frye in Angus Fletcher's 'Frye and the Forms of Literary Theory': 'He not only watches the forest as well as the individual trees; he watches to see what lies beyond the forest.' The subject of Part IV is Frye as a great thinker, shaper of a metacriticism or *theoria* of language and literature that has given new perspectives on the whole range of human culture. This part of our book begins theatrically, with a lively invitation from composer John Beckwith and poet-playwright Reaney to imagine ordinary noises heard by Frye in Moncton and Toronto in the early part of a life that extended from 1912 to 1990. This imagining leads to a consideration of how in the 1920s the sound of a train whistle, the soft tinkling of bicycle spokes, a singer's voice battling through the scratching static of early radio, and the sound of a typewriter all gave way in a highly formative imagination to Purcell's *Golden Sonata*, Mendelssohn's *Song without Words*, and Mozart's *Clarinet Trio* K.498, and so led to an understanding of the rudiments of music and, in due course, to the structural rhythms of literature. In his essay Fletcher recalls how in *Anatomy* Frye 'discovered in literature the seemingly endless sources of symbolic energy' and made clear that it is literature's two central processes, myth and metaphor, that deliver this energy, which otherwise would remain bound up and unreleased in the inert language of the dictionary. *Anatomy* treats literature 'as a kind of nature, a living system, a vital nexus,' and the task of theory becomes one of isolating the myriad ways in which literature aptly expresses the whole range of human desire and frustration. Fletcher finds in Frye's 'featural' and 'motivic' criticism a kind of 'musical, polyphonic analogizing' (positioned within Blakean visionary purposes) which concerns the very nature of theorizing, every bit as much as the nature of literature. Like Bach musically, and Borges verbally, Frye 'invents fables and myths of our mental capacity to perceive linkages between widely and even wildly remote parts of a symbolic or actual world.'

Nella Cotrupi's '*Verum Factum*: Viconian Markers along Frye's Path' identifies 'jarring contradictions' in Frye's acknowledgments of his debt to Vico and then examines the ways in which the two thinkers 'interrogate the social and epistemological implications of the *verum factum* principle.' It is this principle that leads both men to try to come to terms with human nature and its distinctive relation to the rest of the given cosmos, and so to focus on the products of human creative activity, on culture, on what Frye calls 'the total body of imaginative hypothesis in a society' (*AC*, 127). In both Vico and Frye there is a concentration on metaphorical language that is profoundly connected with the *verum factum* conception: the operation of metaphor is 'the originary process' that allows human beings, in Cotrupi's words, 'not to discover or uncover the world but to call it into being ... from the raw data of sensory perception.' In their deep realization of the centrality of language in culture, and of the constructive possibilities of illusion in recreative *praxis*, Vico and Frye are unlike the many postmoderns who, once they have recognized the metaphorical and hypothetical nature of language, end up seeing language as 'a prison house' that cannot be escaped.

There has been a good deal of confusion about Frye's view of history, and of literature in relation to history. A number of the essays touch on this subject but two in particular bring it to the fore: Hayden White's paper in Part I and Eva Kushner's 'Frye and the Historicity of Literature' here. Kushner's essay shows how Frye finds literary history useful and necessary for understanding the literary work in its own time and place but accurately observes that his main interest is in the ever-renewed life of the work in its new setting: 'every new appropriation makes cultural history in its own time and place.' This is because, in Frye's words, the 'culture of the past is not only the memory of mankind, but our own buried life, and the study of it leads to a recognition scene, a discovery in which we see, not our past lives, but the total cultural form of our present life' (*AC*, 346). Kushner's paper reminds us that Frye does assert historicity, a historicity that is specifically literary, and that he in no way denies the multiple cultural specificities for which his system (her word not his) is supposed to account.

Jan Gorak, in 'Northrop Frye and the Legacy of Communication,' takes up a conversation with Salusinszky, Fischer, and Dolzani. He defines his subject as two separate channels of communication in contemporary societies: one, expressed in Frye's concept of literature as a supreme fiction, central both to the integrity of 'the inner mind' and to a visionary mission of human liberation; the other, the rule-bound, predictable, coercive communications of the media, especially eletronic ones, through which the legal, religious, commercial, and political transactions of modern societies take place. It is this latter channel, powerfully described by Frye in *The Modern Century*, through which the monoliths of coercive order may have the capacity to form a total environment in which nothing real or genuinely human is left to be communicated. Gorak, disagreeing with Salusinszky's use of the term 'liberal' to describe Frye and with Fischer's phrase 'residual anarchist,' points instead to a revolutionary Frye who, unlike literary critics earlier in this century, came to see that the social or cultural dominance of rhetorical, dialectical communication is not necessarily an unfortunate mistake, and that the real task for criticism is to explore the relationship between the world of visionary desire and the cycle of rhetorical exchange. This is an emphasis in the late writings of Frye, also identified by Dolzani, which so far has received little attention; if delved into, it could renew or strike up illuminating conversations with postmodern theorists who have ignored or dismissed Frye as an old-fashioned critic wedded to an outdated metanarrative.

Ross Woodman, in 'Frye, Psychoanalysis, and Deconstruction,' tries to catch a glimpse of Frye the 'introspective thinker' (whom Frye kept well in the background), as a way of understanding and explaining how the radically different working assumptions about the origins of literary language of Frye and deconstructionist thinkers (Derrida, Lacan, Kristeva, and de Man) do not preclude complementarity and interpenetration between the two kinds of criticism. Because of its Freudian roots and its emphasis on the materiality of language, deconstruction opens up a contesting of Frye's logocentric view of literary language as the mythical and metaphorical displacement of the Word, ultimately answerable to the Word. Woodman cites Kristeva as an example: she describes the dismemberment within poetic language as the traces of the mother's body, which she calls semiotics, and sees the Logos as being subverted and overthrown. But, Woodman concludes, deconstruction does not overthrow the logocentric system. Rather, it 'releases it from the closure which otherwise as system continues to threaten its ongoing life.' Readers of this book will find it useful to bring to Woodman's essay Kristeva's own statements about Frye's criticism, in the last essay in this collection.

'The Function of Riddles at the Present Time' by Eleanor Cook relates Frye's theory to deconstruction from a quite different vantage point. Cook is interested in the fact that, although deconstructionists deeply mistrust most rhetorical figures, they 'adore,' 'desire,' and 'remain faithful to' riddle or enigma. 'Enigma is to deconstruction what metaphor is to so-called logocentrism.' Cook's purpose is 'to outline a proposed anatomy of the enigma or riddle, considered as masterplot.' This involves recognition of the major difference between the Oedipal riddle beloved of Freudians, which moves downward to darkness, and the Pauline riddle, which ends in revelation, light, and the clarifying of the obscure. Cook agrees with many others that Frye's criticism is a romance or quest, but she goes one step further and sees its masterplot as this Pauline riddle. She recognizes that it is no longer easy for criticism either to see authority in the masterplot or to imagine alternative end-directed readings. Still, like Gorak, Dolzani, and others, she reasons that, living as we do in a world in which 'knowledge about means increasingly outstrips wisdom about ends,' criticism might think again about masterplots. In this task no body of work would help more than that of Frye.

It will come as a surprise perhaps that the last essay in this book, Julia Kristeva's 'The Importance of Frye,' is a strong affirmation of the importance of Frye's criticism for contemporary literary theory and for Kristeva's own work. Although, as she says, everything separates her from Frye – age, social and political experience, sex, technical interest, and a linguistics for the materiality of language and its unconscious logic – she is convinced that Frye's three encyclopaedic works have major significance, and she says why they have. She herself read *Fearful Symmetry* in the late sixties, while trying to get beyond formalism and structuralism, and was struck by the way Frye's inclusion of the poetic texts of British literature within the biblical tradition which nourished it makes possible a criticism focused on relationships and symbolic models. This enterprise confirmed for her what at that time she had proposed under the term 'intertextuality.' Frye's second major work, *Anatomy of Criticism*, inspired strongly by Aristotelian terminology, can, in Kristeva's judgment, make criticism seem excessively ambitious but only in this way can it come near to the extraordinary polysemy of literary art. She recognizes that the different modalities of criticism described in Essay 2 of *Anatomy* can be contested or added to, but she welcomes the fact that Frye brings them together, thus breaking down the habitual technical compartmentalization of contemporary literary theory and opening the way 'to a competent interdisciplinarity.' She goes further, and sees Frye's emphasis on the archetype – as a means of linking one poem with another and thus integrating literary experience – as an ethical requirement: so that we will not lose the content that carries the rhetorical play; so also that we can anchor this content in the Western metaphysical tradition and see how our literature is contrapuntally inseparable from Western religion and philosophy. From this emphasis Kristeva moves logically to strong support of Frye's spiritual aspiration in *The Great Code*, to his attempt to preserve, through the richly diverse literatures over the centuries, both the biblical evangelical message and the tradition of Greece and Rome. This aspiration of Frye, this valorizing of cultural memory and probing of the roots of our civilization, Kristeva sees as 'the primordial task of literary criticism.'

Frye recognized that we are all products of our social conditioning (our ideologies), but throughout his life he searched for ways that we might ground our study of culture on something more than ideology. He provided incisive intellectual analyses of particular ideologies (applied mythologies), but he himself cannot be contained or fully explained within any one conceptual or theoretical formulation. He realized of course that his own work was a 'social construction,' that what he wrote about was deeply influenced by his roots in a Western tradition, a Canadian tradition, a dissenting low-church tradition, a university tradition, a musical tradition, and any number of other traditions that made him what he was. But no one fought more mightily than he to prevent the products of our culture from being seen simply as counters in an ideological warfare. It was important to him to demonstrate that not everything can be reduced to ideology. To the question of whether there is anything beyond or behind ideology, anything other, that is, than the social and psychological and political anxieties that usually emerge in criticism, his answer was a resounding yes. Much of his writing in his last decade was an effort to say what this is. The most extended form of his answer is set out in the first half of *Words with Power*, in terms of what he calls the modes of *langage*. Here, and in the posthumously published *Double Vision*, he revises significantly what he said on the theory of language as recently as *The Great Code* (1982). Several of the essays in this present book provide illuminating entries into this still largely unexplored part of the Frye legacy.

For Frye, literature and the language of the imagination were primary to all other forms of expression. Since, moreover, literature is a field not of conflicting arguments but of interpenetrating visions, endlessly inventive and various in the recreation of perennial human stories and desires, it invites a comparable flexibility and comprehensiveness from criticism. It was Frye's hope, by no means realized in his lifetime, that criticism – the consciously organized intellectual and imaginative understanding and use of literature in the transforming of human lives and societies – would not fragment and disintegrate into warring schools of self-absorbed specialties. He was aware that it might seem 'the height of absurdity' to hope for 'a larger perspective that the assumption of coherence for criticism as a whole could give,' but – and this is a matter not addressed directly in any of the essays in this book – he was convinced that 'a consensus does exist in criticism,' even though it is largely concealed by the dialectical divergences and pluralistic tendencies working themselves out among the contemporary schools (*WP*, xviii–xix). The clue to recognizing such a consensus, I suggest, lies in the growing realization among many critics that the different schools of criticism all have their blind spots, inadequacies, and limitations, and that these are analogous to what Frye, in his account of the different modes of verbal language, calls 'excluded initiatives.' In other words, we may be arriving at a stage – the Frye of *Words with Power* thinks that we are – in which there is a growing sense of a need for an overarching *theoria* that can find a place for a multiplicity of critical theories.

Although it is not likely that all the contributors to this book would agree that there is such a consensus, or even that it is desirable, it seems to me that all of them without exception have responded positively to the extraordinary catholicity and freedom of thought and imagining that is characteristic of Frye. Collectively, they bring to their accounts of him a very wide range of descriptive terms but, even as they do so, they do not claim adequacy for any of the terms used, and none of them pretends fully to have understood or described the whole legacy of Frye. Rather, there is a pervasive sense that the writings of this man are at once so wide in their reach and implications, and contain so many brilliant insights and nuggets of wisdom aphoristically expressed, that they will need to be returned to over and over again. Above all, perhaps, and this would please Frye, there is a feeling in most of these essays that the work to which he devoted his life is by no means done, that human civilization and even the survival of our species are precarious at best, and that creative responses in the form of powerful new visions and formulations are radically necessary.

The story of Frye's life contains many elements and can be told in numerous ways. Whatever shape the particular telling takes, it must give prominence to three major intellectual adventures he involved us in – *Fearful Symmetry* (1947), *Anatomy of Criticism* (1957), and the Bible books, *The Great Code* (1982) and *Words with Power* (1990) – for it is around these heroic efforts that Frye's many other writings gather, like so many preliminary or retrospective skirmishes in a tale whose protagonist's monster-slaying comes to three prodigious climaxes. It is perhaps appropriate, then, while examining the ways in which Frye would have us recreate the verbal treasures of our legacy, to remember one particular image from the last, most contemplative phase of his ironic yet exuberant imaginative life: the rose window in *The Great Code* and *Words with Power*. This visual symbol is placed prominently above the titles of parts 1 and 2 and at the heading of each of the eight chapters in both books. In the metanarrative that taught Frye how to imagine and think – and which he spent the years of his chronological, historical life decoding in arrestingly fresh and powerful ways – the figure of the eight-petalled rose, traditionally found on the western, sunset end of Gothic cathedrals, is richly suggestive. Among its many resonances, this rose signifies above all a renewal of the first day of Creation. It is at once an echo for Frye of the eternal generation of the Word and a figure of the future world which we human beings always have yet to create. As the seven days of historical time meet the eighth day of eternity, forming a perfect octave once known as the ancient 'Rest of God,' we can be sure that for Frye recognition of this frontier between burial and resurrection was meant to lead the awakened mind not to a flight from history and moral obligation but, through what he called the participating apocalypse, back into the work of creation.

ROBERT D. DENHAM

Frye's International Presence

'Frye's pervasive influence': that was the phrase used in the jacket copy of *Northrop Frye and Modern Criticism*, the proceedings of the 1965 English Institute session devoted to Frye's work. In his early fifties, Frye was already seen by the director of the session, Murray Krieger, as having 'had an influence – indeed an absolute hold – on a generation of developing literary critics greater and more exclusive than that of any one theorist in recent critical history' ('Northrop Frye and Contemporary Criticism,' 1). *Anatomy of Criticism* was clearly a book for its time, and the theories developed there are, in this age of theory, no longer in the vanguard. Even so, the thirty books by Frye published since *Anatomy* have attracted wide readership, and *The Great Code*, a bestseller in Canada, was reviewed in more than 160 publications. Frye may no longer have a 'hold' on a generation of critics, but the efforts to grapple with his thought have not diminished in the past thirty years, and the bibliographic record of commentaries on Frye, of rereadings of *Anatomy* and his other books, and of applications of his theories suggests that he is still a large presence in Anglo-American criticism.[1] But how has Frye fared on the international scene? The holding of an international conference on Frye's legacy provides an occasion for reflecting on that question.[2]

One index of Frye's international presence is the degree to which his books have been made available in languages other than English. The first translations of Frye were in German: *Anatomy of Criticism* in 1964 and *A Natural Perspective* in 1966. These were followed by the French translation of *The Modern Century* in 1968. The next year three more of Frye's books appeared in French, two in Italian, and one each in Japanese and Spanish. Since that time there has been a steady stream of translations: except for the year 1982, at least one translation of a Frye book has appeared every year since 1971. In addition to German, French, Italian, Japanese, and Spanish, one can read Frye's books in Portuguese, Romanian, Serbo-Croatian, Danish, Dutch, and Korean. Altogether there have been fifty-one translations of his books. The Italians have been the most industrious, having translated sixteen books, followed by the Japanese with nine. Of the sixteen books Frye wrote before 1977, all but *Spiritus Mundi* have been translated into at least one language, and translations of the books written after that time continue to appear. One can read *The Great Code*, for example, in French, Serbo-Croatian, Italian, Dutch, Spanish, and Danish, and a Japanese translation is under way. In addition, Frye's essays can be read in Hungarian, Chinese, Hebrew, Polish, and Turkish. In summary, Frye's work is now available in seventeen languages. (For a list of translations see Appendix.)

The reception Frye's work has received in countries as different as Italy, Japan, and India gives further evidence of his international standing. Baldo Meo has contended that there are only a few disciples of Frye's archetypal criticism in Italy. But the Italians have, nevertheless, shown an uncommon interest in Frye: they flocked to the lectures he gave in Italy in 1979, sponsored a conference on his work in 1987, have written widely about him (his Italian bibliography has now grown to almost 200 items), and awarded him the prestigious Mondello Prize in 1990. At Frye's death, the Italian media carried a dozen major stories about his life and career.[3] Similarly in Japan, Frye's ideas have been widely disseminated through the translation of his books there, and Shunichi Takayanagi reports that among Japanese students of English literature Frye's critical theories, as well as his role in the study of Romanticism, are well known. 'All the major Japanese newspapers,' according to Takayanagi, 'reported [Frye's] death' ('Northrop Frye and Endo Shusaku,' 3), and *Eigo Seinen* (*The Rising Generation*), a periodical devoted to English studies, recently published articles by five Japanese scholars in a special section entitled 'The World of Northrop Frye's Criticism.' Takayanagi himself has offered graduate seminars on *The Great Code* and *Words with Power*.

Frye's influence in India has been profound and far-reaching, especially in the 157 Indian universities where English is taught. His ideas were assimilated earlier in India than in most countries, because the teaching of his criticism did not have to wait for translations to appear. Mohit Ray, in a paper presented at the Toronto conference, observed that Frye's popularity in India began not with *Anatomy* but with *Fearful Symmetry*. This was an important book for Indians not simply because it treated a seminal English poet but also because of 'the connections Frye had suggested between Blake and the *Bhagavadgita*' ('The Influence of Frye,' 2). *Fearful Symmetry*, Ray continues, 'immediately found a place in all university libraries and gave a new direction to Indian literary criticism in regional languages. By the time English critics, mostly with a sound background of English education, became familiar with Frye as a critic, *Anatomy of Criticism* (1957) had appeared. The book more than fulfilled the expectations roused by *Fearful Symmetry*. Since literary criticism is a part of the M.A. syllabus in English in almost all the Indian universities, *Anatomy of Criticism*, soon after its publication was recommended as a standard reference book in most universities ... It will not be an exaggeration to say that [*Anatomy of Criticism*] revolutionized Indian literary criticism' (2,3).

Ray goes on to trace the influence of Frye not simply in English criticism in India but in sixteen regional languages as well, concluding that after the publication of *Anatomy* and *Fables of Identity*, Indian literary criticism underwent a 'sea-change' (8).

The records we have of the reviews of Frye's books in foreign languages are sketchy at best, as there are no indexes to reviews in some languages; but more than 170 reviews in languages other than English have been recorded – reviews of both the English and the foreign-language versions of Frye's books. In addition, there is a long list of reviews written in English that appear in foreign-language periodicals. Although some of Frye's books have received little or no notice in other languages, others have been reviewed extensively. Of the eighty recorded reviews of *Anatomy*, for example, fifty-three are in languages other than English. While these data say little directly about Frye's influence, they do suggest a substantial world-wide visibility.

Of the thirteen books devoted completely to Frye (three more are forthcoming), only one has been in another language – Jan Ulrik Dyrkjoeb's *Northrop Fryes litteraturteori*, published in Copenhagen in 1979. But there have been more than 150 articles, essays, and portions of books about Frye's work in other languages. Mario Praz was writing about Frye in 1955, and in the late 1950s and early 1960s, other Italian critics, most notably Remo Ceserani, Beniamino Placido, and Claudio Gorlier began to take notice.[4] Perhaps the most important early essay on Frye not written in English was Robert Weimann's 'Northrop Frye und das Ende des New Criticism,' published in *Sinn und Form* in 1965. Throughout the late 1960s, *Anatomy of Criticism* having by then established itself, a number of essays began to appear in other languages, including Italo Calvino, 'La letteratura come proiezione del desiderio';

Hélène Cixous, 'Une science de la littérature'; Gianni Celati, 'Archetipologia sistematica: Per una iniziazione all'opera di Northrop Frye'; Hiroshi Ebine, 'Northrop Frye and the Novel' (in Japanese); Pierre Dommergues, 'Northrop Frye et la critique américaine'; Maurits Engelborghs, 'Frye en den mythekritiek'; Hiroshi Izubuchi, 'Anatomy of Criticism and Its Environs' (in Japanese); and Sonja Basic, 'Northrop Frye kao mitski i arhetipski kriticar.' From these beginnings the international response to Frye's work in non-English-speaking countries, during the past two decades, blossomed.

A decade ago Terry Eagleton remarked that 'Northrop Frye and the New Critics thought they had pulled off a synthesis of [liberal humanism and structuralism],' and he asked, 'but how many students of literature today read them?' (Literary Theory, 199). Eagleton assumed that the obvious reply to his rhetorical question was 'not very many.' But in the Anglo-American world the proper response, even if we use only the record of written responses to Frye, is 'a considerable number.' It was only a few years before Eagleton's remark – in the late 1970s – that Frye was the third most frequently cited writer in the arts and humanities born in the twentieth century (see Eugene Garfield). Given the numerous translations of Frye's books, the reviews they have received outside Canada and the United States, and the large body of writing his criticism has generated in other languages, I rather suspect that from the international perspective the answer to Eagleton's question is also 'a considerable number.'

Influence and reputation are difficult things to measure, and even though Frye has entered into the common currency of criticism, we cannot yet speak with authority about how his work will be viewed fifty or one hundred years from now. Many stories are yet to be told. When asked to speak on Frye's Shakespearean criticism several years ago to the Hungarian Shakespeare Committee, I approached the task somewhat nervously, wondering what I should say by way of introducing Frye to a group of Shakespeareans gathered in Budapest. I quickly discovered, however, that they knew more about Frye's Shakespearean criticism than I did, that one among them had translated Anatomy of Criticism, that still another taught a course devoted entirely to Frye, and that Frye's views were a frequent topic in the courses of others.

There are doubtless similar stories to be told by the Chinese students who have been introduced to Frye's work at Wuhan Teachers' College and Hubei University; from Korean students who have only recently been able to read Frye in their native language; from the writers, teachers, and translators Frye met with in Moscow, Kiev, and Leningrad in 1988; from Julián Rodriguez at the University of Murcia and Tibor Fabiny at Atilla József University, who have spent a great deal of energy in making Frye's ideas available to Spanish and Hungarian students, respectively; and from the Croatian faculty members who, as Frye discovered on his trip to Zagreb only four months before he died, regularly use his criticism in both their scholarship and teaching.[5] These are the kinds of stories that do not make their way into the *MLA Bibliography* and the citation indexes, but in the final reckoning they will perhaps have as much to say as anything else about Frye's international presence.

NOTES

1 For a fairly complete account of the writings about Frye's criticism (books, essays, reviews, and dissertations), see part 2 of my *Northrop Frye: An Annotated Bibliography* and the supplements that appear in the *Northrop Frye Newsletter*; and for the kinds of evidence one might use in considering the range and the weight of Frye's influence, see my 'An Anatomy of Frye's Influence' and 'Auguries of Influence.'

2 There have been two other international conferences devoted to Frye's criticism: 'Ritratto di Northrop Frye,' held in Rome in May 1987, and 'The Legacy of Northrop Frye in the East and West,' which took place in Korea in May 1992. A fourth such conference is planned for July 1994 at Peking University in Beijing, China.

3 Eleven Italian newspapers devoted more than 200 column-inches to recounting Frye's achievements. For a list of the stories – doubtless a partial list – see 'Obituaries, Tributes, Memorials,' *Northrop Frye Newsletter* 3 (Spring 1991): 21–3. A tribute to Frye was also broadcast on Italian Radio (RAI).

4 On Frye's reputation in Italy, see Meo.

5 Although Frye seemed uncomfortable when he had to leave the familiar confines of Victoria College, he did speak to many international audiences over the course of his career; altogether, he lectured in fifteen different countries.

WORKS CITED

Denham, Robert D. 'An Anatomy of Frye's Influence.' *American Review of Canadian Studies* 14 (Spring 1984): 1–19.
– 'Auguries of Influence.' In *Visionary Poetics: Essays on Northrop Frye's*

Criticism, edited by Robert D. Denham and Thomas Willard. New York: Peter Lang, 1991.

– *Northrop Frye: An Annotated Bibliography of Primary and Secondary Sources.* Toronto: University of Toronto Press, 1987.

Eagleton, Terry. *Literary Theory: An Introduction.* Minneapolis: University of Minnesota Press, 1983.

Garfield, Eugene. 'Most-Cited Authors in the Arts and Humanities, 1977–78.' *Current Contents* 32 (6 August 1979): 5–10.

– 'The 250 Most-Cited Authors in the *Arts & Humanities Citation Index*, 1976–83.' *Current Contents* 48 (1 December 1986): 3–10.

Krieger, Murray. 'Northrop Frye and Contemporary Criticism: Ariel and the Spirit of Gravity.' In *Northrop Frye and Modern Criticism*, edited by Murray Krieger. New York: Columbia University Press, 1966.

Meo, Baldo. 'La fortuna di Frye in Italia.' In *Ritratto di Northrop Frye*, edited by Agostino Lombardo. Rome: Bulzoni Editore, 1989.

Northrop Frye Newsletter. Vol. 1 (1986) Salem, Va: English Department, Roanoke College.

Ray, Mohit K. 'The Influence of Frye on Contemporary Indian Literary Criticism.' Paper presented at the conference 'Legacy of Northrop Frye,' Toronto, Ontario, 29–31 October 1992. 8 pp. Photoduplicated typescript.

Takayanagi, Shunichi. 'Northrop Frye and Endo Shusaku: Myth, Creative Imagination, and Salvation.' Paper presented at the conference 'The Legacy of Northrop Frye in the East and West,' Seoul, Korea, 22 May 1992. 14 pp. Photoduplicated typescript.

Abbreviations

AC	*Anatomy of Criticism: Four Essays* (1957)
BG	*The Bush Garden: Essays on the Canadian Imagination* (1971)
CP	*The Critical Path: An Essay on the Social Context of Literary Criticism* (1971)
CR	*Creation and Recreation* (1980)
DG	*Divisions on a Ground: Essays on Canadian Culture* (1982)
DV	*The Double Vision: Language and Meaning in Religion* (1991)
EAC	*The Eternal Act of Creation: Essays, 1979–1990* (1993)
EI	*The Educated Imagination* (CBC, 1963)
EIi	*The Educated Imagination* (Indiana University Press, 1964)
FI	*Fables of Identity: Studies in Poetic Mythology* (1963)
FS	*Fearful Symmetry: A Study of William Blake* (1947)
FT	*Fools of Time: Studies in Shakespearean Tragedy* (1967)
GC	*The Great Code: The Bible and Literature* (1982)
LT	*By Liberal Things* (1959)
MC	*The Modern Century* (1967)
MD	*The Myth of Deliverance: Reflections on Shakepeare's Problem Comedies* (1983)
MM	*Myth and Metaphor: Selected Essays, 1974–1988* (1990)
NFC	*Northrop Frye in Conversation* (1992)
NFCL	*Northrop Frye on Culture and Literature: A Collection of Review Essays* (1978)
NFS	*Northrop Frye on Shakespeare* (1986)
NP	*A Natural Perspective: The Development of Shakespearean Comedy and Romance* (1965)
OE	*Northrop Frye on Education* (1988)

RCLI   *Reflections on the Canadian Literary Imagination: A Selection of Essays by Northrop Frye* (1992)

RE   *The Return of Eden: Five Essays on Milton's Epics* (1965)

RTW   *Reading the World: Selected Writings, 1935–1976* (1990)

SeS   *The Secular Scripture: A Study of the Structure of Romance* (1976)

SM   *Spiritus Mundi: Essays on Literature, Myth, and Society* (1976)

SP   *Sound and Poetry* (1957)

SR   *A Study of English Romanticism* (1968)

StS   *The Stubborn Structure: Essays on Criticism and Society* (1970)

TSE   *T.S. Eliot* (1963)

WGS   *A World in a Grain of Sand: Twenty-Two Interviews with Northrop Frye* (1991)

WP   *Words with Power: Being a Second Study of 'The Bible and Literature'* (1990)

WTC   *The Well-Tempered Critic* (1963)

Chronology

1912 Herman Northrop Frye born in Sherbrooke, Quebec, 14 July, to Herman Edward Frye and Catharine Mary Maud Howard.

1919 Moved to New Brunswick.

1928 Graduated from Aberdeen High School in Moncton, New Brunswick. Enrolled for a short time in a business course.

1929 Entered Victoria College, University of Toronto.

1933 Graduated from Victoria College. Entered Emmanuel College, University of Toronto.

1934 Spent the summer as student minister near Shaunavon in southwestern Saskatchewan on a circuit of the United Church of Canada.

1936 Graduated from Emmanuel College. Ordained in the United Church of Canada. Received a Royal Society of Canada fellowship to study the prophecies of William Blake. Entered Merton College, Oxford.

1937 Married Helen Kemp, 24 August. Appointed as lecturer in the honours course in English literature at Victoria College.

1938 Returned to Merton College, Oxford, to complete studies for BA degree.

1939 Began tenure as member of the faculty at Victoria College.

1940 Received MA degree from Merton College.

1943 Promoted to assistant professor at Victoria College. Supervised the first of thirty-one theses written under his direction.

1947 Published *Fearful Symmetry*. Promoted to associate professor at Victoria College and became literary editor of *Canadian Forum*.

1948 Promoted to rank of professor at Victoria College. Became editor of *Canadian Forum*, a position he held until 1954.

1950 Received a Guggenheim Fellowship. Began writing an annual survey of Canadian poetry for *University of Toronto Quarterly*.

1951 Elected fellow of the Royal Society of Canada.

1952 Became chair of the English Department at Victoria College.

1953 Served as chair of the English Institute.

1954 Appointed Class of 1932 Visiting Lecturer at Princeton University.

1957 Published *Anatomy of Criticism*. Was visiting lecturer at Harvard University. Received from Carleton University the first of thirty-seven honorary doctorate degrees.

1958 Received the Lorne Pierce Medal from the Royal Society of Canada.

1959 Became principal of Victoria College.

1963 Published *The Educated Imagination*, *Fables of Identity*, *The Well-Tempered Critic*, and *T.S. Eliot*.

1965 Published *A Natural Perspective* and *The Return of Eden*.

1967 Appointed University Professor at the University of Toronto. Received the Canada Council Medal. Published *Fools of Time* and *The Modern Century*.

1968 Published *A Study of English Romanticism*.

1969 Elected a foreign honorary member of the American Academy of Arts and Sciences.

1970 Received the Pierre Chauveau Medal from the Royal Society of Canada. Published *The Stubborn Structure*.

1971 Published *The Bush Garden* and *The Critical Path*. Received the Canada Council's Molson Award.

1972 Elected Companion of the Order of Canada.

1974 Elected Honorary Fellow of Merton College, Oxford.

1975 Became corresponding fellow of the British Academy. Named Charles Eliot Norton Professor of Poetry at Harvard University.

1976 Published *The Secular Scripture* and *Spiritus Mundi*. Became foreign member of the American Philosophical Association. Served as president of the Modern Language Association.

1978 Published *Northrop Frye on Culture and Literature*. Became Chancellor of Victoria University. Received the Royal Bank Award.

1979 Made lecture tour of Italy, speaking to large audiences in Rome, Florence, Venice, Milan, and other cities.

1980 Published *Creation and Recreation*.

1981 Elected honorary member of the American Academy and Institute of Arts and Letters.
1982 Published *The Great Code* and *Divisions on a Ground*.
1983 Published *The Myth of Deliverance*.
1986 Published *Northrop Frye on Shakespeare*.
1987 Attended an international conference in Rome, Italy, 25–27 May, devoted to assessing his work. Received the Governor General's Award. Began fiftieth year of teaching at Victoria College.
1988 Published *Northrop Frye on Education*.
1989 Published *Mito Metaphora simbolo*. Northrop Frye Centre at Victoria University, University of Toronto, inaugurated.
1990 Published *Myth and Metaphor*, *Words with Power*, and *Reading the World*. Received the Mondello Prize at the University of Palermo. Delivered a series of lectures at Emmanuel College, published posthumously as *The Double Vision* (1991).
1991 Died of cardiac arrest, 23 January, in Toronto.

PART I

The Double Vision:
Culture, Religion, and Society

A.C. HAMILTON

The Legacy of Frye's Criticism in Culture, Religion, and Society

Matthew Arnold made critics aware of their legacy when he lamented that, because his own age lacked 'the true life of literature,' criticism could only beckon towards the promised land: 'That promised land it will not be ours to enter, and we shall die in the wilderness: but ... to have saluted it from afar, is already, perhaps, the best distinction among contemporaries; it will certainly be the best title to esteem with posterity.' Since Arnold's time, critics – and Frye was one – have claimed that their work shares 'the true life of literature' by being creative, its relation to literature being, then, neither parasitic nor symbiotic but for some – Frye was not one – capable of flourishing without it. Possibly, then, our major critics will be subject to the same test applied to our major writers: who among them will be found freshly challenging and inexhaustible? who among them just will not go away? Frye had his own legacy in mind when he said in a hopeful mood: 'All [a] poet or critic can do is to hope that somehow, somewhere, and for someone, the struggle to unify and to relate, because it is an honest struggle and not because of any success in what it does, may be touched with a radiance not its own' (*StS*, 89). In a practical mood, he said he would like to become 'a kind of lumber room for later generations ... a resource person for [anyone] to explore and get ideas from' (*NFC*, 157–8). In a belligerent mood, he said: 'I have no worries about my own place in [future criticism]. If posterity doesn't like me, the hell with posterity – I won't be living in it anyway' (*WGS*, 287).

The social context of literature and therefore its study is, for Frye, broadly cultural, and that social-cultural context is deeply religious. Accordingly, he refers to a great work of literature as 'a place in which the whole cultural history of the nation that produced it comes into focus' (*EIi*, 123); he defines literary criticism as 'the conscious organizing of a cultural tradition' (*GC*, xviii); and he sees that tradition from the vertical perspective provided by religion. The most important fact about his criticism is that, for him, the three areas of society, culture, and religion are one: each interpenetrates the others, and together they interpenetrate literature even as they are interpenetrated by it.

In considering Frye as a social-cultural-religious critic, I shall begin by citing what he says about the end of the critical path, which he followed in all his writings, because I believe it suggests the distinctiveness and scope of his legacy. In these concluding four sentences of his book, *The Critical Path*, Frye discusses the concerns that bind individuals to society as they are countered by the desire of the individual for freedom within society:

> It is out of the tension between concern and freedom that glimpses of a third order of experience emerge, of a world that may not exist but completes existence, the world of the definitive experience that poetry urges us to have but which we never quite get. If such a world existed, no individual could live in it, because the society he belongs to is part of himself, including all those who are too cold and hungry and sick ever to get near it. No society, even the smallest and most dedicated community, could live in it, because the innocence needed to live continuously in such a world would require a nakedness far beyond anything that removing one's clothes could reach. If we could live in it, of course, criticism would cease and the distinction between literature and life would disappear, because life itself would then be the continuous incarnation of the creative word. (*CP*, 170–1)

This is one of the many passages in Frye's writings where we may stand with him at the centre of his thought in a moment of revelation that potentially contains everything he has ever said or tried to say. It is a visionary moment of identity or unity that I would call 'mystical', though he would never have accepted that term.

In studying Frye's criticism, I have attributed the two major contexts – the cultural and the literary – within which he treats any literary work to two early seminal influences, respectively, Spengler's *Decline of the West* and Blake's canonical works. But after reading *The Double Vision*, John Ayre's biography of Frye, the interviews published in Robert Denham's *A World in a Grain of Sand*, and especially David Cayley's lengthy interview, *Northrop Frye in Conversation*, I realize that these two influences were a consequence of personal visions. In *The Double Vision*, in the course of describing how 'one has glimpses of the immense foreshortening of time that can take place in the world of the spirit,' Frye defines inspiration as 'the coming or breaking through of the spirit from a world beyond time,' and adds: 'One may, as I have done myself, spend the better part of seventy-eight years writing out the implications of insights that have taken up considerably less than an hour of all those years' (55).

Chiefly in the intimacy of interviews, Frye recorded several of these ecstatic 'moments' that inspired his writings. He told John Ayre that when he was about fifteen, walking to high school in Moncton, 'just suddenly that whole shitty and smelly garment (of fundamentalist teaching I had all my life) just dropped off into the sewers and stayed there' (*Northrop Frye*, 44). This moment of rebirth, informed by Zechariah's night vision of Joshua clothed with a filthy garment, which the angel of the Lord ordered to be taken away, brought a strong apocalyptic element to Frye's thought. As he told David Cayley, what is 'really very central to what I believe' is a dialectic 'which moves toward the separation of a world of life from a world of death.' In effect, he recalls his first mystical moment when he adds: 'when you make choices, when you make decisions, you are always moving toward an apocalyptic vision of something that doesn't die, and throwing off the body of death that you ought to be delivered from' (*NFC*, 211).

This moment also brought him to his identification with Blake, the one poet who enjoyed a full vision of the world of 'definitive experience' described in *The Critical Path*. When he says later, 'I wasn't really brought up with that garment on me at all' (*NFC*, 49), he is explaining rather why that garment could drop off: the Methodism he absorbed from his mother emphasized religious experience rather than doctrine, and the story element in the Bible rather than its record of historical fact. Such religious conditioning as a child, he explains, 'may have helped to propel me in the direction of a literary criticism that has kept revolving around the Bible, not as a source of doctrine but as a source of story and vision' (*DV*, 3).

The second recorded moment, which reinforced the first, came to him as an undergraduate early in the morning – variously fixed at 2, 3, and 3:30 – while he was writing an essay on Blake's connection to Milton through their use of the Bible. As he told Pelham Edgar, he had 'glimpses of something bigger and more exciting than I had ever before realized existed in the world of the mind,'[1] 'a sudden expansion of the horizon' (*WGS*, 275), 'a different kind of intuition' that took him, he said, 'twenty years to articulate' (*SM*, 17). This was the sudden insight that the two poets 'were connected by the *same* thing, and sameness leads to individual variety, just as likeness leads to monotony.' The perception of their identity, and the identity of all poets through the Bible, allowed him to make what he calls a 'particular discovery [that] was a natural one for me to make at a time when I was actually a student of theology' (*SM*, 17), namely, that the Bible provided the mythological framework for Western culture.

The third recorded moment came when, still an undergraduate, he encountered Spengler. He told David Cayley what happened while he was reading *The Decline of the West*: 'I suddenly got a vision of coherence. That's the only way I can describe it. Things began to form patterns and make sense' (*NFC*, 48). In response to Cayley's cogent questioning, he went on to explain why Spengler enraptured him:

> Finally I've more or less figured out, I think, what I got from Spengler. There's a remark in Malraux's *Voices of Silence* to the effect that he thought that Spengler's book started out as a meditation on the destiny of art forms and then expanded from there. And what it expanded into is the key idea that has always been on my mind, the idea of interpenetration, which I later found in Whitehead's *Science and the Modern World*, the notion that things don't get reconciled, but everything is everywhere at once. Wherever you are is the centre of everything. And Spengler showed how that operated in history, so I ... kept those two intuitions, which I felt were going to be very central. (*NFC*, 61–2)

As he recounts in *Spiritus Mundi*, Spengler showed him 'how all the cultural products of a given age ... form a unity that can be felt or intuited, though not demonstrated, a sense of unity that approximates the feeling that a human culture is a single larger body, a giant immersed in time' (111). It was Spengler, then, who led Frye to regard a literary work as primarily a cultural text, to define criticism as a 'theory of society,' and to see that the modern critic's 'total subject embraces not merely literature, but the areas of concern which the mythical language of construction and belief enters and informs. These areas ... include large parts of religion, philosophy, political theory, and the social sciences' (*CP*, 98). In sum, Spengler made Frye a cultural critic.

I call these three moments 'mystical' for three reasons. First, because an insight that may be only 'felt or intuited' cannot be fully explicated: despite Frye's gift of language, the mystery remains, and he can only point to it. Hence 'feeling' and 'glimpse' became two key words in his criticism: he will begin with a 'feeling' about something inchoate and end with a 'glimpse' of its place within the total order, which he hopes his readers will share. Second, because these moments afford a vision of order and comprehensiveness, of totality and wholeness, where others find only differences or, at best, similarities. They taught him to organize his thought by frameworks and structures, patterns and charts designed as mnemonic devices to help us see with him. Third, because these moments forged his identity with what he had seen, as he suggests in *The Educated Imagination* when he refers to 'those rare moments' when we feel that 'we are also a part of what we know' (33). They made him, as he acknowledged, distinctive as a critic: to think 'as poets think – in terms of metaphors' (*NFC*, 145), and therefore to build his critical theory around metaphor. The identity of all things becomes the key concept in his criticism.

However, I am not going to fight for the word. Frye objected to its application to Blake's poetry because to the mystic the direct apprehension of communion with God is an end in itself while to the poet it is 'but a means to another end, the end of producing his poem' (*FS*, 7). So one may say of Frye's apprehension of the identity of all things: it was a means to the end of writing his many books in order to communicate that apprehension to his readers. The term 'visionary', which he applies to Blake, rightly applies to him: intuitions, perceptions, and insights provided the initiative for everything he wrote. Often these consolidate into aphorisms but more often they remain apocalyptic, as when he speaks of 'catch[ing] glimpses of the powers and forces of a far greater creative design' (*DG*, 190); or when he claims that in the process of seeking imaginative identity the initiative is seen to come 'not from some unreachable "in itself" world, but from an infinitely active personality that both enters us and eludes us' (*MM*, 107); or when he refers to that final moment when 'some of us may catch a glimpse of a boundless energy which ... has always the power to create all things anew' (*SM*, 227). If there is a final mystery in his criticism, it is the mystery of revelation, one element of which is that all literary works including works of popular culture form an order of words aligned to God's Word within all culture as a verbal universe. It is this revelation that he sought desperately to communicate to others, as far as words may do so.

There must have been an unrecorded fourth moment early in Frye's life when he realized that the physical world is unreal and that reality is found in human fictions. The trauma of the recognition that human beings fell from a higher level of reality with which they had been identified to a lower world of illusion from which they feel totally alienated is written all over Frye's works. For example, it provoked him to say that 'a serious human life, no matter what "religion" is invoked, can hardly begin until we see an element of illusion in what is really there, and something real in fantasies about what might be there instead' (*GC*, 50). It determined what writings always confronted him, such as *The Tempest* and the Book of Job. It led him to claim that '[the] story of the loss and regaining of identity is ... the framework of all literature' (*EI*, 55); and to understand by that term 'not the feeling that I am myself and not another, but the realization that there is only one man, one mind, and one world' (*RE*, 143).

I stress these early visionary moments in Frye's life because he said that 'you keep revolving around your childhood all your life,' that 'I'm really building everything around a highly personal vision, a vision that I think I've had since I was a child' (*WGS*, 263, 219), and that 'everything I write *I* consider autobiography' (*OE*, 211). His criticism may be regarded, then, as an attempt to explicate these moments.

Frye's early religious conditioning in which he read the Bible for its stories rather than for its doctrine determined his interest in myth or story in literature, and the encyclopaedic drive of his mind determined his special interest in the canonical stories derived from the Bible which had consolidated into the mythology that characterizes the culture of Western Europe. That conditioning also made him aware that we live in two worlds: the alien world of physical reality and the human world of culture. The first is the world in which we must live though we remain unadjusted to it; the second is the world in which we want to live. Frye calls this second world a mythological universe because originally it formed a canon of interconnected myths or stories, 'a single encyclopaedic form' or 'a total body of vision' (*AC*, 55) which expresses our human concerns, hopes, desires, anxieties, and ideals. It is the world of culture built out of nature, and within which literature descends in a manner that recreates and recovers the original myth. Society later constructs an ideology out of this mythology, in effect kidnapping it, in order to support its authority.

Since most cultural critics, especially those with a Marxist bent, treat ideology as a political power-struggle, Frye is generally dismissed as a cultural critic. Raymond Williams saw in him 'the features of a familiar enemy';[2] and Terry Eagleton calls him a liberal humanist: 'the impotent conscience of bourgeois society' that was ineffectual in opposing the dominant ideologies of late industrial capitalism (*Literary Theory*, 199). The hostility was mutual. In *Words with Power*, Frye refers disparagingly to critics who 'are still unwilling or unable to get past the ideological stage in dealing with literature, because they are less interested in literature than in the relation of literature to some primary ideological interest,' and he places himself among those 'interested in dealing with literature in terms of its own mythical and metaphorical language, for whom nothing is prior in significance to literature itself' (27).

Frye allows, grudgingly, that poets 'normally reflect the ideologies of their own times, and certainly they are always conditioned by their historical and cultural surrounding,' but he adds: 'there has always been a sense of something else that eludes this kind of communication' (*MM*, 21). His sense of this 'something else' characterizes him as a social and cultural critic. For him, works of literature chiefly reflect one another through their use of conventions, myths, and genre, and this helps us 'to get a glimpse into the authority of literature, an authority which derives from its integrity as a structure rather than from its fidelity as a mirror of its time' (*MD*, 11). Accordingly, he turns from the ideological content of a literary work to its structure of images and metaphors which reveals the underlying mythology from which it descends. Interest in literary structure led him to see through any literary work to literature as a whole, and only then to its cultural context. Of the three worlds of human consciousness expressed in literature, philosophy, and religion, the first appealed most strongly to him for the reason he gave in an address to the Victoria University alumni in 1983: 'The glimpses I have had of the imaginative world have kept me fascinated for nearly half a century, and no one life could begin to exhaust the fascination' (*MM*, 78).

I trace a development of Frye as a cultural critic, though it may be more of a clarification in his thought. In his earlier writings, he relates literature's mythical language directly to society's dominant mythology, which he describes as 'a structure of ideas, images, beliefs, assumptions, anxieties, and hopes which express the view of man's situation and destiny generally held at that time' (*MC*, 105). Later he refers to this mythology as 'the mythology of concern' which 'crystallizes in the centre of a culture,' and which, with 'its roots in religion,' serves to bind the community in common acts and assumptions (*CP*, 35, 36). Still later, he returns to Blake who restructured the traditional mythological universe 'on a basis of human desire and ambition rather than anxiety' (*SM*, 109). Using this distinction, he separates a primary mythology, which he identifies with literature, from a secondary mythology, which he identifies with ideology. The first addresses the individual's primary concerns: the desire for food, shelter, sexual relations, survival, freedom, and happiness; the second, society's concerns: the anxiety to maintain its authority and prestige by preserving its hierarchy and class structure, its religious and legal institutions, and its defence against all rival ideologies (see *MM*, 88). While he still allows that every work of literature, which descends from mythology, 'is an ideological product, an expression of the culture of its age,' now he argues that the critic's task is 'to distinguish ideology from myth, to help reconstitute a myth as a language, and to put literature in its proper cultural place as the central link of communication between society and the vision of its primary concerns' (*MM*, 268, 103). His very strong message in a number of later essays – as close as he ever gets to exhortation – is that primary concerns must now become primary. It may be part of Frye's legacy as a cultural critic to be labelled a member of the Green Party.

Among the primary concerns, he includes 'the concern of a conscious being to enlarge that consciousness, to get at least a glimpse of what it would be like to know more than we are compelled to know' (*MM*, 22). For him, that concern is evident in his effort to see beyond literature in its cultural context: not other than but more than literature. That brought him to treat the Bible as 'literature plus'; and using that term, he may be called a cultural critic 'plus'.

Religion may be added to that 'plus', and even be regarded as primary, provided that it is divorced from dogma, doctrine, or sectarian belief of any kind, that it is never extracted 'from the culture in which it is embedded' (*NFC*, 195), and that its vertical dimension on human life always focuses on the present and not on the future. Frye's criticism is sustained by the faith that once the human imagination, as expressed in culture, recovered the myths originally projected upon God, we may 'pass from state to community, from exploitation to imaginative work, from culture as the privilege of a few to culture as the inner condition of everyone' (*SM*, 110). The faith may be indebted to Blake but the language suggests Arnold's claim that culture 'seeks to do away with classes' (*Culture and Anarchy*, 70).

As a cultural critic, Frye endorses Arnold's concept of culture as 'the human source, at least, of spiritual authority' (*WTC*, 154) because it 'tends to create out of actual society an ideal order of liberty, equality, and fraternity' (*StS*, 254). As a religious critic, he shares a kinship with Blake that was initiated by their shared evangelical conditioning. In a 1983 interview, he refers obliquely to the effects of that first ecstatic moment when the garment of fundamentalism dropped from him: 'The sudden realization from Blake that one didn't have to [see life as "a progressive spiritual impoverishment"] and still keep a wide-open perspective on whatever words like *infinite* and *eternal* mean, was the revelation that Blake was to me. He had the same kind of middle-class, Anglophone Biblical training that I had had. He saw structures in it that made human sense and didn't discourage the full use of the human faculties' (WGS, 263–4). All three – Blake, Arnold, and Frye – saw the Bible as the foundation and superstructure of the culture in which they were embedded: a culture within which, and for which, they wrote.

In this essay, I have been considering one dimension of Frye's legacy, his work as a social-cultural-religious critic, and I want to conclude with two general remarks. But first, a preliminary question: Will any contemporary critic have a legacy? Frank Kermode believes not. 'All criticism has its season,' he remarks, 'in which it lives, if it lives at all, by a dazzle or minor radiance that cannot be expected to last. The best it can aspire to is a shadow of the condition Wallace Stevens thought a poem might achieve, a sort of August moment, a moment of illusory fixity.'[3] Yet Frye held that 'our reception ... comes nearer to being our real selves than anything stowed away inside us,' and he cites approvingly the suggestion in Milton's Lycidas that fame 'is a secular counterpart of what in Christian revelation is the hope of immortality' (StS, 37, 147). The burden of his reputation in his own day weighed on him like the stone of Sisyphus. 'As one's reputation grows, and as continuous effort is needed to sustain it,' he wrote in 1983 about a speech in Shakespeare's Troilus and Cressida, but surely not without personal reference, 'one finds the stone getting heavier each time it is rolled up the hill' (MD, 68). Will that reputation survive?

Several readers have hazarded an answer to that question. Notorious among them, Frank Lentricchia saw Frye as Wallace Stevens's 'The Man on the Dump' (After the New Criticism, 30). Robert Denham believes that 'Frye will continue to be read ... beyond [the 1980s] because he does not speak from himself; he speaks, rather, with the voice of impersonal authority, to us.'[4] Ian Balfour believes that Frye's writings will 'continue to pose a challenge for the future of criticism, a future in part made possible by [his] work' (Northrop Frye, 110). Geoffrey Hartman believes that after the flood of contemporary criticism ebbs, Anatomy of Criticism and The Great Code 'will rank as monumental relics of an exceptional moment of Freemasonry in our discipline' (Minor Prophecies, xxx). (By that term, I assume he means that Frye's criticism is free from any doctrinal religious bias.) In 1990 I raised the question of his legacy by asking, 'if in the 1990s and beyond [he] may assume once again the role of the prophet whose voice reminds us that the creative power of the human imagination revealed through literature breaks vertically into society with a transcending vision of a higher human order' (Northrop Frye, 215). I concluded that he would, provided that criticism 'focuses its interest on literary works in their entire literary and cultural contexts, both past and present, and reveals how literature in these contexts remains central to the primary and ultimate human values and concerns of all readers' (*Northrop Frye*, 223). I have no reason now to change my mind except that I am less sanguine about future criticism. But to come to my final two remarks.

First, Frye believed that an individual may develop by 'transforming' himself or herself 'into a focus of a community' (*SM*, 120). His greatest strength as a cultural critic – and it may prove his greatest legacy – is that he always speaks within and through the best in Western culture, within and through its mythology rather than its ideology. Yet he was fully aware that he spoke as 'a Canadian intellectual' (*StS*, 61) living in the mid-twentieth century, a 'bourgeois liberal,' one who was 'middle-class, English-speaking, white, [and non-conformist] Protestant' (*WGS*, 263). For that very reason his criticism may seem increasingly alien to an increasingly multicultural society. When Mahatma Gandhi was asked what he thought of Western civilization, he responded, devastatingly, that he thought it would be a very good idea. While Frye was very tolerant of other religions, saying that he was prepared to learn from them, he added that 'we have to remember the rock from which we were hewn' (*NFC*, 195) – here acknowledging Isaiah's injunction 'Look unto the rock whence ye are hewn.' Certainly he spoke always within the Western biblical tradition, but the religion he espoused was more ecumenical than sectarian. Those of another religion are not excluded when he refers to the Bible, not as a unique Christian revelation, but as 'the body of words through which I can see the world as a cosmos, as an order, and where I can see human nature as something redeemable, as something with a right to survive.' Or when he speaks of God as transcendent because otherwise there is only physical nature with which we cannot communicate, and human nature which, without some sense of God, remains a psychotic ape. Or when he sees that Christianity, by uniting the divine and the human, has opened a path of freedom to human beings which is infinite (*NFC*, 189, 190).

My second point is that literary critics may be among the most expendable of all writers, but Frye strikes me as unique, and permanently valuable, because of the insights that sustained him in a lifetime of critical endeavour. In the future they should sustain others. Of course, many – perhaps most – may choose not to respond to his visionary criticism: to the critical presbyopia which he enjoyed even as a young man, to the ever 'expanding eyes' with their dizzying perspectives, or to the encyclopaedic cast of his mind that finally included everything. Yet the insights, intuitions, and visionary moments scattered throughout his writings were not so much his own as he was their persuasively articulate medium, which forced him to write, as he acknowledged: 'my writing isn't something I run, it runs me. I have to do what it says' (*NFC*, 140). Hence he adopted his characteristic ironical pose in which he remains transparent to his subject, saying that the teacher and student – and he could have added his reader – 'are all united in the same vision' (*WGS*, 286). One cannot quarrel with a vision, especially one that offers only to show us what we have always known but have forgotten. Frye said of Blake that 'a theory of symbolism broad enough to develop the critical and appreciative side of contemporary culture will almost have to draw heavily on him' (*FS*, 423), and I would say the same of Frye's theory of culture.

I suspect that his legacy will be preserved by his general readers, or at least by a saving remnant among them: those who share his sense of the primary importance of our primary concerns, who feel that there is a reality outside the unreal society in which we live and are prepared to entertain a vision of something far greater. At the outset, I suggested that the distinctiveness and scope of Frye's legacy are illustrated in his remarks on a third order of experience to which religion, philosophy, and literature can only point, and now I conclude by saying that his legacy will be shared by those who are persuaded by him that they may find in culture what (in his words) 'will give our imaginations a depth and a perspective that can take in other possibilities, chiefly the possibility of a more intense mode of living' (*MD*, 89–90). In the future, such readers should respond to him as they do to any literary classic: one who will not go away but always confronts them as a freshly challenging presence. The more he is read, the more inexhaustible he will be found; the more that is seen in him, the more there remains to be seen.

NOTES

1 Ayre, *Northrop Frye*, 92.
2 Williams, 'A Power to Fight,' 9.
3 Kermode, 'The Men on the Dump: A Response,' 93.
4 Denham, 'An Anatomy of Frye's Influence,' 12.

WORKS CITED

Arnold, Matthew. *Culture and Anarchy*. Edited by J. Dover Wilson. Cambridge: Harvard University Press, 1972.

- 'The Function of Criticism at the Present Time.' In *Representative Essays*, edited by E.K. Brown. Toronto: Macmillan, 1936.

Ayre, John. *Northrop Frye: A Biography*. Toronto: Random House, 1989.

Balfour, Ian. *Northrop Frye*. Boston: Twayne Publishers, 1988.

Denham, Robert D. 'An Anatomy of Frye's Influence.' *American Review of Canadian Studies* 14 (1984): 1–19.

Eagleton, Terry. *Literary Theory: An Introduction*. Minneapolis: University of Minnesota Press, 1983.

Hamilton, A.C. *Northrop Frye: Anatomy of His Criticism*. Toronto: University of Toronto Press, 1990.

Hartman, Geoffrey. *Minor Prophecies: The Literary Essay in the Cultural Wars*. Cambridge: Harvard University Press, 1991.

Kermode, Frank. 'The Men on the Dump: A Response.' In *Addressing Frank Kermode: Essays in Criticism and Interpretation*, edited by Margaret Tudeau-Clayton and Martin Warner. London: Macmillan, 1991.

Lentricchia, Frank. *After the New Criticism*. Chicago: University of Chicago Press, 1980.

Williams, Raymond. 'A Power to Fight.' *The Guardian*, 12 November 1970.

THOMAS WILLARD

Archetypes of the Imagination

Twenty-one years ago, Frye introduced me to the work of Henry Vaughan's twin brother. Frye had found a copy of *The Works of Thomas Vaughan*, edited by a famous esotericist, while browsing in Britnell's Book Shop on Yonge Street in Toronto and had incorporated his thoughts about the creative word in a chapter on Blake's literary tradition (*FS*, 151, 158). But his remarks did not prepare me for the puzzles I found as I began reading a copy in the Renaissance and Reformation section of the Pratt Library – for example, the use of 'archetype' in a poem by Thomas Vaughan written after the death of his beloved metaphysics teacher, William Cartwright:

> When he did read how did we flock to hear;
> Sure some professors became pupils there.
> He would refine abstractions: it was he
> That gave the text all its authority.
> ...
> He plunder'd not the heavens , nor brought he down
> Secrets from thence which were before unknown;
> Yet some there are believe their wits so ripe
> That they can draw a map of the Arch'type,
> And with strange optics tutor'd they can view
> The emanations of the mystic Jew.
> In this his pious ignorance was best
> And did excel his knowledge of the rest. (476)

I caught the reference to Kabbalah but had to ask, Which archetype? And with that question began a major strand in the conversation that I was privileged to have with Frye for the next two decades.[1] He explained that this was an older, Neoplatonic view of Godhead as the archetypal pattern imposed on the creation – a view I found in Vaughan's first prose tract when I eventually unravelled it. The poem could be a tribute to Frye himself, whose lectures drew fellow professors and showed a tactful restraint in the face of students seeking, what a piece of street theatre called, 'Apocalypse Now'; Frye included God (or heaven or identity) on the blackboard maps he offered, but never tried to map the ultimate. In conversation, he was always happier to talk about other people's systems, and reluctant to explain his own. Therefore, I must at once confess that I owe many of my thoughts about archetypal theory to Frye and that he would surely not agree with everything I shall say. What he would probably agree with is that, just as the archetypal critic must stand back from the individual work, the study of archetypal criticism demands intellectual distance.[2]

When we stand back and look at the overall contours of Frye's canon, we find that he spent ten years developing the theory of archetypes, from 1947 when *Fearful Symmetry* appeared to 1957 when *Anatomy of Criticism* appeared with an essay entitled 'Archetypal Criticism.' He explained the term for another twenty-five years until *The Great Code* appeared in 1982, and there he abandoned the word, saying he would never have used it had he known how completely Jung's usage would dominate the field (48).[3] He did not use the word at all in *Words with Power*, so far as I can see; and this seems ironic because the book's second half, where Frye plays elaborate variations on four biblical images, is probably the most sustained piece of archetypal criticism he wrote after *Fearful Symmetry*. From a long-range perspective, Frye took centre stage for a while as chief spokesman for archetypal criticism, but returned to his first vision of the mythological universe – a vision that he said first came to him at a very young age.[4] His archetypal theory explained the analogical sort of thought that made his study of Blake possible, but Frye did not need its acceptance in order to keep on writing criticism.

Frye had spoken of the 'archetypal vision' in *Fearful Symmetry* (108), but he used the word 'archetypal' in a traditional Christian sense to refer to Jesus as the pattern of creation 'through whom all things are made,' the original creative Word from which all other words have sprung. Here we are at the edge of cosmology, which archetypal critics ignore at their peril. Here we encounter the ancient theory (voiced by Martianus Capella in the Middle Ages and by Robert Fludd in the Renaissance) that there are three worlds: the macrocosm, the microcosm, and the archetype, which is to say, the great world of nature, the little world of human beings, and the world of God's mind.[5] That is how the word 'archetype' is first used in Philo Judaeus's book *On the Creation of the World* (I, 69), and how it appears in Dionysius the Areopagite's commentary *On the Celestial Hierarchy* (II, 4). It refers to the world beyond the *primum mobile* that Dante enters in canto 27 of the *Paradiso*. The Christian *mundus archetypus* is close to Plato's world of the ideal form (εἶδος), and Plotinus spoke of rising above the physical world to its archetype (*Enneads*, V. 1.4). Syncretic works drawing from Gnostic Christianity and Neoplatonism began to speak about the 'archetypal form' (ἀρχέτυπον εἶδοσ, mentioned in the *Corpus Hermeticum*, I.8.a).[6] In Neoplatonism, the logoi or seminal reasons (*rationes seminales*) were said to flow out of the archetype, through the World Soul, and into the World Spirit, the last concept being close to what Shakespeare called 'great creating Nature' (*Winter's Tale*, IV. iv. 88; see Economou, chap. 1). The image in God's mind thus made its stamp on the creation, and for people in the biblical tradition, humankind was made in God's image (Gen. 1:26); for those in the Christian tradition, the ultimate human image was that of Jesus, who became the archetypal pattern for poets like Blake.

The archetypal cosmology was familiar to Frye from two scholarly studies that he recommended to his graduate students, one by Irwin Panofsky and another by Francis Yates ('Myth and Myth Criticism'). It was more familiar still from two poems he regularly taught. Milton's *De Idea Platonica* asked the freshman question, where do ideas come from?, and imagined that the original 'archetype of man' (*hominus archetypus*) was still walking about somewhere in the wilds of creation. Yeats's *The Second Coming* evoked by its very title a 'vast image' which any self-respecting Neoplatonist would recognize at once as an archetypal image because it came 'out of *Spiritus Mundi*.' However, the archetypal cosmology did not fit Frye's four-level world of poetic imagery any better than it had fitted Milton's, and its occasional use by Yeats seemed positively antiquarian. The 'archetypal world' belonged to the old cosmology that placed value 'up there' beyond the stars, and it hardly survived the Romantic revolution. C.G. Jung used geological, as opposed to cosmological, imagery when he spoke about archetypes residing in the substrata of the psyche; and his own dreams about the collective unconscious involved descent into an underground shrine or an old cellar, rather than ascent through the spheres.[7] He consistently dodged the question: Where do archetypes come from? Frye sounded a bit old-fashioned using the old sense of 'archetype' even to explain Blake; he could hardly use it to explain modern literary criticism.

Fortunately, as he found, the word 'archetype' had assumed a modern meaning in the eighteenth century. He discovered an example in James Beattie (*EAC*, 94), and his early follower Lauriat Lane found one in

Samuel Johnson.[8] Ironically, however, Johnson and Beattie (actually Beattie's editor) used the word in the very way that Locke had used it in *An Essay Concerning Human Understanding*.[9] Moreover, Locke used the term 'archetype' to explain that most un-Blakean of mental phenomena, the generalization. Locke wanted to show why people can communicate about justice (in the Johnson example) and, in doing so, wanted to show where communication goes amiss and why language can only approach the ideal (Beattie's concern). He revived the old word 'archetype' but turned philosophy on its ear by suggesting that the 'archetype' of an idea was not some pre-existent reality but what would now be called a social construction, to be arrived at by commonsense experience. Worst of all, for those who think of Frye's criticism as emerging from Blake's 'case against Locke,' the empirical Lockean archetype seems exactly what Frye began talking about in the fifties. When he spoke about the Cinderella archetype, for example, he was generalizing from his own reading experience, knowing that most of his readers would have had a similar experience of it. When he envisioned a science of criticism, he was building the case *for* Locke.[10] To be sure, he did not take the Lockean tradition so far as did Kenneth Burke, who drew from Jeremy Bentham's theory of 'archetypation' as well as from Aristotle's concept of entelechy and proceeded to argue that critical archetypes were creations after the fact, 'mythic ways of formulating entelechial implications (or possible summings-up in principle) by translating them into terms of a vaguely hypothetical past' (*Dramatism and Development*, 43–4). However, inasmuch as Frye made the case for Locke he built a case against Jung, whose archetypes were as innate as the instincts, indeed were said to be images that the instincts have of themselves.[11] On this account, of the innate versus the socially constructed, Jung's archetypes are fundamentally different from Frye's. But that is not to say that they are incompatible.

A fair bit has been said already about Frye's relation to Jung, and a good bit more remains to be said, but I must let it suffice to say the obvious. Reading Jung in English in the late forties, when Frye studied his work most intently,[12] was very different from reading him even a decade later. Frye had to settle for incomplete and often inadequate translations, which were completely redone when Jung's collected works began to appear in English in the fifties. He therefore read Jung as he might have read a difficult foreign poet like Rilke. He poured over Jung's analyses of two dream sequences, the first from *Symbols of Transformation* and the second from the opening of *Psychology and Alchemy*. He could not have known at the time that the chapter on sacrifice in the first book was written just as he himself was coming into the world and soon led to a break between Jung and Freud, or that the analysis in the second would be followed by a thoroughgoing study of alchemy that opened the symbolic world of the alchemists for the modern students of literature. Nor could he have realized that Jung did not use the term 'archetype' until a decade after *Symbols* was written. Frye only had Jung's method, which consisted in amplifying dreams with a wealth of learning from anthropology and religion, and by the late forties he felt he had the method down pat.

When *Psychology and Alchemy* appeared in something like its present form in 1953, as one of the first volumes in what would become Jung's *Collected Works*, Frye wrote the longest book review of his career, 'Forming Fours.' In the review, he described the structure of Jung's theory as he might describe the world of Dante or Blake; and although he was a bit overschematic, he was remarkably right. His one mistake of any significance was a common one, and reflected Frye's nervous memories of Naziism: he explained that Jung's archetypes came from the collective unconscious and complained that Jung assigned specific racial content to what should be the common possession of humanity. A critic can easily answer this complaint, as Eugene Williamson has done, by drawing attention to the title essay in Jung's *Archetypes of the Collective Unconscious*, but that essay was first published in German in 1954, the year Frye's review appeared, and was not available in English until the volume appeared in 1959, two years after Frye's comments reappeared in *Anatomy* (111–12). Jung's readers are still confusing archetypes with archetypal images; the archetypes are pure relationship like mother or lover, while the archetypal images contain content that the individual brings from his or her own sensory experience.[13] This confusion could be avoided by reading Jung's *Memories* (e.g., 347) or his contribution to *Man and His Symbols* (96), both published in the sixties, but Frye read little of Jung after the fifties and can perhaps be forgiven.[14] When he last talked with me about Jung, during a luncheon conversation in Tucson in 1990, and he raised his old complaint about racially motivated archetypes, I decided to correct him. He took a swig of beer, looked me in the eye, and said: 'If that's what he says, then I have no problem with Jung.' Temperamentally, Frye was always more interested in showing where he differed from another critic, and thus in defining his own position. But he regarded Jung, at the basis, as a fellow critic.

Towards the end of *Fearful Symmetry*, Frye observed that 'psychology and anthropology have worked great changes in our study of literature' and suggested that the emerging criticism might cast light on more than literature. 'It is conceivable,' he said, 'that such a study – the study of anagogy, if a name is wanted – would supply us with the missing piece in contemporary thought which, when supplied, will unite its whole pattern' (424, 425). Frye soon assigned the word 'anagogy' to its medieval sense (already found in pseudo-Dionysius)[15] of a divine overview and began using the word 'archetype' instead. For his second appearance at the English Institute, in 1950, he wrote 'Blake's Treatment of the Archetype.' Towards the close of his paper, he drew parallels between Jung's anima and Blake's emanation, and stated that Blake's poetry 'consisted almost entirely in the articulation of archetypes' (189). But lest he sound like a Jungian, he hastened to add: 'By archetype I mean an element in a work of literature ... which can be assimilated to a larger unifying category.' And here he came to a critical act of faith: no archetype, no totality; and its corollary: no totality, no science of criticism. He had wrestled with the problem since chapter 1 of *Fearful Symmetry*, where he tried to explain how his own cultural associations could open up Blake's world and where he had taken the offensive, asserting that source-hunting was for literalists and that with a poet as symbolically sophisticated as Blake the 'analogue' was all (11). In the late forties, 'archetype' was the magic word, used in at least one title in the 1949 *PMLA*, and Frye's contribution to *The Kenyon Review* series entitled 'My Credo' was naturally enough 'The Archetypes of Literature.' Pressed for further definition, he presented 'The Literary Meaning of "Archetype" ' at the MLA convention in 1952, and from there it was only a short step to *Anatomy* and its 'Theory of Archetypal Meaning.' We may not be quite so surprised that he dropped the term 'archetype' in the end if we remember that his career followed the myth of return, which in his case meant back to Blake. I suspect that the word 'analogy' (with its link to the Logos) will become a more important word for Frye's readers, even as αναλογια is the crucial word for pseudo-Dionysius.[16]

Archetypal criticism, so called, has gone out of fashion during the last decade or two, partly because poststructuralism has rejected the very possibility of a 'totally intelligible' criticism such as Frye hoped to derive from archetypes, and partly because the old determinisms that he rejected – Marxism, Thomism, and the like (*AC*, 6, 17) – have been replaced by the new determinisms of race, class, and gender, which resist anything that smacks of élitism. It is commonplace to say, as Charles Baldick does in *The Concise Oxford Book of Literary Terms*, that archetypal criticism is reductive and ignores 'cultural differences' (17). These changes remind me of a remark that Alfred Harbage made in the early fifties, not long after having been selected over Frye for a

Shakespeare position at Harvard.[17] Harbage suggested that literary criticism was in need of a word like 'anarchetype' to account for radical innovations in the drama (*Shakespeare and the Rival Traditions*, xii). If Frye had been the debating type, he would have shot back that an archetype has no more politics in it than a metrical form does, and that it remains for the individual poet to put a revolutionary or conservative spin on the archetype in question. At about the same time, Leslie Fiedler was drawing his distinction between the archetype and the writer's signature on it (*No! in Thunder*, 309–28), which was not wholly unlike Eliot's distinction between the tradition and the individual talent, and Frye had rather more sympathy with these later distinctions. But I must not give too dim a picture. Although many critics now seem bent on something like Harbage's 'anarchetypes,' some genuine archetypal criticism continues to be written after the school of Frye. To give only two recent instances: Femi Euba has written a book on the 'origins and development of satire in Black drama' which relies on Frye for its conception not only of satire but of its archetypal victims (chap. 3), and Meredith Powers has drawn upon Frye's later theories of codified literature in a book on the heroine archetype in the West.[18] Further archetypal criticism is being written after the school of Jung, and it seems likely that Frye's legacy as an archetypal critic will remain linked with Jung's. If anything, they will probably get linked more closely.

Frye and Jung had a remarkable amount in common. They both grew up in relative isolation, in religious families of limited means; both came into their own at university, and both found that they needed to go their own way. In the shorthand of Jung's character typology, both were introverted thinking intuitives. Both were strongly attracted to mystical religion yet felt compelled to write in the language of science in order to win acceptance for their ideas, and both stepped outside that science in their last days. I think it is precisely as we lose those scientific and positivistic anxieties that we will find they have more and more in common.[19] When Jung turned from 'the language of science,' he told his 'personal myth' in his *Memories* (3), and it turned out that he had lived a life of allegory: he had made the Orphic quest to rescue his anima from the underworld of the unconscious. Meanwhile, as Frye withdrew from his more polemical public persona and spoke more as a representative of his generation in Canada, he got past his anxiety about personal readings and what he had called impressionistic criticism. He had long resisted comparison to Maud Bodkin (see *CP*, 16), an early proponent of reader-response criticism, in part

because she was professedly introspective; but he came to admit that
his aperçus were also personal. In giving up their claims to scientific
authority, then, Jung and Frye spoke even truer of the unconscious and
the imagination, respectively, and thus proved the old Romantic axiom
of Emerson's *American Scholar*: the further one descends into oneself,
the more one speaks for all selves.

The Jungians who seem to have learned Jung's lessons best are those
who have followed their own quests; and of these, the most helpful for
literary critics in North America may well be James Hillman, whose
archetypal psychology is premised on what he calls 'the poetic basis of
mind.' Hillman realized early on that 'all ways of speaking of archetypes are translations from one metaphor to another' and therefore
talked explicitly about 'the *genres* and *topoi* in literature' (*A Blue Fire*,
23). Hillman, for one, has drawn upon the work of Jung's friend Henri
Corbin, a French scholar who discovered the archetypal imagination at
work in the devotional literature of Persia. Corbin was scholar enough
to recognize that he was describing the Neoplatonic concept of the
mundus archetypus, stripped of its early Christian colouring, and he was
philosopher enough to suspect that this sort of imagination was not the
creation of the individual poetic genius but rather the creator of
individual genius, as expressed in what he called the *mundus imaginalis*
or 'imaginal world.' The imagination, he explained, 'is the mirror *par
excellence*, where the images of the archetypal world have their epiphany; this is why the *mundus imaginalis* is the foundation of a theory
of the imagination's knowledge and function.'[20] Frye only knew of
Corbin as a name, but Corbin's theory seems remarkably close to much
that he held dear – to Blake's holy city of the imagination (called
Golgonooza because it existed 'beyond time') and to Stevens's 'Description without Place' (which Frye taught frequently):

> Even the seeming of a summer's day
> Is description without place. It is a sense
>
> To which we refer experience, a knowledge
> Incognito, ... (343)

This is a world that does not literally exist anywhere but exists forever
as a consequence.

This transpersonal world would seem to embrace the collective unconscious, on the one hand, and the Romantic imagination, on the other
– indeed, would seem to show them in similar light. This may be why

Frye saw no need for the conception of a collective unconscious, at least for a literary critic (*AC*, 112); in any case, it is why I have titled my essay 'Archetypes of the Imagination' echoing Jung's 'Archetypes of the Collective Unconscious.' Like the unconscious, the literary imagination is both a process and a product, a power and an accomplishment. If we ask where Frye's legacy is to be found, we will find that he has been telling us ever since he wrote about Blake's *Jerusalem*. Like all true acts of the imagination, Frye's words and thoughts are always available in the archetypal world:

> Permanent, & not lost not lost nor vanish'd, & every little act,
> Word, work & wish, that has existed, all remaining still ...
> ...
> Shadowy to those who dwell not in them, meer possibilities:
> But to those who enter into them they seem the only substances
> (Jerusalem, plate 13, lines 60–1, 64–5)

NOTES

1 I have encouraged the conversation with many students of Frye's work, and am happy to thank Alvin Lee, who encouraged me to write on this subject, and Bob Denham, who provided bibliographical and moral support.
2 There is a large body of literature on the subject: van Meurs and Kidd, *Jungian Literary Criticism, 1920–1980*, includes 902 items, with 12 on archetypal criticism and 28 on Frye; Duncan, 'Archetypal Criticism in English, 1946–1980,' includes 330 items with 7 on Frye.
3 Frye made similar points in interviews in 1979 and 1990: See *RTW*, 203–4; *NFC*, 75–6, and 'Expanding Eyes,' in *SM*, 117. For a good survey of his thoughts about archetypes, see Hamilton, *Northrop Frye*, 108–10.
4 *Journey without Arrival*, 1976 (documentary film).
5 See Godwin, *Robert Fludd*, 14–16.
6 Frye noted the Neoplatonic background in an interview (*WGS*, 203).
7 Jung, *Memories*, 158–60. A traditionalist could easily complain about Jung's 'use – or rather his usurpation – of the term "archetype"' to refer to psychic content without the spiritual origin (Burckhardt, *The Mirror of the Intellect*, 59). I have discussed the archetypal theories of Jung and Frye in relation to the cosmology of Renaissance alchemy in 'Alchemy and the Bible,' 121–2.
8 Lane, Jr, 'The Literary Archetype,' 226–7. This latter essay deserves to be

known for its remarks on Frye, 'the outstanding advocate of archetypal criticism at the present time' (228–9). Perhaps ironically, Lane begins by noting that critical terms go out of fashion when there is too much disagreement about what they mean.

9 See, for example, Book II, chap. 30, section 1, and Book III, chap. 6, section 51. The second passage makes the famous argument that even Adamic language must have been conventional; however, it refers to 'Archetypes made by Nature' and so leaves a door open to a deistic view of design. The word 'archetype' is not of great significance for Locke, and is not glossed in Nidditch's glossary.

10 Cook has discussed Frye's case against Blake in his Northrop Frye: A Vision of the New World, 48–54; for 'The Case against Locke,' see FS, chap. 1.

11 Jung, Archetypes of the Collective Unconscious, 44.

12 See Ayre, Northrop Frye, 216–17, and NFC, 77.

13 See Kugler, The Alchemy of Discourse, chap. 1, for a response to this common misconception and for Jung's claim to be known as a structuralist.

14 Frye has made relatively few references to Jung's other works. See his reference to Jung's essay on synchronicity in GC, 74, and the unflattering reference to Jung's study of alchemy in MM, 90.

15 For a good study of pseudo-Dionysius's theories, see the reference to archetype in Roques, L'univers dionysien, 123; for information on anagogy as developed in the medieval sensus quadruplex, see Pelikan, The Melody of Theology, 119–23; on the similarity between the anagogue and the archetype, see Hinton, 'Anagogue and Archetype,' 57–63.

16 See, for example, Areopagite, The Celestial Hierarchy IV, 1. The word 'analogy', unlike 'anagogy' and 'archetype', appears in the Bible; see Frye's discussion of Romans 12:6 in GC, 61, 219.

17 Ayre, Northrop Frye, 229.

18 An earlier feminist critic, Annis Pratt, though dismayed by the sexism of the archetypes that Frye took from European literature for Anatomy, is impressed by the victim archetypes that he finds everywhere in Canadian literature; see her 'Spinning Among Fields.'

19 Frye told Cayley he would now favour a view of criticism as software (NFC, 63); Joseph Campbell voiced a similar thought in his work with Bill Moyers, The Power of Myth, 20.

20 This passage was quoted in Corsetti, Histoire de l'ésotérisme et des sciences occultes, 321. For a good introduction to this aspect of Corbin's thought, see Bamford, 'Esotericism Today,' 127, and throughout.

WORKS CITED

Ayre, John. *Northrop Frye: A Biography*. Toronto: Random House, 1989.

Baldick, Charles. *The Concise Oxford Book of Literary Terms*. Oxford: Oxford University Press, 1990.

Bamford, Christopher. 'Esotericism Today: The Example of Henry Corbin.' *Alexandria* 1 (1991): 121–61.

Blake, William. *The Poetry and Prose of William Blake*. Edited by David V. Erdman. New York: Doubleday, 1965.

Bodkin, Maud. *Archetypal Patterns in Poetry: Psychological Studies of the Imagination*. London: Oxford University Press, 1934.

Burckhardt, Titus. *The Mirror of the Intellect: Essays on Traditional Science and Sacred Art*. Translated and edited by William Stoddart. Cambridge: Quinta Essentia, 1987.

Burke, Kenneth. *Dramatism and Development*. Barre, Mass.: Clark University Press, 1972

Campbell, Joseph, and Bill Moyers. *The Power of Myth*. Edited by Betty Sue Flowers. New York: Doubleday, 1988.

Canadian Broadcasting Corporation. *Journey without Arrival: A Personal Point of View from Northrop Frye*. Toronto: Canadian Broadcasting Corporation. 1976. Documentary film.

Cook, David. *Northrop Frye: A Vision of the New World*. New York: St. Martin's, 1985.

Corsetti, Jean-Paul. *Histoire de l'ésotérisme et des sciences occultes*. Paris: Larousse, 1992.

Duncan, Joseph E. 'Archetypal Criticism in English, 1946–1980.' *Bulletin of Biography* 40 (1983): 206–30.

Economou, George. *The Goddess Natura in Medieval Literature*. Cambridge: Harvard University Press, 1972.

Euba, Femi. *Archetypes, Imprecators, and Victims of Fate: Origins and Developments of Satire in Black Drama*. New York: Greenwood Press, 1989.

Fiedler, Leslie. *No! in Thunder: Essays on Myth and Literature*. Boston: Beacon, 1960.

Frye, Northrop. 'Archetype' and 'Jungian Criticism.' In *The Harper Handbook to Literature*. With Sheridan Baker and George Perkins. New York: Harper, 1985.

– 'Literature and Myth,' and 'Myth and Myth Criticism: An Introductory Bibliography,' compiled with Jay Macpherson. In *Relations of Literary Study*, edited by James Thorpe. New York: MLA, 1967.

– 'Blake's Treatment of the Archetype.' In *English Institute Essays, 1950,* edited by Alan S. Downer. New York: Columbia University Press, 1951.

Godwin, Joscelyn. *Robert Fludd: Hermetic Philosopher and Surveyor of Two Worlds.* London: Thames and Hudson, 1979.

Hamilton, A.C. *Northrop Frye: Anatomy of His Criticism.* Toronto: University of Toronto Press, 1990.

Harbage, Alfred. *Shakespeare and the Rival Traditions.* New York: Macmillan, 1953.

Hillman, James. *A Blue Fire: Selected Writings by James Hillman.* Edited by Thomas Moore. New York: Harper, 1989.

Hinton, Norman. 'Anagogue and Archetype: The Phenomenology of Medieval Literature.' *Annuale Medievale* 7 (1966): 57–63.

Jung, C.G. *Collected Works.* Translated by R.F.C. Hull et al. Twenty volumes. Vol. 5, *Symbols of Transformation.* Vol. 9, part 1, *Archetypes of the Collective Unconscious.* Vol. 12, *Psychology and Alchemy.* New York: Pantheon; Princeton University Press, 1953–79.

– *Memories, Dreams, Reflections.* Recorded and edited by Aniela Jaffé; translated by Richard Wilson and Clara Wilson. New York: Random House, 1961.

Kugler, Paul. *The Alchemy of Discourse: An Archetypal Approach to Language.* Lewisburg: Bucknell University Press, 1982.

Lane, Lauriat, Jr, 'The Literary Archetype: Some Reconsiderations.' *Journal of Aesthetics and Art Criticism* 13 (1954): 226–32.

Locke, John. *An Essay Concerning Human Understanding.* Edited by Peter H. Nidditch. Oxford: Clarendon, 1975.

McQuaid, James Stanley. 'Robert Grosseteste on *The Celestial Hierarchy* of Pseudo-Dionysius the Areopagite: An Edition, Translation and Introduction of His Text and Commentary.' PhD diss., Queen's University, Belfast, 1961.

Panofsky, Irwin. *Studies in Iconology.* New York: Oxford University Press, 1939.

Pelikan, Jaroslav. *The Melody of Theology: A Philosophical Dictionary.* Cambridge: Harvard University Press, 1988.

Powers, Meredith A. *The Heroine in Western Literature: The Archetype and Her Reemergence in Modern Prose.* Jefferson, NC: McFarland, 1991.

Pratt, Annis V. 'Spinning among Fields: Jung, Frye, Lévi-Strauss.' In *Feminist Archetypal Theory: Interdisciplinary ReVisions of Jungian Thought,* edited by Estella Lauter and Carol Schreier Rupprecht. Knoxville: University of Tennessee Press, 1985.

Roques, René. *L'univers dionysien.* Paris: Aubier, 1954.

Stevens, Wallace. *The Collected Poems of Wallace Stevens*. New York: Albert A. Knopf, 1955.

van Meurs, Jos, and John Kidd. *Jungian Literary Criticism, 1920–1980: An Annotated Critical Bibliography of Works in English (with a Selection of Titles after 1980)*. Metuchen, NJ: Scarecrow Press, 1988.

Vaughan, Thomas. *The Works of Thomas Vaughan*. Edited by Arthur Edward Waite. London: Theosophical Publishing, 1919.

Willard, Thomas. 'Alchemy and the Bible.' In *Centre and Labyrinth: Essays in Honour of Northrop Frye*, edited by Eleanor Cook et al. Toronto: University of Toronto Press, 1982.

Williamson, Eugene. 'Plato's *Eidos* and the Archetypes of Jung and Frye.' *Interpretations* 16 (1985): 94–104.

Yates, Frances A. *Giordano Bruno and the Hermetic Tradition*. London: Routledge; Chicago: University of Chicago Press, 1964.

HAYDEN WHITE

Frye's Place in Contemporary Cultural Studies

On wild trees the flowers are fragrant; on cultivated trees, the fruit.
– Kierkegaard

In this essay I want to reflect on what I take to be Frye's enduring contribution to cultural studies. I once characterized him in print as the greatest natural cultural historian of our time; and I want to expand on that generalization in order to pay tribute to Professor Frye's brilliance as a theorist of culture and renovator of humanistic studies in the second half of our century.

I cannot pretend to any special intimacy of acquaintance with Professor Frye. We met and talked a few times, first at Cornell University in the spring of 1970, at the Society for the Humanities, where we occupied contiguous offices for a few weeks. He would stop by from time to time and lean on the door-frame to chat. I attended some seminars he gave on Blake, Stevens, Joyce, and Yeats. We met a few times afterwards, when I was visiting lecturer at the University of Toronto, at the MLA celebration of his seventy-fifth birthday, and finally, during the summer before his death, for a moment at the entrance of Massey College. I recall that, on the last two occasions we met, we talked about 'mode' and the relation between the musical and the literary or poetic notions of modality. He was unfailingly courteous although always slightly reserved; I had the feeling that he was always in that shop in the back of the mind of which Montaigne spoke, working on some intellectual issue.

The name Frye has always been, since the moment I first opened *Anatomy of Criticism* in 1960 or thereabouts, a metonymy for serious, systematic but flexible and always developing reflection on the nature of culture, the conditions of cultural creativity, and the fate of our civilization. Frye remarks somewhere that 'the great synthesis of Marx and Spengler has yet to be written.' Whether Frye thought such a synthesis could be written or should even be attempted is difficult to say, but only a scholar with Frye's range of interests and desire to make sense of history could even have envisioned such a project. It might be instructive to reflect on some of the implications of his envisioned coupling of Marx and Spengler, the radical and the reactionary, the would-be scientist of history and the Nietzschean aesthete. Presumably, a synthesis of these two 'metahistorians'[1] would have resulted, not in a monstrous mixture of species, but in something quite new and radically different from earlier philosophies of history. It would be a comprehensive theory of history that refused either to reduce culture to a function of material determinations, on the one side, or to inflate, spiritualize, and fetishize it, on the other – the kind of theory of culture that is implicit in Frye's *Anatomy of Criticism*.

Contemporary practitioners of what has come to be called 'cultural studies' have not on the whole found much of use in Frye's work. In part this is because cultural studies is a neo-Marxist activity, inspired by the example of such figures as Gramsci, Raymond Williams, Stuart Hall, Jürgen Habermas, and Louis Althusser, adamantly historicist therefore and paranoically hostile to anything smacking of formalism, structuralism, idealism, or organicism. Insofar, then, as Frye's work is noted at all by practitioners of cultural studies, it is as an example of these fallacious or misguided (insofar as they are ahistorical) ideologies. He is put down as one who believed that literature was paradigmatic of culture, that culture itself was autonomous vis à vis society and the modes of material production that determine dominant social formations, and that, accordingly, both culture and society can be studied only in an ahistorical, which is to say, a synchronic, structuralist, or formal manner. The panorama of historical occurrence which Frye is thus supposed to have confronted consists of a finite set of forms of cultural expression of which literature is a paradigm. These interact significantly only with one another and not at all with the more mundane world of economic, political, and social praxis, and they develop only insofar as they succeed one another in positions of dominance and subordination cyclically (rather than progressively or developmentally or dialectically). For Frye, it would seem, everything happens in cycles. So goes the negative account of Frye's system.

It seems incredible that anyone who has taken the least trouble to read any of Frye's work would credit him with such a banal conception of culture, literature, and history. It would take someone profoundly ignorant of history to think that history develops in either a cyclical or a linear (or for that matter a spiral) form. And I have never understood why historians of historical thinking attribute such models to sophisticated thinkers like Spengler or Nietzsche or Mill or Hegel. It will not do, however, simply to dismiss this hostile characterization of Frye's position as a product of prejudice or ignorance alone. First, because the cultural-studies Marxists who criticize Frye for his formalism, structuralism, idealism, and so on, are not equally prejudiced against Frye's critical practice, his theory of criticism, and his idea of the relation of criticism, literature, and culture. Some of them have read Frye closely; a number are sympathetic to his larger project of systematizing literary studies; and a few even consider him to have provided a viable model for a Marxist theory of culture. (In this last category I place Fredric Jameson in particular.)[2] Then, too, it must be said that a good number of conservative critics and students of culture concur with Frye's Marxist critics in their suspicion of his systematicity, the formalist-taxonomic bent of his work, his demystification of tradition, and what appears to be the determinism of those patterns he purports to find not only in literary criticism, but in the historical development of literary styles as well.

It is this agreement across what would otherwise be radically opposed ideological positions on the seemingly ahistorical nature of Frye's system that must give us pause in our effort to identify Frye's enduring contribution to contemporary cultural studies. For, on the face of it, there is some truth to the charge that Frye's system is ahistorical, in the way, for example, that Spengler's system, so subtly analysed by Frye in an essay of 1974,[3] was, and indeed still is, thought to be ahistorical. The alleged ahistoricity stems from what appears to be a cyclical model of literary, critical, and cultural change. In this model progress is measured, if at all, only by an originary displacement of mythic structures of consciousness into a variety of kinds of fiction, of which literature or poetry is one, and then a recurrence within fiction of a discrete set of kinds of modes, symbols, story forms or myths, and genres, the natures of which are defined primarily in terms of their relationships with one another, rather than with some extraliterary, social, or material causal principle that would allow us to explain their transformations in other than autotelic terms. Progress in this system, if such there be, consists only in the recombination of a finite (though unbounded) set of discrete elements and a rearrangement of hierarchies of relationships among them in ways that appear to render useless any effort to identify the intentions of individual human agents or authors, the expectations of patients or readers, or the constraints imposed by social and cultural institutions that might be appealed to as causal forces in order to explain why any given change in the field of literature, and by extension in culture in general, occurred when, where, and in the way that it did. Changes in modes (from romance through high and low mimetic to ironic), in symbols (from sign through image and archetype to monad), in archetypes (from romance through tragedy and comedy to satire), and in genres (from epic through lyric and dramatic to encyclopaedic) appear to replicate the sequence of the main kinds of critical practice (from historical through ethical and archetypal to rhetorical), never breaking the cycle but only going back to the first in order to permit the pattern to be repeated again – and again. Whence the opinion, often expressed, regarding Frye's similarity not only to Spengler but also, and above all, to Jung.

While this understanding of the nature of Frye's system can be justified by a reading of his work that focuses on his exploitation of the technique of synchronicity for characterizing the structure of literature, culture, and civilization, it yields insight into only one aspect of his system and neither the whole nor the essential element of it. Frye was nothing if not a philosopher of human freedom, of artistic creativity, and beyond that of a generally human power of species self-creation. This is the Viconian component in his thought, and it is absolutely essential for an understanding of both his project and his articulation of it across a very long and very consistent career of intellectual work. Frye often cites Vico's famous formula *verum factum est*. This is usually translated as 'the true is the made' and cited as a tag for Vico's idea that one can truly know only that which one has oneself made or is capable of making. Vico used the idea to distinguish between the kind of knowledge that human beings can have of culture and that which they can have of nature. This theory is called 'maker's knowledge,' and it holds that, since nature was made by God, human beings can never hope to have the kind of knowledge of it that only God could possess. However, the theory also says, since culture is a distinctively human creation, human beings can aspire to a knowledge of culture of a kind and degree utterly different from that which they can have of the rest of nature. And since history is the record of this process of cultural creation, human beings can legitimately aspire to a knowledge both of history and of themselves as the agents of a specifically historical mode of existence that is both more true and more certain than any knowledge they can ever hope to have of nature. Historical knowledge, in short, is human self-knowledge and specifically knowledge of how human beings make themselves through knowing themselves and come to know themselves in the process of making themselves.

Vico's theory of 'maker's knowledge' provides an epistemological basis for an ethics and pedagogy of humanism radically different from that of Enlightenment rationalism.[4] 'Maker's knowledge' is not only a way of characterizing the kind of activity we might wish to call 'poetic'; it is also a way of characterizing the kind of knowledge we get from reflecting on human creativity. Recall that it was Vico who, against the emergent rationalist dogmas of the Enlightenment, purported to find the secret of human creativity, of culture, and therefore of human history, not in reason or even in the will, but rather in the imagination, specifically in the human capacity to think in images as well as in concepts, to coin metaphors and then use them as a basis for action in, against, and with the rest of nature, and thereby to humanize nature and make of it a dwelling place adequate to the satisfaction of distinctively human, as against generally animal, needs and desires.[5] Whereas Kant and the Enlightenment in general viewed metaphor as the source of all error, Vico viewed metaphor as the basis of a uniquely human kind of intellection, an intellection that was projective as well as reflective, capable not only of registering and combining experiences but of shaping them as well – in precisely the same way that the poet shapes language and, in shaping it, revivifies it, remakes it, makes it new, at once revealing hitherto unapprehended potentialities for expression in it and permitting the world to appear in a new and unexpected light at the same time. For Vico, metaphor and image were not presumed to stand over against concept and perception as madness to reason or error to truth. On the contrary, Vico envisioned a continuity between metaphoric thinking (what he called 'poetic logic' [*The New Science*, Book III]) and rational or scientific thinking, the former being related to the latter not as an inferior or childish kind of thinking to a superior or adult kind of thought, but rather as an opening stanza of a poem might be related to its final stanza or, more pertinently, as a poetic prefiguration is related to its fulfilled form.

This relationship of the beginning of a poem to its conclusion, or of a prefiguration to its fulfilled form, served Vico as a model of the relationship between primitive and civilized consciousness, of that between the earliest age or originary period of a civilization and its latest or decadent period, between the imagination and reason, between popular culture and high or élite culture, and between the human body and the human mind. He did not view the relations thus posited as being either causal or teleological in kind. Those aspects of human nature and culture conventionally regarded as higher or more advanced were not to be regarded as effects of causes more basic nor were they to be seen as aims, ends, or purposes inherent in things by virtue of genetic endowment, in the manner of an Aristotelian oak-in-acorn. They are, rather, more in the nature of modal transformations of the kind encountered in music or mathematics, with the difference that they exist in things human and historical rather than only in concepts or in algorithms.

Like Vico, and, it might be added, like Hegel, Marx, Nietzsche, Freud, and Weber – thinkers who have learned to see dialectically[6] – Frye apprehends continuities and interanimations, rather than oppositions, between those phenomena conventionally called truth and error, sanity and madness, good and evil, objectivity and subjectivity, the letter and the spirit, the literal and the figurative, and even between art and life or, within literary art, between poetry and prose, and within each of these, between great, noble, or high forms, on the one side, and their humble, popular, or low counterparts, on the other. As thus envisaged, the world of cultural forms is a stable plenum which, rather than undergoing the kind of change we would call historical, would seem to resemble more a field of electromagnetic force or a mathematical matrix marked less by evolution than by changing intensities, displacements, and modalities. Certainly, this is the kind of thing suggested by those numerous schemata and descriptions of modular relationships (as between mythic archetypes, genres, modes, symbols, and the like) encountered in works like *Anatomy*, *Words with Power*, or the essays collected in *Fables of Identity*.

But such schemata apply only to those moments in which Frye – drawing back from the panorama of Western cultural history or the history of Western literature from the Greeks and the ancient Hebrews to the present – seeks to view it whole and synchronically and to capture its most prominent structural features as if in a kind of still photograph or holographic reproduction. That this system has undergone change and continues to undergo change goes without saying. The crucial role of the concept of displacement in Frye's work from first to last indicates as much. But displacement is a concept used to characterize the translation of the structures and imagery of myth into literature; it is a concept that makes it possible to conceive of literature as having a history.[7] And while displacement continues within literature – for example, 'displacement in the direction of the moral' (*AC*, 155) when desire is subjected to 'ethical refinement,' as with the Victorians (*AC*, 156) – it can hardly be conceived as a principle of qualitative change of the kind we associate with real historical development. The displacement of a genre, mode, myth, symbol, or whatever, from one place to another in the system of literature would be an example of what Spengler called 'pseudo-morphosis.'[8] Like another fundamental concept in Frye's system, condensation (the equivalent of Freud's *Dichtungsarbeit*, in *The Interpretation of Dreams*), displacement indicates a quantitative rather than a qualitative change. The field of literature, or criticism, or culture undergoes change, but only of either local intensities (condensations) or pseudo-morphosis (displacement).

But this is as it should be for any builder of a system. A systematization is a spatialization of a process which must, in the nature of its operations, suppress awareness of temporality and change and fix attention solely upon what remains constant. But when it comes to historical phenomena, which is to say, phenomena that have as their fundamental mode of being in the world their responsiveness to time and its effects, it is necessary to switch, as it were, from the synchronic to the diachronic mode in order to theorize a model, not of structure but of sequentiation, for which the notions of condensation and displacement, with their suggestions of intensification, on the one hand, and of movement, on the other, must be inadequate.

I think it is fair to say that Frye had trouble with history, and he had trouble with it because, first of all, he believed in it, which is to say, he believed that culture and society did change and changed in qualitative as well as quantitative ways; but, secondly, he believed that the ways in which culture and society changed were quite different from the ways in which nature or different aspects of nature changed. And I think it fair to say that historical change was a problem for Frye, because unlike, say, Freud, he did not believe that things had to be viewed from the perspective of the final entropic 'blah.' Nor did he believe, at least as a principle of professional, as against personal, faith, that everything was going to come out all right in the end. What Frye needed was some kind of equivalent to Kant's idea of the purposiveness of the art object, which is to say, an idea of nonpurposive purposiveness, in order to be able to say that both literature and criticism and, finally, culture itself displayed evidence of the kind of progressive closure with reality as that promised in the Book of Revelations. In my view, this is the idea that reappears, again and again, in Frye's work, at least since *Anatomy*, but especially in both *The Great Code* and *Words with Power*.

Frye explicitly rejected a conception of historical inquiry directed at a perfect recovery or even minimally adequate reconstitution of the past. In *Anatomy*, he cited 'a fascinating little book called *Repetition*' by Søren Kierkegaard, and proposed using 'repetition' as an alternative to the

'Platonic' notion of anamnesis or 'recollection.' By 'repetition,' Frye tells us, Kierkegaard apparently meant, 'not the simple repeating of an experience, but the recreating of it which redeems or awakens it to life, the end of the process ... being the apocalyptic promise: "Behold, I make all things new"' (AC, 345). 'Without this sense of "repetition,"' Frye concludes, 'historical criticism tends to remove the products of culture from our own sphere of interest. It must be counterpoised, as it is in all genuine historical critics, by a sense of the contemporary relevance of past art' (AC, 346).

In his 'fascinating little book,' Kierkegaard used the notion of repetition to characterize those aspects of life in which what otherwise would seem to be mere 'transition' is grasped as a 'becoming.' And he writes: 'Repetition and recollection are the same movement, only in opposite directions; for what is recollected has been, is repeated backwards, whereas repetition properly so-called is re-collected forwards' (Repetition, 4).

'Repetition' or 'recollecting forwards' constitutes the basis of Frye's conception of an 'ethical criticism,' a criticism which 'relates culture ... to the future, to the ideal society which may eventually come,' just as 'the imaginative element in works of art ... lifts them clear of the bondage of history' (AC, 346–7). It is the utopian impulse that provides Frye with his unique conception of historical change and historical understanding.

It is interesting to note that Frye returns to the idea of repetition again and again over the course of his career, especially in the two late works, The Great Code and Words with Power. For example, in the former work, he cites the notion as marking a difference between 'a past-directed causality and a future-directed typology. The mere attempt to repeat a past experience,' he observes, 'will lead only to disillusionment, but there is another kind of repetition which is the Christian antithesis (or complement) of Platonic recollection, and which finds its focus in the Biblical promise: "Behold, I make all things new" (Revelation 21:5).' Frye goes on, then, to identify Kierkegaard's 'repetition' with 'the forward moving typological thinking of the Bible' (GC, 82).[9] And he argues that typology is 'essentially a revolutionary form of thought and rhetoric,' the 'metaphorical kernel' of which is the 'experience of waking up from a dream, as when Joyce's Stephen Dedalus speaks of history as a nightmare from which he is trying to awake.' The kind of transition indicated here is like that of waking from sleep: 'one world is simply abolished and replaced by another.' We have revolutionary thought, he says, whenever 'the feeling "life is a dream" becomes geared to an impulse to awaken from it.' It is the 'typological structure and shape of the Bible' which makes 'its mythology diachronic, in contrast to the synchronic mythology characteristic of most of the religions outside it' (GC, 82–3). Thus Frye concludes: 'What typology really is as a mode of thought, what it both assumes and leads to, is a theory of history, or more accurately of historical process: an assumption that there is some meaning and point to history, and that sooner or later some event or events will occur which will indicate what that meaning or point is, and so become an antitype of what has happened previously' (GC, 80–1).

Here we get to the crux of Frye's theory of historical change, or what amounts to the same thing, his theory of cultural/literary change. Repetition – 'not the simple repeating of an experience, but the recreating of it which redeems or awakens it to life' – names the process productive of the type/antitype relationship by which a later event, text, period, culture, thought, or action can be said to have 'fulfilled' an earlier one – in the same way that a figure of speech such as metalepsis or irony can be said to have 'fulfilled' another figure – such as prolepsis or metonymy – that may have preceded it in a verbal sequence. 'Fulfillment' here is to be understood as the product or effect of a kind of reverse causation – a kind of causation peculiar to historical reality, culture, and human consciousness, by which a thing of the past is at once grasped by consciousness, brought into the present by recollection, and redeemed, made new, by being put to a use theretofore unforeseeable by human beings responding to the press of what Frye calls 'secondary concerns' and having been diverted from their 'primary concerns': food and drink, sex, property, and 'liberty of movement' (WP, 42–6). Fulfillment (or 'antitypicality') is less like the kind of thing that happens as a result of a process of mechanistic causation than the kind of thing that happens when a person fulfills a promise, honours a vow, remembers an oath, or performs a duty. It is a peculiarly human kind of 'construal' of a relationship between a past and a present.

The archetype or paradigm of this process of change Frye found, of course, in the Christian appropriation of the Hebrew Bible (or the whole of ancient Judaic culture in general) treated as a prefiguration (or type) of which the New Testament (or Christianity in general) was held to be the fulfillment (or antitype). Needless to say, his seeming valorization of this process of cultural appropriation by virtue of his treatment of it as the very paradigm of cultural creativity did not endear him to critical theorists – both Jewish, like Harold Bloom, and not Jewish, like Barbara Johnson – for whom a notion of creativity based on a concept of what they regarded as 'expropriation,' however benign or merely 'symbolic' it was presumed to be, was repugnant. Thus, for example, Bloom feels 'moved to reject ... idealized modes of interpretation ... stimulated [by the historical triumph of Christianity], from the early typology on to the revival of *figura* by Erich Auerbach and the Blakean *Great Code* of Frye. No text,' Bloom informs us, 'fulfills another text and all who insist otherwise merely homogenize literature' (' "Before Moses Was," ' 13).[10]

Bloom's criticism of Frye's typological or figural model of historical change[11] seems unduly harsh inasmuch as Bloom's own theories of the 'anxiety of influence,' or 'misprision,' and the necessarily 'agonistic' nature of all writing can legitimately be viewed – or so it seems to me – as another version of the prefiguration-fulfillment model. And far from leading to an 'idealized mode of interpretation' which promotes the notion of a 'homogenized literature' (or history, for that matter), the prefiguration-fulfillment model provides a way of construing the processes of cultural production which we alone wish to call 'historical'. For this notion of the relation obtaining between the earlier aspects or periods of a culture's history and later ones allows us to take into account the fact that – in history at least – there is no such thing as creation *ex nihilo*. It dispels thereby the myth of a creativity without violence. Moreover, it allows us to conceptualize the problem of the relationship between tradition (that body of cultural artifacts inherited from the past) and the kinds of cultural innovation which, though manifestly different from what had come before, still appear to be linked in some essential, but nongenetically, determined way to the past. The prefiguration-fulfillment model, indeed, provides a notion of genealogical affiliation as an historically responsible alternative to the physical and biological conception of a genetic relationship. Finally, and this strikes me as the most importantly realistic aspect of Frye's idea of cultural history (as against its alleged 'idealism'), the prefiguration-fulfillment model of cultural change, with its notion of retrospective expropriation of the products of past creative efforts, reminds us of the 'fallen' nature of any exercise of merely human creativity, namely, that it is always an exercise of power, that it is violent, and that it redeems itself only in the extent to which it 'makes new' the cultural artifacts it used as the material cause of its own operation.

NOTES

Epigraph, in Kierkegaard, *Repetition: An Essay in Experimental Psychology*, 2. Kierkegaard published this essay in 1843 under the pseudonym Constantine Constantius. He claims to have found the saying in 'Stories from Heroes by Philostratus the Elder.'

1 This was a term which Frye used in an essay, 'New Directions from Old,'

many years ago and from which I took the title of one of my books. I first
encountered the term, used in a derogatory sense, somewhere in the work
of Collingwood. Frye's use of the term was not derogatory, although in
later life he sometimes grouped it with a number of other *meta* words
which he used to connote an overly ambitious kind of system-building.
Yet Frye's own enterprise, from his book on Blake on through *Anatomy of
Criticism* to *Words with Power*, is nothing if not 'metacritical.'

2 See especially Fredric Jameson, Introduction to *The Political Unconscious*,
  68–74.

3 Frye's 'Spengler Revisited,' in *SM*, 179–98. The essay originally appeared
  in *Daedalus* (Winter 1974).

4 Cf. Isaiah Berlin, 'Vico's Theory of Knowledge and Its Sources,' in *Vico and
  Herder*, 99ff.

5 Lest this be considered as little more than a namby-pamby Enlightenment
  progressive thought, I should stress that Vico recognized that humanity
  contained within itself the capacity for its own and nature's (or at least the
  world's) destruction as well as a capacity for transforming 'nature' into
  'culture.' Had humanity not had the capacity to destroy as well as to
  create, it could not be considered free.

6 By 'dialectically' I mean, literally, 'reading across', not what is supposed to
  be the Hegelian trinitarian concept of 'thesis, antithesis, synthesis.' Frye's
  system is not trinitarian but what biblical scholarship called 'diatessaron-
  ic,' consisting of the 'fourfold' rather than the 'trinitarian' web of relationships. I invite readers curious about this notion of the fourfold, which has
  nothing to do with number mysticism but, rather, everything to do with
  the theory of taxonomy which requires at least a 'dual binary' in order to
  be what mathematicians might call interesting, I invite such readers to
  look at the *OED* entry under 'diatessaron'.

7 'The presence of a mythical structure in realistic fiction ... poses certain
  technical problems for making it plausible, and the devices used in solving
  these problems may be given the general name of *displacement*' (*AC*, 136).

8 Frye's 'displacement' resembles, of course, Freud's notion of '*Verschiebung-
  sarbeit*' (usually translated as 'displacement'). It is an aspect of 'primary
  process' thinking which, in the 'dreamwork,' transfers an affect from one
  ideation to some other one in the service of denial or negation.

9 Frye writes: 'Kierkegaard's "repetition" is certainly derived from, and to
  my mind is identifiable with the forward moving typological thinking of
  the Bible' (*GC*, 82).

10 It was mentioned to me after the lecture at which this text was originally
   presented that the Christian and specifically the Pauline notion of 'fulfillment' implies or presumes or connotes, in addition to the sense of 'realiza-

tion' or 'consummation', the idea as well of 'abolition'. This secondary (or primary) connotation would thus account for the resentment that Jewish scholars might feel for the typological thinking in general and the versions of it which take as unproblematical the idea that Christianity might be a 'fulfillment' of Judaism. The notion that the Christian Testament might be a 'fulfillment' of the Hebrew Testament would imply that Christianity not only 'realizes' or 'consummates' ancient Judaism but also 'abolishes' it. It should be said, however, that the idea of 'fulfillment' found in the Christian Testament (in Romans, 2 Corinthians, and Galatians) is expressed in ηλερόω and ηλερομα, neither of which, as far as I can tell, connotes 'abolish' or 'abolition' (rendered in the Christian Testament as κατάργεο). There can be no doubt that later Christian theology treated the idea of fulfillment as entailing the abolition (in the Hegelian sense of *Aufhebung* or 'sublimation'?) of Hebrew law and therewith the religion of the Hebrews. But this does not seem to me to be sufficient reason to reject the Christian idea of typology or *figura* as providing a model of historical change and transformation. What typology or figure-fulfillment suggests is that a later generation may choose to view itself as an heir of an earlier idea, value, or institution. Like it or not in a specific case, the fact of the matter is that this is the way 'history' works.

11 Which was explicitly embraced by Frye in 1957 as that which led him to the conceptualization of *Anatomy*. Cf. *AC*, vii.

WORKS CITED

Berlin, Isaiah. 'Vico's Theory of Knowledge and Its Sources.' In *Vico and Herder: Two Studies in the History of Ideas*. New York: Viking Press, 1976.

Bloom, Harold. ' "Before Moses Was, I Am": The Original and Belated Testaments.' In *Notebooks in Cultural Analysis: An Annual Review*, edited by Norman F. Cantor and Nathalia King. Vol. 1. Durham: Duke University Press, 1984.

Jameson, Fredric. Introduction. In *The Political Unconscious: Narrative as a Socially Symbolic Act*. Ithaca: Cornell University Press, 1981.

Kierkegaard, Søren. Epigraph. In *Repetition: An Essay in Experimental Psychology*, translated by Walter Lowrie. Princeton: Princeton University Press, 1946.

Vico, Giambattista. Book III. In *The New Science of Giambattista Vico*. Rev. ed. Translated from 3rd ed. of 1744 by Thomas G. Bergin and Max H. Fisch. Ithaca: Cornell University Press, 1970.

CRAIG STEWART WALKER

Religious Experience in the Work of Frye

1

One of the characteristic preoccupations of the modern age has been the problem of how to account for human identity. The question hinges on the degree to which human identity is externally determined or predetermined, and the degree to which human beings are free to determine their own identity. It is an anxious question, in part because, while the advances made in disciplines such as biology, sociology, and psychology have improved our understanding of the various forces that fix or predetermine a human being's identity, we find that our ability to account for the aspect of the self that is not determined by these forces, but continues to exercise free will, has scarcely improved at all.

Any concept of freedom will require two elements: the first is the will at the centre of the self that is free to choose; and the second is a context within which the free will operates. In other words, in order to experience freedom, one must believe that the free act has meaning. The English novelist Nicholas Mosley made such an argument in a theological essay written in the sixties, arguing that what gives freedom meaning in everyday life is our general sense of the kind of people we choose to be. Accordingly, we experience this freedom less through our ability to compel others to do our will than through our courage to face any rationalizations and self-deceptions, to move beyond the circumstances that might blind us. The question of how this position of authority is to be attained 'was once the business of religion,' Mosley suggests. 'Religion was what let men be free, gave men an area of freedom; suggested what to make of themselves in it. Religion was about the sort of disciplines, guides, there were in the achieving of this in oneself; about what could be done about it for others' (*Religion and Experience*, 35–7, 47). Yet it is obvious that the language of religion is widely regarded with suspicion or indifference today.

There are several good reasons for such misgivings about religion. In the first place, religion has too often placed itself on the defensive by taking any new idea that requires a modification of religious faith as a kind of attack. That attitude has resulted, argues Alfred North Whitehead in *Science and the Modern World*, in the degeneration of religion 'into a decent formula wherewith to embellish a comfortable life,' because of its apparent inadequacy to engage the modern world in any serious manner (168). Whitehead remarks on the contrast between religion and science in this respect: 'when Darwin or Einstein proclaims theories which modify our ideas, it is a triumph for science. We do not go about saying that there is another defeat for science, because its old ideas have been abandoned. We know that another step of scientific insight has been gained. Religion will not regain its old power until it can face change in the same spirit as does science. Its principles may be eternal, but the expression of those principles requires continual development' (168). In the second place, there is an understandable reluctance to engage one's personal identity with any authority that has so often proved itself unreliable in the direction of human enterprises. But such misgivings about religion carry a price, which Charles Taylor in *Sources of the Self* has called 'the dilemma of mutilation.' Taylor frankly admits that 'the great spiritual visions of human history have also been poisoned chalices, the causes of untold misery and even savagery. From the very beginning of the human story religion, our link with the highest, has been recurrently associated with sacrifice, even mutilation, as though something of us has to be torn away, or immolated if we are to please the gods' (519). On the other hand, says Taylor, 'adopting a stripped-down secular outlook, without any religious dimension,' also results in a 'mutilation,' insofar as it entails 'stifling the response in us to some of the deepest and most powerful spiritual aspirations that humans have achieved' (520). It would seem, moreover, that despite all our misgivings about the possible dangers of such spiritual aspirations, they remain an indefatigable element in our thought, which may retire from explicitly religious domains only to reappear in other cultural guises, be they artistic or metaphysical.

The predicament, then, can be described in this way: it seems necessary to locate, and find a way of speaking about, an aspect of human experience that in some way can transcend the realm of materialist reason and thereby provide identity with an escape from an ultimately determinist conclusion. Yet, at the same time, it seems impossible to accept the kind of surrender of self that the acceptance of a divine authority so often demands. One way of approaching the predicament is to revisit the question of religious experience with a view to determining whether there is something in this concept that is compatible with the modern mind. In other words, we would want assurance that some meaningful way of understanding human spirituality was possible, which did not necessitate a repudiation of reason or an acceptance of what seemed to be superstitious nonsense; which would help to clarify our sense of individual freedom with regard to both the human community and our material environment; and which would not require the kind of self-surrender that would rob us of our need for a sense of self-determination. This essay attempts to show how one such version of religious experience may be construed from the work of Frye.

2

The phrase 'religious experience' commonly refers to two ideas. When someone speaks of having had a religious experience, it refers to an event, a finite and present sense of spiritual communion. When there is discussion of whether some statement or action is commensurate with religious experience, the phrase refers to a body of wisdom which has been accumulated through contemplation of spiritual matters – in other words, a general spiritual outlook. Both ideas are pertinent to this essay, which attempts to show, first, that certain specific moments of insight in Frye's life have the character of particular events of spiritual communion, and, second, that these inform and are interrelated with Frye's general spiritual outlook, which in turn pervades all aspects of his thought. Having established these points, I will suggest how Frye's version of religious experience relates to some other trends in religious experience in the twentieth century.

In *The Double Vision*, Frye declares that he has spent 'the better part of seventy-eight years writing out the implications of insights that have taken up considerably less than an hour of all those years' (55), and I intend to take him at his word by isolating and discussing a few of these moments of insight. In some cases, the details are too sketchy to allow for much discussion: for example, Frye spoke of the importance of a particular reading of Spengler's *Decline of the West* at the Edmonton YMCA in 1931,[1] but the precise character of the experience itself remains obscure. On the other hand, there are at least three other occasions during which Frye underwent an experience of what might be called a religious kind, of which he was able to provide a more precise account.

All three of these experiences occurred fairly early in Frye's life, the first two in his teenage years, the third in his early twenties, yet each had a decisive effect that stayed with him for the rest of his life. Frye's first such experience took place while he was a student at Aberdeen High School in Moncton. In a 1979 interview with Bob Sandler, he remembered

walking along St. George St. to high school and just suddenly that whole shitty and smelly garment (of fundamentalist teaching I had all my life) just dropped off into the sewers and stayed there. It was like the Bunyan feeling, about the burden of sin falling off his back only with me it was a burden of anxiety. Anything might have touched it off, but I don't know what specifically did, or if anything did. I just remember that suddenly that that was no longer a part of me and would never be again.[2]

Frye explained something of the effect of that Damascene experience in a letter to Roy Daniells, saying that he had decided,

without realizing it at the time, that I was going to accept out of religion only what made sense to me as a human being. I was not going to worship a god whose actions, judged by human standards, were contemptible. That was where Blake helped me so much: he taught me that the lugubrious old stinker in the sky that I had heard so much about existed all right, but that his name was Satan, that his function was to promote tyranny in society and repression in the mind. This meant that the Methodist church down at the corner was consecrated mainly to devil-worship, but, because it did not know that, it would tolerate something better without knowing what that was either.[3]

John Ayre includes this story in his biography of Frye, calling the event 'a parody of the Methodist conversion experience his Howard and Demorest predecessors so earnestly demanded of themselves' (44). That Frye's religious experiences bear some relation to the Methodist tradition in which he was raised is an important issue; but, in my view, Ayre's comment begs rather than answers the question of the degree to which Frye's experience is parodic or genuine, a point to which I shall return shortly.

The second particular experience has been less precisely explained, but one finds fragments referring to the event scattered throughout Frye's work.[4] The kernel apparently lies in a train ride which Frye took in 1927 to visit his sister, Vera, in Chicago at age fourteen (*NFC*, 44). This initial experience was later augmented by a number of other overnight train rides, but it was that first long journey that left the deepest impression on Frye's mind. The phenomenon that precipitated the insight is familiar to all those who have sat awake on a train overnight: as one sits drowsily watching the world pass by outside the window and the sky gradually darkens, there comes a moment of discovery that what one is looking at is no longer the scenery outside the window, but rather reflections in the window pane of objects that are actually inside the carriage. The period of mesmerized ambiguity about what is inside and what is outside, what is illusion and what is reality, gradually gives way to a point at which the outside world is all but invisible, and one is left merely staring at one's own reflection. As the dawn breaks, the process is reversed, and by stages one's focus and understanding of the objects of perception are taken up by the outside world again.

The phenomenon itself is not so remarkable, of course, as the insight which it occasioned for Frye. In essence, this was the realization that nature and the world at large always appear within an envelope of human interpretation; accordingly, the passive mind will find itself gazing at an illusion it believes is reality and, unaware of the projected character of what it perceives, numbed and satisfied by this illusion, it will end by staring complacently at its own narcissistic reflection. Set against the deluded passive mind is the active imagination, which struggles to detach its projections from its perceptions through a process of critical analysis.

Frye's third experience occurred in an academic context, and belongs to a species of insight known to many a desperate undergraduate; as Frye describes it, the 'one split second when, cramming for an examination and dizzy with lack of sleep and benzedrine, he suddenly kn[ows] that something of which his own mind form[s] a part [is] much more deeply involved in the nature of things than he had ever dreamed' (*LT*, 19). Frye's version of this experience took place in Bowles Lunch, an all-night diner on Bloor Street, where he was working on an essay discussing Blake's poem *Milton*, a paper, he tells us,

I sat down to write, as was my regular bad habit in those days, the night before. The foreground of the paper was commentary, which was assuredly difficult enough for that poem, but in the background there was some principle that kept eluding me. On inspection, the principle seemed to be that Milton and Blake were connected by their use of the Bible, which was not merely commonplace but seemed anti- literary as well. If Milton and Blake were alike on this point, that likeness merely concealed what was individual about each of them, so that in pursuing the likeness I was chasing a shadow and avoiding the substance. Around about three in the morning a different kind of intuition hit me, though it took me twenty years to articulate it. The two poets were connected by the *same* thing, and sameness leads to individual variety, just as likeness leads to monotony. I began dimly to see that the principle pulling me away from the historical period was the principle of mythological framework. The Bible had provided a frame of mythology for European poets: an immense number of critical problems began to solve themselves as soon as one realized this. (*SM*, 17)

Frye adds, 'So far from hitching literature to a structure of belief, this principle actually emancipates literature from questions of belief altogether' (*SM*, 18).[5] *The Great Code* and *Words with Power* are only the most obvious derivations of that insight.

3

Before looking at the place of these individual experiences within Frye's general outlook, I should like to say a word about my criteria for calling these experiences religious. It is obvious enough how the first experience falls into the category (although undoubtedly even it would be deemed irreligious rather than religious by many), but it may seem that the other two experiences are moments of critical or philosophical insight that have less apparent connections with religion. To help clarify this matter, I shall refer (as practically any serious discussion of religious experience must) to William James's classic, *The Varieties of Religious Experience* which, though ninety years old, remains the most provocative and one of the most comprehensive studies of the subject available. James devotes most of his book to documenting the details of personal testimonies, then attempts to draw some general conclusions about the nature of religious experience, working from the most neutral (and yet still useful) definition of religion possible, as a 'total attitude of a serious nature.' He suggests that what this broad array of experiences shares is a dialectical pattern, which begins with 'a sense that there is *something wrong about us* as we naturally stand' and moves to 'a sense that *we are saved from the wrongness* by making proper connection with the higher powers.' This latter sense results in the subject's consciousness 'that this higher part is coterminous and continuous with a MORE of the same quality, which is operative in the universe outside of him, and which he can keep in working touch with, and in a fashion get on board of and save himself when all his lower being has gone to pieces in the wreck' (507–8). In the three moments of insight I have chosen from Frye's life, we see this saving connection with higher powers in the form of, respectively, the liberation from anxiety encountered in the sense of a divinity superior to the literalist, fundamentalist dogma; the recognition that what the passive mind takes for reality is illusion and that the active, critical mind is the connection to truth; and the recognition of the principle by which a mythological framework may be used as a structure that transcends specific ideological attachment.

However, James makes a point of the sense of 'the exteriority of the helping power' in these accounts of religious experience, and this raises the question of whether there is a corresponding sense of 'exteriority' in Frye's insights. The answer is not simple, and is additionally complicated because the question is effectively rendered moot by James himself, who suggests that 'whatever it may be on its *farther* side, the "more" with which in religious experience we feel ourselves connected is on its *hither* side the subconscious continuation of our conscious life' (512). Moreover, he argues that, in the end, the origin of religious experience is hardly what is important anyway; rather, the value of the experience must be judged according to its effects. I am not willing to let the question of origins slip from sight as easily as this; however, further remarks must be deferred until some other points have been made.

James's book also provides support for the legitimacy of the 'religious experience' label in the resemblance that the pattern of some of his accounts bears to Frye's insights. The letting drop of the shitty fundamentalist garment, for example, echoes the 'self-surrender' type of conversion detailed by James, where anxiety and the burden of sin is shucked off, and Frye's own comparison of the experience to Bunyan's conversion shows his awareness of this. The railway journey through the night is comparable to the experiences described by James in which the self is momentarily effaced in a kind of implosion of self-despair and then brought to life again. Finally, the recognition of the unity that gave Blake and Milton their individuality is essentially a variation of recognizing the interpenetration of all things, the sense of the oneness of the universe. Indeed, these insights of Frye's are close enough to the classic patterns of religious experience described by James to warrant the hypothesis that they might have been, to some degree, an effect of his Methodist upbringing.

This is to take the view of Hans Küng, who argues in *Theology for the Third Millennium* that 'religious experience is *a priori* interpreted experience, and for that reason it is stamped by the religious tradition in question and by its different expressive forms' (234). Certainly a Methodist upbringing would be particularly fertile in this respect, for religious experience has always been central to Wesleyan thought. Indeed, it was in part the unease and suspicion with which the religious experiences claimed by John Wesley and his brother, Charles, were received that prompted their decision to secede from the Church of England. In their view, justification through faith had been one of the main tenets of the Protestant reform, and the apparent drift away from this concept towards a more doctrinal emphasis was a serious theological error. In the event, their secession was not nearly so abrupt nor absolute as those of many other sects have been, and the centrality of religious experience to Methodism in no sense signified an abjuration of structured worship.[6] Rather, the main significance of their secession was a shift to emphasize the necessity of a personal sense of spiritual communion and the responsibility of Christians to realize their faith in their daily lives. The corollary of this latter point was that faith included a belief in the perfectibility of human nature, that life could be lived without sin, and this was the other major distinguishing feature of Methodism.

Of course, as with all revolutions, atrophy gradually crept into the Methodist movement, and what had been visionary simply became a new standard for conformity. Like any religion, Methodism has had its share of petty, rule-obsessed, officious bigots, and these ensured that what had begun as a liberating shift of authority to the individual became in many cases a dogmatic insistence, a positive demand that the individual declare a conversion experience or risk the disapprobation of the entire congregation. Hence, religious experience became, as Walter Houston Clark has argued, 'often nothing more than a shallow emotionalism, followed either by a rigid dogmatism or backsliding that left the worshipper in a worse state than before' (*Religious Experience*, 6). It is in part because of the apparent falsity and shallowness of such witness that this requirement has receded during the twentieth century. In Frye's youth, however, the expectation that all church members would experience conversion was still strong, and this was a burden placed especially on the adolescent, as a sort of requisite for adult church membership.

In *The Psychology of Religion* (1899), E.D. Starbuck suggests that conversion is, by its very nature, an experience most suited to adolescence, when character formation is most precipitous; many religions, recognizing this, promote religious conversion as a kind of intensification of the natural growth into adulthood. Starbuck's idea is discussed by William James, who agrees that there are many adolescent conversions that bear the mark of their religious traditions to such a degree that they have an air of preappointment to them, but he also reminds us that all such imitations have a presumably authentic original, and that the element of tradition in the form of a conversion experience is no proof against its authenticity or the possibility that it possesses unique content (224, 262).[7] Moreover, James makes a distinction between the nonvolitional and the volitional conversion experience: that which occurs as a kind of unexpected release and that which is the result of an active search for enlightenment.

Frye's own version of the conversion experience occurred in adolescence, and though it would fall into the nonvolitional category, it is quite probable that the climate of his religious upbringing and the character development endemic to adolescence both played a role in preparing his mind for this moment of insight. But, returning to Ayre's remark that Frye's doffing of the shitty garment of fundamentalism was a parody of the traditional Methodist conversion, the question is begged as to whether it may not be more accurate to say that the conversions-by-rote typical of fundamentalist Methodism were the parodies, and that Frye's experience was closer to the sort of conversion Wesley originally had in mind. The answer may be indeterminable, because it is not the sort of matter that can be definitively settled with a straightforward appeal to history; but the ambiguity is in itself suggestive, given that, despite the extremely heterodox nature of some of Frye's views (e.g., his statement that 'the God of official Christianity' was 'invented as a homeopathic cure for the teachings of Jesus' [FS, 61]), there is every sign that he understood his own religious experience as belonging to the Protestant tradition rather than standing apart from and against it. If the fact that he was an ordained minister of the United Church of Canada were not evidence enough of this opinion, Frye makes the point explicitly in a number of writings.[8]

There is, moreover, an apparent continuity or analogy of approach between Frye's ideas and the teachings of the Methodist Church. Aside from the stress on personal experience and responsibility, the idea of the perfectibility of the self is a powerful driving force behind all Frye's work, and this leads to another point of emphasis which he shares with Methodism – his evangelical insistence on speaking over the heads of academics to an audience of lay readers. One also detects a strong current of Methodist social outreach in Frye's thought. In Canada this became a movement called the Social Gospel, which was based on the idea of applying Christianity to the relief of social suffering, and one finds a version of this idea in Frye's public activities, particularly his involvement with The Canadian Forum and his championing of the CCF (the Co-operative Commonwealth Federation, which later became the New Democratic Party, Canada's social democrats), a social activism that seems always to have coexisted with a belief that no social or political invention could ever decisively and adequately replace Christianity.[9] Finally, the Methodist combination of the structure of the Church of England articles with an emphasis on personal experience finds a kind of parallel in Frye's thought; while he insists on the necessity of a disciplined assimilation of cultural structures, at the same time he insists on leaving the particular encounter with art, including value judgments, for the individual to relate to personal experience.

4

Does this mean, then, that Frye's version of religious experience is simply a derivation of the Methodist outlook? I think not, because, while certain structures and assumptions have been discussed, we have yet to consider the aspect of Frye's religious experience that is unique, which is to say the mystic element in his outlook. The word 'mystic' is a somewhat problematic term because it invites so many confused, pretentious, or obfuscating connotations. It is a problem that Frye wrestled with in an afterword to *Fearful Symmetry*, in which he discussed the question of Blake's mysticism. Frye likens Blake's art to the spiritual discipline of Yoga,

> which liberates man by uniting him with God. The true God for such visionaries is not the orthodox Creator ... who must always be involved with either an eternal substance or an eternal nothingness ... but an unattached creative Word who is free from both. Unity with this God could be attained only by an effort of vision which not only rejects the duality of subject and object but attacks the far more difficult antithesis of being and non-being as well. This effort of vision, so called, is to be conceived neither as a human attempt to reach God nor a divine attempt to reach man, but as the realization in total experience of the identity of God and Man in which both the human creature and the superhuman Creator disappear ... If mysticism means primarily a contemplative quietism, mysticism is something abhorrent to Blake, a Selfhood-communing in Ulro; if it means primarily a spiritual illumination expressing itself in a practical and (in spite of its psychological subtlety) unspeculative piety, such as we find in the militant monasticism of the Counter- Reformation, the word still does not fit him. But if mysticism means primarily the vision of the prodigious and unthinkable metamorphosis of the human mind just described, Blake is one of the mystics. (*FS*, 431–2)

As we would expect, Frye's own 'vision of the prodigious and unthinkable metamorphosis of the human mind' is similar in many ways to Blake's; but Frye's ideas about religion developed over the course of the twentieth century and it is in the context of twentieth-century theology that they are best understood.

In his 1949 essay called 'The Church: Its Relation to Society,' Frye seems to echo Whitehead when he argues: 'The Church has been tempted by the world to present its faith as an obstinate reiteration of traditional myths, insisting in the teeth of all natural law that they are facts, and defying the advance of science as a dog howls at the rising moon. It must learn to present its faith again as the emancipation and fulfillment of reason' (RTW, 219). Of course, Frye and Whitehead are not the only people to complain about hidebound literalism in the modern church's teachings. Indeed, some of these complaints about religious conservatism have been preludes to programs of theological reform. Yet it is apparent that with some of the alternative theologies comes an alternative problem.

One of the most prevalent alternative theologies pursues the vein of thought that Rudolph Bultmann termed 'demythologization.' The main idea is that religious faith should not be contingent on the historical truth of events recorded in the Bible, a notion which is reasonable enough. However, the thrust of this reaction to literalism has been, in large part, towards an internalization of religion, an attempt to maintain certain religious attitudes by locating their authority entirely within the psyche. The difficulty with this approach is explained by Colin Falck in *Myth, Truth and Literature*:

> it is hard to see how on the internalized view of religious belief there can be any such thing as a *religious* way of life or a *religious* dimension of experience at all. The internalized account of religion, while being able to tell us certain – essentially ethical – things about what it calls 'the religious requirement' or the need for behavioural authenticity, can in fact tell us nothing whatever about ... the kinds of concepts or images in terms of which the world which we inhabit needs most authentically to be seen, and can therefore tell us nothing about what the notion of self- overcoming, or self-transcendence ... can really amount to ... there is no way in which the self which is to be overcome or transcended can be defined in terms of its grasp, or lack of grasp, of a reality or truth ... which our pursuit of self-transcendence might reveal to us. (130–1)

In other words, once one has made the decision to abandon the conservative emphasis on scripture as the ultimate source of religious authority and decided to locate that sense of authority in the self, one necessarily forfeits the clear notion of an 'other' towards which one's religious affections can aspire.

Frye saw this two-sided problem with great clarity, and articulated it in *The Secular Scripture*:

> Not all of us will be satisfied with calling a central part of our mythological inheritance a revelation from God, and, though each chapter in this book closes on much the same cadence, I cannot claim to have found a more acceptable formulation. It is quite true that if there is no sense that the mythological universe is a human creation, man can never get free of servile anxieties and superstitions, never surpass himself, in Nietzsche's phrase. But if there is no sense that it is also something uncreated, something coming from elsewhere, man remains a Narcissus staring at his own reflection, equally unable to surpass himself. Somehow or other, the created scripture and the revealed scripture, or whatever we call the latter, have to keep fighting each other like Jacob and the angel, and it is through the maintaining of this struggle, the suspension of belief between the spiritually real and the humanly imaginative, that our own mental evolution grows. (60–1)

At this point, the idea that there is such a struggle seems clear enough, but to simply state the fact is not to give any sense of the real nature of the problem, which hangs on the question of how the individual may make such a struggle comprehensible. In other words, given that neither one outlook nor the other is adequate, what does it mean to say that there must be a struggle between the two outlooks? What sort of a religious experience does this imply?

As with so many philosophical questions, to restate the problem is to come halfway towards articulating the solution. Such a rearticulation is provided by F.W. Dillistone in his book *Religious Experience and Christian Faith*, a study of the idea of religious experience through the lives and works of ten prominent thinkers of the twentieth century. Dillistone suggests that there are two overarching patterns revealed: one is centripetal, the other centrifugal. The centripetal pattern concentrates on the particular event in space and time – the location and moment of the crucifixion – as that which bestows meaning on the whole of Christian experience (96–7). Dillistone sees such an outlook evinced, for example, in the work of T.S. Eliot and Paul Tillich. He cites Eliot's declaration that 'To apprehend / The point of intersection of the timeless / With time, is an occupation for the saint' and Tillich's insistence that the meaning of his whole system proceeds from the historic moment of the crucifixion as evidence of the centripetal pattern of their thought (104–5).

The centrifugal pattern, by contrast, tends to find meaning by spinning away from the constrictions of the particular world to discover the immanent divinity of a broader and deeper experience. Two examples which Dillistone cites of the centrifugal pattern of religious experience are Arnold Toynbee's notion that historical patterns evince a spiritual and eternal reality beyond all worldly phenomena and Wallace Stevens's belief that ultimate meaning lies in 'a reality that forces itself upon our consciousness and refuses to be managed and mastered,' a meaning that Stevens suggests can only be glimpsed momentarily through the 'incessant conjunctionings' of imagination and reality (106–9).

For the centripetal pattern, an individual's relation to transcendence finally rests upon the concept of reconciliation; for the centrifugal it is fulfillment. In other words, the centripetal attitude looks at a specific point in the mythological framework for ultimate spiritual authority, whereas the centrifugal attitude finds the ultimate authority in a personal experience which is independent of scripture. The identification I am making between these ideas and the previous articulation of the problem may be somewhat confusing because the centripetal pattern corresponds to the sense that the authority is placed externally, whereas the centrifugal pattern sees the encounter with authority as an internal matter. But the matter is somewhat clarified when one recognizes that the difference amounts to where the centre of religious experience is placed. If the centre is located in a specific moment in time and space, as revealed through scripture, there is a centripetal movement of religious experience which leads all individual minds from any other location in time and space (i.e., the periphery) inward to that location, the centre. If, however, one locates the centre within the individual's mind, the movement is an expansive one, a process of projection, or a progressive accommodation of the larger world to the central experience of spiritual immanence located in the individual; the movement is from the centre to the periphery.

Dillistone concludes his study of Christian religious experience in the twentieth century by asking rhetorically whether we must 'settle for one *or* the other' or whether some kind of dialectic or 'mutual interchange' is possible (116). Of course, such a mutual interchange is precisely the solution suggested by Frye, but the presentation of the problem in terms of centripetal and centrifugal patterns evokes another of Frye's theories which can assist our articulation of the religious experience implied.

On a number of occasions, Frye remarked that whenever we read we find our attention moving in two opposite directions: centripetally to comprehend the order of words and centrifugally to relate what we are reading to our experience of the outside world. It is this same framework which provides the pattern for Frye's version of religious experience: both the centrifugal emphasis on the individual experience and the centripetal emphasis on the specificity of the passion of Christ are integrated in the attitude which, following Blake, Frye called the 'double vision.' It is a version of the vision through the window pane of the train, the deliberate and ambivalent shifting from one mode of seeing to another, and that metamorphic process becomes a liminal point through which Frye's overarching vision is achieved.

5

Having understood Frye's general spiritual outlook, his 'double vision,' in those terms, one may see the relationship of the specific religious experiences described at the beginning of the paper in a new light. The experiences form a sequence that passes from what William James would call a nonvolitional through to a volitional conversion with an intermediate stage. That is to say, the first experience, in which the shitty garment of fundamentalism was let drop, was not sought after, but represented a kind of release of the mind to apprehend what was already latent in experience. The second experience, in which there was a metamorphosis of perception from window to mirror to window over the course of a train journey, involved a liminal recognition of the difference between the passive and the active role – in a sense it was a revelation of the necessity of assuming a volitional attitude towards experience. The third insight, in which the Bible was seen to provide a code for art which existed independently of personal interpretation, was the product of concentrated study, and although it also has the character of a kind of release of the mind from one level to another, because of the element of discipline and self-application, it resembles what James would recognize as a volitional conversion.

These three moments of insight may be regarded as a series of transactions between the individual imagination and God. In the first instance, the escape from fundamentalism is experienced as a kind of withdrawal of divine presence from inhibiting and neurotic social imperatives. This results in a sense of release, a recognition that the realm of myth is separable from individual experience. There is a centrifugal aspect to this experience, for in escaping from a dogmatic interpretation of myth, the authority of the religious experience is thrown onto the relation between one's conscience and one's experience of the world.

In the second event, the transaction is experienced as an exchange of one's sense of the origin of perception from an exterior to an interior source and then back again. That exchange prompts the recognition that one creates much of one's own world, and that such self-creation can become a trap when one fails to perceive one's own projections disguised in what Hans Robert Jauss would call the 'horizon of expectation' or E.H. Gombrich would call the 'grid of perception,' meaning the interpretive structure endemic to human perception.[10] Hence, it is recognized that to escape from a narcissistic reading of oneself will require an effort of critical thought. Essentially, this insight implies that one may, with effort, pass from a centripetal to a centrifugal pattern of experience and back again.

The third transaction involves an insight achieved through the process of self-detachment, or at least the repudiation of passive assumptions which was discovered in the second experience. There is a recognition that a society's mythology (considered as a complete structure) approaches neutrality to the degree to which it can be stripped of its literal, denotative aspect; that the Bible, for example, may serve as a structure which may be used in any number of ways. The experience of liberation is earned through a disciplined process whereby one appropriates the central structure, internalizes it and makes it one's own, thereby enabling a release of one's own energy.[11]

The integration of these three discrete Frye experiences into a general spiritual outlook provides not only an answer to the question of how to reconcile the competing versions of Christian religious experience, but also the philosophical ground on which Frye's theories stand, having answered the postmodern theoretical question of where the centre is located in which experience finds its root. Speaking of the New Testament at the 1984 MLA conference, Frye argued: 'the text is not the absence of a former presence but the place of the resurrection of the presence ... In this risen presence text and reader are equally involved. The reader is a whole of which the text is a part: the text is a whole of which the reader is a part: these contradictory movements keep passing into one another and back again. The Logos at the center, which is inside the reader and not hidden behind the text, continually changes place with the Logos at the circumference that encloses both' (MM, 26). As A.C. Hamilton remarks, this is what Frye would say of any literary work (Northrop Frye, 218). In other words, Frye's critical outlook is of a piece with his spiritual outlook because his religious experience has been developed into a total philosophy.

The theological dimensions of this philosophy are expressed in perhaps their most compressed and lucid form in Frye's reading of the Book of Job. 'Anyone interested in the Bible and literature,' wrote Frye in *Words with Power*, 'will eventually find himself revolving around the Book of Job like a satellite' (310). That is because the Book of Job neatly represents our ambivalence and anxiety about setting any faith in a spiritual life when we live in this evidently material world. There are various levels at which the Book of Job may be read: the first sections seem to pose fewer difficulties, but in the interpretation of Job's religious experience, understandings diverge sharply, often losing themselves, it would seem, in the whirlwind out of which Yahweh speaks. The least sophisticated, and unfortunately probably the most prevalent, reading sees Job's experience as a simple lesson of humility in the face of an inscrutable deity – a hard lesson admittedly, but for which Job is duly rewarded with a restored and even augmented fortune and family. A closer and more thoughtful reading shows that Job is indeed reduced to humility, but that the lesson he learns, from Yahweh's relentless prodding, is that persisting in a simplistic view of guilt and innocence as the ruling principles of the world is wrong-headed.[12] One conclusion drawn from this is that, given the complexity of the deity's concerns, as exemplified by the existence of monsters like Behemoth and Leviathan, it is naive to think that the simple attempt to maintain one's moral innocence should be sufficient to ensure a happy life.

Frye takes Job's vision in a different direction, insisting that what Yahweh attempts to show Job, after relieving him of his obsession with moral rewards and punishments, is that to insist on thinking in terms of causes at all is to arrive back at the First Cause – the Creation – which is not much help in itself. However, the vision of Behemoth and Leviathan which follows represents the possibility of seeing with God-like eyes, for the vision suggests that these forces of evil can be seen to be external to Job, if Job employs the context for perception implied in Yahweh's recapitulation of the creation (see *GC*, 196–8; *WP*, 310–13). The exegetical validity of this reading is less important to my argument here than the continuity between it and the pattern which, I have suggested, is assumed by Frye's version of religious experience. Once dogmatism has been shed and Job's tendency to project his own ideas has been revealed, the vision of the Creation as recapitulated by Yahweh restores Job's sense of a centre within himself. From this centre it is possible to perceive a complete framework, offering the imagination a kind of nontemporal, spatial orientation, as it were, a context within which the individual is able to participate in the creative process, rather than remaining a passive observer. In other words, both the centripetal goal of reconciliation and the centrifugal goal of fulfillment are integrated in Frye's version of the religious experience.

I began this essay by talking about the modern predicament of identity, and I suggested that one means of confronting and possibly mitigating the problem would be a version of religious experience that affirmed spirituality as a significant aspect of identity without, however, repudiating reason or embracing superstition. Frye's version of religious experience is built on the principle that a sense of spirituality may be recovered through an effort of imagination, and his work itself is the best evidence that such an understanding redeems faith as 'the emancipation and fulfillment of reason.' Of course, such an approach to faith will by no means satisfy everyone: for example, the role of imagination in Frye's theological ideas has led William Fennell to complain that Frye seems to deny 'the objective reality of God' ('Theology and Frye,' 113–21). But Frye's argument is precisely that any experience that one might have of a god must transcend questions of subjectivity and objectivity, because the best means we have at our disposal for comprehending such an encounter is the word, and the word is metaphorical: hence the importance of understanding the relationship between the Bible and literature.[13]

The paramount concern mentioned at the outset of this essay had to do with the role of freedom in determining identity. In Frye's version of religious experience, the question is reformulated somewhat by identifying freedom with responsibility. In other words, Frye's spiritual outlook, far from striving to deny material experience, takes as its starting point the experience of the individual as a social being within a modern environment, and insists that any dependence upon passive assumptions about these surroundings is effectively a form of mental slavery. To escape this slavery it is necessary, first, to cultivate a sense of humility about one's passive assumptions and, secondly, to transcend such assumptions through critical thought within the framework provided by mythology. That framework is neutral insofar as it places any specific concerns within the totality of all human concern, and hence provides a vantage point from which the world may be reconceived by the creative imagination. The 'self-surrender' implicitly demanded by so many spiritual outlooks is, therefore, inverted in Frye's version of religious experience; the spiritual insight is achieved by a separation of the active, truth-seeking imagination from the passive acceptance of illusion. Hence, liberation of the self is achieved, not through a simple, absolute denial of authority, but through a careful resurrection of the divinity latent in the human imagination. Freed from the clamour of personal and societal neuroses, the individual may once again hear a 'still small voice' through an encounter with the Logos, and the process of creating the world anew begins once again.

NOTES

1 Frye made reference to this event on several occasions; e.g., Ayre, *Northrop Frye: A Biography*, 68.
2 Interview with Bob Sandler, 20 September 1979; cited by John Ayre, *Northrop Frye*, 44.
3 Frye to Roy Daniells, 1 April 1975; cited by Ayre, *Northrop Frye*, 45.
4 E.g., *MC*, 26–49; *BG*, vi; *CR*, 6.
5 See also Ayre, *Northrop Frye*, 92.
6 For example, Wesley's group continued to observe the articles of the Church of England, although Wesley did reduce the original list of thirty-five articles to a more compact version of twenty-five. In fact, the Methodists were so called because of their methodical and disciplined attempt to integrate religious faith with daily life.
7 Cited and discussed by James, *The Varieties of Religious Experience*, 198–204.
8 E.g., 'The Church: Its Relation to Society' (1949), in *RTW*, 203–19; 'The Search for Acceptable Words' (1973), in *SM*, 3–26; and *NFC*, 139. Non-Canadian readers may be unaware that the United Church of Canada, founded in 1925, was mainly comprised of people from three churches: Methodists (who formed a majority of the founding United Church members, nearly all of the Methodist congregations in Canada having opted for union), Presbyterians, and Congregationalists.
9 For a full discussion of this idea and its effects on the international activities of the Canadian Protestant Church, see Wright, *A World Mission*.
10 See Jauss, *Toward an Aesthetic of Reception*, passim; and Gombrich, *Art and Illusion*, part 1.
11 There is not room in this paper to pursue the analogies which these experiences have with Frye's literary theories. Suffice it to say that they correspond to three central tenets of his liberal-oriented criticism. And while these tenets may have been derived from other writers (as the quotations below will show), they are worked into a coherent system by Frye. For brevity's sake, the analogues to the three experiences may be expressed, respectively, as three axioms: 'the content of literature is hypothetical, assumed rather than asserted' (*EAC*, 7); literature 'is like a picnic to which the author brings the words and the reader the meaning' (*FS*, 427–8); and 'the mythical and imaginative forms of verbal discourse ... may be unlimited in depth and complexity, but they are finite in range' (*EAC*, 6).

12 See, for example, Greenburg, 'Job,' in *The Literary Guide to the Bible*, 298–9; Good, 'Job,' in *Harper's Bible Commentary*, 430–1.
13 See *NFC*, 188–95, for Frye's direct response to Fennell's remark.

WORKS CITED

Ayre, John. *Northrop Frye: A Biography*. Toronto: Random House, 1989.

Clark, Walter Houston, ed. *Religious Experience: Its Nature and Function in the Human Psyche*. Springfield, Ill.: Charles C. Thomas, 1973.

Dillistone, F.W. *Religious Experience and Christian Faith*. London: SCM Press, 1981.

Falck, Colin. *Myth, Truth and Literature: Towards a True Post-modernism*. Cambridge: Cambridge University Press, 1989.

Fennell, William O. 'Theology and Frye: Some Implications of *The Great Code*.' *Toronto Journal of Theology* 1, no. 1 (1985): 113–21.

Hamilton, A.C. *Northrop Frye: Anatomy of his Criticism*. Toronto: University of Toronto Press, 1990.

Gombrich, E.H. *Art and Illusion: A Study in the Psychology of Pictorial Representation*. Rev. ed. Princeton: Princeton University Press, 1969.

Good, Edwin M. 'Job.' In *Harper's Bible Commentary*, edited by James L. Mays. San Francisco: Harper & Row, 1988.

Greenburg, Moshe. 'Job.' In *The Literary Guide to the Bible*, edited by Robert Alter and Frank Kermode. Cambridge: Harvard University Press, 1987.

James, William. *The Varieties of Religious Experience*. 1902. Reprint. Harmondsworth: Penguin, 1985.

Jauss, Hans Robert. *Toward an Aesthetic of Reception*. Translated by Timothy Bahti. Minneapolis: University of Minnesota Press, 1982.

Küng, Hans. *Theology for the Third Millenium: An Ecumenical View*. 1988. Reprint. Translated by Peter Heinegg. New York: Doubleday, 1990.

Mosley, Nicholas. *Religion and Experience: A Lay Essay in Theology*. Philadelphia: United Church Press, 1965.

Taylor, Charles. *Sources of the Self: The Making of the Modern Identity*. Cambridge, Mass.: Havard University Press, 1989.

Whitehead, Alfred North. *Science and the Modern World*. 1925. Reprint. New York: Mentor Books, 1962.

Wright, Robert. *A World Mission: Canadian Protestantism and the Quest for a New International Order, 1918–1939*. Montreal: McGill-Queen's University Press, 1991.

MARGARET BURGESS

The Resistance to Religion: Anxieties Surrounding the Spiritual Dimensions of Frye's Thought; OR, Investigations into the Fear of Enlightenment

The original title of my essay was simply 'The Resistance to Religion: Anxieties Surrounding the Spiritual Dimensions of Frye's Thought.' Religion and anxiety are touchy subjects, however, and I confess that it took an inordinate number of false starts and preliminary drafts before I had worked through enough of my own anxieties to be able to focus on the issues that I found most compelling in the topic and that seemed to me to be most essential to it. Eventually it became necessary to limit even these to two general areas of concern, both of which derive from my experience of observing and working with Frye over a period of ten or so years of his teaching the legendary Bible course, and both of which take their point of departure from statements in the introduction to *The Great Code* regarding the kinds of resistance to the biblical material that he personally encountered among readers and students. Then, as these considerations themselves underwent a series of progressive shifts in emphasis as a result of still further rounds of modifications and revisions, the expanded title suggested itself as an indication of the increasingly specialized nature of the essay's central preoccupations and as a more accurate representation of its final content.

The typical patterns of resistance that Frye describes involve fears of being led either towards or away from existing positions of either acceptance or rejection of religious belief, but if one reads closely one eventually realizes that the kind of belief to which he is referring is somewhat more complex and considerably more all-encompassing than the formalized doctrinal positions of the traditional institutional religions. Belief and disbelief as they are ordinarily understood, he elaborates, are 'so often and so intensely anxious and insecure' because they are closely connected in even the most enthusiastic and receptive of his youthful students' minds with the 'powers of repression' that keep them from recognizing what they already potentially know. The material that he is dealing with is therefore emotionally explosive because it is the anxieties rather than the rational faculties of the student that make the primary response to whatever is being said (*GC*, xv, xx).

There is a highly paradoxical quality to Frye's encounter with and response to the patterns of resistance which he describes. On the one hand is his acknowledgment of the powers of repression that he picks out as the teacher's first point of active attack. On the other is his insistence on the importance of teaching under the rubrics of academic freedom and professional ethics and his extreme reticence in the face of any direct discussion of his personal beliefs. Far from imposing these beliefs on others, he developed what he described as a strategy of 'deliberate elusiveness on my part' to contend with the inevitable questions of students and interviewers. The teacher is not, he insisted, 'primarily someone who knows instructing someone who does not know,' but rather 'someone who attempts to *re-create the subject in the student's mind.*' For this reason 'something [must always be] kept in reserve, suggesting the possibility of better and fuller questions, [or] the student's mental advance [will be] blocked' (*GC*, xv, emphasis added). Ironically, then, the attack of which he speaks consists of evasion, and the teaching models which he invokes in support of this technique are the dialogic method of Socrates, the exercises in paradox of the Zen Buddhist koan master, and, more immediately connected with his specific subject material, the parables of Jesus.

There seem to be several principles operative in the intentional impeding of the learning process implied by such indirect and evasive approaches to teaching. Primary among these is the kind of counterattack which they are designed to provoke: the powerful internal resistance referred to can only be overcome by an intense desire to learn and a corresponding intensity of effort on the part of the student. As D.T. Suzuki says of Zen, 'the truth of Zen can never be attained unless it is attacked with the full force of personality' (*Essays in Zen Buddhism*, 1st ser., 16).

A second central principle would appear to derive from the suggestion of a direct relationship between the authority of a spiritual truth and its ineffability – the actual impossibility of its direct articulation. *Tao Te Ching*, for example, begins with the proviso, 'The tao that can be told / is not the eternal Tao / [and] The name that can be named / is not the eternal Name' (1), while in the Bible Paul tells of a vision in which he experienced himself as being 'caught up into paradise,' where he heard 'unspeakable words,' words, he goes on to add, which it was also '*not lawful* for a man to utter' (2 Cor. 12:4, emphasis added).[1] Beyond the claims of ineffability, therefore, there is evidence of a further tendency towards intentional secrecy and even of prohibition. 'Those who know don't talk / [and] Those who talk don't know,'[2] Lao-tzu also notes cryptically, and in the Gospels Jesus implies to his disciples that he speaks to the multitudes in parables precisely in order 'that seeing they might not see, and hearing they might not understand' (Luke 8:10).[3]

The usual explanation for this air of secrecy and prohibition is that the ill-considered and untimely exposure of truths which can only be 'spiritually discerned' (as in 1 Cor. 2:14) to an audience that is incapable of such discernment will merely result in a reception of mockery or worse for both the truths and the teacher. 'Cast [not] your pearls before swine,' Jesus warns in the famous biblical passage, 'lest they trample them under their feet, and turn again and [attack] you' (Matt. 7:6),[4] while the punch line of a contemporary joke that asks for an explanation of the difference between a psychotic and a mystic informs us that 'the mystic knows who not to talk to.'

It gradually becomes clear, however, that what all of these tactics of evasion ultimately add up to is a long-standing and deeply ingrained cross-cultural taboo against the direct articulation and sharing of the most profound spiritual knowledge and experience. Such a taboo, in my opinion, cannot help but have powerful ramifications for any teacher attempting to approach the great spiritual traditions in anything resembling the traditional attitudes of deference and respect, and especially for any teacher venturing to utilize or to teach in its own right Frye's work on the biblical material. For Frye's remarkable diplomacy in honouring simultaneously and at all times the mythical and metaphorical integrity of his sacred textual material, the unconscious internal resistance of his readers and students, and the subtle technical stratagems of his chosen teaching tradition is epitomized in his own haunting dictum that to answer a question is to consolidate the mental level on which it is asked (*GC*, xv, 196). And what this suggests to me is that the mandate implied for the successor who would presume to undertake the task of the further transmission of his teachings – or, as one of the possible purposes of this book, the perpetuation of his legacy – includes, in the area of his biblical subject material at least, the virtually impossible assignment to speak the unspeakable and teach the unteachable.

The first of the general areas of concern that I referred to at the beginning of my essay therefore reflects my own growing awareness of, and frankly my increasing frustration with, constraints which I undoubtedly experienced more intensely and perceived as more binding than others because of my unique proximity to Frye and the requirement that I simultaneously complement and support his specific teaching situation, as well as because of my respect for and personal loyalty towards him. This first area of concern includes such issues as the possibilities for misinterpretation and misrepresentation of material that has never been directly stated; the sense of a massive betrayal of tact, if not the actual violation of a taboo, related to any failure to adhere to Frye's established model of elusiveness and indirection; and the levels of authenticity and personal credibility that can be maintained in the attempt to remain true to the original power and authority of what is essentially a mediated vision. The second area of concern, to which I will now turn, derives from my personal inclination to question the appropriateness, and perhaps even the legitimacy, of retaining the inherited model of elusiveness in the present day, and represents an attempt to diffuse some of the tension associated with it by uncovering what is at stake behind it and by explaining why a certain amount of anxiety not only is justified but represents an entirely natural reaction under the circumstances.

I cited earlier Frye's definition of the teacher as 'someone who attempts to re-create the subject in the student's mind,' and it is time now to consider more closely just what that subject really is. It is often forgotten that the course that was known for years as the Bible course, and which eventually produced *The Great Code*, was in its final version taught in conjunction with classical and Near Eastern mythology as 'The Mythological Framework of Western Culture.' What this means is that, however prominent the Bible was as the chief attraction and the principal focus of attention of the course, its main subject was not so much the actual text of the Bible as the overall vision of reality or world-view represented by the Bible and the other mythological texts studied in juxtaposition with it. The attempt to recreate the subject in the students' minds thus represents, in my understanding of it, a subtle but systematic attempt to reconstruct their mythological model of reality, or to recreate their world-view. In other words, what the student is being led to is a general expansion of consciousness, and the powers of repression identified as the teacher's first point of attack correspond to the boundaries circumscribed by conventional ego-consciousness, while the attack itself is necessitated by the tendency of the socially and ideologically conditioned ego to turn its regulating mechanisms of balance and control into a self-defeating tyranny of repression.[5] A challenge of this enormity is not without its dangers and must obviously be handled with utmost integrity, and that the process was fraught with undeniable tensions even for Frye is evidenced by the cautiousness with which he broaches the subject towards the end of *The Double Vision*. 'Such a phrase as "consciousness-raising" may often refer to niggling pedantries of no real importance,' he states almost apologetically, 'but,' he then continues, 'behind it is something that could be of revolutionary religious significance' (*DV*, 82–3). And what this revolutionary religious significance ultimately refers to, if I may be so indiscreet as to finally come right out and state what at the same time seems to me painfully obvious, is essentially an enlightenment vision, 'enlightenment' being understood in its Eastern sense as a radical and total 'reconstruction of one's entire personality' (*Essays in Zen Buddhism*, 1st ser., 56) that results in a cutting through of the illusions of ordinary perception (in their Eastern designation, *maya*) to an entirely new vision of reality.

Frye was very careful in *The Great Code* and elsewhere to qualify his introduction of Eastern concepts and terminology with the assertion that they merely represented oriental analogues of less clearly recognized elements of Western tradition (*GC*, 105–6; *DV*, 55–6). Nevertheless, it is important to note the frequency with which he draws such parallels and the extent to which they have permeated his thinking, or his reconstruction of the subject in his own mind, even when the references are not overt. Among the comparisons that are overtly drawn are the relationships between the *shunyata* or 'void' of Buddhist thought and the 'vanity' of the book of Ecclesiastes (*GC*, 123), between the ecstatic meditative states of *samadhi* and *satori* and such New Testament conceptions as '"born of the spirit," "fullness of time," or the sudden critical widening of the present moment expressed by the word *kairos*' (*DV*, 55), between 'enlightenment' and 'salvation' (*WGS*, 140–1; cf. also *GC*, 105), and between the concept of 'interpenetration' and the 'metaphors of particularity' expressed in such images as Blake's 'world in a grain of sand' (*GC*, 167)[6] and Paul's conception of the body of Christ as both including and being included within each member of the body of the Christian church (*GC*, 100; *WP*, 89, 126).[7]

Less immediately apparent because they are not always as explicitly stated are connections between the Eastern 'ways of liberation' (including Buddhism, Taoism, Vedanta, and Yoga) and Christ's 'way of salvation'[8] (*WP*, 91–2), between 'enlightenment' or 'liberation' (*DV*, 55–6) and the 'liberty' asserted to be 'the chief thing that the gospel has to bring to man' (*GC*, 232),[9] between 'awakening' and 'resurrection' (*GC*, 101), and between 'enlightenment' and its diverse articulations as 'disillusionment' understood as a release from the self-constructed prison of illusion (*GC*, 123), as the sudden illumination represented by the metaphor of 'seeing' (*MM*, 96, 188, 244; cf. also *GC*, 116–17), as the transformation or metamorphosis of consciousness represented by the concept of *metanoia* (*GC*, 130–1, 193), and as the 'way the world looks after the ego has disappeared' in the 'participating' apocalyptic vision (*GC*, 137–8).

Least evident and most illuminating of all, however, is the light which the Eastern traditions shed on Frye's insistent and repeated emphasis on a primordial separation of subject and object and on the importance of metaphor in re-establishing the original connection between the two. In *The Double Vision* he invokes the 'program of spiritual awareness' laid down in Hegel's *Phenomenology of Spirit* to describe how 'the gap between a conscious perceiving subject and a largely unconscious objective world confronts us at the beginning of experience' and to explain that 'all progress in knowledge, in fact in consciousness itself, consists in bridging the gap and abolishing both the separated subject and the separated object' (*DV*, 36). But it is only when we look at the Eastern equivalent of this formulation that we begin to understand just why this process is so important. In the Yoga Sutras of Patanjali, a treatise on yogic meditation which Frye referred to on numerous occasions in his lectures as well as in *The Great Code* (212–13), we read that it is precisely 'this achievement of sameness or identity with the object of concentration [that] is known as *samadhi*,'[10] and elsewhere in the literature on Yoga it is explained that 'enlightenment, or liberation, is that condition of being in which the gulf between subject (mind) and object (matter) does not exist,'[11] or, alternatively, that 'the last achievement of all thought is a recognition of the identity of spirit and matter, subject and object.'[12] The Sanscrit term *yoga* is etymologically derived from the root *yuj*, meaning 'to bind together, to yoke,'[13] and is most frequently interpreted as 'union,' specifically the union of the individual self with the transcendental Self,[14] or the individual soul with the absolute Spirit;[15] thus the purpose of Yoga is said to be 'to transcend the ego-personality in order to recover our original Identity, the transcendental Self (*atman, purusha*), or Spirit,'[16] a process also referred to as 'God- or Self-*realization*.'[17] Applied to Frye's explication of 'the central expression of metaphor [as] the "god," the being who, as sun-god, war-god, sea-god' – or, I would add, although Frye himself was too discreet to do this here, Father-God – 'identifies a form of personality with an aspect of nature' (*GC*, 7), the union, or re-union, of the subject and object in metaphor therefore implies a union, or re-union, of the human with the divine, or the radical atonement (understood as 'at-one-ment') of God and humanity

(*GC*, 134). And with this realization it finally becomes possible to further identify the 'powers of repression' referred to in the introduction to *The Great Code* with the natural tendency of human beings to repress the memory of their original divine nature, an identification which is confirmed later on in the book when we are informed that 'the spiritual body [the *soma pneumatikon* of which Paul speaks in 1 Corinthians 15:44] is the most deeply repressed element of experience' (*GC*, 136; cf. also *DV*, 13–14; *WP*, 124–6).

That Frye himself could possibly have been aware of, much less intended, this unexpected and initially somewhat startling association between Yoga (the disciplines of which were practised in conjunction with all of the major Eastern religions) and the Christian atonement may upon first reading seem rather incredible; however, that he was in fact thoroughly familiar with both the process described here and its larger implications is demonstrated indisputably by the General Note on Blake's Mysticism appended to *Fearful Symmetry*, in which he writes:

> the struggles of the mystics to describe the divine One who is all things, yet no thing, and yet not nothing; to explain how this One is identical with the self yet as different from the self as it can be; to make it clear how the creaturely aspect of man does not exist at all and yet is a usually victorious enemy of the soul, begin to have more relevance to Blake. From this point of view, *Blake's 'art' becomes a spiritual discipline like the Eastern 'yoga,' which liberates man by uniting him with God* ... Unity with this God could be attained only by an effort of vision which not only *rejects the duality of subject and object* but attacks the far more difficult antithesis of being and non-being as well (*FS*, 431; emphasis added).[18]

Moreover, the 'existential' or 'ecstatic' metaphors (*WP*, 75–6, 82) of union and of interpenetration constitute the very essence of both the formulation of the apocalyptic vision presented on page 166 of *The Great Code* and the enlightenment vision of the Buddha described by Suzuki in the essay on the Gandavyuha or Avatamsaka Sutra[19] which Frye cites as his source for the concept of interpenetration on the following page (*GC*, 167–8). In Frye's words: 'The apocalyptic vision, in which the body of Christ is the metaphor holding together all categories of being in an identity, presents us with a world in which there is only one knower, for whom there is nothing outside of or objective to that knower, hence nothing dead or insensible. This knower is also the real consciousness in each of us' (*GC*, 166). And in Suzuki's words:

'When the Buddha enters into a certain kind of Samadhi, the pavilion where he is situated all of a sudden expands to the fullest limits of the universe; in other words, the universe itself is dissolved in the being of the Buddha. The universe is the Buddha, and the Buddha is the universe' (*Essays in Zen Buddhism*, 3rd ser., 78–9). And in a second essay, 'The Doctrine of Enlightenment,' Suzuki states, further echoing Frye, that 'in Enlightenment thinker and thinking and thought are merged in the one act of seeing into the very being of Self' (*Essays in Zen Buddhism*, 1st ser., 56).

The worst fears of those apprehensive about religious or spiritual content in Frye are thus fully realized, for what we have here is undeniably a full-blown mystical vision, and what Frye says of Blake at the conclusion of his General Note on Blake's Mysticism is shown to be equally applicable to himself: namely, that 'if mysticism means primarily the vision of the prodigious and unthinkable metamorphosis of the human mind just described, then [Frye] is one of the mystics' (*FS*, 432).

The question that remains, then, is just why these experiences, which are after all purported to be ecstatic, are perceived to be so threatening. The answer to this question appears to be twofold. The first factor to enter into consideration is the psychological response of the ego, which, understandably in light of the apparent threat to its existence suggested by the assertion that 'the apocalypse is the way the world looks *after the ego has disappeared*' (*GC*, 138; emphasis added), fears the expansion of consciousness involved as a potential source of its own annihilation. The crucial point to be recognized here is that the threat is in fact only apparent, for as Alan Watts points out, and as Frye himself seems to understand,[20] in a highly evolved consciousness 'liberation does not involve the loss or destruction of such conventional concepts as the ego; it means *seeing through them*,' for, 'instead of falling below the ego, liberation surpasses it' (*Psychotherapy East and West*, 19; emphasis added). Also relevant in this regard is the suggestion that at least a part of the previously mentioned taboo against the direct disclosure of the most profound spiritual knowledge and experience derives from a more generalized 'unspoken cultural taboo against ecstasy' – and this includes ecstasy of either the sexual or the spiritual variety, for the two exist on a continuum – which constitutes a variation on the ego's fears of annihilation and which has further produced the phenomenon, reported to be widespread in contemporary society, of the so-called 'closet mystic.'[21] Ever since the advent of Freud, Western culture has been working on its sexual taboos; the implication here is that in order to complete this process it will be necessary to start working on its spiritual taboos as well.

Underlying the frequently neurotic and self-limiting 'anxieties of self-interest' (*WP*, 251) generated by the defensiveness of the control-oriented ego, however, there lurks a deeper and more genuinely insidious problem represented by the element of escapism inherent in the traditional emphasis of both Eastern and Western dualistic world-views on the necessity for a total renunciation and denial of nature and the limitations of a negatively perceived and valued-embodied earthly existence before transcendence can be achieved. Whether or not it is recognized as such, inherent in this aspect of the resistance to religion, or what might be better described in this context as the fear of enlightenment, is a healthy mistrust of mythological constructs of reality that have in fact to a very great extent been anti-life.

To illustrate the issue first in terms of Eastern thought: the detachment and separation from the natural and the worldly which have been presumed to be the paradoxical prerequisite for unification with the spiritual and the divine are conveyed very explicitly by Mircea Eliade in a standard work on the philosophy and practices of Yoga: 'if, etymologically *yuj* means 'to bind,' it is nevertheless clear that the 'bond' in which this act of binding is to result presupposes, as its preliminary condition, breaking the 'bonds' that unite the spirit to the world. In other words, liberation cannot occur if one is not first 'detached' from the world, if one has not begun by withdrawing from the cosmic circuit ... Even in its 'mystical' acceptation – that is, as signifying *union* – Yoga implies a preliminary detachment from matter, emancipation with respect to the world' (*Yoga*, 5). And he reiterates, further underlining the negativity of this position: 'Again and again Indian texts repeat this thesis – that the cause of the soul's 'enslavement' and, consequently, the source of its endless sufferings lie in *man's solidarity with the cosmos*, in his participation, active and passive, direct or indirect, in nature. Let us translate: solidarity with a *desacralized* world, participation in a *profane* nature' (10).

The picture that is thus created is hardly one that is attractive to modern Western sensibilities, and it is for this reason that more recent interpreters of Yoga, such as Georg Feuerstein, have expressed preference for the teachings of the nondualistic schools (Patanjali's system of classical Yoga being held to belong to the dualistic tradition), among them Advaita Vedanta and Tantrism, the 'great dictum' of which, according to Feuerstein, is that 'the transcendental Reality and the conditional world are coessential – nirvana equals samsara' (*Yoga: The Technology*, 7).

The various schools of Buddhism as well – including the Hinayana or Theravada tradition, on the one hand, and Mahayana and Zen

Buddhism on the other – hotly debated the question of how the attainment of nirvana was to be reconciled with the problems and limitations of earthly existence and the 'bondage of birth and death.'[22] Suzuki cites one Zen master as taking vehement exception to the suggestion that nirvana should be construed as providing an escape from such existence. 'No matter how you struggle, Nirvana is to be sought in the midst of Samsara (birth-and-death)' (*Essays in Zen Buddhism*, 1st ser., 13), he insists, echoing the Tantric position cited above: 'Salvation must be sought in the finite itself, there is nothing infinite apart from finite things; if you seek something transcendental, that will cut you off from this world of relativity, which is the same thing as the annihilation of yourself. You do not want salvation at the cost of your own existence' (12).

Suzuki, who was known to have himself attained the enlightenment he taught, corroborates this point of view. 'Nirvana [is] nothing else in its essence than Enlightenment,' he affirms. 'Enlightenment [is] Nirvana reached while yet in the flesh, and no Nirvana [is] ever possible without obtaining Enlightenment' (51).

Translated into Western terms, the issue corresponds to the question of whether the apocalypse occurs within time or is to be anticipated only as an abstract event in an indefinite future marking either death or the end of history and of the natural order as we know it. Frye appears to fall firmly on the side of Zen in this matter, in that he holds that the apocalyptic vision can break in on one at any moment in a timeless present (*GC*, 136), and yet there seem to me to be disturbing residues of dualism in his thinking. These make themselves felt primarily in connection with his negative attitude towards nature, which derives from its identification with the 'fallen' world in the traditional Christian cosmology, and which is reflected in pronouncements such as 'Human nature is corrupt at the source because it's grown out of physical nature ... I feel there must be something that *transcends* all this,'[23] and in his repeated assertion that, of the two parents, the mother, symbolic of 'the embryonic life in Mother Nature,' is 'the one we have to break from in order to get born' (*GC*, 108; cf. also *WP*, 218). It is in the apocalyptic vision that nature, 'this permanent objective body which nourishes and incubates the imaginative form,' has been viewed by Frye, in conformity with tradition, as 'drop[ping] out,' for 'Nature,' he writes in *Fearful Symmetry*, 'is Mother Nature, and in the perfectly imaginative state there is no mother' (75). In other words, as David Cayley has observed, Frye does appear to 'accept the Bible's apocalyptic either/or.' ' "The only either/or dialectic that I'm interested in,"' he records Frye as saying, '"is the apocalyptic one, which moves towards a separation of a world of life from a world of death,"' the equation of nature with death implied here appearing to align him with the anti-life positions of the dualistic mythological world-views referred to previously. And yet, he further states, this 'final separation of life and death has to be in the form of an *imaginative vision*' ('The Ideas of Northrop Frye,' part 3, 17; emphasis added), that is, it is not to be taken literally. For as he has explained earlier in *The Great Code*: 'What is *symbolized* as the destruction of the order of nature is the destruction of a *way of seeing* that order that keeps man confined to the world of time and history as we know them' (GC 136; emphasis added).[24]

Given the contemporary insight into the correlation body:nature: woman:sexuality,[25] however, and given the fact that throughout his career Frye has consistently represented nature as subhuman, alien, and hostile to man,[26] one cannot help but be frustrated by imagery that appears to say one thing but is asserted to mean another. And one cannot help but be troubled by mythologies, or possibly by misreadings of mythologies, that do not accept as a fundamental tenet the essential meaningfulness and validity of human life in its natural form and environment. A genuinely enlightened spirituality or consciousness, one feels, should be based on a vision of integration rather than of separation, and should therefore affirm and include rather than exclude and deny nature, the body, sexuality, and the feminine principle. It therefore comes as a great relief when, towards the end of his long career, we begin to notice a change in Frye's attitude towards nature. In an interview conducted in 1983 he retracts a statement made in *Fearful Symmetry* regarding 'the imaginative conquest of nature,' explaining that his original opinion had been shaped by Blake's view that 'where man is not, nature is barren' and his 'resistance against everything that Graves means by the White Goddess' (WGS, 250), which would include 'natural religion' and 'the worship of a female principle' in nature (FS, 75). He would prefer to speak now, he says, of the 'identification' with and 'participation of man in nature' (WGS, 250).

In *Words with Power* Frye speaks of 'a new kind of alliance with nature, cemented two centuries ago' by the 'Romantic mythological revolution' (WP, 251–2) and cites the view of Rousseau, the 'herald' of this revolution, 'that the natural came from man's setting in physical nature, that reason was not a faculty separating man from this nature, but one uniting him with it, that man should recover the perspective in which he was a child of nature as well as a child of God, and that the old upper level of nature to be reached by virtue and religion and the benefits of civilization was not really a fulfillment of nature, as it claimed, but an impoverishing of large elements of it' (*WP*, 241). However, since Frye is still discussing redemption in terms of a separation from 'the predatory and destructive elements acquired from [man's] origin in nature' (*WP*, 135) and advocating the 'break' from the 'mother' which he regards as representative of an escape from imprisonment in 'nature's cycle of life, death and rebirth in a different form' (*WP*, 218), one is inclined to suspect that, two centuries after Rousseau, he has not quite completed the transition in his own mind. It is only in *The Double Vision* that he finally becomes fully reconciled to nature and presents as the 'central theme' of that work a revised vision of 'the harmony of spirit and nature,' 'the double vision of *a spiritual and a physical world simultaneously present*' (*DV*, 84–5; emphasis added).[27]

One senses from following a mind like Frye's struggling with and finally coming to terms with the age-old dilemma of the nature of the relationship between human embodiment and a spiritual principle that this is a portentous moment in the development of the mythological framework of Western culture, a moment that brings us to a possibility that is receiving considerable attention among contemporary investigators, that is, of the imminence of a major 'paradigm shift.' The term is used by Frye himself in the introduction to *Words with Power* in conjunction with his discussion of the response to his ahistorical reading of the Bible in *The Great Code* (*WP*, xvi). In *The Great Code* itself, however, as part of his elaboration of 'the radical meaning of "atonement" as "unifying," ' he speaks instead, appropriately in light of his metaphorical formulation of the divine-human relationship, of a fundamental change in metaphor or 'metaphor shift' to describe a new attitude in which 'a channel of communication between the divine and the human is now open' (*GC*, 134), a channel which can only be facilitated by this revised vision of 'the harmony of spirit and nature.'

It is in this formulation of the reconciliation of spirit and nature or matter, therefore, that we find the clue to the alleviation of our anxieties regarding the tensions between the secular and the spiritual, for their interpenetrating energies may now be explained in the more neutral terms of the 'implicate' and 'explicate' orders of modern physics (*DV*, 84),[28] and thus in terms of a principle of complementarity rather than of duality. And it is here also, I would suggest, that we find the key to the understanding of the relationship between the two apparently opposing mythological cosmologies, one of which sees salvation as coming from 'above' and the other 'from below and within,'[29] the possibility for the amalgamation or 'union' of which was first glimpsed as Job was seen to look both 'up' and 'down' at the end of *Words with Power* (311–13). No longer mutually exclusive, and therefore together representative of a new world view or construct of reality, these may now be imaged in terms of that other treatment of the 'double vision' which was presented by Yeats in his *A Vision*, namely, as the two interpenetrating gyres said by Yeats to be 'dying each other's life, [and] living each other's death' (120) in the manner of one of Frye's favourite aphorisms from Heraclitus.[30]

NOTES

1 In Frye's estimation the emphasis seems to fall on Paul's inability to make the language of his vision intelligible rather than on his being forbidden to do so (*GC*, 231), but a sense of prohibition nevertheless remains.

2 *Tao Te Ching*, 56. One of the older translations includes a commentary which refers to this as 'the Mysterious agreement'; see Legge, trans., *The Texts of Taoism*, pt. 1, 100.

3 It should be noted, however, that the equivalent passage in Matthew 13:13 conveys a slightly different nuance regarding the situation: 'Therefore speak I to them in parables: *because* they seeing see not; and hearing they hear not, neither do they understand' (emphasis added).

4 I have taken the liberty of substituting the Revised Standard Version's 'attack' for the Authorized King James Version's 'rend' here.

5 The problem involved here is articulated by Frye in *The Double Vision* in terms of Michael's explanation to Adam of the mechanisms of tyranny in Book XII of *Paradise Lost* and Paul's distinction between the *soma pneumatikon* and the *soma psychikon*, or the 'spiritual body' and the 'natural man,' made in 1 Corinthians 2:14 and 15:44 (*DV*, 12–14; cf. also *WP*, 124–5).

6 It is striking to note the resemblance between Blake's formulation and the imagery of the Buddhist Gandavyuha Sutra, in which the Buddha is said to have 'the miraculous power of manifesting all the images of the Dharmadhatu within one single particle of dust,' and the Bodhisattvas are said to be 'able to expand their own bodies to the ends of the universe' and to 'reveal in each particle of dust all the worlds, singly and generally, with their different conditions and multitudes.' Quoted in Suzuki, *Essays in Zen Buddhism*, 3rd ser., 89, 90.

7 Cf. also Gal. 2:20 and Col. 1:27.

8 Acts 16:17.

9 The formulation is attributed to Milton, but it clearly coincides with Frye's own thinking about the gospel.

10 Prabhavananda and Isherwood, trans., *How To Know God*, 54. Hegel does not appear to refer directly to the doctrines of Yoga in his *Phenomenology of Spirit*. He does discuss them in his published lectures on the philosophy of religion; however, these are dated some twenty years later. See his *Lectures on the Philosophy of Religion*, 283ff.

11 Feuerstein, *Yoga*, 153–4.

12 Ibid., 252. The differing identifications of the subject with mind and with spirit create some confusion for the nonspecialist. One is inclined to speculate about indications of different levels of meditative absorption, or of a rift said by scholars to exist between dualistic and nondualistic schools of Yoga; however, the issue appears to be best resolved by the fact that the concept of 'mind' is a highly complex one in Eastern thought and may represent either the emotional and rational functions of the 'heart' or 'lower mind' or the more intuitive and inspirational faculties of a 'higher mind' or 'spirit,' depending upon the context in which it appears. I thank Professor Joseph O'Connell of the Department of Religious Studies at the University of Toronto for his very kind assistance with this question.

   The complete passage from which this particular quotation is excerpted is striking for its unmistakably Blakean formulation: 'The last achievement of all thought is a recognition of the identity of spirit and matter, subject and object; and this reunion is the marriage of Heaven and Hell, the reaching out of a contracted universe towards its freedom, in response to the love of Eternity for the productions of time. There is then no sacred or profane, spiritual or sensual, but everything that lives is pure and void. This very world of birth and death is also the great Abyss.' For the original, see Coomaraswamy, *The Dance of Shiva*, 140.

13 Feuerstein, *Yoga*, 16.

14 Ibid., 12.

15 Ibid., x.

16 Ibid., xx.

17 Ibid., 2.

18 My thanks are due to John Ayre for drawing my attention to the General Note, which I had forgotten about when I first started working on the paper.

19 The Gandavyuha Sutra forms the final part of the massive Avatamsaka Sutra.

20 The 'disappearance' of the ego would appear to be analogous to the 'destruction' of the order of nature which is said to be symbolic of the 'destruction of the way of seeing that order' (*GC*, 134).

21 Feuerstein, *Sacred Sexuality*, 27.
22 Suzuki, *Essays in Zen Buddhism*, 1st ser., 49. The debate referred to here has apparently been complicated in the West by misunderstandings perpetuated before Buddhist texts became accessible to Western scholars. According to one of the more recent sources, Sangharakshita in *Survey of Buddhism*, the traditional explanations of nirvana as 'the "blowing out" of the fires of greed, hatred and delusion' and as 'the state wherein the thirst for sensuous experience, for continued existence, and even for non-existence is altogether absent' are derived from the etymologies of the Sanscrit 'Nirvana, from the root *va*, meaning to blow, and the prefix *nir*, out or off' and its Pali equivalent '*nibbana*,' 'made up of the negative particle *ni* and *vana* meaning selfish desire or craving.' 'Notwithstanding these etymologies,' Sangharakshita asserts, 'the goal of Buddhism is far from being a purely negative state, a metaphysical and psychological zero wherein individuality disappears, as some of the older orientalists maintained that the Buddhists believed.' However, the difference which does nevertheless exist between the two main streams of Buddhism is explained as follows: 'Psychologically, Nirvana is a state of absolute illumination, supreme bliss, infinite love and compassion, unshakeable serenity, and unrestricted spiritual freedom. Ontologically, it is for the Hinayana the eternal, unchanging, extra-mental spiritual entity wholly unconnected with the cosmic process, and for the Mahayana the Absolute Reality transcending all oppositions including that between itself and the Samsara.' See Sangharakshita, *A Survey of Buddhism*, 26–7.
23 Cayley, 'The Ideas of Northrop Frye,' part 3, 10; emphasis added.
24 To translate again into Eastern terms, the 'uncovering' or 'unveiling' implied by the process of 'revelation' or 'apocalypse' (Latin *apocalypsis*; Greek *apokaluptein*, from *apo*, 'off', plus *kaluptein*, 'to cover') corresponds to the removal of the veils of *maya* (Sanscrit) or 'illusion'.
25 The insight has become almost universal; however, the formulation of it employed here is taken from Feuerstein, *Sacred Sexuality*, 17.
26 I adhere to the traditional 'male metonymy' (*WP*, 190) advisedly here because of the tension between the masculine and the feminine principles implied by this attitude.
27 The significance of this vision cannot, to my mind, be overestimated, for what is involved here is not merely a revised evaluation of nature as positive but an entirely new conception of a *spiritualized* or *resacralized* nature, or what contemporary psychologists are translating into human terms as a fully 'embodied' spirituality or consciousness. What this means in terms of the central line of argument of this paper is that, even in the West, enlightenment is beginning to be perceived as attainable by conscious

individuals within our own cultural context rather than merely as an abstract ideal dimly associated with some distant and alien culture. For an example of one individual's experience of this process I would refer those who are interested to the remarkable story told by Mary Hamilton, a teacher of dance in the Faculty of Kinesiology at the University of Western Ontario in London, Ontario. See Hamilton, 'Redeeming Eve's Body,' in *Leaving My Father's House*, 127–96.

28 The concept of 'implicate' and 'explicate' orders derives from physicist David Bohm. See Bohm, *Wholeness and the Implicate Order*, especially chap. 7, 'The Enfolding-unfolding Universe and Consciousness.'

29 Cayley, 'The Ideas of Northrop Frye,' part 1, 7.

30 Cf. also *WP*, 161, 166; *MM*, 13, 224.

WORKS CITED

Bohm, David. *Wholeness and the Implicate Order*. London: Routledge and Kegan Paul, 1980.

Cayley, David. 'The Ideas of Northrop Frye.' Part 1. *Northrop Frye Newsletter* 3, no. 1 (Winter 1990–91).

– 'The Ideas of Northrop Frye.' Part 3. *Northrop Frye Newsletter* 4, no. 1 (Winter 1991–92).

Coomaraswamy, Ananda. *The Dance of Shiva: Fourteen Indian Essays*. Bombay: Asia Publishing House, 1948.

Eliade, Mircea. *Yoga: Immortality and Freedom*. 2nd ed. Princeton: Princeton University Press, 1969.

Feuerstein, Georg. *Sacred Sexuality: Living the Vision of the Erotic Spirit*. Los Angeles: Jeremy P. Tarcher, 1992.

– *Yoga: The Technology of Ecstasy*. Los Angeles: Jeremy P. Tarcher, 1989.

Hamilton, Mary. 'Redeeming Eve's Body.' In *Leaving My Father's House: A Journey to Conscious Femininity*, by Marion Woodman with Kate Danson, Mary Hamilton, and Rita Greer Allen. Boston: Shambhala, 1992.

Hegel, Georg Wilhelm Friedrich. *Lectures on the Philosophy of Religion*. In *The Lectures of 1827*, edited by Peter C. Hodgson. Berkeley: University of California Press, 1988.

Lao-tzu. *Tao Te Ching*. Translated by Stephen Mitchell. New York: Harper and Row, 1988.

Legge, James, trans. *The Texts of Taoism*. Part 1. New York: Dover, 1962.

Prabhavananda, Swami, and Christopher Isherwood, trans. With commentary. *How to Know God: The Yoga Aphorisms of Patanjali*. New York: Mentor, 1953.

Sangharakshita. *A Survey of Buddhism: Its Doctrines and Methods through the Ages*. 6th ed. London: Tharpa Publications, 1987.

Suzuki, D.T. *Essays in Zen Buddhism*. 1st ser. London: Luzac, 1927.

– *Essays in Zen Buddhism*. 3rd ser. London: Rider, 1953.

Yeats, W.B. *A Vision and Related Writings*. Selected and edited by A. Norman Jeffares. London: Arena, 1990.

Watts, Alan. *Psychotherapy East and West*. New York: Vintage, 1975.

IMRE SALUSINSZKY

Frye and Ideology

My primary text is *The Critical Path*, subtitled 'An Essay on the Social Context of Literary Criticism,' and I want to trace two paths from it: forward to *Words with Power* in 1990, and then backward to *Anatomy of Criticism* in 1957. *The Critical Path* was published in 1971, but written, and compulsively rewritten, between 1968 and 1970. Parts of it were composed, and delivered as lectures, at Cornell, at Indiana, and also at Berkeley, where Frye was visiting professor in the spring of 1969. These dates remind us, when we read *The Critical Path* today, that the book is inseparable from its own social context: that is, a profound crisis in the universities, reflecting the broader social crisis over the war in Vietnam, the crisis that had been threatening to tear apart the cohesive ideology of the Western liberal societies.

Frye's response to the virtual civil war raging around his head in the late 1960s is in character: he thinks back through the entire history of the way that the West has related social belief, individual freedom, and the creative arts and sciences, and the way that the university has participated in this network of relations. The cardinal idea around which Frye arranges the whole network is his idea of the 'myth of concern,' which he describes in *The Critical Path* as comprising 'everything that it most concerns its society to know.' He says: 'The myth of concern exists to hold society together, so far as words can help to do this. For it, truth and reality are not directly connected with reasoning or evidence ... What is true, for concern, is what society does and believes in response to authority, and a belief, so far as a belief is verbalized, is a statement of willingness to participate in a myth of concern' (36).

This description makes the myth of concern sound a great deal like an ideology. 'Ideology' is a notoriously slippery term, but according to

Terry Eagleton, one of its foremost students, its sense always has to do with the legitimating of society's power-structure through a variety of strategies of signification: through promoting the society's values; through naturalizing those values into apparently commonsensical pre-suppositions; through marginalizing rival forms of thought; and through mystifying the true power-relations that obtain in society (*Ideology*, 5–6). Softer, by which I mean less overtly Marxist, accounts of ideology than Eagleton's tend to emphasize ideology as a contestive space of significa-tion, rather than as a mechanism serving the exclusive interests of the dominant social group. Nevertheless, everyone seems to agree that ideol-ogy is the place where social belief, social value, and social power are inculcated in, and then expressed by, social subjects as meanings and interpretations.

Frye, as usual, is well ahead of us, because he remarks in *The Critical Path* that the reader would have no problem in substituting the word 'ideology' wherever he uses 'myth of concern' (112). So, given that *The Critical Path*, like so much of Frye's later work, is precisely about the relation of literature to concern, to ideology, we have reason to wonder – even leaving aside Hayden White's demonstration of 'counterideologi-cal' elements in the *Anatomy* – whether Frye was really the idealizer and mystifier and dehistoricizer that much of contemporary commentary wants to make him out to have been. Expressing the form of the relation between literature and concern in *The Critical Path*, Frye says that, while a society's literature grows out of its myth of concern, it is not identical with it: literature 'represents the *language* of human concern' and 'dis-plays the imaginative possibilities of concern' (98). Unlike concern, 'Lite-rature is not to be believed in: there is no "religion of poetry": the whole point about literature is that it has no direct connection with belief' (128).

In *The Modern Century*, written just before *The Critical Path*, Frye says that some modern myths of concern, most notably the democratic myth of concern, are 'open' or 'liberal' myths, in that they are able to moderate their own ideological anxieties sufficiently to allow other kinds of dis-course – based not on pure belief, nor on pure rhetoric, but on critique and argument and truth of correspondence – a space in which to operate (114–15). In *The Critical Path*, Frye calls this objective, scientific kind of discourse a 'myth of freedom.' He associates it explicitly with whatever is 'liberal' in a society, and says that it grows out of, and then enters into a permanent tension with, concern itself (44–5). Certain ideologies, in other words, open spaces for the performance of their own critique, their own partial demystification.

I have a hunch that the relation of literature to ideological concern, as he tries to set it out in *The Critical Path*, troubled Frye so much that that is the reason why, as he informs us strangely in the preface, he kept sitting down simply to revise the book, and then rewrote it completely. And still, in *The Critical Path*, the relation seems unsettled, nervous. Literature, rather than being concern, is supposed to represent the 'language of concern.' But was not the myth of concern only ever a language in the first place? Frye's difficulty is that of finding, as he puts it, a 'middle way': a path between the deterministic fallacy of subsuming literature into social history and the aestheticist fallacy of cutting it off completely from its sustaining social roots and potential social force (32–3). The fact that *The Critical Path* places Frye there – between determinism on the one side and aestheticism on the other – makes it an emblematic text for his whole career.

The suggestion that Frye was never quite satisfied with the way that he worked out the relation of literature to ideology is confirmed when we open his last book and find that there, in *Words with Power*, he spends the first hundred or so pages tinkering with, and rewriting yet again, the picture of concern, ideology, and literature that he had presented twenty years earlier in *The Critical Path*. In addition, this indicates how aware, even near the end of his life, Frye remained of the critical currents that were flowing around him. In other words, he knows in *Words with Power* that a new 'historicism,' a new integration of literature with social ideology, a new account of the relation of words to power, is underway in the discipline; and he knows that he needs to address it.

Frye is willing to concede in *Words with Power* that 'ideology seems to be the delta which all verbal structures finally reach' (19). But here he divides the myth of concern into 'secondary concerns,' the hard-core ideological matters, and 'primary concerns,' which are concerns about things so basic that any direct statement of them can only take the form of platitude: 'that life is better than death, happiness better than misery, health better than sickness, freedom better than bondage, for all people without significant exception' (42). As in *The Critical Path*, literature is seen as related to secondary concern, but as distinguishable from it, except that here the distinction seems to consist less in literature as being the 'language of concern' than in literature's ability to relate secondary concerns to 'the primary ones of making a living, making love, and struggling to stay free and alive' (*WP*, 42–3).

This sense of primary concern was only gestured at in *The Critical Path* in its passing suggestion of a 'concern behind concern' (103). Unfortunately, though, all of this belief in some 'primary' terrain sounds exactly like an ideology itself. Indeed, such an invocation of a realm of 'natural' or 'primary' human needs, transcending all distinctions of race, class, and gender, and connected with the aesthetic, is precisely what contemporary left cultural critics mean when they talk about an 'aesthetic ideology.' By defining, as it were, the minimum of what is essential for all human beings you can end up producing a highly distilled version of the Western liberal ideology itself.

Suspending that issue, I want now to return to my primary text, and to the point in his potted cultural history of the West that brings Frye to the English Renaissance. In *The Critical Path* Frye describes the 'typical humanist' as follows: 'The typical humanist strives to be sane, balanced, judicious; he is not a prophet nor an angry man ... He avoids both technical and colloquial language, and has a deep respect for conventions, both social and literary. As a professional rhetorician, his instinct is to save the face of the situations he encounters by finding the appropriate words for them' (90). It would have been hard for informed readers in 1971, and it would be impossible for us now, to miss the hint in this passage: the hint that, in so describing the 'typical humanist,' Frye is also giving a pretty fair description of himself. He, too, is someone who constantly seeks to 'save the face of the situations he encounters,' either by finding new contexts that will allow what were previously thought of as opposites to coexist or by finding a 'middle way' between them, or by showing that they are not really opposites at all. The last of these is precisely what he does, in *The Critical Path*, with the social turmoil going on around him in the late 1960s: those who prosecute war have lost sight of primary concerns, and can only see secondary ones; but those who seek to end war by 'harassing and bedevilling the university' (164), trying to turn it into a church or political party, have given in to secondary concern as well – they cannot see that where the university belongs is in the myth of freedom, and that the road to primary concern goes via freedom, not via secondary concern.

This habit of seeking the 'middle way' is of course what marks Frye as a liberal. It is interesting to reflect that to be a liberal was a deeply unfashionable thing both at the very beginning and then again at the very end of Frye's writerly career, but he never cavilled at the label. Indeed, when, in an interview with Marylou Miner recorded less than a year before his death, Miner compared him to Matthew Arnold, he replied: 'Except that Matthew Arnold had yellow streaks in him which prevented him from being a proper liberal at times. It's the streak of cowardice in Arnold that seems to make him a flawed liberal from my point of view' (Interview with Northrop Frye,' 13). Frye's legacy, therefore, is bound up inextricably with the destiny of the liberal mind, or rather the two destinies are bound up together. Although we cannot answer it, we can ask the question: Was Frye the last great liberal thinker?

The word 'liberal' takes us back to the 'myth of freedom.' That is where Frye places the university in society, and it is also where he places his own vision of criticism in *The Critical Path*, where he says that the critic 'is not himself concerned but detached. His criteria are those of the myth of freedom, depending on evidence and verification ... Once the critic is released from the preoccupations of a moral and evaluating approach, he is obliged to preserve a tolerance for every variety of poetic expression and a respect for every poet's individuality' (99). However Frye tries to rework it over the years, literature retains a connection with secondary concern, and hence with ideology. But criticism belongs inside the myth of freedom, and it is criticism that continually performs the rescue operation that lifts an element in all literature clear of its origins in ideology. This is why Frye's idea of 'primary concern' is not necessarily just the 'aesthetic ideology' revisited: the relation between literature and primary concern is a constructed relation, not a natural one. And criticism is the place where the construction occurs.

This complicates our sense of Frye's liberalism. When he talks about human apocalypses and revelations (*Eli*, 105), Frye sounds like what Richard Rorty calls a 'liberal metaphysician,' someone who believes that there are real essences behind our philosophical vocabularies (*Contingency*, 73). But when he talks about the spirit of inquiry as a 'myth' of freedom, Frye sounds more like what Rorty calls a 'liberal ironist': someone who thinks that the only real choices are between old and new vocabularies (*Contingency*, 74–5). Frye says in *Words with Power* that reducing a work of literature to its ideological dimension, or what he calls its 'overthought' (57), is a critical decision. His own decision – and *Anatomy* makes it quite clear that this is simply an assumption you make if you believe that such a subject as criticism can exist as an objective study – is to examine the formal 'underthought' of poetry, the progression of images and metaphors and narrative structures that connect the work of literature to the whole literary universe; this grand poem then images forth the triumph of primary over secondary concern, and thus rediscovers the social power of words in a renewed context.

This is the central argument that Frye reiterates in *Words with Power*: 'I think of a poet, in relation to his society, as being at the center of a cross like a plus sign. The horizontal bar forms the social and ideological conditioning that made him intelligible to his contemporaries, and in fact to himself. The vertical bar is the mythological line of descent from previous poets back to Homer' (47). Frye's work tells us this one story, over and over: it is criticism, and criticism alone, not something essential to literature, that can free literature from becoming or remaining a mere counter in the historical process of the legitimating of ruling-class interests.

Imagine that you are confronted by two stark alternatives. On the one side is a historical determinism so powerful that it cannot see anything like an autonomous 'aesthetic space' for literature, condemning all such notions as bourgeois illusions. On the other side is a linguistic nihilism so intense that it cannot see any social function for literature whatsoever, reducing it to an endless 'free-play' of ambiguous signifiers.

Is this a description of last year's MLA convention? It could be, but in fact I am trying to describe the dialectical situation that confronted Frye in the 1940s and 1950s, as he worked his way towards *Anatomy* and tried to reconcile what is now called 'vulgar' Marxism, on his left-hand side, with what is now called 'old' New Criticism, on his right. In *Anatomy*, Frye sees these alternatives as, simply, ideologies: as 'dialectical crowbar[s]' or 'determinisms,' all 'substituting a critical attitude for criticism' (12, 6). It is impossible to overestimate the extent to which *Anatomy* emerges out of Frye's sense that such ideological approaches, such surrenderings of criticism to secondary concern, such 'definite positions' as he calls them (19), had reached a dead end.

But they had not. In our own time, the linguistic nihilists seem to be retreating; and the social determinists – the new historicists, the Foucauldians, the gender-studies and subaltern-studies people, the 'polite' Marxists, the British cultural materialists – all seem to be in the ascendant. Let me close by glancing at 'cultural criticism,' a term I use to describe three of the most influential strains in current theory, all of which have the word 'cultural' somewhere in their titles: 'cultural materialism,' with its centre of gravity in Sussex; 'cultural studies,' with its centre of gravity in Birmingham; and 'cultural poetics' (Stephen Greenblatt's preferred term to 'new historicism'), with its centre of gravity on the west coast of the United States.

Cultural criticism does not see any distinction between what it studies – culture, including literature – and ideology. In his recent *British Cultural Studies: An Introduction*, Graeme Turner says that ideology saturates language, and that it 'not only produces our culture, it also produces our consciousness of our selves' (26–7). Cultural criticism takes ideological criticism to a point that Frye could not have imagined: it folds not only literature and other forms of representation, but all previous attempts to study these representations, back into secondary concern.

But here cultural criticism runs into the problem of circularity: if the ideologies that cultural criticism studies are, as Turner says, 'unconscious' (27), and have been placed in all social subjects, then how do the students of cultural criticism know what further ideologies are motivating their curriculum? Interestingly, cultural criticism responds to this problem by reverting to the metaphor that Frye so heartily disliked: the metaphor of positioning. Louis A. Montrose, for example, lays great stress on the way that, in cultural poetics, the critic's own position is made part of the problem under investigation ('Professing the Renaissance,' 25–6). But this really only delays the problem of circularity: even after I have carefully positioned myself, there must be yet further positions that I unconsciously reflect, but do not know. And so there commences an endless positioning and repositioning, until finally I find myself firmly positioned at last: in a corner, with wet paint on every side. And this is precisely where my opponents – the writers of fear-mongering books on political correctness and tenured radicalism – most want to see me positioned.

Frye's legacy will not depend upon disciples, which are the last thing he wanted anyway; he once told me that gathering disciples around yourself was simply inviting the 'Judas reaction.' Rather, Frye's legacy will depend upon the power of his ideas to continue to compete within a changing critical market-place, at least in my view (I am aware that Frye himself would not have used such pragmatist language to describe the evolution of critical ideas). So far, the lessons of *Anatomy* regarding the dead end of ideological criticism have not been taken. But now, more than ever, many books of criticism seem like smart bombs fired across discursive minefields, making me wonder whether Frye's 'middle way,' between determinism and aesthetic indeterminacy, may yet turn out to be the truly critical path.

WORKS CITED

Eagleton, Terry. *Ideology: An Introduction*. London: Verso, 1991.

Miner, Marylou. 'An Interview with Northrop Frye.' *Northrop Frye Newsletter* 4, no. 2 (1992): 8–13.

Montrose, Louis A. 'Professing the Renaissance: The Poetics and Politics of Culture.' In *The New Historicism*, edited by H. Aram Veeser. New York: Routledge, 1989.

Rorty, Richard. *Contingency, Irony, and Solidarity*. Cambridge: Cambridge University Press, 1989.

Turner, Graeme. *British Cultural Studies: An Introduction.*
Boston: Unwin Hyman, 1990.
White, Hayden. 'Ideology and Counterideology in the *Anatomy.*' In *Visionary Poetics: Essays on Northrop Frye's Criticism*, edited by Robert D. Denham and Thomas Willard. New York: Peter Lang, 1991.

DEANNE BOGDAN

The (Re)Educated Imagination

In January 1980, one month after the defence of my doctoral dissertation, my thesis supervisor said to me in a throwaway line, 'Now that the oral is over, you'll have to get some distance on Frye.' Over the years, that remark has remained with me as one of those utterances that Frye said chases itself around in your head and takes on a life of its own.[1] Perplexed then and for some time afterwards, I did not know what it would mean to 'get some distance' on Frye nor why anyone would have to. As I had tried to show in my thesis, Frye was the twentieth-century's archetypal apologist for poetry, in the tradition of Sidney, Shelley, and Arnold, all of whom in their own way were answering Plato's charge to the poets.[2] Trying as much as possible to look at the structure of Frye's thought from the inside, I focused on his theory of poetic creation and response within its anagogic context, that sense of the infinitude of verbal meaning brought about by the 'swallow[ing]' (*EI*, 33) of life by literature, the containment of fallen existence by the imaginative process.[3] With anagogy, you just did not get outside even if you wanted to.

So powerful was the influence of Frye's thought on my own that only after my thesis was completed did I recognize its structure as the quest myth. In the years following, all my writing in poetics and its application to educational theory was grounded in my constructions of Frye's constructions. With respect to poetic creation, I used his architectural and musical metaphors to explore his flight from truth-of-correspondence ('From Stubborn Structure to Double Mirror'); and I developed a taxonomy of his theory of literary response as a dialectical activity ('Taxonomy of Literary Response'). These efforts all supported my acceptance of his acceptance of belief in literature as the corner-stone of a liberal education and the arts as the life-blood of society.

Since then, I have been making what Frye called an 'involuntary journey': for me, a critical path which, in hindsight, I now connect to my unconscious need to 'get some distance' on him. As Frye wrote: 'if the journey is a metaphor for life, life has to be followed to the end, but the end is the point of the journey, or at least the quality of the end is. It is conceivable, however, that a journey might have a value in itself. If so, obviously there would have to be something inside the traveller to resonate against the experience, so the theme of journeying for the sake of the experience of journeying would often be at the same time a journey into oneself' (MM, 221). My interior journey has taught me that the only way I could distance myself from Frye was indeed to travel in and through him through the three stages of the quest myth: initiation, separation, and return. This paper recapitulates that structure while attempting to delineate my relationship to Frye from a particular standpoint – that which Marion Woodman has called a 'father's daughter' (Ravaged Bridegroom, 9), that is, a woman who is especially vulnerable, by dint of her very aspiration to the intellectual and creative life, to the savagery of the Cartesian split between mind and body. I have been only one among countless daughters and sons who have recognized in Frye their intellectual and spiritual father; and my story offers, through the three stages of my journey, a defence, critique, and reconception of literary education. The period of initiation was devoted to adherence to the principles laid down in The Educated Imagination: separation, to reversing them; and return, to reconfiguring them.

Initiation: The Educated Imagination

Frye's legacy to culture and society can be said to be encompassed within the two covers of The Educated Imagination, his most accessible articulation of his theory of the relationship between literature and education. During my initiation period, I laboured lovingly as a father's daughter, embracing the paternal tradition, propounding his deep-browed humanism, confident in my task: to elaborate the implications of the educated imagination for what has loosely come to be called reader-response theory and practice in the classroom. Frye probably would have regarded the phrase 'reader-response theory' itself as something of an oxymoron if A.C. Hamilton is right, as I think he is, that for Frye any theory of reader response that does not distinguish between

reading and criticism (especially those theories derived from phenomenology) 'has not been shaped out of an inductive survey of English literature but depends upon a reader's *ignorance* of most of it' (*Northrop Frye*,
221; emphasis added). Notwithstanding Frye's claim that there is nothing to be wrought from literature except the experience of literature,
there was still such a thing for him as 'incomplete' or 'incompetent' 'half-
reading' (*GC*, 58): the importance of what readers bring to the text was,
within the swirling galaxies of the 'order of words' (*AC*, 17), relatively
minor, criticism being for him a 'monument to a failure of experience'
(*CP*, 27). It is Frye's ambivalence about experience[4] which, I think, made
him an Aristotelian rather than a Longinian critic.[5] It is both his acceptance and his mistrust of experience which underwrites the three tenets
of the educated imagination: the sharp distinction between ordinary
existence and imaginative experience (*WTC*, 149–50); the apolitical nature of the literary; and the logical priority of the critical response over
the direct or 'participating' response (*NP*, 9).

Within the ethos of the educated imagination, these three principles in
turn devolve upon a triad of premises which informed Frye's humanist
fervour about the educational value of literature: the distinction between
ordinary existence and imaginative experience, on the assumption that
literature influences for good but not for ill; the apolitical nature of the
literary, on the assertion that literature does not say that it is a hypothetical construct which needs criticism to speak for it (*WP*, 27);[6] and the logical priority of the critical response, on a poetics of total form, in which
literary response consists of the dialectical activity of alternating states
of engagement and detachment.

For several years, the foregoing provided me with a secure context,
culturally and dispositionally, for working through three main issues
related to the educational value of literature, what I have come to call the
justification problem (why teach literature), the censorship problem
(what literature to teach), and the response problem (how to teach it).
Each of these problems found its conceptual home within three tenets of
the educated imagination: the justification problem within the belief that
literature constitutes 'the best subject matter in the world' (*OE*, 10); the
censorship problem within the dictum that a 'man is defiled by what
comes out of him and not by what goes into him' (*WP*, 263);[7] and the response problem within the postulate of the autonomous reader for
whom consciousness is all, who, through greater and greater exposure
to literary experience and increasing knowledge about literature, strives
to overcome dissociation of sensibility as an inescapable fact of reading
life. For the autonomous reader, what might be deemed false content or

painful literary experience by any one reader at any one time in any given reading act is subsumed instrumentally under literary understanding (*DV*, 76, 80).

Separation: The Metaproblem

While my labour was, I hope, fruitful, one could hardly say that I was getting any distance on Frye. What I was getting was an induction into the educated imagination so intense that distancing from it necessitated a separation stage that shook my entire cultural identity. The first phase of separation was what we might call the 'politics of literary engagement,' brought about by my work on the censorship of Margaret Laurence's novels in Peterborough County in 1985. Here I came to the gradual realization that the epistemological assumptions underlying the social effects of literary reading held by educators wanting to alter the curriculum in order to keep pace with changing cultural norms bore a disconcerting similarity to those held by book-banning religious fundamentalists.[8] The second phase, inspired by my first experience teaching women's literature and feminist literary criticism a year later, marked my formulation of a 'poetics of refusal.' Based on feminist philosophers and reader-response theorists, such as Sandra Lee Bartky, Judith Fetterley, and Shoshanna Felman, and on Lawrence Lipking's conception of a 'poetics of need,' the poetics of refusal had pointed up the artificiality of the infinite regress of delayed critical judgment, especially if one is reading for one's life as many women are when introduced to feminist literary criticism.[9] For all of Frye's ardency about the educated imagination as 'education for life,' his literary epistemology, it seemed to me, posited a disembodied, certainly ungendered, reader.

Both phases of this stage of separation brought into relief the educational implications of 'direct' literary experience as a form of 'real' experience in a way that rendered thoroughly problematic the three tenets of the educated imagination. (I put both words in quotation marks because we know, of course, that both kinds of experience are always mediated.) Though it had always been clear to me that Frye's distinctions – between literature and life, the direct and critical response, imaginative experience and ordinary existence, primary and secondary concern, mythology and ideology, literary convention and reality, scholarship and evaluation, and the like – were conceptual categories, not actual divisions (*WP*, 42), my research into the censorship problem and my teaching from a feminist perspective impressed upon me the enormous practical difficulties, if not the impossibility and even the undesirability, of maintaining those distinctions in classrooms full of real readers reading. Above all, I came to take seriously what students know, overtly and tacitly, not just about literature but about their own literary experience, experience which was, it seemed to me, based quite legitimately on something other than either the possession or the lack of literary knowledge.

From a theoretical standpoint, my work in censorship had resulted in my having effectively conflated the issues of selection and censorship. (The line between them is much finer than we think.) In other words, once literary reading is set within an expressly educational context, in which we acknowledge expansion of a canon or restructuring of a curriculum, we must also confront the fact that the hypothetical dimension of literature notwithstanding, literature does say things. My work in feminism showed that the notion of the autonomous reader traded on an ordering of literary response that was both hierarchical and androcentric. All of this eventuated in my coming to see that rationales for the teaching of literature were on a collision course with arguments against the censorship of school texts, in that educators could too readily and inconsistently shift the focus from engagement to detachment according to the dictates of political expediency. As well, it became increasingly apparent to me that the classroom handling of students' literary response was not a discrete issue to be addressed apart from those of justification and censorship, each oblivious to the others in shoring up unproblematic belief in literary education as unconditionally benign. Rather, justification, censorship, and literary response formed interdependent aspects of a metaproblem, which was itself testimony to the dual power of literary experience as a form of real experience: within cultural diversity and ideological schisms, this intrication of the why, what, and how of teaching literature disclosed that literary experience could be negative as well as positive. So palpable were the intellectual, personal, and social implications of the effects of my discoveries that I was not content to have them either fobbed off as category mistakes or relegated to the Frygean twilight zone of the subliterary or the extraliterary. After all, it was Frye's work that had taught me about the normative influence of direct literary experience to begin with. As he wrote in *The Critical Path*, 'Our structures of reason and imagination are ... analogical constructs designed to recapture, within the mental processes that belong to our present state, something of a lost directness of apprehension' (31).

Through this facet of my journey, the tripartite conceptual framework of the educated imagination was turned inside out. First, with the dismantling of the disembodied reader, imaginative experience became integrated with ordinary existence. Second, the literary could no longer remain apolitical, but was imbued with the particularities of the social and cultural biases and the power relations of students who are located with respect to race, class, and gender. Finally, direct response assumed an ethical, even ontological priority over the critical response. That is, the participating or direct response does not just happen first, but takes on a philosophical importance that supersedes criticism: the educational value of literature becomes as much a matter of the fact that student readers respond according to their difference as it is a matter of where their responses might fall within any taxonomical continuum. In short, the order of words cannot claim epistemic superiority over my affective life, for what is at stake is not just the educational potential of *dianoia* but my prior right to experience *nous* as autobiographically significant. Your literary interpretation, even though it might be better than mine, cannot make me mean.[10]

Feminist theories of reading, having successfully reconceptualized the ethical dimension of literature by questioning the grounds of literary importance in terms of a gendered divided consciousness, reinforced my reconception of direct response. Under the gaze of a woman reading with the passion of her subjectivity, literary taxonomies topple, hierarchical categories dissolve, and 'strong writers turn pale.'[11] When a 'recovering' father's daughter seeks to reassociate sensibility, she uses her body as prime consultant; and I could no longer rationalize under the mantle of the educated imagination the mental and emotional anguish of some respondents – their refusal to delay value judgments, or even their impulse to reject a text because of how it had acted on them – as a species of what Frye would have regarded as partial form. The imperative for readers to move from partial form to 'literature as a total form' (*AC*, 115), as it is represented by a 'full' or 'genuine' 'literary' response, an imperative whose *telos* resides in the very distinction between 'part' and 'whole,' to me entailed a literal self-denial, whose psychological and ethical implications for education clamoured to be addressed. Did I really believe, with Frye, that it 'does not matter a tinker's curse what a student thinks and feels about literature until *he* can think and feel, which is not until *he* passes the stage of stock response' (*StS*, 83, emphasis added)?

Return: The Re-Educated Imagination

The effect of this experience was to catapult me into a 'double ontological shock ... first, the realization that what is really happening is quite different from what appears to be happening; and second, the frequent inability to tell what is really happening at all.'[12] Impelled to subvert the hierarchy between the direct and critical response, yet lacking the full awareness of what I was undertaking, I began to redraw for myself the map that had thus far guided my journey. For this, I had to supply my own vocabulary for my ideas, which, while they were doubtless influenced by poststructural and postmodern theory, were still primarily rooted in the initial three premises of the educated imagination, now rendered inapplicable to the metaproblem within their original context, but still relevant, it seemed, to its resolution. In order then to support a theory that both politicized and privileged direct response, itself a concept that contemporary criticism called into question, I supplemented the metaproblem of justification, censorship, and response with the complicating factors of the feeling, power, and location problems, hoping thus to lend ethical and ontological weight to the psychological evanescence of the participating response. That the who, where, and when of literary reading were just as important as the what, why, and how of the metaproblem, for me, made the context of literary response a primary concern rather than an invisible taken-for-granted ideological positioning, as it would be within the educated imagination. New terminology, such as 'the poetics of ordinary existence,' attempted to show that literary experience was not so impoverished as to need critical compensation for its failure; and the notion of women's post-tragedic stance – that women come to the text knowing already what Oedipus had to find out, namely, that they are betrayed by their gods – provided theoretical ballast for the experiential descent of literature into life.[13]

In thus getting some distance on Frye, I was propelled to ask the question Jane Miller poses in *Seductions: Studies in Reading and Culture*: what is it that can sweep a woman into complicity with a metaphysic, the very breadth of whose explanatory power excludes her (121–2).[14] For me, it was precisely the deep knowing of the anagogic perspective, the 'recognition scene' (*AC*, 346) of standing inside Logos. You have only to go to Pythagoras to see the force of the connection, the mathematical certainty of the 'I am that am' radiating as the music of the spheres, the Great Chain of Being, microcosm as macrocosm. And you can go there solely by way of your own patterned logic of noticing and unnoticing[15] as you orbit the dizzying universe of Frye's order of words. But when you see that the pattern is not yours and the journey not on your terms, that you have been absent from the very first incarnation of the Word, this knowing is necessarily also an unknowing, an archetypal misrecognition scene. It is the double vision, not as the spiritual distinguished from the natural, but as the awareness of a radical displacement from such a vision, in which the category 'woman' is inexorably identified with the category 'natural' (see especially *DV*, 22–4, 31).

In order to relate the re-educated imagination to the educated imagination one must be both inside and outside anagogy at the same time, while seeing from below. Seeing from below, according to Donna Haraway, is a privileged sight-line because it exposes modes of knowing based on 'denial ... repression, forgetting, and disappearing acts.' Seeing from below gives its viewers 'a decent chance to be on to the god trick and ... its dazzling – and, therefore blinding – illuminations,' its 'ways of being nowhere while claiming to see comprehensively' ('Situated Knowledges,' 584). Viewing from below is the only way that I, as both woman and educational theorist within the academy, could possibly have gotten any distance on Frye. The re-educated imagination is perhaps a subaltern defence of poetry written from the 'partial perspective' of my 'situated knowledge' as a father's daughter. It represents my attempt to embody vision by stressing the feeling, power, and location problems, not as subcategories of the mythological, but as essential conditions of knowing, as the tangible realities that make 'claims on people's lives' ('Situated Knowledges,' 590, 589) primary rather than secondary concerns.

The re-educated imagination respects anagogic vision as the goal of the educated imagination, but is wary of it as possibly a god trick that can too easily evade critical responsibility for the effects of its own insights and the premises of its own construction.[16] As an antidote to conceptions of objective reality founded on abstraction, anagogic vision nobly purports to reintegrate body and spirit. But a spiritual vision can never be fully present to itself unless it regards 'the violence implicit in [its] visualizing practices' as integral to its seeing, unless the question of 'with whose blood ... [one's] eyes [have been] crafted' ('Situated Knowledges,' 585) becomes a primary concern.

For a father's daughter seeing from below, anagogy as the double vision of religious experience is accompanied by the mundane operation of the double take, which looks again at the value dimension of critical categories and literary structures to discover what they foreground and what they erase, what they enable and what they efface.[17] When logical distinctions precede the conditions under which these distinctions are applied, one can hide behind categories if people get too close. For example, in one of his later essays, Frye simply differentiated between the literalist and the imaginative as a way of 'pass[ing] over the more pathological and racist forms of such attitudes, merely saying that hysteria, by insisting that an inner state of mind is united when it is actually divided, is bound to project its frustrations sooner or later on some outward scapegoat who symbolizes the objecting inner self' (*MM*, 98). The re-educated imagination would appreciate the insight but notice that the comparative freedom with which one can distinguish but pass over racism, sexism, or homophobia is won in this case by reasserting the hierarchy between mythology and ideology, a position that makes it easier for some more than others to be able to say 'merely say.'

In his introduction to *Northrop Frye in Conversation*, David Cayley, commenting on the social function of literary archetypes in Frye's work, observes that it 'is in the wrestle between the archetype and the individual life' that we become humanized (22). The re-educated imagination is concerned with the conditions of that struggle at a historical moment when mythology is particularly being played out as ideology. This is nowhere more apparent than in the social function of female archetypal images. Even Frye's quasi-mystical double vision of a perfectly integrated humanity, one that makes of schematizing a profound spiritual exercise, presumes a system of noticing and un-noticing that is complicit with the disincarnation of women. While I agree with him that 'there is a strong resistance within an ideology to placing its excluded initiative, the myth it lives by, into focus and examining it in a broader perspective' (*WP*, 24), I would suggest that the excluded initiative of the educated imagination is the silent Beatrice (*WP*, 28), an image which might be examined within its broader context – the gendered hierarchy between subject and object.

So long as Beatrice does not speak, bodies fall or disappear in support of the second sight of him who is continually straining to look beyond; and the flexibility afforded by double vision will tend to be defined less as divine energy 'humble enough to return to its human dimensions'[18] and more as 'the same man ... actually get[ting] both heroines, one in his imaginative and the other in his everyday life' (*WP* 269). The flexibility of the latter is perilously close to mere fluidity – of the flip between convention and reality that can sweep us clear of 'the world of facts' too readily and too soon (*DV*, 18; *AC*, 347): the historical Regine becomes the material cause of Kierkegaard's redemptive quest; and the dead victims of the Montreal massacre erased in Frye's efforts, real and sincere doubt-less though they were, to identify with the alien 'other,' when he ac-knowledged feeling 'some involvement even with the fantasies of a psychotic murdering women who want to be engineers' (*DV*, 80, 34).

It would be easier for me to pass over this and admit to having made huge category mistakes. Rather, I would say that Norrie Frye was seduced by the breadth of his own vision, which became both a defence against and release for his intense inner life.[19] His involuntary journey compelled him to unseat Nobodaddy, to seek a form in which the Word could be pure utterance; to this end, he needed the educated imagination and the order of words, a structure stubborn enough to resist the 'wandering of desire' (SeS, 30). His hypothetical gaze, ever struggling for embodiment, ultimately informed the relationship between literary genres and what the world calls reality. Whether the effects of these relationships are ethical problems teachers of literature should worry about is the business of the re-educated imagination.

Involuntary journeys produce, by virtue of the very attempt to go home again, involuntary returns – to a different location from where we begin. I have been led out of my father's house but only across Bloor Street, where a host of critical disciplines, through their partial vision, work inter alia with literature to ask such questions as: Who gets to see the world in a grain of sand?

NOTES

1 Frye, 'Literature as Therapy,' 31.
2 See Deanne Bogdan, 'Instruction and Delight.'
3 'Anagogically, then, poetry unites total ritual, or unlimited social action, with total dream, or unlimited individual thought. Its universe is infinite and boundless hypothesis: it cannot be contained within any actual civilization or set of moral values, for the same reason that no structure of imagery can be restricted to one allegorical interpretation ... The *ethos* of art is no longer a group of characters within a natural setting, but a universal man who is also a divine being, or a divine being conceived in anthropomorphic terms' (AC, 120).
4 See especially David Cayley's NFC, 39–48. I am not sure that Frye would completely agree with Cayley's claim in his introduction that 'the test of the imagination's truth is in experience' (33).
5 For an analysis of *Anatomy* as a formulation of Aristotle's conception of narrative understanding, see Ricoeur, 'Northrop Frye's *Anatomy of Criticism*.'
6 Also, 'Poetry seeks the image rather than the idea, and even when it deals with ideas, it tends to seek the latent basis of concrete imagery in the idea' (FI, 57).
7 This text is taken from Matthew 15:11. The use of 'man' here – Matthew

also uses it – is in keeping with the masculinist bias of the concept of the educated imagination, which I elaborate on later in the paper.

8 See Bogdan, 'The Rhetorical Fallacy,' 197–211.

9 See Bartky, 'Towards a Phenomenology of Feminist Consciousness'; Bogdan, 'Censorship, Identification, and the Poetics of Need'; Fetterley, *The Resisting Reader*; Gold, *Read for Your Life*; Felman, 'Psychoanalysis and Education,' 21–44; Lipking, 'Aristotle's Sister.'

10 See *StS*, 74ff; Campbell, 'Expression and the Individuation of Feeling,' 291. Campbell presents a compelling analysis of the relationship between expression and affect as an explanatory category at the ontological level. See also Felman, *Jacques Lacan and the Adventure of Insight*, 119.

11 Lipking, 'Aristotle's Sister,' 103.

12 Bartky, 'Towards a Phenomenology of Feminist Consciousness,' 256.

13 See Bogdan, *Re-Educating the Imagination*.

14 In *Cassandra*, Wolf writes, 'I claim that every woman in this century and in our culture sphere who has ventured into male-dominated institutions – "literature" and "aesthetics" are such institutions – must have experienced the desire for self-destruction' (299).

15 Morgan, *The Demon Lover*, 60.

16 Frye certainly acknowledged his own bourgeois underpinnings. But his liberalism was too unruffled in its assumption of an unproblematic coherence: 'I am what I am: let others be what they are' (*NFC*, 215; see also 66).

17 If I take seriously literary experience as a form of real experience, a certain discomfiture overcomes me when Frye presumes to speak for me by insisting on the absolute distinction between literature and life in all literary conventions at all times and for all people; as, for example, when he says in *Words with Power* that the 'preposterous sexist ideology' of Shakespeare's *The Taming of the Shrew*, which is subordinate to the 'sure-fire drama' of the work, is 'never taken very seriously' (215). I do not regard my desire to put quotation marks around 'forgiven harlot' (214), 'suppliant heroines in a fix' (93), and 'poetic mistresses' as 'available' or 'unavailable,' (79) used unproblematically within the context of literary convention, as something I need to 'get over,' or at least, 'beyond.' Nor do I believe that the low-level anxiety I experience at the repeated metaphor of penetration (110, 112, 117) to describe the highest level of verbal revelation makes me an ideologue stuck in the rut of stock response.

18 Woodman, *Leaving My Father's House*, 43.

19 Like his countryman, the late Glenn Gould, Frye was in his own way an ecstatic. See Bogdan, 'From Stubborn Structure to Double Mirror,' 42; see also *NFC*, 63.

WORKS CITED

Bartky, Sandra Lee. 'Towards a Phenomenology of Feminist Consciousness.' In *Philosophy and Women*, edited by S. Bishop and M. Weinzweig. Belmont: Wadsworth Publishers, 1979.

Bogdan, Deanne. *Re-Educating the Imagination: Toward a Poetics, Politics and Pedagogy of Literary Engagement*. Portsmouth: Boynton-Cook/Heinemann, 1992.

– 'Censorship, Identification, and the Poetics of Need.' In *The Right to Literacy*, edited by A. Lunsford, H. Moglen, J. Slevin. New York: MLA, 1990.

– 'From Stubborn Structure to Double Mirror: The Evolution of Northrop Frye's Theory of Poetic Creation and Response.' *The Journal of Aesthetic Education* 23, no. 2 (1989): 33–43.

– 'A Taxonomy of Literary Response and Respondents.' *Paideusis: Journal of the Canadian Philosophy of Education Society* 1, no. 1 (1987): 43–54.

– 'Literary Response as Dialectic: Modes and Levels of Engagement and Detachment.' *Cuadernos de Filologia Inglesa* 2 (1986): 45–62.

– 'The Rhetorical Fallacy: Values as Literary Representation.' Deanne Bogdan and Stephen Yeomans, 'School Censorship and Learning Values through Literature,' pt. 2. *Journal of Moral Education* 15, no. 3 (1986): 197–211.

– 'Instruction and Delight: Northrop Frye and the Educational Value of Literature.' PhD diss., University of Toronto, 1980.

Campbell, Susan Leslie. 'Expression and the Individuation of Feeling.' PhD diss., University of Toronto, 1992.

Cayley, David. Introduction. In *Northrop Frye in Conversation*, edited by David Cayley. Toronto: Anansi, 1992.

Felman, Shoshanna. *Jacques Lacan and the Adventure of Insight*. Boston: Harvard University Press, 1987.

– 'Psychoanalysis and Education: Teaching the Terminable and Interminable.' *Yale French Studies* 63 (1982): 21–44.

Fetterley, Judith. *The Resisting Reader: A Feminist Approach to American Fiction*. Bloomington: Indiana University Press, 1981.

Frye, Northrop. 'Literature as Therapy.' *Northrop Frye Newsletter* 3, no. 2 (1991): 23–32.

Gold, Joseph. *Read for Your Life: Literature as a Life Support System*. Markham, Ont.: Fitzhenry & Whiteside, 1990.

Hamilton, A.C. *Northrop Frye: Anatomy of His Criticism*. Toronto: University of Toronto Press, 1990.

Haraway, Donna. 'Situated Knowledges: The Science Question in Feminism and the Privilege of Partial Perspective.' *Feminist Studies* 14, no. 3 (1988): 575–600.

Lipking, Lawrence. 'Aristotle's Sister: The Poetics of Abandonment.' In *Canons*, edited by R. von Hallberg. Chicago: University of Chicago Press, 1983.

Miller, Jane. *Seductions: Studies in Reading and Culture*. London: Virago Press, 1990.

Morgan, Robin. *The Demon Lover: On the Sexuality of Terrorism*. New York: Norton, 1989.

Ricoeur, Paul. 'Northrop Frye's *Anatomy of Criticism*, or the Order of Paradigms.' In *A Ricoeur Reader: Reflection and Imagination*, edited by Mario J. Valdés. Toronto: University of Toronto Press, 1991.

Wolf, Christa. *Cassandra: A Novel and Four Essays*. Translated by Jan Van Heurck. New York: Farrar-Straus-Giroux, 1984.

Woodman, Marion. *Leaving My Father's House: A Journey to Conscious Femininity*. Boston: Shambhala, 1992.

– *The Ravaged Bridegroom: Masculinity in Women*. Toronto: Inner City Books, 1990.

MICHAEL DOLZANI

Wrestling with Powers:
The Social Thought of Frye

St Paul, or whoever wrote Ephesians, said that we wrestle not against flesh and blood but against powers, against the rulers of this world of darkness, against spiritual wickedness in high places. In recent years, literary and cultural criticism have wrestled – mostly in the dark, like Jacob – with the question of the relationship between language and power. When the title of Frye's last major work, *Words with Power*, became known even before it was published, it was natural to assume that Frye, despite his aversion to polemics and direct confrontation, had become interested in the debate and intended to take part in it, responding at last to the heavy criticism, even the dismissal, of his own theories during the poststructuralist era. And sure enough, when the book finally appeared, there was at least one sign of possible influence. Revision in such an extraordinarily consistent thinker is highly significant, and *Words with Power* quietly revises *The Great Code* by adding rhetoric – the ideological phase of language – exactly in the centre of its sequence of descriptive, conceptual, metaphorical, and kerygmatic phases.

But if *Words with Power* approaches its subject by means of current issues and vocabulary, the subject itself had been long meditated. I was startled to find the phrase 'words with power,' echoing the clause 'for his word was with power' from the Gospel of Luke (4:32), in one of Frye's notebooks from the 1940s, in the context of a meditation on the latent and largely unrecognized powers of language. From the outset he recognized, to borrow the title of one of his essays, that language is the home of human life; therefore a theory of society has to begin with a theory of language and its various functions.

Frye's literary theory gives a central place to myths and archetypes, and, though he had many other interests, that is still the chief legacy with which his inheritors must wrestle. Indeed, my first premise is this: that anyone who has a problem with Frye's literary theory is likely also to have a problem with his social perspective – and that these will be two versions of the same problem. My second premise is that one's evaluation of both his literary and his social thought will depend upon whether one accepts or rejects the central principle of *Words with Power*, that which Frye calls existential or ecstatic metaphor, because that is the latest name he found for the experience – I think it has to be evaluated as an experience as well as an idea – on which all his writing depends. From ecstatic metaphor springs the *axis mundi* which forms the anatomy of the entire order of words; from it springs the quest or journey which is the total narrative of literature; but from it also blossoms a vision of society progressively transformed in history through being recreated by its revelatory, or apocalyptic, power. The standard complaint about the mythical and archetypal perspective is that it is reductive: it forces all the diversity of literature into the mould of a few predictably repetitive universals. The educational implications of such a point of view are authoritarian and conformist: education's job is to condition people into thinking within the categories of a few universal truths which work to reinforce social unity. Attacks on Frye during the fifties and sixties tended to take the form of calling *Anatomy of Criticism* unscientific; the question was whether the archetypal patterns were there or not in an empirical sense. Attacks on Frye during the seventies and eighties often took another form: it is easy enough to find recurrent patterns, for we are all conditioned in a hundred ways to find them, and writers are conditioned willy-nilly to repeat them. The question now is: Who has decided what the universals shall be, and whose is the authority to interpret, and therefore impose, their meaning? And this is a social, not just a literary, question. Literary patterns and meanings may remain within the realm of the hypothetical, the imagination's 'as if,' but the same myths and metaphors that organize literature serve as a model for the myths and metaphors that organize culture and society; if the two realms were not synergetic, Frye would have no means of speaking in *Words with Power* of the social authority of the poet.

It is hardly a profound observation that the chief social and cultural problem of the contemporary world is the reconciliation of unity with diversity, common identity with difference. In the United States, 'multiculturalism' and 'diversity' have become buzz words; Canada is trying to decide whether it is one nation or ten provinces and a congregation of native peoples; Europe is the chrysalis of an unknown species; the Soviet Union is 'former'; and Yugoslavia burns like a comet hung in the sky to warn us. The so-called 'hermeneutics of suspicion' seems to me largely a reaction among intellectuals to the ideology of the Cold War years. Now the era of superpowers seems to be over: China and the United States may not fall apart like the Soviet Union, but it is clear that both are on the verge of transformation into something much less monolithic and overshadowing; and the false unities and orders, both foreign and domestic, imposed during the imperialistic period are crumbling like a mummy exposed to air. Speaking of legacies, it seems to me that among the more unfortunate legacies from the Cold War period is the reaction in the opposite direction against all forms of order, unity, or pattern, on the grounds that these are nothing but ideologies in disguise. It is not that I do not see that this is often in fact quite true; and as a product of the sixties I have a predisposition to sympathize with what seems at bottom a kind of anarchism whose goal, if anarchism can have a goal, is the addressing of some very real social injustices. But the feeling often seems to be that diversity is enough, that unity is invariably the sheep's clothing of some wolf's ideological program. First of all, this courts a dangerous tribalism, as people huddle together in various ethnic, religious, economic, or other in-groups. Secondly, the modern world is a very lonely place, as people increasingly lose not only their sense of community but even a sense of personal identity. Nor am I convinced that life would be one exuberant carnival if only we could learn to live without such unhealthy security symbols as stable relationships, families, communities, and strong egos, and celebrate total mutability with a Nietzschean dancing step. Old orders and unities must change, and change to something at once more equitable and more flexible, but a choice between order that denies difference and difference that denies order is no choice at all. It is what Blake called a 'cloven fiction.'

My thesis is that for Frye myths and archetypes, the units of unity and order in literature, are not, thirty-five years of criticism to the contrary, categories of sameness and uniformity, but of something more paradoxical which the Romantics called unity-in-diversity, identity-in-difference, multeity-in-unity, the unity of opposites, and other designations of a have-your-cake-and-eat-it-too variety. The verbal means of expressing the identity of two different things is the metaphor, but in literature, as we noted, metaphor remains in the realm of the hypothetical or 'as if.' Therefore the social concerns of *Words with Power* drove Frye behind literary metaphor, so to speak, into the more experiential realm of ecstatic metaphor, of which literary metaphor is a descendant.

To ordinary consciousness, one thing is never also something else, except tautologically, so ordinary consciousness has, or thinks it has, little use for metaphor. It follows for ordinary consciousness, including what we call reason and commonsense, that unity and diversity, the universal and the particular, the One and the Many, can never be integrated. All there can be are a series of compromises, usually involving some form of hierarchical subordination, or an oscillation from one mode of perceiving to the other. In the paranoia of our times, what used to be dismissed as mystical or irrational – metaphor's paradoxical statement that *A* is *B* – is now more likely to be suspected as ideological double-talk hiding a political motive: if we say that All is One (or else should be) we have a good paradigm for a 'totalizing' social order. Therefore, if ecstatic metaphor is something more than wish-fulfillment or brainwashing, where is it available to us?

Its more intense forms occur, as its name denotes, in the kind of epiphanies or peak experiences characteristic of shamans, prophets, etc., and their latter-day descendants, the artists. Blake speaks of knowing the world in a grain of sand, eternity in an hour; more pertinent to our social theme, he speaks of One Man who is all human beings when viewed close up, and who is also identified with God and nature. Abraham Maslow claimed that such peak experiences are not unique to religious or artistic visionaries, but are the major identifying mark of self-actualized personalities. But what of those who have not been privileged enough to have had such an experience? Some of them may rather resent, in fact, the privileging of those who claim to have done so. Blake wished that all God's people were prophets, but in fact God's people are a lot more like Blake's patron, William Hayley, who concluded that Blake was either irresponsible or just plain mad.

Not all forms of ecstatic experience are so epiphanic: every time we identify ourselves with something else – a lover, a cause, a country, even our name – we bind together that which we know is also other than ourselves. Of course, it is possible to insist on the ironic discontinuities in all of these instances, or on the illusory nature of all identifications in the 'real' world. Frye's stock example is when we identify ourselves with the person we were as a child; yet the spooky, uncanny feeling I get when I stare at the clay impression of a child's hand made when I was in kindergarten reminds me that we by no means always feel identical even with ourselves. Much less with others: how could I ever have loved that person? we say. Nevertheless, when the centre cannot hold, things fall apart, psychologically or socially. The important thing is not so much to have a centre as to have one that includes differences. It is when our capacity for metaphorical identifications fails that we begin excluding or suppressing more and more.

Metaphors considered as units of structure build up the framework we call a cosmology; considered as units of process they build up the narratives we call myths. There is a misconception that myths are inherently conservative, that they are deterministic patterns imposed out of an anxiety about time and change. It is certainly true that myths, up to the Romantic period, have most often been pressed into the service of ideologies interested in controlling or preventing change: the natural order and social contract set down at the Creation by gods or culture heroes is renewed cyclically, is meant to endure eternally without deviation, and is the paradigm for every social activity down to eating and love-making. Frazer, one of the two influences on Frye's early social thought concurrently with Blake, showed how this was true of traditional nonhistorical societies, both archaic and contemporary; the other early influence, Spengler, showed that a cyclical decline-and-fall pattern survives in the sequence of historical civilizations, despite attempts of an ideology of linear progress to disguise it. Thus, the power of myth gets perverted by what Frye calls the secondary concerns of the social contract into a cycle of eternal sameness; Frye calls Blake's version of this the Orc cycle. In it, the fiery-haired Orc embodies both the organic energy of physical nature and the social energy of revolution; but eventually such energy always declines, and Orc is made subservient to the icy-haired law-and-order figure Urizen; or else is sacrificed to Urizen in his prime, like an Adonis; or simply ages into him, as a hippie may age into a yuppie and vote Republican. In any case, the historical cycle merely turns round again, as law is imposed upon freedom, restraint upon desire, coercive unity upon diversity.

Blake realized, as did Freud and Jung after him, that this struggle of opposites is not a vestigial remnant of a savage time, as Frazer thought, but is fought out in the mind of every individual in every society. The humanities have become much more polemical in recent decades because certain writers have forced us to recognize that, like it or not, the humanities can find no sequestered ground apart from this struggle. Blake would have understood those writers, and up to a point sympathized with them: if there were ever a writer in the margins it was the neglected poet-prophet who scribbled some of his best aphorisms literally in the margins of books whose reactionary social opinions infuriated him.

The great social need of our time, as of Blake's own, is for a means to break the Orc cycle, the war between unity and diversity. Blake recognized that there is no fatalistic inevitability about that cycle, for when the power of ecstatic metaphor is liberated from its Samson-like subservience to the ideology of sameness, it becomes a force working progressively through history for recreation; through it, unity-in-diversity becomes not a static state of being but a dynamic process of evolving revelation, or apocalypse.

This may all sound naively idealistic enough. Yet the postmodern period is hardly likely to survive into a period that is 'post-' anything – except perhaps posthumous – if we do not figure out how to achieve an individuality that is neither a falsely-unified egotism nor a disintegrated paranoid schizophrenia; a community that is neither an authoritarian hierarchy nor an ideologically-polarized tribalism. Let me suggest that the kind of society we need to create finds a possible model in Frye's vision of the 'order of words' in Anatomy, a liberal democracy of texts that 'privileges' less than any work of criticism I know. In fact, the most notorious idea in Anatomy, that we should expand our vision by subordinating value judgments to our experience of the whole order of words, canonical or noncanonical, popular or élitist, Western or non-Western, explodes the very idea of a canon as either the basis or the goal of our literary experience. Not a canon, then, but a tradition: an interpenetrating body of texts. The members of that body often disagree with, disapprove of, or dislike one another, yet they belong, even despite themselves, to a single community. The analogy with a possible social community is obvious. To say that such a thing does not and could not exist is beside the point. To wrestle against powers, one must possess power, and the vision's power to recreate those whom it inspires is what truly matters. For those of us who have been recreated by the power of Frye's vision, that is his true legacy. And knowing this, we may realize that the power against which we wrestle in the darkness might be Jacob's angel – might be the Word which lames us, but which does not depart without a blessing.

PART II

Imagined Community: Frye and Canada

LINDA HUTCHEON

———

Frye Recoded:
Postmodernity and the Conclusions

The last few decades appear to have witnessed every possible extreme of response to, and evaluation of, the work of Frye,[1] but few commentators on the cultural scene have been able to ignore it. As early as 1976, Malcolm Ross claimed that Frye 'caught up all our national anxieties, all our moral and metaphysical concerns, all our critical and formal queries about the nature and purpose of arts, reordered them, transubstantiated them, made of them a great *Summa*, made of criticism itself a total *gestalt*, a substitute for religion' ('Critical Theory,' 167–8). Frye's largely occasional pieces on Canadian cultural topics find their place in this *Summa*, but they too are not exempt from extremes of response. For some, the 'dean of Canadian critics' was responsible for proclaiming 'the merit and grandeur and existence of a vital Canadian literature,' defining 'the Canadian imagination for this century.'[2] For others, his influence on Canadian literature and criticism was 'pervasive' but 'bad,' destructive of 'the distinctive qualities of the Canadian identity.'[3] For still others, his impact was 'minor' and 'overestimated.'[4] Most have noticed the discrepancy between Frye's grand systematic structures of literary myth (in general and in the literature of the past) and his more 'immediate and formally more fragmentary pieces on the literature of his own country.'[5]

My own approach to one particular part of Frye's corpus – his Canadian writings, and in particular his Conclusion to the first (1965) and the second (1976) editions of *Literary History of Canada* – is what some would call a typically 'postmodern' one that eschews this kind of binary opposition in order to explore the both/and logic of the middle ground. Like many Canadians educated at the University of Toronto, I was once Frye's student, though I never knew him outside the classroom, then or later. My personal debt to him comes not only from what he taught me directly in his lectures and in his writing, but also from what he did to make English departments 'safe' (if not always hospitable) for a later generation of literary theorists who were also interested in Canadian literature and culture. On the surface, that is where the similarity ends between Frye – the modernist and the humanist – and many of those who followed – the postmodernists and the poststructuralists or feminists or 'postcolonialists.' But perhaps we should not stop at superficial differences.

It is not hard to see why Frye has been located in the modernist camp.[6] Even in his Canadian writings, Frye insisted upon an 'international' style (reminiscent of architectural modernism's 'international style') and upon an antimimetic, modernist view of the autonomy of art: as he taught, 'the poet's quest is for form' (BG, 176). But aesthetic modernism is a particular manifestation of modernity, a broader cultural and social 'paradigm' (Huyssen via Kuhn) or 'project' (Habermas) or 'episteme' (Foucault) or 'condition' (Lyotard) – depending on whose term and definition you choose to adopt. Nevertheless, what philosophers and social analysts seem to agree upon is that what all call modernity began with the shift from Renaissance humanism to Cartesian rationalism, with a move onto what Stephen Toulmin characterizes as 'a higher, stratospheric plane, on which nature and ethics conform to abstract, timeless, general, and universal theories' (Cosmopolis, 35). It is on this general, universal, totalizing plane that are born and flourish both Frye's totalizing, visionary order of myth and his fervent humanist belief in the value and function of art. Frye's work has been seen by some either to anticipate,[7] or actually to be itself, an example of structuralism at work. While both obviously share this modern systematizing impulse, the nature of the system and its derivation could not be more different.[8] The even more evident difference, however, is less with structuralism – which, arguably, remains on one level very much a product of modernity – than with those diverse theories grouped together under the label of poststructuralism, for they belong squarely in the domain of postmodernity: almost twenty years ago, Edward Said had already contrasted Frye's centred theory with the decentred ones of Derrida, Foucault, and Deleuze (Beginnings, 375–7). While there are some critics who see Frye as prefiguring,[9] or even initiating,[10] certain poststructuralist notions, they do not take sufficiently into account what Andreas Huyssen calls the major 'shift in sensibility, practices, and discourse formations which distinguishes a postmodern set of assumptions, experiences and propositions from that of a preceding period' (After the Great Divide, 181). Dealing in the most general of terms, in the postmodern (non-)scheme of things, foundational concepts like system, order, and rationality are called into question by nonfoundational notions like contingency, ambiguity, and provisionality. The universal, the general, and the timeless are undermined by a valuing of the particular, the local, and the timely. In what follows, I would like to address the magisterial, totalizing work of Frye, the 'Mandarin,' modern, Canadian theorist, but I will do so in what Dick Hebdige has called a somewhat 'smaller voice,' that of 'a finite, gendered being bounded by particular horizons, perspectives, experiences, knowledge' (*Hiding in the Light*, 11). This voice can only offer a partial (and postmodern) reading of Frye's Canadian writings and of both their links to, and their breaks with, the paradigm of postmodernity.

To begin with the obvious and move to the more contentious (and more interesting perhaps) is also, in this context, to move from the general and theoretical to the specifically Canadian. Despite Terry Eagleton's views of Frye's classificatory scientificity as antihumanist (*Literary Theory*, 91–6), I think for most of us it would be Frye's passionate humanist commitment that likely marks the greatest divergence from such postmodern stances as Derridean deconstruction with its emphasis, to use A.C. Hamilton's terms, on 'difference not identity, temporality not spatiality, fissure not fusion, gaps not continuity, dissemination not polysemy, fragmentation not unity, aporias not vision' (*Northrop Frye*, 218).[11] In a very different sense from Derrida's much discussed challenge to Western metaphysics, Frye's system of mythic patterns is also vast in its implications, because it is 'epistemologically constitutive, conditioning our basic perceptions of the structure of the universe.'[12] The teaching of literature, therefore, becomes the teaching of 'the ability to be aware of one's imaginative social vision, and so to escape the prison of unconscious social conditioning' (*BG*, 29). The step from humanist educational mission to, say, certain kinds of feminist or poststructuralist teaching may not, at times, seem a great one: all share a desire to defamiliarize the 'givens' of culture and to raise consciousness. But Frye's 'mythological universe, a body of assumptions and beliefs developed from ... [human] existential concerns' (*GC*, xviii) is conceptually quite distant from a Barthesian or Althusserian postmodern concept of ideology. Indeed, what Frye called 'ideology' was always secondary to the mythic, derivative rather than creative.[13]

This emphasis on the imaginative and the creative (rather than on any postmodern stress on the subjection to, and seduction of, ideology as what 'goes without saying' in culture) is a sign of Frye's roots in a tradition that is both idealistic and romantic. However, it also signals his modernist faith in the autonomy of art that is the core of his 'militantly non-referential view of literature'[14] as 'a disinterested structure of words.'[15] In his discussion of Canadian literature before 1965 – in his Conclusion to the first edition of *Literary History of Canada* – Frye asserted that the 'forms of literature are autonomous: they exist within literature itself, and cannot be derived from any experience outside literature' (347), but that Canadian literature is still 'more significantly studied as a part of Canadian life than as part of an autonomous world of literature' (334). As we shall see shortly, this particular judgment exemplifies one of the major tensions in Frye's work, a tension that is arguably *post*modern in its paradoxical recognition of both the reflexivity and the worldliness of literature.

For the moment, however, let us remain within the modernist frame of reference of Frye's detached and autonomous mythology (349), a frame that shows (as did Eliot's before it) romantic roots and classical aspirations: 'the imagination is the constructive element in the mind,' argues Frye, while noting that its 'intensity cannot be conveyed except through structure, which includes design, balance, and proportion' (Conclusion [1976], 330–1). Frye's mythic theorizing, as many have pointed out, is itself definable in these terms as a high modernist work, a triumph of the totalizing, organizing imagination; of course, a postmodern view might well see such an 'Apollonian'[16] ordering impulse as also manifesting a certain 'will to power over the field of contemporary criticism.'[17] Frye's 'elaborate and beautiful structures,'[18] as they have been called, are nothing short of a total, and overtly utopian, scheme for interpreting the universe. In other words, in direct opposition to what Jean-François Lyotard calls the postmodern 'incredulity toward metanarrative,' and in strong contrast to the postmodern suspicion of the power behind such hermeneutics and its possible suppression of difference, Frye's inclusive 'master' or metanarrative could be seen to elide difference in the name of both the commonality (indeed universality) and the coherence characteristic of the paradigm of modernity. Aiming to reconcile, rather than foreground, differences, this 'synoptic' view (*AC*, 3) of literature and criticism may well be an 'artistic achievement,'[19] but its achievement would have to be defined within a very particular context – that of modernity. In that frame of reference, the postmodernly plural – the contingent, the provisional, the multiple, the different, and the indeterminate – would have to be homogenized: Frye, the humanist, the modern, argues that 'the imagination is occupationally disposed to synthesis' (*BG*, x). When Hamilton interprets this synthesizing disposition as a 'distinctively Canadian response to an overwhelming, alienating, and therefore self-alienating physical environment' (*Northrop Frye*, xiii), he is therefore aptly interpreting Frye very much in his own terms. But are all tensions and contradictions really resolved so easily? For example, Frye may indeed debunk the notion of the romantic genius in the first Conclusion (335), but he simultaneously invokes (over thirty times in as many pages) an equally romantic notion of the imagination, interpreted in characteristically liberal humanist (paradoxical) terms as both individual and universal. To complicate matters even more, Frye also adds something called the 'social' or the 'Canadian imagination' – and this is where things start to get interesting, and maybe even *postmodern*.[20]

Of all the theoretical positions that Frye took over the years, perhaps none caused more debate than his famous stand on the danger of making value-judgments the goal or starting point of criticism (*AC*, 18–24; 'On Value Judgments'). Almost everyone who has written on Frye has had his or her own (mis)understanding of this position,[21] and I am no exception. Even if *Anatomy of Criticism* were the 'memorable and influential piece of counteraxiology' that Barbara Herrnstein Smith makes it out to be (*Contingencies of Value*, 12), the view Frye offers in two Conclusions to *Literary History of Canada* is not so far from Smith's own theories of the necessarily mutual implication of criticism and the 'history of taste' (22), and thus of the historical relativity and contingency of values in the light of intellectual, social, and institutional contexts. In 1965, Frye was willing to make a judgment call, to say that there was not yet any 'classic' writer in Canada, classic in the sense of 'possessing a vision greater in kind than that of his [or her] best readers' (Conclusion [1965], 333). Having done so, however, he could then safely deny that *Literary History*, as a whole, was evaluative: it could not be an act of canonization because there was nothing yet worthy enough to canonize. The postmodern challenges to canon-formation over the last decades might make Frye's contradictory remarks about evaluating the quality of Canadian writing seem disingenuous to some, but I would argue that they represent precisely what we have come to see as the postmodern tension between the local and the particular versus the universal and the general. This and other tensions forced Frye into the seemingly contradictory position of valuing in our literature that which 'pulls us away from the Canadian context toward the centre of literary experience itself' (Conclusion [1965], 334), and yet being unable to ignore the Canadian 'social and historical setting' (334). By 1976, when he published the second Conclusion, Frye could happily celebrate 'a bulk of good writing,' with an 'extraordinary vitality and morale behind it' (Conclusion

[1976], 319): 'Canadian literature is here' (319), he proclaimed, but still added: 'perhaps still a minor but certainly no longer a gleam in a paternal critic's eye' (319). By 1991, just before his death, Frye could go even further: 'English Canada, the land nobody wanted, the land that seemed unable to communicate except by railways and bridges, began, from about 1960 on, to produce a literature of a scope and integrity admired the world over.'[22]

Frye did steadfastly refuse to rank Canadian writers, saying: 'The differences in value will emerge after a century or so and we don't need to hurry about them';[23] but he thereby obscured his own, very considerable role (as reviewer, critic, teacher, and editor) in that very act of canonization and differentiation. Indeed, he has been called one 'of the most significant canon-makers of postwar criticism,'[24] and not only within Canada. It has been pointed out that many of his so-called factual terms are in fact value-judgments – 'naive allegory,' 'superficial convention,' and so on[25] – and that his reviews are obviously full of evaluative statements (see P.J.M. Robertson), especially his 'Letters in Canada' reviews of Canadian poetry in the 1950s. There, aware of writing for a specifically Canadian readership, not for 'invisible posterity' (BG, 126), Frye chooses to deal with 'the positive merits of what is before him' rather than with 'vague relativities of "greatness"' (BG, 126). His reason is not unlike the one he would give a short time later in the first Conclusion: 'while much Canadian verse could be honestly described, by the highest standards of the best twentieth-century poets, as metrical doodling, it could also be described, just as honestly and perhaps more usefully, as the poetic conversation of cultivated people' (57). I suspect this tension between his humanist/universalist or his modernist/internationalist 'standards' of the 'classics' and the Canadian contextual specifics is what brought about the diverse responses to Frye's position: on the one hand, he was praised for honestly judging the quality of Canadian writing and thus being in 'the grandest Western tradition of self-criticism;'[26] on the other hand, he was called, in Heather Murray's memorable image, a 'wolf in sheepdog's clothing,' standing guard 'over a fledgling Canadian literature, protecting it from the ravages of evaluation – but is he really the leader of the pack?' ('Reading for Contradiction,' 73).

This very argument, however, can only be carried on within the frame of reference of the *modern* paradigm, where foundational truth supports firm and accepted universal standards of judgment. But what if we chose to examine Frye's position from a postmodern perspective, one which, in Zygmunt Bauman's terms, 'does not seek to substitute one truth for another, one standard of beauty for another, one life ideal for another ... [but] braces itself for a life without truths, standards, ideals' (*Intimations*, ix)? In other words, what if we changed the turf utterly? Suddenly, instead of sounding like a failed nation with a deficient or at least immature culture (according to the model of modernity), Frye's Canada might start to sound postmodernly open and provisional. Maybe it would not be a negative, as (a modernly read) Frye implies in the first Conclusion, to be 'trying' to do something and 'not quite [to have] done it' (333). If the universal were undermined (were shown, in fact, to be very limited in terms of class, race, gender, and so on), then maybe it would not be a bad thing to ask, 'Where is here?' (Conclusion [1965], 338) – that is, to position oneself locally and specifically. Perhaps what (the modernist, progressivist) Frye disliked as Canada's romantic 'fixation on its own past' (338) could be recoded in terms of the postmodern queries about, and challenges to, the ontology and epistemology of history itself (see Hutcheon; White).[27] In short, the contradictions that Heather Murray ('Reading for Contradiction,' 73) wants us to read for in Canadian writing by means of Marxist, deconstructionist, psychoanalytic, and feminist theories are to be seen in Frye too – at least, when we are not blind to the pesky postmodern eruptions that break through the modernist order of his thought. That these eruptions occur most often in his Canadian writing, I want to argue, is not an accident.[28]

Most of the time, however, the tensions that mark what I would like to call these 'eruptions of the postmodern' have been read as simple contradictions: for Frank Lentricchia, Frye is 'half-structuralist, half-aesthete' (*After the New Criticism*, 10). In his Canadian writings, Frye gives us, according to A.J.M. Smith, 'paradoxes which, as he presents them, seem like truisms' (*Towards a View*, 202). Eli Mandel reads the simultaneously 'nationalist, internationalist, regionalist' Frye as inconsistent (*Another Time*, 158) and contradictory ('Northrop Frye,' 284). Indeed, within the *modern* paradigm, any postmodern inclusive, *both/and* thinking – that would accept and seek to value such seeming opposites – is literally inconceivable: the modern is the realm of the binary *either/or*.[29] But if we are willing to accept the multiple and the tentative instead of the single and the sure, if we can live with the relational instead of the oppositional, then maybe those tensions that are so (modernly) troublesome can become the (postmodern) complexities that might enrich our understanding both of Canadian culture and of Frye's position on (and in) it.

We have already seen the most obvious of these tensions – the non-evaluating Frye evaluating Canadian literature, both reinforcing and calling into question the validity of universal standards of judgment. Part of the tension here no doubt results from the two different – but often simultaneous – roles Frye played (or was made to play) in Canadian letters, including in writing the two Conclusions: he was at once (to use his own distinction) an 'academic critic' and a 'public critic,' at once the detached analyst of autonomous art and the 'Tory radical,'[30] concerned with the social and historical function of art, and particularly of Canadian art.[31] So, often at one and the same time, Frye was the Olympian, detached theorist and the engaged field-worker as teacher and reviewer. His faith in humanist universals and his modernist internationalism sat side by side with his belief in the power and value of Canadian regionalism; his view of art as autonomous rubbed shoulders with his commitment to the local roots of imagination: 'Poets do not live on Mount Parnassus, but in their own environments, and Canada has made itself an environmental reality,' he wrote in *The Bush Garden* (10). Typically these so-called contradictions are expressed in the same sentence: sometimes he is writing about himself, such as when he mentions his 'writing career which has been mainly concerned with world literature and has addressed an international reading public, and yet has always been rooted in Canada and has drawn its essential characteristics from there' (*BG*, i); at other times, he is referring to such things as Canadian poetry, where he has seen how 'the echoes and ripples of the great mythopoeic age kept moving through Canada, and taking a form there that they could not have taken elsewhere' (*BG*, ix). In either case, the paradoxes remain.

Or do they? Some have argued (e.g., P.M. Cummings) that Frye actually managed to synthesize disinterested aesthetic criticism with socially conscious humanistic criticism; but perhaps that too is a modern, totalizing position that resolves (and dissolves) the tensions instead of dealing with them. The existence of many commentators who have constantly remarked on such tensions suggests that they need to be thought through, not reconciled, or – in another typically modern response – denied. Readers of Frye have often chosen, of course, to ignore one half of the contradiction, on the grounds that it does not fit their particular vision of consistency and right order. For instance, some see only his interest in the Canadian social and historical context, and then either celebrate that or condemn it as a reduction of the 'study of literature to that of various aspects of Canadian life'[32] or, worse, as the founding principle of the much derided 'thematic criticism' that is said to have dominated Canadian literary thinking, leading to what Frank Davey once called 'sociology – usually bad sociology ... extra-literary, normative and polemic' (*Surviving the Paraphrase*, 5). Others have seen only the other side, only the interest in 'literature as some kind of separate, total system.'[33] There is no doubt that Frye believed in the 'order of words,' the 'total structure of literature itself' (*StS*, 88); but he also said that the role of criticism was 'to examine first the literary and then the social context of whatever it's studying.'[34] The subtitle of *The Critical Path*, after all, was *An Essay on the Social Context of Literary Criticism*; that of *The Stubborn Structure* was *Essays on Criticism and Society*. But it is in his writings on Canadian culture that this side of his work comes out most clearly, and those critics who have not looked at these writings frequently miss this important tension in his thought.

Those who have studied these texts, though, often take what I would see as a postmodern stance, accepting the tensions and seeing them, in fact, as productive. Ian Balfour notes that Frye's writings on 'Canadian culture qualify and complicate (for his readers) the rest of his oeuvre,' because they force a 'reconsideration of many sides of his work, especially with regard to the status of history and the role of regionalism in cultural production' (*Northrop Frye*, 79). However contradictory it may seem within the paradigm of modernity, Frye's Canadian writing displays postmodern *both/and* thinking, offering *both* a theory of archetypes and the autonomy of art *and* a theory of the 'rootedness' of texts in social, political, economic, and cultural terrain. Similarly, his analysis of the Canadian cultural situation was usually much more provisional than later commentators have wanted to grant. As Russell Brown has pointed out, most have conveniently forgotten that even the most infamous concept of the first Conclusion – that of the 'garrison mentality' – was introduced with the words: 'what we may provisionally call' (342). But even granting that postmodern gesture to the provisional, we would not be wrong to see the defining of the overarching concept of the garrison mentality as a most *modern* act: 'Small and isolated communities surrounded with a physical or psychological "frontier," separated from one another and from their American and British cultural sources: communities that provide all that their members have in the way of distinctively human values, and that are compelled to feel a great respect for the law and order that holds them together, yet confronted with a huge, unthinking, menacing, and formidable physical setting – such communities are bound to develop what we may provisionally call a garrison mentality' (342). It is also within the paradigm of modernity that Frye is here defining the garrison – as a 'closely knit and beleaguered society' within which one can be 'either a fighter or a deserter' (342). The general context for this structuring *either/or* binary opposition of the human and the natural can only be a modern one. In other words, we are dealing here not simply with the description of a state of mind in the past[35] – though it is that – but with an entire frame of reference that excludes other possible conceptualizations of the social.

In that light, rather than try to suggest what a postmodern version of Frye's garrison might look like, I would like to take from his definition of it one word – the word 'communities' – and show how that concept, from the perspective of postmodernity, might offer a 'recoding' of Frye's insights that could account for our current cultural scene more adequately than would any simple applying of the totalizing metanarrative of the (historical) garrison image to describe living and creating in Canada of the 1990s. Typically, however, a few words of (problematizing) caution are in order. Taking off from Benedict Anderson's theory of nation as 'imagined community,' Zygmunt Bauman points out that 'community is now expected to bring the succour previously sought in the pronouncements of universal reason and their earthly translations: the legislative acts of the national state' (*Intimations*, xix). But perhaps Canada, as a nation state whose fragile legislative identity has been under severe scrutiny recently, already is itself a community that defies 'the pronouncements of universal reason' to define itself in terms of linguistic and cultural duality, even multicultural multiplicity. But such a community, Bauman insists, 'does not grow in the wilderness: it is a greenhouse plant, that needs sowing, feeding, trimming and protection from weeds and parasites' (xix). Somewhere between the garrison and the wilderness, then, is the greenhouse community, precarious and in constant need of loving care. Bauman continues: 'It is precisely because of its vulnerability that community provides the focus of postmodern concerns, that it attracts so much intellectual and practical attention, that it figures so prominently in the philosophical models and popular ideologies of postmodernity' (xix). Frye too had seen that artists drew strength from their community (*DG*, 24), but for him this was regionally and historically defined: 'No Muse can function outside human space and time, that is, outside geography and history' (31). As Bauman illustrates, within the postmodern paradigm community lacks that kind of 'stability and institutionalized continuity' and so requires 'overwhelming affective commitment' even to come into being (*Intimations*, xix); put in other words, the postmodern community is as likely to be organized around the fluctuating and shifting allegiances, loyalties, obligations, and responsibilities of daily life as it is to be defined by gender, race, ethnicity, class, sexual choice, or religion. Region does not go away, but takes its place as one of many variables that define community. The E-mail computer network or the social or medical support group would therefore be as much a community, in this postmodern sense of the word, as Pratt's Newfoundland (see *BG*, 194).

Of course, community is a word that appears often in Frye's writing, whether the focus is generally liberal humanist or specifically Canadian. He often speaks of 'fraternity,' of 'a society of neighbours, in the genuinely religious sense of that word' (*MC*, 102). Marxist critic Fredric Jameson has located the 'greatness of Frye' in 'his willingness to raise the issue of community and to draw basic, essentially social, interpretive consequences from the nature of religion as collective representation' (*The Political Unconscious*, 69).[36] Based on what David Cook has called an 'educational contract' (*Northrop Frye: A Vision*, 83), Frye's view of the university was also one of a scholarly community[37] that could 'play an active role in the national intellectual life.'[38] In the seventies and eighties, Frye also wrote about ethnicity and community in Canada, about how the postwar immigrants found their place in the larger community of largely Scots-Irish Toronto 'with a minimum of violence and tension, preserving much of their own cultures and yet taking part in the total one' (*DG*, 68). Acknowledging that this ease of communal integration was likely made possible by the already double nature of the Canadian self-definition, Frye also came to value the resultant 'decentralizing rhythm that is so essential to culture' (*DG*, 68). But that very 'decentralizing' is what makes the notion of multiple (postmodern) communities unintelligible within the context of modernity's totalizing and centring rage for order.

The postmodern writing being done from within the plural and shifting communities of Canada today cannot, I suspect, be understood (at least, not in its own terms) within the modernist terms of reference Frye set up, for example, in the first Conclusion to *Literary History of Canada*. What would feminist or gay, socialist or conservative, native or black or Asian writers make of Frye's distinction between the 'rhetorical' and the 'poetic,' between the 'impulse to assert' and the 'impulse to construct' (346)? The modernist Frye believed that the genuinely 'imaginative writer' might well begin 'as a member of a school or group' but would 'normally' pull away from it, as he or she develops (354). Within the postmodern paradigm, such a pulling away would be illusory, if not impossible: the particular and the local cannot be left behind. Today, to write from such a 'situated' position is not to produce 'propaganda' (345) or 'reportage' (348); it is to produce Daphne Marlatt's *Anahistoric* or Michael Ondaatje's *Running in the Family*.

There are obviously differences – major ones – between the stances of Frye, the modern and the art of postmodernity, between the garrison and the community. To his insight into class structures – that the garrison mentality was the 'conservative idealism of its ruling class, which for Canada means the moral and propertied middle class' (Conclusion [1965], 350) – we would have to add today a self-consciousness about that class's race, gender, religion, sexual orientation, and European culture. In other words, we cannot simply argue that Frye was a closet postmodernist. But there are perhaps postmodern moments in his writing, most especially in his Canadian writing. These are moments in which the postmodern erupts into the systematic and rational order of modernity – moments in which *both/and* thinking is the only way to explain (without explaining away) the paradoxes and the contradictions, what I have been calling the tensions between autonomy and historical/social context, between evaluation and explication, between detachment and engagement, between the universal and the local, between the international and the national. Eli Mandel once said that Frye's Canadian criticism was 'cogent and powerful' but 'still ... puzzling, widely misunderstood.' He added that 'misreadings of it form one of the fascinating chapters of Canadian literary history' ('Northrop Frye,' 284). As a provisional and tentative contribution to that chapter, I offer this 'misreading,' not in the name of any modern 'fearful symmetry,' but in the hope of a postmodern 'fearless asymmetry.'[39]

NOTES

1 See Hamilton, *Northrop Frye: Anatomy of His Criticism*, for summary.
2 St Andrews, 'The Canadian Connection: Frye/Atwood,' 47.
3 Jackel, 'Northrop Frye and the Continentalist Tradition,' 228.
4 Cameron, 'Frye Talking,' 114.
5 Woodcock, 'Diana's Priest in the Bush Garden,' in his *The World of Canadian Writing*, 227; see also Davey, *From There to Here*, 108; Pacey, 'The Course of Canadian Criticism,' 26.
6 E.g., Cook, *Northrop Frye: A Vision of the New World*, 14; Sullivan, 'Northrop Frye: Canadian Mythographer,' 5; Scobie, 'Leonard Cohen, Phyllis Webb, and the End(s) of Modernism,' 67.
7 Sparshott, 'Frye in Place,' 144.
8 Todorov, *The Fantastic*, 17–19. For summary of the relationship, see Denham, 'An Anatomy of Frye's Influence'; Riccomini, 'Northrop Frye and Structuralism.'
9 O'Hara, *The Romance of Interpretation*, 190.
10 Hamilton, *Northrop Frye*, 216.
11 However, Derrida, the high priest of decentred narratives, admits to Imre

Salusinszky that when he was writing *Of Grammatology* he finally got 'a coherent vision of Western culture and its relation to writing and speaking' (*Criticism in Society*, 23).

12 Gorak, *The Making of the Modern Canon*, 144.

13 In Salusinszky, *Criticism in Society*, 31.

14 Gorak, *The Making of the Modern Canon*, 136.

15 Frye, Conclusion, in vol. 2, *Literary History of Canada*, 344. For clarity, I will refer to Frye's conclusion to the first edition as Conclusion (1965) and to the second edition as Conclusion (1976), though I will use the pagination of the second edition throughout.

16 Jones, *Butterfly on Rock*, 18.

17 O'Hara, *The Romance of Interpretation*, 189.

18 Woodcock, 'Diana's Priest in the Bush Garden,' 225.

19 Denham, *Northrop Frye and Critical Method*, 224.

20 The combination of universalism and individualism, without this admixture of the social, can be seen in Frye's response to what today would be considered trademarks of the postmodern aesthetic: the use of parody and the challenge to the accepted borders between high and popular art forms. In reviewing Canadian poetry in the 1950s, Frye felt that the frequent use of parody to solve 'the problem of form' (*BG*, 174) was a weakness, not a virtue: 'in every age Echo is merely the discarded mistress of Narcissus' (175). In a feminist or postmodern age, we might well recode this as 'in some ages and in some places Echo is the challenging and generative partner of a self-deluded Narcissus.' (It may not read as well, but that is often the fate of the problematizing postmodern.) Similarly, Frye's hierarchical modernist view of popular art (see Huyssen for the relation of modernism to mass culture) as 'formula-writing' (Conclusion [1965], 349), good for relaxation because it reinforces social values and does not prod us 'into making the steep and lonely climb into the imaginative world' (350), is one that has been contested by postmodern critics such as Jim Collins, who argues a view of popular culture as much more resistant and much more complex and decentred than modernism had allowed. For Frye, writing in 1965, one could separate the 'genuinely imaginative' (354) and the 'mass market'; but by 1976, in part thanks to the success of Leonard Cohen as both a 'serious poet' and a 'genuinely popular' singer (Conclusion [1976], 331), he too came to see that this typically modern binary opposition at least needed questioning.

21 See Hamilton, *Northrop Frye*, 21–5.

22 Frye, 'Northrop Frye's Canada,' A13.

23 Slopen, 'Climate, Distance Shape Canada's Writers,' 66.

24 Gorak, *The Making of the Modern Canon*, 121.

25 Davey, *From There to Here*, 107–8.
26 Clark, 'Bibliographical Spectrum and Review Article' in *Review of National Literatures*, vol. 7, 155.
27 Within a postmodern paradigm, Frye's championing of *homo ludens* (Conclusion [1965], 343) would also not have to be read, as his (equally modern) critics have, as reducing all literature to a 'verbal game' (Conclusion [1976], 331). Play could become 'that for the sake of which work is done' (331–2).
28 Even in his general theorizing, though, at least one recent critic has noted what could be read as postmodern tendencies – the 'rich intertextual shape' of Frye's canon (Gorak, *The Making of the Modern Canon*, 129) or the 'dynamic, unsettling energy' that myths come to have within what is seen as a destabilizing rather than consolidating 'visionary canon' (143).
29 Kaplan, *Postmodernism and Its Discontents*, 5.
30 Czarnecki, 'Reflections of a Radical Tory,' 50.
31 See Solecki, 'Criticism and the Anxiety of Identity,' 1029.
32 Stuewe, *Clearing the Ground*, 12.
33 Edward Said in Salusinszky, *Criticism in Society*, 141.
34 Ibid., 33.
35 Delany, 'The Letter and the Spirit,' 56.
36 Jameson then goes on to use Frye's views on myth as informing literature to argue for literature as informed by 'a political unconscious': 'all literature must be read as a symbolic meditation on the destiny of community' (*The Political Unconscious*, 70). He also argues that Frye ends up 'recontaining' this radical possibility of 'collective and social interpretation which his hermeneutic had seemed to open' (71).
37 In Salusinszky, *Criticism in Society*, 39.
38 Woodcock, 'Northrop Frye,' in *Oxford Companion to Canadian Literature*, 283.
39 I thank Len Findlay for this line, one he fittingly presented in describing a notion of community today, in his remarks at the University of Saskatchewan's conference, 'Realizing Community,' April 1992.

WORKS CITED

Balfour, Ian. *Northrop Frye*. Boston: Twayne, 1988.
Bauman, Zygmunt. *Intimations of Postmodernity*. London: Routledge, 1992.
Belsey, Catherine. *Critical Practice*. London: Methuen, 1980.
Brown, Russell. 'On Reading for Themes in Canadian Literature.' Manuscript.

Cameron, Barry. 'Frye Talking.' *Canadian Literature* 101 (1984): 113–14.

Clark, Richard C. 'Bibliographical Spectrum and Review Article: Is There a Canadian Literature?' In *Review of National Literatures*, edited by Richard J. Schoeck. Vol. 7, *Canada*. New York: Griffon House, 1976.

Collins, Jim. *Uncommon Cultures: Popular Culture and Post- Modernism*. New York: Routledge, 1989.

Cook, David. *Northrop Frye: A Vision of the New World*. Montreal: New World Perspectives, 1985.

Cummings, P.M. 'Northrop Frye and the Necessary Hybrid: Criticism as Aesthetic Humanism.' In *The Quest for Imagination: Essays on Twentieth-Century Aesthetic Criticism*, edited by O.B. Hardison, Jr. Cleveland: Press of Case Western Reserve University, 1971.

Czarnecki, Mark. 'Reflections of a Radical Tory.' *Maclean's* 95, no. 25 (21 June 1982): 49–50.

Davey, Frank. *Surviving the Paraphrase: Eleven Essays on Canadian Literature*. Winnipeg: Turnstone Press, 1983.

– *From There to Here: A Guide to English-Canadian Literature since 1960: Our Nature – Our Voices II*. Erin, Ont.: Press Porcépic, 1974.

Delany, Paul. 'The Letter and the Spirit.' *Saturday Night* 97, no. 5 (May 1982): 55–6.

Denham, Robert D. *Northrop Frye: An Annotated Bibliography of Primary and Secondary Sources*. Toronto: University of Toronto Press, 1987.

– An Anatomy of Frye's Influence.' *American Review of Canadian Studies* 14 (1984): 1–19.

– *Northrop Frye and Critical Method*. University Park: Pennsylvania State University Press, 1978.

Eagleton, Terry. *Literary Theory: An Introduction*. Oxford: Blackwell, 1983.

Foucault, Michel. *The Order of Things: An Archaeology of the Human Sciences*. New York: Pantheon, 1970.

Frye, Northrop. 'Northrop Frye's Canada.' *The Globe and Mail* (15 April 1991).

– 'On Value Judgments.' *Contemporary Literature* 9 (1968): 311–18.

– Conclusion. In Klinck, vol. 2.

– Conclusion. In Klinck, vol. 3.

Gorak, Jan. *The Making of the Modern Canon: Genesis and Crisis of a Literary Idea*. London: Athlone, 1991.

Habermas, Jurgen. 'Modernity – An Incomplete Project.' In *The Anti-Aesthetic: Essays on Postmodern Culture*, edited by Hal Foster. Port Townsend, Wash.: Bay Press, 1983.

Hamilton, A.C. *Northrop Frye: Anatomy of His Criticism*. Toronto: University of Toronto Press, 1990.

Hebdige, Dick. *Hiding in the Light: Of Images and Things*. New York: Routledge, 1991.

Hutcheon, Linda. *A Poetics of Postmodernism: History, Theory, Fiction*. London: Routledge, 1988.

Huyssen, Andreas. *After the Great Divide: Modernism, Mass Culture, Postmodernism*. Bloomington: Indiana University Press, 1986.

Jackel, David. 'Northrop Frye and the Continentalist Tradition.' *Dalhousie Review* 56, no. 2 (1976): 221–39.

Jameson, Fredric. *The Political Unconscious: Narrative as a Socially Symbolic Act*. Ithaca: Cornell University Press, 1981.

Jones, D.G. *Butterfly on Rock: A Study of Themes and Images in Canadian Literature*. Toronto: University of Toronto Press, 1970.

Kaplan, E. Ann, ed. *Postmodernism and its Discontents*. London: Verso, 1988.

Klinck, Carl F., ed. *Literary History of Canada: Canadian Literature in English*. 2nd ed. 3 vols. Toronto: University of Toronto Press, 1976.

Kuhn, Thomas S. *The Structure of Scientific Revolutions*. 2nd ed. Chicago: University of Chicago Press, 1970.

Lentricchia, Frank. *After the New Criticism*. Chicago: University of Chicago Press, 1980.

Lyotard, Jean-François. *The Postmodern Condition: A Report on Knowledge*. Translated by Geoff Bennington and Brian Massumi. Minneapolis: University of Minnesota Press, 1984.

Mandel, Eli. 'Northrop Frye and the Canadian Literary Tradition.' In *Centre and Labyrinth: Essays in Honour of Northrop Frye*, edited by Eleanor Cook, Chaviva Hosek, Jay Macpherson, Patricia Parker, and Julian Patrick. Toronto: University of Toronto Press, 1983.

– *Another Time*. Erin, Ont.: Press Porcépic, 1977.

Murray, Heather. 'Reading for Contradiction in the Literature of Colonial Space.' In *Future Indicative: Literary Theory and Canadian Literature*, edited by John Moss. Ottawa: University of Ottawa Press, 1987.

O'Hara, Daniel T. *The Romance of Interpretation: Visionary Criticism from Pater to de Man*. New York: Columbia University Press, 1985.

Pacey, Desmond. 'The Course of Canadian Criticism.' In Klinck, vol. 2.

Riccomini, Donald R. 'Northrop Frye and Structuralism: Identity and Difference.' *University of Toronto Quarterly* 49 (1979): 33–47.

Robertson, P.J.M. 'Northrop Frye and Evaluation.' *Queen's Quarterly* 90 (1983): 151–6.

Ross, Malcolm. 'Critical Theory: Some Trends.' In Klinck, vol. 2.

Said, Edward. *Beginnings*. New York: Basic Books, 1974.

Salusinsky, Imre. *Criticism in Society*. New York: Methuen, 1987.

Scobie, Stephen. 'Leonard Cohen, Phyllis Webb, and the End(s) of Modernism.' In *Canadian Canons: Essays in Literary Value*, edited by Robert Lecker. Toronto: University of Toronto Press, 1991.

Slopen, Beverley. 'Climate, Distance Shape Canada's Writers.' *Publishers Weekly* 215, no. 10 (5 March 1979): 66–9.

Smith, A.J.M. *Towards a View of Canadian Letters: Selected Critical Essays, 1928–1971.* Vancouver: University of British Columbia Press, 1973.

Smith, Barbara Herrnstein. *Contingencies of Value: Alternative Perspectives for Critical Theory.* Cambridge, Mass.: Harvard University Press, 1988.

Solecki, Sam. 'Criticism and the Anxiety of Identity.' *Queen's Quarterly* 90, no. 4 (1983): 1026–33.

Sparshott, Francis. 'Frye in Place.' *Canadian Literature* 83 (1979): 143–55.

St Andrews, B.A. 'The Canadian Connection: Frye/Atwood.' *World Literature Today* 60, no. 1 (1986): 47–9.

Stuewe, Paul. *Clearing the Ground: English-Canadian Literature After Survival.* Toronto: Proper Tales Press, 1984.

Sullivan, Rosemary. 'Northrop Frye: Canadian Mythographer.' *Journal of Commonwealth Literature* 18, no. 1 (1983): 1–13.

Todorov, Tzvetan. *The Fantastic: A Structural Approach to a Literary Genre.* Translated by Richard Howard. Ithaca: Cornell University Press, 1973.

Toulmin, Stephen. *Cosmopolis: The Hidden Agenda of Modernity.* New York: Free Press, 1990.

White, Hayden. *Metahistory: The Historical Imagination in Nineteenth-Century Europe.* Baltimore: Johns Hopkins University Press, 1973.

Woodcock, George. 'Diana's Priest in the Bush Garden: Frye and His Master.' In *The World of Canadian Writing: Critiques and Recollections.* Vancouver: Douglas and McIntyre, 1980.

– 'Northrop Frye.' In *The Oxford Companion to Canadian Literature*, edited by William Toye. Toronto: Oxford University Press, 1983.

JAMES REANEY

The Inheritors Read the Will

Trying to think, one day, what absolutely minimal group of words could be used to express what Frye has given us, I finally came up with 'stories'. Other candidates were 'metaphor' & 'Word.'

Perhaps I'm partial to 'stories' because I'm a playwright, but it does seem to me that Frye is on to something when he implies that stories account for the different shapes of societies; once arranged in a charismatic way, they become irresistible patterns; they become controllable, sometimes uncontrollable, driving forces for good, for bad, for nothing, for identity; for power over us they fight each other, and Frye's master, William Blake, writes that there are stories that control all the others.

Not only that, stories are the secret manipulators of philosophers, of historians, of politicians; just lately, even science has succumbed to producing creation stories that involve wicked witches called black holes and elastic space & time scenarios the Brothers Grimm might have collected. Gone, at last, is the unnerving mechanism Sir Isaac Newton trapped us in, and I have always thought it ominously significant that Sir Isaac's world picture had its beginning in the behaviour of an Apple.

In a moment, I'll go into the excitement of how Frye sees stories coming together for maximum arrow-power, but what I would like first to underline is that as a critic he emphasizes that care has to be taken in how you retell the stories.

It seems civilized to put on Shakespeare plays over & over again, but not so civilized if you castrate them by missing the conventions they're written in. Read Frye on *Comedy of Errors*, and his imagery analysis pegs it as a dry run for *Pericles*; see *The Comedy of Errors* produced at a local theatre some years ago, and the twins' mysterious mother comes out of her abbey (disguised as a covered waggon) firing a shotgun!

For years, I have always wondered why you never seemed to see a good production of *Macbeth*. Was it because all that Malcolm can muster up when informed of his father's murder is 'O, by whom?' or is it supposed to contrast with the others expressing their grief so volubly and so well? Both Malcolm & his father, Duncan, the anointed king, seem always to be played with such effeteness and deliberate un-radiance. Yet Duncan seems decided enough when he orders the execution of the first traitorous Thane of Cawdor. Cut too are the lines about Edward the Confessor, Duncan's English equivalent who heals the sick, and Malcolm's speeches about his own immortality fall very flat.

Well, in Frye's *Natural Perspective* (62) I found the answer: 'If we keep this mythical and conventional element in Duncan's sovereignty at the centre of the play, every word of it fits together into the gigantic and terrifying tragic structure that we know so well. Take it away, and Thomas Rymer himself could hardly do justice to the chaos of what remains.' In their own way, Duncan & Malcolm have to appear as riveting as 'the butcher and his fiend-like queen.'

Well, one way a director could improve ineffectual versions of *Macbeth* is to make sure that Malcolm's command to cut down the forest of Birnam Wood is the big moment it is surely intended to be. Because if Malcolm's soldiers had not then proceeded against Dunsinane with Birnam Wood in their hands, Macbeth's will to survive might never have been shattered. Just as theatrical as the murder of Banquo is Malcolm saying: 'Let every soldier hew him down a bough / and bear't before him; thereby shall ...'

In view of the civilization problems that daily face us, this may sound rather picayune, but, to my mind, the reason we get the big problems wrong shows up in the apparently little ones, such as a weak production of a great play. Later on, there's a more crucial turn I'd like to give this, but, right now, let's move on to another kind of theatre-teaching.

I know that Frye has warned several times against mistaking entertainment for education, the sort of situation that develops when your students have watched so much TV they have no attention span left whatsoever, so you reach for some 'Sesame Street' puppets. Still, surely you don't have to be forever solemn about archetypes, displacement, epiphanies, modes, genres, and the *idiotes* figure, in short, the elegant & clear terminology Frye presents in drawing a critical map of the verbal universe.

Accordingly, the image that occurs to me when I describe my imaginative life before I knew the difference between low mimetic and high mimetic is that I was caught in a History of Ideas treadmill with two special dungeons called Historical Influence and Realism. With regard to the last named, it was like another Toronto version of Don Quixote; as I saw it, the landscape was ringed with visible huge and terrifying giants, but fans of James T. Farrell & Theodore Dreiser kept insisting, were under the delusion, that the giants were just hard-working windmills.

But always across the park, through fellow students at Victoria College, came quite different notions of literature that I have always felt were like the sounds of a distant midway.

What I could hear was the music from carousels of revolving modes spinning from inscape to outscape and up to inscape & epiphany again; the Test-Your-Weight animal/vegetable/mineral paradigms with the work in question as the sledge hammer rattling out its authorial apocalyptic & demonic hounds & greyhounds, demiwolves, shoughs; the Siamese Twins of Lyric & Epos.

Upon graduation, I fell into New Criticism at Manitoba & faced the awesome task of having to teach *The Heart of Midlothian* in twelve hours, the smallest amount of time in which my course captain felt one could do justice to its verbal texture. To a friend who told him of my predicament on Bloor Street, Frye suggested that I could fill in the oversupply of time by parsing the whole novel, sentence by sentence.

And then, I found out how to enter the midway and work the machinery myself. I think it was when I figured out a displacement exercise for my Creative Writing students – rewrite *The Robber Bridegroom* in terms of the Winnipeg you've grown up in. That worked so well that I could begin to hope my own verbal expertise might some day overtake my untidy life experience and perhaps get somewhere dramatic.

Perhaps even more enjoyable was the entrée into a world where you were invited to use your midway skills in organizing arrangements of stories for courses, focus a group of identifiers around a literary magazine, watch friends work in teams on the development of such anthologies as the *Uses of the Imagination* whose first reader, delightfully named *Wish & Nightmare*, is aimed at grades seven to ten levels; in other words, enjoy society. In what Frye called the Age of the Tiger, it is really comforting to find a system of insights that can inform a community, not of terrorists, but of identifiers.

All very well, says a bystander, but the world is divided into herbivores & carnivores; carnivores just laugh at better *Macbeth* productions and stories that control all the other stories. So far as this planet is concerned, it's 'Dallas' that controls all the other myths. Look how it brought down the Marxist empire in Eastern Europe singlehandedly, this last insight coming out of a recent CBC 'Ideas' program which dismayed me because if there's one thing I thought Marxism might have been able to exterminate for us it was that boring and oily capitalist butterfly called 'Dallas.'

Then, there is the difficulty of my father who, as a boy, refused to listen to any story unless it had actually happened. My grandmother had to buy him authentic stories about the RCMP, no doubt illustrated by photographs. Now, my father grew up to conquer this problem, but there are others who haven't. They sometimes are found among those who, hearing that the local school library has books that with reference to the Bible use the word 'myth,' dynamite the library.

The answer in Frye is that stories are neither true nor untrue and that the dynamiters have no notion of figurative language; also, these violent objectors are 'closed mythology' attacking 'open mythology' herbivores. The tragedy is that the violent ones really care about 'stories,' and the herbivores don't care enough.

People seem to know how to listen to music (sacred noise), and mathematicians do not threaten to dynamite libraries whose books point out that 2+2=4 is not literally true (sacred engineering), but in large numbers they seem to have lost the ability to participate creatively in what Frye calls 'sacred story.'

The additional problem here is that in between the closed-mythology carnivores and the open-mythology herbivores are crowds & crowds of blind mouths possessed by the sleepwalking spirit of our times, coddled by its consumerist enslavement – everybody in a car sort of thing – who neither against their wills nor with their wills are formed to live on one level. They look up, they look down, they are not fed, and daily more and more of them seek violent vengeance against the society that has mislaid their birthright.

But they seek vengeance without knowing why because when you talk to them about their childhood there are no Bible stories. A couple I admire very much in London, Ontario, go round to the parking lots of low-rental housing developments and from their trailer present children with the Bible in the form of puppet plays. From my own experience with drama workshops on the Bible, I think itinerant theatre may be the answer. One step up and you do contact young people who do remember some of the sacred stories, but one big barrier to this developing into spiritual fertility is God the Father's cruelty. They blame disasters on him, how could he just stand by – or the miracles in the New Testament only disturb them. However, I realize that the problem's not to be solved at this point among the blind mouths; it's further back that we have to find where the pipe from the spring has rusted away, and this occurs when I realize that Blake's 'Single Vision & Newton's sleep' best enunciates the problem, and since it is in *Fearful Symmetry* that I first ran across those words, it's time to turn to a book that came along just in time to help my own despair at there apparently being no other possible levels of existence than just our all too natural selves.

Fearful Symmetry is a book that changed an experience many would-be lovers of Blake used to have in that they took out the *Collected Poems* from a library and never got past the Book of Thel. As a commentary, it then challenges you not only to wrestle with the Blake prophecies but to do other remarkable things.

For example, I always remember the statement near the end of *Fearful Symmetry* that the Crucifixion is an eye through which we are still trying to see. I also remember that, in his analysis of Blake's Israel/Britain symbolism, Frye suggests that the method used was to lay a map of Palestine over a map of Britain. At the time I first read this, my impulse was to try this experiment with the region in which I was then living and reading – southern Ontario. The result of this experiment was that Windsor became Beersheba, North Bay became Dan, with Toronto as Jerusalem, and Lake Ontario as the Dead Sea. Still of great interest to me is that in our local tradition we have a local prophet (like Blake also a follower of Jacob Boehme) who does this sort of thing and he is the visionary of the nineteenth-century Sharon, Ontario, David Willson.

In his discussion of Blake's Job engravings, Frye remarks that there are, like the letters of the Hebrew alphabet, twenty-two of them and the designs are therefore an ideographic epic of which our alphabet itself is a faded example. The idea of a miniature Bible compressed into twenty-two symbols is tantalizing not only to those interested in spiritual education. Blake's illuminated prophecies, like exuberant comic books, are a new way of communicating 'sacred story' to those untouched by telling. Then, too, today we are surrounded by intrusive and well-designed commercial logos that enter our souls like the Trojan Horse. Here is a suggestion of how our side is fighting back. This action, as well as the impulses to see through the eye of the Crucifixion and to see your country as a holy land, not just so much real estate, is all part of a big, overarching drive in the book on Blake and in Blake's vision itself to compel you to read the Bible again. In a letter, Frye once said that 90 per cent of Blake was borrowed from the Bible. Since Blake prophecies obviously refocused the Bible for him, perhaps it is time to examine how he in his later books does this as well.

From *The Great Code* I take: 'why a poet might read the Bible,' and, later on, 'What in the Bible particularly attracts poets and other creative

artists of the Western world?' In my own case, as a very young proto-
poet, the attraction to the Bible was the stories. There was a tradition in
our neighbourhood of people reading the Bible through many times,
even of copying it out, so at first I didn't skip and, as a result, got stuck
in Leviticus. Waiting for some years to go by before I tackled that again,
I fell upon Saul & the Witch of Endor – and Elijah & the Ravens – propelled thereto by the illustrations.

My own experience with reading the Bible to children – little boys – is
that, when, by accident, I read them the story of Ahab & Jezebel, they
asked for more. No wonder, for if you remember that story it has a great
Gothic climax where Jezebel is thrown off the palace balcony to dogs
below who lick up her blood; the next day nothing is found of her except
the palms of her hands. For those of us who may have worried about the
Bible's lack of interest in impartial history, Frye points out that there is
serious doubt that Ahab & Jezebel were that bad, but 'the sense of
urgency in the writing comes out much more freely for not being
hampered by the clutter of what may have actually occurred.' In other
words, Ahab & Jezebel were enemies of Elijah, and that's that. After
Jezebel, what next do some children like to hear about? Why, the two
she-bears that finished off the forty-two children who made the big
mistake of mocking the prophet Elijah's baldness. Later on when they
read *Finnegans Wake*, this will come in handy, but just in case you think
that my getting children to pay attention to Bible stories is to terrify
them, I should tell you that in drama workshops on the Bible they like
building the Tower of Babel out of cardboard boxes and seeing them
come tumbling down.

Yes, the first response to the Bible may indeed have been as raw &
primitive as that sketched above, but what *The Great Code* early establishes is that there is, in reading the Bible through, a slow & steady
'further intensifying of the prophetic vision.' As the stories acquire more
and more levels of meaning, there is a cumulative transforming effect on
the listener. How this works is clarified by seeing the Bible as a week in
which each day presents us with a different challenge to our creativity:
Monday – Creation; Tuesday – Revolution & Exodus, Wednesday – Law,
where young readers are apt to get stuck, Thursday – Wisdom, Friday
– Prophecy, Saturday – Gospel, and Sunday – Apocalypse, Revelation.

What could be more attractive to a would-be poet than the Book of
Revelation, the Sabbath Fair where all the threads of the previous six
days are woven together in a midway of seven-headed monsters, a
creation dismantled, a final threshing out of the worthless chaff in us
separated from the grains worth keeping? As well, there is the hair-

breadth escape of a snow-white bride and her baby from a beautiful witch (Jezebel again and 'Who is the fairest of them all?'); there is even a prince on a white horse, who, after the opening of Seven Seals, takes his Bride, that's us!, away to a city built out of giant fiery stones – jewels – and in the centre of that city is a familiar garden and tree, but this time only one tree beside a river that flows from the side of the enthroned Lamb of God.

To this very day, I can still remember the effect of that book when it was first taught to me, a fairly rare thing in today's Sunday schools. I do not know why. Its effect on me was that of the metamorphosis of spirit which *The Great Code* singles out as the effect of 'sacred story.'

At this point, *The Great Code*, you should know, points out one of the reasons for the transforming effect of the Biblical Week is that Christ has become the Bible. As you read the Gospel day of the Bible week, you can't help but notice how so many turns in his life are a fulfillment of some situation set up long before he was born in the previous days of the Biblical Week. Since his story fills the Sixth Day, which in Genesis was reserved for the creation of Adam, Christ too is a new man made out of the dust of the other five previous days.

Dust! I'm reminded of that Zen gravel garden in Japan where the covered side of a courtyard architecturally designed to force perspective and organize response in a special way, the onlooker sees, made out of gravel raked in delicate curvings and boulders carefully placed and half submerged in the gravel 'water' – the onlooker sees a spiritual seascape. One tourist from Texas is reported to have said, 'It's just a bunch of gravel.' In the same way, those not in the know probably find the Bible just a cobbling together of old stories. But no, the stories' arrangements, the conventions in which they are written, their modulations into prophecies and reprises, all this takes over the listeners' consciousness and expands it.

We become the Bible too.

How do we extend this to a sick society that desperately needs re-newal? I'm sure it has to start among the grassroots in very small, quiet ways. If you could persuade just 2 people in a class of 300 that it isn't just a bunch of gravel! When I read hysterical articles on what is happening to the schools – 'the butcher and his fiend-like queen' have got loose in the corridors and parents are buying their children bullet-proof vests – the last thing you ever hear is '*Comedy of Errors* is a dry run for *Pericles, Prince of Tyre*' or 'Please leave in the part about Edward, the Confessor.' Yes, you do hear about commercial culture gutting the minds of youth with what Frye calls TV stories written for the mob, glorifying the victimizers; but just where are the stories on our side and how do we retell them? The cultural critics I've been describing are more likely to suggest that the teachers take target practice.

Because its directors don't really find 'anointed temples' as much fun as murder, a production of *Macbeth* falls to pieces. Well, we're never going to defeat mobs & tyrannies that way. I suggest that defeat of the tyrant is more likely to follow the strategic advice of some young, scholarly shrimp – perhaps just as callow-seeming as Malcolm, and even 'to women yet unknown,' who happens to be good, maybe, at the art of camouflage. 'Let's raise some tree branches,' he advises, apparently to hide the smallness of our numbers from the foe. But, the moment we raise those branches, the giant's castle falls down!

SANDRA DJWA

Forays in the Bush Garden:
Frye and Canadian Poetry

It is appropriate when honouring the legacy of Northrop Frye to speak of his literary antecedents, for a part of what we leave to others proceeds from what we have inherited. Accordingly, I am taking a semiauto-biographical approach to a young and sometimes feisty Frye and the early moulding of his intellectual career at Victoria College, University of Toronto. This essay, supplementing John Ayre's helpful biographical account of the thirties and forties, draws upon correspondence, letters, and diaries from this same period and several interviews with Frye which took place between 1973 and 1989. My argument is that Frye came to know Canadian poetry through the poems of E.J. Pratt, familiarly known as Ned, a professor at Victoria College who became Frye's friend and mentor; more importantly, Frye continued to see Canadian poetry (and to formulate his criticism of it) from the perspective of Pratt's vision and cosmology. A further intriguing possibility, suggested by Frye himself, is that his first book on Blake, *Fearful Symmetry* (1947), was influenced in significant ways by Pratt's poem, 'The Truant' (1942).

Some time ago, when working on an introduction to E.J. Pratt's *Complete Poems*, I asked Frye to characterize the primary figures at the University of Toronto in the thirties. He described Milton scholar A.S.P Woodhouse as 'a rotund person with a broad face ... at certain angles he had a remarkable resemblance to [Samuel] Johnson ... he himself was very well aware of this: he kept the portrait of Johnson over his desk.' Of Pelham Edgar, the professor who first encouraged his work on Blake, Frye recalled that he was a staunch supporter of Canadian literature and 'really quite sold on [Charles G.D.] Roberts.' And of Pratt: 'Well, Pratt ... was as kindly ... as everybody said he was. At the same time, it was a mask that he was deliberately cultivating ... The geniality ... covered ... a very considerable sense of conflict ... I've got Barker Fairley's portrait of him ... and it's a very tragic, harrowed face. Barker always said that it doesn't look like what you see when you see Ned, but it looks like the man who wrote those poems.'[1] We speculated on what the portrait of Johnson had meant to Woodhouse: aside from a common interest in Milton, it was possibly confirmation of his position as lawgiver. When I asked what had happened to Pratt's portrait, Frye replied that for much of his academic life it had hung above his own desk.[2] The question I was left with is one that I propose to explore: if Woodhouse identified with Johnson, the lawgiver, what did Frye find in Pratt and Canadian poetry?

To get to Frye and Canadian poetry in the early thirties we have to situate ourselves far down a University of Toronto hierarchy. At the top were Malcolm Wallace and Pelham Edgar, Professors of English and Heads of the English Departments at University College and Victoria College, respectively; in the middle were Professors Pratt, Woodhouse, and E.K. Brown; at the very bottom were students (and later instructors) like Frye and Roy Daniells. Canadian poetry was not the canon we now recognize, but rather the poets of the Confederation as represented by ten pages at the end of *Representive Poetry* (1928), the survey text commonly used in the English pass course at University of Toronto.

A 'Canadian' poetry was identified with a group of poet-personalities (primarily Charles G.D. Roberts and Bliss Carman) and their supporters; both were viewed with suspicion by young intellectuals. Although Canadian poetry was a tenuous entity, the Canadian Authors' Association had launched a 'Buy Made-in-Canada Goods' campaign that equated the buying of books of Canadian verse with the supporting of Canadian culture. Then, too, poets from the 1880s like Roberts and Carman were promoted by the association as 'our younger moderns' and sent on cross-country tours to read Canadian poems. Given the satirical temper of the twenties and the pervasive influence of American satirist H.L. Mencken, a debunking reaction was inevitable. This occurred in April 1925 in the so-called 'battle of the books,' a response to a claim by Roberts in *Saturday Night* that Carman was 'the greatest living lyric poet with the possible exception of Mr. W.B. Yeats' (28 March 1925).

Distrust of this partisan criticism was reflected in A.J.M. Smith's 'Wanted – Canadian Criticism,' published in *The Canadian Forum* in 1928. This essay, combining Mencken's tone with T.S. Eliot's thought, announced: 'Modernity and tradition alike demand that the contemporary artist ... shall be an intellectual. Sensibility is no longer enough, intelligence is also required. Even in Canada' (601). Similarly, in 1931–2 Frye, in *Acta Victoriana* (sometimes under the *nom de plume* of Monocle which he associated with Roberts) wrote lampoons and limericks[3] and spoke of the improbability of a Canadian culture and the 'frenzied enthusiasm and intellectual jingoism' of Canadian drama (56 [Mar. 1932], 33). When Frye became editor of *Acta* in May 1932 the 'Canadian' vanished from the journal's annual Canadian poetry contest, and Frye, also paraphrasing Eliot, urged poetry contributors to 'make an exhaustive survey of the kind of work done by [their] most distinguished contemporaries, and trace out the precedents and traditions they follow' (57 [Feb. 1933], 7).

As a contributor to *Acta*, Frye had seen, in successive issues of the journal, two poems that embodied the difference between the new verse and the old: 'The Highway' by Pratt and 'Pan and the Rose' by Roberts. 'Came Pan to the garden on a golden morning, / The dew of the thickets adrip on his thighs'[4] – these two lines indicate why Roberts came to represent all that Frye rejected in bad Canadian verse. In 1941 Roberts, by then Sir Charles, published a chap-book which Pelham Edgar praised extravagantly.[5] Frye recalled 'a most embarrassing luncheon that Pelham gave': 'Pelham said that Roberts had just written a poem – this was the first year of the war – which in his view was one of the great poems of the English language ... Roberts read it and it was horrible. And there was a kind of submerged whinny that was supposed to be appreciation going around.'[6] This incident marked a nadir in Frye's views of the older Canadian poetry. What seems to have stuck in his craw was this ridiculous praise of Roberts, a man Frye considered 'a ... model of the phoney genius with his title and his monocle and his knighthood.'[7] The next year, 1942, Frye heard Pratt read 'The Truant,' and the following year, 1943, was an *annus mirabilis*: Smith published *The Book of Canadian Poetry*, which established a poetic canon; Brown published *On Canadian Poetry*, which defined a critical context; and Roberts, at the close of the year, died.

Of these events I would judge that the most important for Frye was hearing 'The Truant' read aloud. Frye had known Pratt since the early thirties when he had regularly gone to see him 'to talk about plays.'[8] After his graduation in 1933, while studying theology at Emmanuel College, Frye earned extra money by marking Pratt's papers. Pratt, he said, would explain to 'all and sundry' that Frye's presence at Emmanuel, then quite unfashionable, was because of 'a promise to a mother.' It was true, Frye recalls, but he did not know how Pratt knew.[9] As Pratt had made the same promise to his own mother,[10] there must have been a high degree of mutual identification. These years saw the height of Pratt's party-giving days, clubby Chestertonian 'stag nights,' where the writing of verse, especially parodied sonnets, was part of the evening's wit. Frye was always included: 'Ned knew I was broke.'[11] Pratt's 'boundless generosity and kindliness,' Frye later observed, were qualities founded on 'a genuine enthusiasm for human life and personality, and a sense of the reality of love'[12] – and by this last comment I take it that Frye means *agape*.

About Pratt, the thirties' poet, the most important point to remember is that he is a highly mythic and symbolic poet whose narratives sometimes verge on allegory. 'The Highway,' for example, draws upon Darwin's science and the Bible to develop a sweeping vision where cosmic and human evolution culminate in the birth of Christ: 'But what made *our* feet miss the road ... / O star! O rose! O Son of Man?'[13] In his later Introduction to Pratt's *Collected Poems* (1958), Frye speaks of this 'misstep or falling away' (xxii). His implict equation of 'misstep' and 'sin' reminds us that when Frye was first reading Pratt he was a student of philosophy and theology. For Pratt's generation, poetry was the natural expression of his religious concerns; for Frye's generation, such concerns sometimes found their way into criticism.

I have managed to unearth one exception, a sonnet written by Frye on his twenty-third birthday. This sonnet, a *jeu d'esprit*, is a pastiche of several of Milton's well-known sonnets, where Frye explores, not altogether flippantly, the Miltonic question of vocation:

> Milton considered his declining spring
> And realized the possibility
> That while he mused on Horton scenery
> Genius might join his youth in taking wing;
> Yet thought this not too serious a thing
> Because of God's well-known propensity
> To take and re-absorb inscrutably
> The lives of men, whatever gifts they bring.
> Of course I have a different heritage
> I have worked hard not to be young at all,
> With fair results; at least my blood is cooled,
> And I am safe in saying, at Milton's age
> That if Time pays me an informal call
> And tries to steal my youth, Time will get fooled.[14]

Frye's line 'The lives of men, whatever gifts they bring' recalls Milton's 'God doth not need / Either man's work or his own gifts' (Sonnet XIX). And there is a ring of truth as well as self-parody in the statement 'Of course I have a different heritage.' Like Pratt, the Newfoundlander, who had followed the same path at Victoria twenty-five years before, Frye was a product of the Maritimes where education as a preacher or teacher was often the only way out of poverty. Here he identifies with the equally struggling young Milton whose 'three and twentieth year ... no bud or blossom show'th' (Sonnet VII). In effect, Frye is using the world of Milton's sonnets, his poetic cosmology, to express his own questions about God's gifts and 'man's work.' Not surprisingly, this young man who questioned his vocation, wrote verse, and wanted to become a Blake scholar became, as he says, 'quite close' to Pratt,[15] whose early life paralleled his own, who had agonized in verse over his decision to leave the ministry ('Clay'), and who had successfully changed his field from theology to literature.

In January 1936 when Pratt started *Canadian Poetry Magazine* he asked Frye to help him. It was then that Frye discovered that, although Pratt might be a soft touch personally (his financial career could have been scripted by Stephen Leacock), 'Ned's standards were absolutely inflexible when it came to poetry.'[16] Frye recalls that one of Roberts's lady friends had submitted a poem which began: 'Are you sighing on my breast.' 'I said to Ned, "What the hell are we going to do with this poem that begins 'Are you whistling up my arse?' " At that moment the phone rang and it was ... Roberts putting pressure on Ned to publish what he described as one of the most exquisite things he would ever get. Ned said, "That's bilge." He said, "You just don't know what a poem is." And Ned said, "Are you aware that poem has already been parodied?" '[17]

Frye's poetic apprenticeship took place in the first three issues of *Canadian Poetry Magazine* early in 1936. These were lean Depression days and, when the magazine advertised that it would pay for poetry, almost a thousand contributions were received for the second issue. Frye recalled it was mostly 'junk' and his job was to 'winnow through.' What Pratt taught him was 'when a poem was worth five dollars.'[18] As this was the amount given for third prize, this implied a nice degree of poetic discrimination.

Throughout the thirties and forties Frye continued to attend Pratt's parties where he saw Smith and heard several versions of Smith's introduction to *The Book of Canadian Poetry*. This anthology was to provide Frye with, as he said, 'a way into Canadian poetry which I never had before': in effect, Frye was working his way out of his early debunking attitudes.[19] His review of Smith's book in *The Canadian Forum* in December 1943 picked up a hint put forward by Smith in his introduction: 'If their [Roberts, Carman, Lampman, D.C. Scott] theme was narrow, it was an important one ... In general terms, it was nothing less than the impingement of nature in Canada upon the human spirit' (24). Frye noted that, for Smith, the 'outstanding achievement of Canadian poetry is in the evocation of stark terror' (209): 'The immediate source of this is obviously the frightening loneliness of a huge and thinly settled country ... [Man's] thrifty little heaps of civilized values look pitiful beside nature's apparently meaningless power to waste and destroy on a superhuman scale, and such a nature suggests an equally ruthless and subconscious God, or else no God' (209).

Today's reader – or yesterday's reader – browsing through *The Book of Canadian Poetry* will not find 'stark terror.' However, a chronological reading of Pratt's poetry from his *Complete Poems* – 'The Ground Swell,' 'The Ice-Floes,' *The Roosevelt and the Antinoe*, and *The Titanic* – will yield terror and often in conjunction with the threat of death. Julian, the protagonist of Pratt's 'Clay,' fears that a wildly destructive North Atlantic and World War I prove the existence of a ruthless God or else the absence of God – the eighteenth-century clock-maker God who removes himself from his creation.[20]

> The inner courts are thronged with multitudes,
> And crosses – Ah! In cluttered heaps they rose,
> Stacked pile on pile, until they twist and sag
> The rivets on the bolted doors of God ...
>
> (Part 2, 335)

In the years before and after publication of Smith's anthology, Frye had been trying his own hand at poetry and fiction and submitting his work to Pratt, who urged him to concentrate on critical work,[21] especially Blake. During the summer of 1942, Frye submitted drafts of sections of his developing Blake manuscript to Pratt, and Pratt described his new poems to Frye. Pratt's opinion meant a great deal to Frye; on 10 August 1942 Frye wrote in his diary: 'Bitched the day, celebrating because Ned liked the Blake.'[22] Pratt had told Frye he was writing a new poem on Hitler, and the poem that followed was 'The Truant,' an allegory developing from the early years of the war and the blitz of London. This poem has clear affinities with the Romantic cosmologies of Shelley's *Prometheus Unbound* and the prophecies of Blake. When he first heard the poem,[23] Frye immediately saw a Blake connection. In 1942 diary notes headed August 15 he mentions: '[a] stag at Earle Birney's for [Ernest] Sirluck. Ned read us a new poem: general theme of the conflict of Orc and Urizen. Swell poem, too. Infinitely better than a silly fantasia on Hitler's nightmares he'd been discussing with me. The only contribution I made to that was to suggest that in Wagner's general scheme Hitler would not be Siegfried but Alberich [Wagner's evil gnome].'[24] This diary entry indicates that ideas about Hitler, cosmologies, and Pratt's poems were going back and forth between the older poet and the young instructor. Pratt's projected fantasia seems to have taken a more Blakean form, possibly because of concepts gleaned from Frye's sprawling manuscript. The poem, in turn, seems to have helped Frye deal with some of the problems he was experiencing when attempting to organize his material. The degree and sequence of influence is always hard to determine exactly, and my sense that Frye and the structure of *Fearful Symmetry* might have been different without the context of Pratt and the structure of 'The Truant' is not undermined by the possibility of the opposite being true also.

In comments that he made after Pratt's death in 1964, Frye acknowledges his emotional indebtedness to 'The Truant': 'I heard Ned read *The Truant*, and felt not simply that I had heard the greatest of all Canadian poems, but that the voice of humanity had spoken once more, with the kind of authority it reserves for such moments as the bombing of London, when the powers of darkness test the soul and find once more that "The stuff is not amenable to fire" ' ('The Personal Legend,' 9). Frye described himself at that point as, 'nearly running around blind in circles trying to figure out what life was all about. And I could just feel things coming into focus. ['The Truant'] was the kind of confrontation that's very central to Blake as well.'[25] Not only did 'The Truant' provide an entry into *Fearful Symmetry*, but it was a revelation to him that 'not only another poet but a fellow as close to me personally as Ned could think along Blake's lines.'[26]

Curiously, either Frye's critics have not picked up on this suggestion or they find it improbable.[27] Yet, what 'The Truant' offered was a visionary poem which worked through the question that Frye was later to identify as central to Blake: the question of the relation of human beings to nature. This is best seen as an epistemological question: how does one know what one knows?; specifically how does one distinguish between human beings and nature, or between human values and nature's (apparent) values? Pratt presents the debate as an awkward 'flyting' match between man, as perceiver and imaginer, and a tyranical and powerful embodiment of natural mechanical processes. Both truant man and his antagonist are constituted of atoms but, although they share the same chemical and material elements, the distinction between the two, Pratt argues, is mind. Only human beings have the imaginative capacity to comprehend the whole and the ethical sense (here we read 'soul') to make choices which involve necessity and free will. By his use of allegorical structures and by his opposing of two cosmologies – one that might be identified with the eighteenth-century Deists and Locke and the second that has affinities with the Romantics, especially with Blake and Shelley's Prometheus – Pratt provided an example of what Frye was to later describe as 'poetic process.'

In his preface to the 1969 edition of *Fearful Symmetry*, Frye explains that his subject is Blake's 'poetic process' but that he found the book difficult to write until he recognized that symbolic constructs, or cosmologies, are an essential of poetic process. In his text he identifies two kinds of cosmologies. The first, 'designed to understand the world as it is' (n.p.), is the Newtonian system of impersonal power and mechanical force (34) which goes back to the Deists and forward to Darwin and Hardy. In several versions of Frye's introduction this cosmology, as in Pratt's poem, is associated with Nazi totalitarianism. The second, Blake's cosmology, 'is a revolutionary vision of the universe transformed by the creative imagination into a human shape ... not a vision of things as they are ordered but of things as they could be ordered' (n.p.). In the opening chapter of *Fearful Symmetry*, 'The Case Against Locke,' Frye defines Blake's approach as 'allegory addressed to the Intellectual powers' (9) and suggests that 'Blake is protesting against [Locke's] implication that man is material to be formed by an external world and not the former or imaginer of the material world' (23).

Pratt's poem 'The Truant' is also allegory addressed to the intellectual powers. Nature and its mechanical power is personified by the grand Panjandrum who, as Milton Wilson observes, is nonetheless an 'inflated pretender to importance' (*E.J. Pratt*, 39). He is opposed by the Truant, Pratt's generic or Blakean man. The Truant asserts that it is human imagination alone that conceives and contains the universe: ' "You had no name ... / We taught you all you ever knew / Of motion, time and space." '

> 'Boast not about your harmony,
> Your perfect curves, your rings
> Of *pure and endless light* – Twas we
> Who pinned upon your Seraphim their wings,
> ...
> '... one day ...
> We turned a human page

> And blotted out a cosmic myth
> With all its baby symbols to explain
> The sunlight in Apollo's eyes,
> ...
> That day we learned how to anatomize
> Your body, calibrate your size
> And set a mirror up before your face
> To show you what you really were – a rain
> Of dull Lucretian atoms crowding space ...
>   (Part 2, 129–30)

In this poem Pratt draws upon the cosmology of Lucretius's *De Rerum Natura*. Lucretius argues that human beings, including their souls, are simply an aggregation of atoms and thus without hope of immortality. The Truant, echoing Henry Vaughan's 'The World' ('I saw eternity the other night / Like a great ring of pure and endless light'), speaks as an artist-creator to assert his faith in the human imagination and the soul. He also rejects Lockean cosmology which posits the separation of human beings and nature. It is precisely because, in Pratt's view, man's imagination contains his universe, and because his 'soul' is not amenable to physical process, that he can briefly play 'truant' from the natural order. To adapt Frye's terms, the Truant's cosomology, taking a human shape, rejects things as they are in favour of things as they should be. What Frye seems to find in Pratt's poem is a dramatization of the conflict between Blake's cosmology and Locke's: as such, it may well have provided a paradigm for 'The Case Against Locke,' his introduction to Blake's thought.

In 'The Truant,' Pratt very briefly unifies human beings and nature by arguing that the human imagination contains nature, a positive 'accomplishment' of the sort that Frye liked to call 'comic.' Throughout all his early poetry, however, up to the forties and *Towards the Last Spike*, Pratt's poetry presents human beings and nature as divided and in perpetual struggle: his greatest fear is that a ruthless nature will prevail over puny human beings and their moral values. That Frye views Canadian poetry through the contrast of cosmologies (with the tragic one dominating) is suggested by his 1956 essay 'Preface to an Uncollected Anthology,' where he writes: 'It is Pratt who has expressed in *Towards the Last Spike* the central comic theme, and in *Brébeuf* the central tragic theme, of the Canadian imagination,' and who combines the two in ' "The Truant," '... the greatest poem in Canadian literature' (*Contexts of Canadian Criticism*, 190). Frye traces the beginnings of the tragic theme back to the 1860s and a scene depicting Canadian nature as 'a mystery of mindless power' in Charles Heavysege's *Jephthah's Daughter* (1865). But, in fact, this scene owes more to literature than to nature as it is highly derivative of Tennyson's *Morte d'Arthur*. The bleakness of the landscape, the alliteration of the passage, and the development of character all echo aspects of Tennyson's poem. Jephthah, like Sir Bedivere, must be rebuked until he keeps his oath; his sword 'whirl[s]' as does Excalibur and 'clang[s]' on the sloping rocks as does Sir Bedivere's mail.[28] When as sensitive and as experienced a critic as Frye overlooks obvious literary allusion, we can only assume he is reading deductively rather than inductively. And, indeed, it is only if Frye stands in the 1950s with Pratt's tragic poetic perspective on Canadian nature and looks back at the Canadian tradition that it is possible to construe *Jephthah's Daughter* as an example of an amoral Canadian nature.

An extension of what I see as Frye's explication of Pratt's cosmology is developed in the Conclusion to the first edition of *Literary History of Canada* (1965) where Frye finds in Canadian writing 'a tone of deep terror in regard to nature ... The human mind has nothing but human and moral values to cling to ... yet the vast unconsciousness of nature in front of it seems an unanswerable denial of those values' (830). Frye suggests that the human response to a formidable physical and psychological frontier is a community 'garrison mentality' found in Pratt's poetry with his 'infallible instinct for what is central to the Canadian imagination.'[29] But a 'garrison mentality' is not unique to Canadian poetry.[30] As I noted in 1973, Frye's 'garrison mentality' has affinities with the mental 'palisade' of W.C. Williams's *In the American Grain*, where he suggests that the early Puritans, confronted with the wilderness, turned in upon themselves, falling back for greater security upon a doctrinaire religion and its community manifestations.[31] This view of a community garrison is also cited by Lawrence in his 'Study of Thomas Hardy' where he speaks of 'The little fold of law and order, the walled city,' from which human beings have to defend themselves against 'the vast, uncomprehended and incomprehensible morality of nature.'[32] The psychological paradigm of a garrisoned individual confronted with the wilderness is, at root, a theological issue given new currency in the 1870s, and it is not surprising that Frye should share these concerns and associate them with Pratt, who was influenced by the late Victorian crisis in belief, by Darwin and by Hardy.

However, to work backwards from the forties and fifties and Pratt is to distort our perspective on Canadian poetry. It does so in the same way as does Alex Colville's well-known painting of the binoculars: the glossy surface of the near-present obstructs the longer view. This is because Pratt's attitude to nature is atypical of Canadian poetry as a whole. Only Pratt begins, as does Hardy, with a vision of a basically amoral, sometimes malignant nature and assigns the possibility of moral action only to human beings.[33] But if we approach Canadian poetry from its first manifestations working forward, from Robert Hayman's *Quodlibets, Lately Come Over From New Britaniola, Old Newfound-land* (1628) through the poets of the Confederation to the moderns, there is abundant evidence that poets writing in Canada see nature as both beneficent and fearful.

If we are to judge from the portrait that hung above Frye's desk for a good part of his working life, Pratt's influence must have been pervasive. Pratt certainly had taken Frye's measure by May 1949: in a letter to Douglas Bush, a graduate of Victoria and former instructor, he remarks, 'There is only one fellow in the Victoria tradition who is close to you, and that's Frye who is going to be heard from in a big way in the future.'[34] However, by the early fifties Frye was beginning to distance himself from certain aspects of Pratt's personality, particularly what he termed the 'compulsive extroversion that began to take over' with *Towards the Last Spike* (1952). He says: 'Ned had a quality which I noticed with Blake ... Blake was so ready to caricature himself, throw himself into any role that he thought his friends would want at the time and I could see Ned doing that ... He wanted to be liked and well, writing poetry, the kind that Pratt wrote – at least his best poetry – is a pretty lonely occupation.'[35] Frye seems to have felt that Pratt, like Roberts before him, had fallen into the pit of personality.

In 1947 Carl Klinck and Henry Wells published *E.J. Pratt: The Man and the Poetry*, and Pratt became more and more 'a smiling public man.' Then, too, in *Towards the Last Spike* Pratt adopts 'holism,' an optimistic view of evolution which pulls the claws from his earlier, fearful nature,[36] and which for Frye may have been a less appealing side of the poem's 'comic' aspect. I suspect Frye is alluding to Pratt in *Fearful Symmetry* when he speaks of the 'dinosaur-haunted mythologies' of those moderns who have been obliged to add Darwin's science and Hardy's 'immanent Will' to the old Copernican god of mindless power (34). Finally, I think that Frye is referring to Pratt when he attacks cosmologies of the kind that structure *Towards the Last Spike*[37] and distinguishes between the man and the poet: 'we speak of So-and-So "the Man," meaning So-and-So when he is not being a poet; but it is only when So-and-So is using the imagination which is the "Real Man" and writing poetry that he is a man' (*FS*, 112). For Blake, as for Frye, a man's 'real life [is] expressed in the total form of his creative acts' (112). Unlike Pratt, Frye seems to have determined to let the work, rather than the man, speak. In this context, Fairley's portrait of the early Pratt as tormented visionary – 'the man who wrote those poems' – may have been a reminder to Frye to stick, like Pilgrim (and his cousin Mr Milton), to the narrow path and the wicket gate.

There is more than a hundred years of English poetry between Bunyan and 'the bush garden' of Susanna Moodie which, as its name implies, is both bush and garden. And there is yet another hundred years of Canadian nature verse between Moodie and Margaret Atwood's poem of the same name. Frye also adopted 'the bush garden' as a title for his collected essays on Canadian poetry, stating they were written at a time when 'Canadian literature was trying to get out of the bush,'[38] which in this sense has a whiff of the second-rate, as in the 'bush league' of Canadian poets. Yet Canadian poetry, with Pratt as its chief exemplar, was an essential part of Frye's early aesthetic development at the University of Toronto.

NOTES

I am indebted to colleagues at Simon Fraser University, Sam Wong, Kathy Mezei, and David Stouck, who read and helpfully commented on this essay.

1 Northrop Frye, interviews with author, 9 September 1988 and 23 August 1988.

2 Several of Frye's friends recall that the portrait eventually migrated to the living-room and hall.

3 In 1931 Frye wrote:

> A young artist's model named Rose
> Refused to take off all her clothes.
> The artist said, 'Model,
> 'Get this in your noddle,
> 'I simply won't draw you in *those!*'
> (*Acta Victoriana* 56, no. 1: 39)

4 Roberts's poem continues:

> ... aloof in garden he spied one blossom,
> A Rose but half open to the insistent sun;
> ...
> His hot heart pounding in his shaggy bosom,

The tender red petals to his lips he drew.
With aching rapture and a wild, wild wonder
He drained the distillage of their honeyed dew.
                                    (*Acta Victoriana* 56, no. 3: 23)

5 Edgar wrote in *Canadian Poetry Magazine*: 'there is superb workmanship in this little volume of war poems ... the pulsing of passionate conviction and the ripened fruit of concentrated thought' (vol. 5, no. 4 [Aug. 1941]: 41).

6 Frye, interview with author, 9 September 1988.

7 Ibid.

8 Ibid.

9 Ibid.; and interview with author, 23 August 1983.

10 Pitt, *E.J. Pratt*, 33, 58.

11 Frye, interview with author, 23 August 1983.

12 Frye, 'Edwin John Pratt, 1882–1964,' *Proceedings of the Royal Society of Canada*, 165.

13 Pratt, 'The Highway,' 15.

14 Northrop Frye to Roy Daniells, n.d. (ca. 1935), Roy Daniells Papers, University of British Columbia Special Collections. The reference to Horton is to the Milton family home where John Milton was thought to have lived between 1635 and 1638 while studying in preparation for his chosen career as a poet. Critics now believe that Milton was at Hammersmith for part of this time. Frye's 'mused on Horton scenery' is relevant because *Comus* was written at Horton and *Lycidas*, the great pastoral that marked the end of Milton's stay at Horton, is dated 'Novemb: 1637.' Frye's lines 'Genius might join his youth in taking wing' and 'And tries to steal my youth' echo the famous opening lines of Milton's Sonnet VII: 'How soon hath Time, the subtle thief of youth, / Stol'n on his wing my three and twentieth year.' Frye, as we have seen, was also writing his sonnet on his twenty-third birthday and, again following Milton's practice, he sent his poem to a close friend, Roy Daniells. Finally, Frye's 'at least my blood is cooled' suggests Milton's early amorous Latin elegies in the style of Ovid. Milton's Elegy V, for example, presents the poet in the guise of the burning lover who seeks in vain for a cooling off. Frye is using the sober verse of the later Milton to comment on the ardent young man who is both the young Milton and the young Frye.

15 Frye, interview with author, 23 August 1983.

16 Ibid.

17 Ibid.

18 Ibid.

19 Ibid. Also, in his review in *The Canadian Forum* in December 1943, Frye says: 'whether Canada is really a national unit in any sense that has a

meaning for culture I could not decide myself until I saw Mr. Smith's book; and even then one has misgivings' (132).

20 See Pratt's 'Clay':

> What Shepherd, this, that so attends his flocks,
> As lead them out into the wilderness,
> What Father, this
> Who cares so little for his children's fate,
> That though he holds the sea within his hands,
> He pours its floods upon their heads, lets loose
> His lightnings, blasts and stalking pestilences,
>
> Named you him, Father?
> God? No. Rather a potter with some clay.
> (Part 2, 324–5)

See also Djwa, *The Evolutionary Vision*, 20–1.

21 Ayre, *Northrop Frye: A Biography*, 168.

22 Northrop Frye, Diary, 15 August 1942, notebook 14, box 21, Northrop Frye Papers, E.J. Pratt Library, Victoria University.

23 That Frye recognized that Pratt's cosmology is Blakean is also apparent from his late-1942 letter to Smith describing 'The Truant': 'It's Blake's conflict of Orc and Urizen, the Prometheus-Jesus agent of humanity revolting against the God of universal machinery' (Ayre, *Northrop Frye*, 182).

24 Ibid.

25 Frye, interview with author, 23 August 1983.

26 Ibid.

27 I suggest this relationship in the introduction to the *Complete Poems of E.J. Pratt* (xxxix–xlii). However, John Ayre finds this relationship unlikely: 'Frye's response to the poem was exaggerated by his own thirst for Blakean heroic imagery' (181–3).

28 Cited in Djwa, 'Canadian Contexts.' See also Djwa, Introduction, *Saul and Selected Poems*, ix–xlvii. Frye argues in 'Preface to an Uncollected Anthology' that Jephthah is sacrificing his daughter to 'nature as a mystery of mindless power, with endless resources for killing man but with nothing to respond to his moral or intellectual feelings' (*Contexts of Canadian Criticism*, 189). However, this reading is not supported by the context of the passage which suggests that God does respond but not as Jephthah desires (49).

29 Frye writes in his Conclusion to the first edition of *Literary History of Canada* (1965): 'A garrison is a closely knit and beleaguered society and its moral and social values are unquestionable ... Here again we may turn to Pratt, with his infallible instinct for what is central in the Canadian imagi-

nation. The societies in Pratt's poems are always tense and tight groups engaged in war, rescue, martydom, or crisis, and the moral values expressed are simply those of that group. In such a society the terror is not for the common enemy, even when the enemy is or seems victorious ... The real terror comes when the individual feels himself becoming an individual, pulling away from the group' (830–1).

30 In general terms, the struggle of the individual against a community social or moral garrison has been the dominant theme of the early modern novel from *The Way of All Flesh* to *Portrait of the Artist as a Young Man*.

31 Djwa, 'Canadian Contexts,' 49.

32 See note 30; also Lawrence, 419.

33 As does T.H. Huxley in his Romanes Lecture of 1893, 'Evolution and Ethics.'

34 E.J. Pratt to Douglas Bush, 24 May 1949.

35 Frye, interview with author, 23 August 1983.

36 Djwa, *The Evolutionary Vision*, 121–36.

37 Frye writes in *Fearful Symmetry*:

The worshiper of 'immanent Will' is extending the subconscious activity of the heartbeat from sense experience to the whole universe. And he does it by exactly the same process of trying to find a least common denominator for his general principles. A man, a dog and a tree are all alive; therefore life must be inherently and really some kind of 'life force' common to them which can only be identified with the lowest possible limit of life – protoplasm, perhaps. But as the boundary between living things and moving things is difficult to trace, the 'immanent Will' is bound to sink below 'life force' to take in all other forms of motion in a more inclusive generalization still.

It is much better, as in the previous case, to go to work the other way. A man, a dog and a tree are all alive; but the man is the most alive; and it is in man that we should look for the image, or form, of universal life. There can be no 'life force' apart from things possessing it: universal life is the totality of living things, and God has intelligence, judgment, purpose and desire because we are alive and possess these things. (35)

38 Ayre, *Northrop Frye: A Biography*, 336.

WORKS CITED

Ayre, John. *Northrop Frye: A Biography*. Toronto: Random House, 1989.

Djwa, Sandra. 'Canadian Contexts.' *West Coast Review* 7, no. 3 (Jan. 1973): 46–50.

- *E.J. Pratt: The Evolutionary Vision.* Toronto and Montreal: Copp Clark and McGill Queen's University Press, 1974.
- Introduction. In *E.J. Pratt: Complete Poems*, Part I, edited by Sandra Djwa and Gordon Moyles. Toronto: University of Toronto Press, 1989.

Edgar, Pelham. Review of *Canada Speaks of Britain*, by Sir Charles G.D. Roberts. *Canadian Poetry Magazine* 5, no. 4 (Aug. 1941): 41–3.

Frye, Northrop [Monocle, pseud.]. 'The Mercury Column.' *Acta Victoriana* 56 (Oct.–Nov. 1931): 38–9.
- 'The Silver Box.' *Acta Victoriana* 56 (Mar. 1932): 33.
- [H.N.F.] 'Editorial in Undress.' *Acta Victoriana* 57 (Feb. 1933): 7–8.
- 'Canada and Its Poetry.' *The Canadian Forum* 23 (Nov. 1943): 207–10.
- Introduction. *Collected Poems of E.J. Pratt.* 2d ed. Toronto: Macmillan, 1962.
- 'The Personal Legend.' *Canadian Literature* 21 (1964): 6–9.
- 'Edwin John Pratt, 1882–1964.' In *Proceedings of the Royal Society of Canada*, series 4, vol. 3 (1965): 161–5.
- Conclusion. In *Literary History of Canada: Canadian Literature in English*, edited by Carl F. Klinck. Toronto: University of Toronto Press, 1965.
- 'Preface to an Uncollected Anthology.' In *Contexts of Canadian Criticism*, edited by Eli Mandel. Chicago: University of Chicago Press, 1971. (Also published in *The Bush Garden*, 163–79. There are some textual differences between these two versions.)
- Papers. E.J. Pratt Library. Victoria University, University of Toronto, Toronto.

Lawrence, D.H. 'Study of Thomas Hardy' in *Phoenix, the Posthumous Papers of D.H. Lawrence.* Edited and with an Introduction by Edward D. McDonald. New York: Viking Press, 1936, 398–516.

Milton, John. *Complete Poems and Major Prose*, edited by Merritt Hughes. New York: Odyssey Press, 1957.

Pitt, David G. *E.J. Pratt: The Truant Years, 1882–1927.* Toronto: University of Toronto Press, 1984.

Pratt, E.J. 'The Highway.' *Acta Victoriana* 56, no. 1 (Oct.–Nov. 1931): 15.
- *E.J. Pratt: Complete Poems*, Part 1, edited by Sandra Djwa and Gordon Moyles. Toronto: University of Toronto Press, 1989.

Roberts, Charles G.D. 'Pan and the Rose.' *Acta Victoriana* 56, no. 3 (1931): 23.

Smith, A.J.M. 'Wanted – Canadian Criticism.' *The Canadian Forum* 8 (1928): 600–1.
- Introduction. In *The Book of Canadian Poetry*. Chicago: University of Chicago Press, 1943.

Wilson, Milton. *E.J. Pratt.* Toronto: McClelland and Stewart, 1969.

MILTON WILSON

Frye as Reviewer of
Canadian Poetry

My topic is not Frye and Canadian culture. Others can discuss the skill with which he relates Canadian literature, historically and geographically, to its social and natural world. I am concerned simply with those annual surveys of newly published English-Canadian poetry which he wrote during the 1950s, and, even there, not with the occasional cultural aside, but with his main business, a practical reviewer's account of the assorted poetic stuff to be found within the covers of a lot of particular books.[1]

Such practical reviewing of poetry hot off the press occurs with one minor exception nowhere else in Frye.[2] I wish to argue that the (for him) unprecedented, start-from-scratch, narrowly focused nature of the job at hand causes Frye to tap the furthest back, the most deep-rooted, of his resources and prejudices as a reader of poetry, the ones his critical career starts with. Well before these reviews, in that extraordinary 1942 essay called 'Music and Poetry,' such Frye basics stand out unmistakably, and they achieve their most notable repetition and development in the first half of *Anatomy*'s Essay 4, where he discusses the verbal rhythms of genres. I say 'notable,' but, comparatively speaking, these pages have been discussed very little.[3] One reason for the neglect is that Frye's analysis of the various patterns of verbal texture needs supplementing with his editor's preface to the *Sound and Poetry* collection of the same year, with *The Well-Tempered Critic* of 1963, and with the 'Charms and Riddles' essay of 1975.[4]

My concern is not to paraphrase Frye's overall argument from these places, but rather to point out how basic to his early criticism, and persistent later on, is that pseudo-Aristotelian *melo-lexis-opsis* scheme with which he leads into Essay 4, and then to demonstrate how some of the scheme's distinctive, even idiosyncratic, qualities stand out in his Canadian reviews, even if the terms themselves are not used. The scheme sets the musical rhythm and motion of *melos* against the imagery and stasis of *opsis*, and puts the diction, idiom, and level of usage of *lexis* in between. But there is an obvious pro-*melos* and anti-*opsis* bias. Of course the scheme, even that bias, has plenty of analogues elsewhere in *Anatomy*, but here it stands in its most immediate relation to verbal texture and to the musical concerns of that seminal 1942 article.[5]

Let me start with the bias against *opsis*. Hearing certainly dominates seeing in Essay 4, as Hamilton has emphasized (*Northrop Frye*, 163–8), at times seems to absorb it, as when imitative harmony and onomatopoeia, and even stanza forms on the page, are included to bolster the meagre pickings of *opsis*. The term's connections with any natural images of sight are minimal. The Frye who grew up against a background of modernist poetry and criticism discovered at an early age strands in them that he liked to react against. Imagism was one of these, with its supposed preference for precise visual imitation. His reaction can be found in many places; but T.S. Eliot's 1936 put-down of Milton's ear-dominated eye was a favourite target (*SP*, xxii). 'Imagism,' Frye says in that connection, 'threw a strong emphasis on *opsis*, and began an almost consciously anti-musical development' (*SM*, 142). Milton's 'musical myopia' is Frye's later parody of Eliot's view. But he makes fun not just of imagistic criticism, but also of the way poets practise their imagism, which turns out to have little of the visual precision they claim.[6]

All this is reflected in Frye's Canadian reviews. Alfred Bailey's imagistic urges prompt Frye to feel 'tired of the critical *cliché* that everything in poetry should be hard, concrete, and precise,' and to insist that you can make 'good poetry out of diffused, muzzy, and generalized language' (*BG*, 18). On Dorothy Livesay's early version of imagism, he comments wryly, 'the virtues of this idiom are not those ... that the imagists thought they were producing [but] those of gentle reverie and a relaxed circling movement,' and on her later version, 'the dangers of imagism are facility and slackness' (84–5). In A.J.M. Smith, Canada's own modernist poet and critic, 'the poetry is intensely visual and conceptual ... but it does not dance' (37). D.G. Jones is at his best 'when he is less preoccupied with visual design and lets his rhythm work itself out' (80). When Miriam Waddington (and others) are praised for 'precise observation,' the observation is almost always social not 'intensely visual' (37). There are, of course, exceptions to this nonvisual emphasis, like the praise of Louis Dudek for his 'quality of ... wet water-colour' (63).

However, the modernist strand that most bothers Frye in Smith is not imagism but the metaphysical conceit. 'Mr. Smith has the reputation,' says Frye, 'of being a metaphysical poet in the tradition of Donne,' and his 'learning perhaps does interfere with his spontaneity' (*BG*, 36–7). Donne's high reputation among up-to-date (and usually anti-Romantic) poets and professors during the twenties and thirties never seems to have meant much to Frye. In the very first of these Canadian reviews, he writes of James Wreford: 'Metaphysical poetry is not a good influence on him' (2). High praise for Earle Birney's *Trial of a City* or P.K. Pages's *The Metal and the Flower* does not prevent him from complaining about 'a few gingerbread conceits' (17) in the one and about 'a conceit ... squeezed to a pulp ... or dragged in by a too restless ingenuity' (39) in the other. A poem by Patrick Anderson 'belongs to that dreary metaphysical interregnum from which poetry now seems to be slowly recovering' (24). In a kind of paradox, the poet praised for the undissociated sensibility ascribed to the metaphysicals by Eliot is the very un-Donnian James Reaney. But when Anne Wilkinson speaks of a snowfall as 'Immaculate conception in a cloud / Made big by polar ghost,' he just calls it 'bad metaphysical poetry' (5). Frye's practical literary ideal (exemplified in Blake's basic unsophistication, despite the elaborate superstructure) remains a kind of popular simplicity, especially in lyric poetry. Observe how he introduces the Anderson review: 'the technical development of a modern lyrical poet is normally from obscurity to simplicity ... he is likely to pass through a social, allegorical, or metaphysical phase ... Finally ... the texture simplifies, meaning and imagery become transparent, and the poetry becomes a pleasure instead of a duty to read' (22–3).[7]

But Frye's anti-*opsis* negatives can be overwhelmed by pro-*melos* positives. He explains at length how Reaney's wide-ranging versification 'puts on an amazing technical show' (*BG*, 89). But instead of Frye's frequent rhythmic analyses, I turn to a more distinctive aspect of his pursuit of *melos*: a fondness for metaphorically reproducing in his own prose a poem's characteristic tone and rhythm. It is a very long-standing fondness. I quote from a revised version of a 1942 passage: 'when we find sharp barking accents, long cumulative rhythms sweeping lines into paragraphs, crabbed and obscure language, mouthfuls of consonants, the spluttering rumble of long words, and the bite and grip of heavily stressed monosyllables, we are most likely to be reading a poet who is being influenced by music' ('Music and Poetry,' 169). Here Browning is the evidence at hand. But Blake's septenarian lines get similar treatment, climaxing with 'the machine-gun fire of auxiliaries and prepositions' (*FS*, 184). Frye is obviously delighted to find that Blake's hero of the imagination, Los, centres his activity on 'the rhythmic clang of the hammer' (*FS*, 292), and that even as engraver Blake focuses on the rhythmic movement of that 'bounding line' (*FS*, 97). In the Canadian reviews when Frye describes 'the percussive vocabulary and wrenched syntax, the pounding and clanging of monosyllables' (*BG*, 106) in Heather Spears's *Asylum Poems*, we are reminded of those earlier descriptions. But sound patterns can stimulate Frye's tropes even more inventively. I think of Fred Cogswell's 'clumping sonnets with rhymes like typewriter bells' (118), of how Alfred G. Bailey's 'accents stick spikily through the metrical feet' and how 'he pulls the last syllable of the line off its stem, like a child picking flowers' (17); of Douglas LePan's 'barbed-wire entanglement of rhyme' (27). Very different, but related to the same *melos*-sensibility, is a comment on Jay Macpherson: 'her melody is of that shaped and epigrammatic quality which in music is called tune' (73).

I can imagine one reaction, perhaps puzzled, to what I have said so far. I have suggested that a few of Frye's rhetorical distinctions from Essay 4 may be implied in his reviewing practice. What about *Anatomy*'s fondness for sweeping and schematic critical categories of other kinds? A further, related question might be: when do we get to myths and archetypes? I will not say too much about my first question. Systematic and explicit organizing principles are relatively rare in these surveys, and when tried they are usually perfunctory and rarely maintained. Of course abstract schemes meet at least some resistance in that early criticism whose relevance I keep invoking. They become fully naturalized, even compulsive, as Frye's theoretical urges develop, but are nevertheless for him a kind of acquired taste, as if he is gradually coming to terms with Blake's systematic 'excess.' In his 1963 essay 'The Road of Excess,' Frye remembers one of his marginalia in his undergraduate edition of Blake. A striking passage of schematic, indeed geometrical, imagery in *Jerusalem* nevertheless includes the phrase 'going forward.' Frye's antistasis note reads, 'something moves, anyhow.' Even in *Fearful Symmetry* his uneasiness about Blake's 'I must create a system' has to be eased by an understanding that it cannot be what Blake rejects as 'mathematical form' (*FI*, 231). In a 1947 essay he thinks disparagingly of Yeats's commentary on Blake as 'an overschematized commentary full of false symmetries' which 'includes all the Euclidean paraphernalia of diagrams, figures, tables of symbols and the like' (*FI*, 232).[8] For a single example from his Canadian reviews of how symmetry can be less than thoroughly applied, I turn to the survey of 1955. Frye starts it with an extreme simplification of patterns currently being assembled for *Anatomy*. 'Poetry ... has two poles,' he asserts, one 'formal' and the other 'representational,' and then includes as many relevant aspects as he can think of under each (*BG*, 44). In due course he divides up the four important volumes of new poetry two and two. Wilfred Watson and Anne Wilkinson are more formal, while Miriam Waddington and Irving Layton (a remarkable pairing) are more representational. Let me just focus on how this works for Layton. At the end of that polarizing introduction, Frye has already started to blur the distinctions between his poles, and even before he gets to Layton, he has dropped 'representational' for based on 'personal experience' (*BG*, 46). As the practical reviewing of *The Cold Green Element* proceeds, aspects more suited to Frye's formal pole flood in, culminating in 'the ironic personal myth' of the title poem, with its 'hanged god ... torn apart and distributed through the landscape,' which turns out to be 'the same image as that of [Wilkinson's] central poem' (53). Frye likes to try out categorical distinctions on Layton ('not a satirist at all, but an erudite elegaic poet,' according to an earlier review [41]), but when he gets to the collected edition of 1959 he just uses a kind of god's-plenty listing of all the very heterogeneous things a poet can do (116–17).

Then there is my second question. Frye's most familiar reputation is as a mythopoeic critic. To what extent do these reviews exemplify it? His favourite mythopoeic ingredient elsewhere is that rhythmic plot-movement ahead and around which he calls *mythos* and uses with such outstanding results in defining the arguments of comedy and romance. The lyric poetry that dominates these reviews offers little scope for such *mythos*. To be sure, when the opportunity comes, with E.J. Pratt's *Towards the Last Spike*, Frye seizes it and, despite the fact that the poem's rhetoric has very limited appeal for him, enters enthusiastically into its unclimactic kind of narrative without narrative (*BG*, 11–12). Displaying what Eli Mandel calls 'uncanny ... prescience,' he sees Pratt's version of *mythos* as a foretaste of technical problems for the long poems that come after the fifties ('Northrop Frye,' 289). Birney's large-scale dramatic poem, *Trial of a City*, provides a related opportunity.

The lyric dominance means that Frye will usually see myth only in its static shape, rather than with its active movement, as archetypes or symbolic levels, not as *mythoi*. These ingredients may represent a less deep-rooted part of Frye, but during the fifties they are being vigorously pursued in the aftermath of *Fearful Symmetry* and for the sake of the imminent *Anatomy of Criticism*. As reviewer Frye finds them very convenient for an opening outline of the themes and conventions that make up a poet's particular world. He tells us that Page's symbolism operates on three levels, comprising (imagistically) the sea at the bottom, 'angels and abstract patterns in white' at the top, and, in between, a 'level of metal and flower, rose garden and barbed wire' (*BG*, 39). These are not exactly the levels of that great chain of archetypal being that he presents in the first half of *Anatomy*'s Essay 3, but they belong recognizably to the same world. On the sword and the net in the title of LePan's collection, Frye hangs an introductory explanation of its overall symbolic design (26). Daryl Hine's brief and still immature collection, *The Carnal and the Crane*, is paid the compliment of a subtle and lengthy definition of its incarnation-surrounded underworld in the context of a wide range of classical and Christian archetypes (76–8). The review of Wilfred Watson's *Friday's Child* is mainly taken up with defining the elaborate archetypal pattern of his two worlds (real and intelligible) and of their apocalyptic reconciliation (46–7). In many such outlines (although not with Page certainly) the archetypal description is at the expense of the rhetorical criticism which (along with the action of *mythos*) I have supposed to be part of Frye's deepest stratum. The skilful simplicity of Watson's handling of his conventional design is praised, but, apart from one line called 'breath-taking' (48), the many quotations are not there for the quality of their utterance. Similarly, Frye moves from the 'richly suggestive intelligence' of Ronald Bates's pattern in *The Wandering World* to what is nevertheless 'unsatisfactory' in the texture of his writing (115). When he does find the texture satisfying, Frye may avoid attributing too much of the poetry's value to its explicit mythopoeia. This reluctance comes out most obviously in the pages on Macpherson's *The Boatman*. While Frye spends a good deal of time defining the context of particular myths within which the book achieves its formal existence, he also (as in an earlier Macpherson review) emphasizes myth as container of the poet's personal and literary emotion, as 'reservoir of feeling' (56). Mythic self-consciousness for either poem or reader is minimized. Her 'myths,' he writes, 'flow into the poems: the poems do not point to them' (74). Myths may be echoed, 'but the lines are not dependent on the echoes, either for their meaning or their poetic value' (75). Frye does not see respect for formal elements such as myth (or metrics) as important signs that Canadian poetry is becoming less amateurish, but presenting the poet of *The Boatman* as a learned poetic mythographer is precisely what he is not trying to do. He finally stresses, not her 'density,' but a 'timeless' and 'transparent' 'style' (74).

'Style' leads me back to those basic rhetorical distinctions. I have said little about *lexis*, the middle and most loosely defined member of Frye's trio of terms, the place where *melos* and *opsis* mingle with each other and which centres on diction, idiom, syntax, voice – on stylistic level of usage. It is being invoked when Frye finds Raymond Souster's epigrams, usually so successful in their concerned but objective social observation of the submerged strata of urban life, sometimes being spoiled by a 'grousing' (*BG*, 62) reflective voice, by 'the moral exasperation that paralyses every comment except the most obvious one' (97). He has similar things to say about the intrusive flatness of the reflective voice in certain of Louis Dudek's poems (53–4). After a *melos* account of John Heath as a jazz pianist whose harmony is more striking than his rhythm, Frye shifts to idiom and syntax, describing how 'most of the protective grease of articles and conjunctions is removed and subject, predicate, object, grind on each other and throw out metaphorical sparks' (104). Frank Scott 'has brought to a high level of technical competence a kind of meditative musing poem through which the longer words of ordinary speech ripple with great colloquial freedom' (38). His account of Reaney's cycle-of-the-year pattern and metrical range in *A Suit of Nettles* does not (in Frye's words) leave 'space ... to dwell on the innumerable felicities of the writing' (90). But a long quotation about one barnyard creature, he cannot resist. His comment on its rhetoric unites the *melos* of 'final spondees ... used so persistently' and the *lexis* of 'tricks of inverted constructions' with the fluttering or zigzagging or upside-down-hanging *opsis* of a bat. Here are charms and riddles indeed. Frye's response to tone of voice and level of usage comes out with special sensitivity on George Johnston's *The Cruising Auk*. It exists throughout the review, even when he is ostensibly summarizing Johnston's overall patterns, but it is underlined at the end. Frye especially praises 'his ability to incorporate the language of the suburbs into his own diction. He does not write in the actual vulgate, but he manages to suggest with great subtlety the emotional confusions behind the pretentious diction and vague syntax of ordinary speech ... Or the elusiveness of large ideas as their shadows pass over an inarticulate mind' (112). The last of many comments on Irving Layton is a *lexis* one: 'if one tires of anything,' Frye writes, 'it is, perhaps, the sense of too insistent a speaking voice, and of being never out of listening range of it ... There is a great variety of theme ... but little variety of tone' (117–18).

In the retrospective paragraphs that end his last annual survey, Frye sees evaluative comparisons with the great works of other times and places as not what these Canadian reviews are trying to offer (*BG*, 126). Yet they do contain plenty of sharp critical judgments. While his mythopoeic criticism allows him to enter a poet's world, but does not necessarily push him to do much more, his deep-rooted rhetorical criticism always seems to be there to take up the evaluative slack.

NOTES

1 Reprinted, nearly in full, in *BG*, 1–127.

2 The reviews are also, even more than those broader essays on Canadian culture, written for an intimate audience quite remote from the international one aimed at in *Fearful Symmetry, Anatomy of Criticism,* and their like. This distinctive awareness that the poets being reviewed are somehow close at hand is an inescapable part of the task he has taken on. I do not just mean academic or private closeness, although of course Frye often finds himself reviewing his former teachers and fellow students, his friends and colleagues, not to mention students he taught in classes. I am thinking also of a more inclusive, even country-wide sort of closeness. Frye here demonstrates in practice what he argues for elsewhere, his sense that community and communication, even literary intimacy, are a characteristic of Canada, in spite of, or perhaps because of, the obvious obstacles. Where else could (or would) Frye, after complaining about a poet's satiric epigrams, take the personal opportunity to add, 'the best of them, I blushingly report, being aimed at me' (*BG*, 21).

3 I can think of just one book (Andrew Welsh's *Roots of the Lyric*) that builds on them, and just one (Hamilton's *Northrop Frye: Anatomy of His Criticism*) that subjects them to really discriminating criticism.

4 The last is collected in *SM*, 123–47.

5 See *AC*, 243–81 and the whole of 'Music and Poetry.' Among the analogues elsewhere would be *mythos* against *dianoia* and the fictional against the thematic.

6 For Eliot's non-imagistic imagism, see *TSE*, 35–6.

7 My sense of Frye's limited empathy with the metaphysicals goes back a long way. I took an undergraduate course in Renaissance poetry and prose with Frye about fifty years ago, and I still remember vividly his teaching of Donne's 'A Valediction: Forbidding Mourning' as a kind of trial-and-error-and-success sequence of conceits. He remarked casually that, after Donne drops that unsatisfactory conceit about 'gold to airy thinness beat,' he at last finds the circle conceit that works. Even in the *Anatomy* one is struck by how infrequently Donne is referred to, not just unlike the expected Romantics, but even compared to an Augustan like Pope.

8 Reading that complaint about Yeats's overschematic criticism reminds one that it is not until *The Great Code* (1982) that Frye himself really allows a 'Euclidean paraphernalia' visually to take over their full share of pages.

WORKS CITED

Frye, Northrop. 'Music and Poetry.' *University of Toronto Quarterly* 11 (1942): 167–79.

Hamilton, A.C. *Northrop Frye: An Anatomy of His Criticism.* Toronto: University of Toronto Press, 1990.

Mandel, Eli. 'Northrop Frye and the Canadian Literary Tradition.' In *Centre and Labyrinth*, edited by Eleanor Cook et al. Toronto: University of Toronto Press, 1983.

Welsh, Andrew. *Roots of Lyric Poetry.* Princeton: Princeton University Press, 1978.

DAVID STAINES

Frye: Canadian Critic/Writer

Frye's writings on Canadian painting, literature, and culture have not always met with approval. There were some, of course, who did acknowledge his singular importance. In 1976 Malcolm Ross observed that Frye, 'more than anyone else, put into perspective and thus into a kind of hierarchical order and coherence the nagging questions that have beset our criticism' ('Critical Theory,' 164). The same year Sandra Djwa noted that Frye's early reviews and essays were 'to provide the critical framework for much of the present writing and study of Canadian poetry' ('The Canadian Forum,' 24). And three years later Clara Thomas asserted that Frye's writings 'offered us liberation from a colonial cringe towards all literature, especially our own ... His work has dignified the study and the teaching of all literature and especially, for me and others like me, the study and teaching of our own' ('Towards Freedom,' 7, 11).

But there have also been many detractors. In 1958 Louis Dudek dismissed Frye as 'the Great White Whale of Canadian criticism' ('Frye Again,' 26). Ten years later, George Bowering wrote that the major concerns of Frye's writings 'seem dated, no matter what truth may lie in them. They are filled with nostalgia for the critical rape of the unconscious that happened in the twenties and thirties. And they are sometimes, for all Frye's talk of the imagination, quite turgidly clerical' ('Why James Reaney is a Better Poet,' 41). In 1978 Robin Mathews denounced Frye as 'one of the worst – certainly one of the most arrogant – critics of Canadian literature' and claimed that his critical writings 'guarantee our quiet colonialism by promulgating a kind of anaemic resignation' (Canadian Literature, 136, 170). And in 1987 Janice Kulyk Keefer was consistently disdainful in her study of Maritime literature: 'Frye's Laurentian paradigm of Canada can, in fact, be seen as an incidental demolition of the Maritimes and that region's vision of the reality it constitutes' (*Under Eastern Eyes*, 27).

The recurring dismissal of his Canadian studies suggests a misreading and/or a misappreciation of them, and Eli Mandel has correctly noted that misreadings of Frye's writings on Canadian literature 'form one of the fascinating chapters of Canadian literary history' ('Northrop Frye,' 284). The title of my essay, 'Frye: Canadian Critic/Writer,' underlines my theme, that Frye is a writer, a writer who deliberately chose criticism as his creative mode, and that his Canadian writings occupy a significant and unique place in his work. In his preface to *The Bush Garden*, Frye refers to the essays in this retrospective collection as 'episodes in a writing career which has been mainly concerned with world literature and has addressed an international reading public, and yet has always been rooted in Canada and has drawn its essential characteristics from there' (i). These 'episodes,' only nineteen in *The Bush Garden*, represent slightly more than one-fifth of his Canadian critical studies. Frye wrote more than ninety reviews, editorials, and essays on Canada. He began with a review of Canadian painting in *The Canadian Forum* of January 1939. And he ended, in his literary criticism, with an afterword to Ethel Wilson's *Hetty Dorval* in the New Canadian Library in September 1990 and, in his cultural studies, with an address two months later to the Social Sciences and Humanities Research Council of Canada at the University of Toronto; in the latter, which was to be his last formal address, he reiterated his vision of Canada, its history, its culture, and his own hope for the future of a tolerant and cosmopolitan country.

These Canadian writings form a whole and reveal a movement from Frye as reviewer to Frye as cultural theorist, a movement that parallels to some degree his shift in his non-Canadian writings from literary critic to protostructuralist. And it deserves emphasis that it is Frye's Canadian writings, which span nearly fifty-two years, that led him from and through reviewing into literary criticism and then into cultural theory. If we see his Canadian studies as a corpus of a writer, we may advance from his detractors' misappreciation and dismissal of these, and move on to a proper appreciation of Frye's writing about things Canadian. Historicizing Frye in his milieu, that milieu which he often claimed as so crucial to his critical thinking, does justice to his place as a Canadian writer. It also suggests that his detractors may be much narrower than they claim Frye himself to be in their attitude to his Canadian writings.

As a student of Canada, Frye began his work as a reviewer, not in his well-known reviews in *University of Toronto Quarterly*, but much earlier, in *The Canadian Forum*. As a reviewer, he saw himself, as he later reflected, 'As a nurse, that is, as somebody bringing along a culture that was not yet wholly mature but showed so many signs of it' (*NFC*, 135). The reviews in *The Canadian Forum* and his role as managing editor of the magazine from 1948 to 1950 form the first period of Frye's Canadian writings.

In this first period of twenty-six essays and reviews, Frye examines Canadian paintings, poetry, and some fiction to find the underlying themes and symbols that seem to characterize his own culture. In these early writings, he moves quickly from the canvas or the text to generalized observations. His first Canadian study, for example, 'Canadian Art in London,' examines briefly the Group of Seven:

> The Group was not badly represented, though I should have preferred bigger and better MacDonalds, and at least one Lawren Harris abstract picture, not only for its own merit but to show that the Group effected a revolution in rhythm and outline as well as in colour. And a good chance to make something of Varley, who seems to me subtler and more emotionally precise an artist than Morrice, was passed up ... The Group of Seven put on canvas the clear outlines of the Canadian landscape in the hard Canadian light, and provided a formula for bright posterish painting, often with abstract tendencies. (304–5)

Two years later, in 1941, a comparison of the paintings of Tom Thomson and Horatio Walker begins no longer with the paintings themselves but with the abstract concepts and even archetypal patterns suggested by them:

> The countries men live in feed their minds as much as their bodies: the bodily food they provide is absorbed in farms and cities: the mental, in religion and arts. In all communities this process of material and imaginative *digestion* goes on. Thus a large tract of vacant land may well affect the people living near it as too much cake does a small boy: an unknown but quite possibly horrible Something stares at them in the dark: hide under the bedclothes as long as they will, sooner or later they must stare back. Explorers, tormented by a sense of the unreality of the unseen, are first: pioneers and traders follow. But the land is still not imaginatively absorbed, and the incubus moves on to haunt the artists. ('Canadian and Colonial Painting,' 377)

Two years later, Frye writes about the landscape of Canadian poetry: 'Canadian poetry is at its best a poetry of incubus and *cauchemar*, the

source of which is the unusually exposed contact of the poet with nature
which Canada provides. Nature is seen by the poet, first as unconsciousness, then as a kind of existence which is cruel and meaningless, then as
the source of the cruelty and subconscious stampedings within the
human mind' ('Canada and Its Poetry,' 210). Already one can see in these
early remarks Frye's characteristic drive towards some greater synthesis,
a re-viewing of the work in a context whose centre is Canadian and
whose circumference is the total structure of the Judaeo-Christian
imagination.

The second period of Frye's Canadian writings centres on the 1950s
when he took over from a dying E.K. Brown the duty of reviewing the
year's poetry for *University of Toronto Quarterly* – and he did regard it as
a duty and a responsibility. These reviews demanded a more constant
and more detailed attention to Canadian literature than did those of the
preceding decade. Given the yearly task of reading all the poetry
published in Canada, Frye approached it as an opportunity to work out
his growing understanding of mythic patterns within the specific
parameters of one art form in one country. These reviews were, as he
later reflected, 'an essential piece of "field work" to be carried on while
I was working out a comprehensive critical theory. I was fascinated to
see how the echoes and ripples of the great mythopoeic age kept moving
through Canada, and taking a form there that they could not have taken
elsewhere' (*BG*, viii–ix). Deliberately and, I suspect, happily, Frye 'dealt
with Canadian poetry for the reader of the *Quarterly*,' to use his own
words, 'as though no other poetry were available to him' (*NFC*, 135). As
a reviewer, he remained the committed, caring, and consistent writer,
seeing his function as a constructive critic, as a 'nurse' helping writers
and, more importantly, readers:

> The reviewer knows that he will be read by the poets, but he is not address-
> ing them, except indirectly ... The reviewer's audience is the community of
> actual and potential readers of poetry. His task is to show what is available
> in poetic experience, to suggest that reading current poetry is an essential
> cultural activity, at least as important as keeping up with current plays or
> concerts or fiction ... The reviewer must take poetry as he finds it, must con-
> stantly struggle for the standards of good and bad in all types of poetry,
> must always remember that a preference for any one kind of poetry over
> another kind is, for him, laziness and incompetence ... The reviewer is not
> concerned with the vague relativities of 'greatness,' but with the positive
> merits of what is before him. And every genuine poet is entitled to be read
> with the maximum sympathy and concentration. ('Letters in Canada 1959,'
> 458–9)

In this final review for *University of Toronto Quarterly*, he concluded: 'The appearance of a fine new book of poems in Canada is a historical event, and its readers should be aware that they are participating in history' (460).

Frye's wish for his readers is his own sense of his mission: situated in a particular moment of Canadian literary history, he considers himself 'participating in history,' and the reviewer must read 'with the maximum sympathy and concentration.'

Frye's concept of the reviewer is not dissimilar to the position of E.K. Brown, a critic Frye admired and his predecessor on the poetry pages of *University of Toronto Quarterly*. For Brown,

> The criticism of poetry as of any art must first interpret. If in the exercise of his interpretative function a critic writes chiefly of what is genuine in a poem, what is notable, what is *there*, rather than of what is spurious, what is negligible, what is not there, his doing so need not mean that he is abandoning another of his functions, the making of judgments. Careful interpretation, conducted with insight and a measure of sympathy, must precede judgment, and in writing of recent or contemporary poets it is much wiser to make sure that one's interpretation is adequate than to press on judgment. ('Letters in Canada 1948,' 255)

Like Frye, Brown refers to the need for sympathy from the reviewer, though he places more emphasis on the interpretative function of the reviewer.

For Frye, these reviews of Canadian poetry, like his earlier reviews, serve the same function in his Canadian writings as does his study of Blake in his non-Canadian writings. 'I think it advisable for every critic proposing to devote his life to literary scholarship,' Frye wrote, 'to pick a major writer of literature as a kind of spiritual preceptor for himself, whatever the subject of his thesis. I am not speaking, of course, of any sort of moral model, but it seems to me that growing up inside a mind so large that one has no sense of claustophobia [*sic*] within it is an irreplaceable experience in humane studies. Some kind of transmission by seed goes on here too' ('The Search for Acceptable Words,' 19).

For Frye's non-Canadian writings, the major writer was, of course, William Blake, and Frye worked his way through Blake's writings to become the creator of *Anatomy of Criticism*. The earlier account of the order and structure of Blake's symbology in *Fearful Symmetry* led directly to Frye's next book, for *Anatomy of Criticism* studies on a grand scale the archetypal or mythic patterns in literature through critical techniques already explored in *Fearful Symmetry*. The student of Blake could later agree with his critics that his writings were a precursor of structuralism, and his insistence on larger patterns may fairly be described as proto-structuralist in its anticipation of later critics' similar concern with schemata and structures.

But Frye, the reviewer of Canadian painting and literature, did not have 'a major writer of literature as a kind of spiritual preceptor' in his own country. In 1965 he observed that his country had 'produced no author who is a classic in the sense of possessing a vision greater in kind than that of his best readers ... There is no Canadian writer of whom we can say what we can say of the world's major writers, that their readers can grow up inside their work without ever being aware of a circumference' (Conclusion [1965], 821). Instead, in lieu of the absent master-worker, Frye collectively made the paintings and books he reviewed his spiritual preceptor, and these works of art serve as his literary training, which in turn prepared for the third and final period of his Canadian writings, those later commentaries that embody a vision of the country, its history, its culture, and its future. Through his reviews, then, Frye became a cultural theorist who articulated the myths he saw shaping the paintings he examined and the books he read. And this third and final period that begins in the sixties includes no reviews but many commentaries and essays on the cultural life of his country.

Frye the reviewer becomes, therefore, Frye the cultural theorist, the mythmaker and the mapmaker of, and for, his own country. In Canada's centennial year of 1967 he affirmed: 'The Canada to which we really do owe loyalty is the Canada that we have failed to create. In a year bound to be full of discussions of our identity, I should like to suggest that our identity, like the real identity of all nations, is the one that we have failed to achieve. It is expressed in our culture, but not attained in our life, just as Blake's new Jerusalem to be built in England's green and pleasant land is no less a genuine ideal for not having been built there' (MC, 122–3). And that identity has found definition in Frye's challenging explorations of the myths he sees as characterizing his country. From his reviews, Frye turned to a consistent articulation of many of the myths that he first found in the paintings and literary works he reviewed. And these myths have become part of our critical vocabulary, indeed of our very language: Canadian nature with its bleak and terrifying desolation; the garrison mentality, that closely knit and beleaguered society at odds with its environment; and, perhaps most crucially, the observation, often repeated and often pondered, that 'Canadian sensibility has been profoundly disturbed, not so much by our famous problem of identity, important as that is, as by a series of paradoxes in what confronts that identity. It is less perplexed by the question "Who am I?" than by some such riddle as "Where is here?"' (Conclusion [1965], 826).

By situating Frye historically in his culture and its development, by seeing him situate himself first in his country's works of art, by seeing him regard his own reviewing as 'participating in history,' we can see his final function in Canada as that of a cultural theorist, giving a voice to his land. And his Canadian writings form a significant part of his total corpus, what, for example, *Seven Rivers of Canada* became to Hugh MacLennan's literary career. But unlike MacLennan, who ventured out of fiction for his geographical and social studies, Frye stayed within criticism, producing steadily and consistently a body of Canadian writings, a legacy that provided, and provides, a context for defining some of the boundaries of critical inquiry about our culture.

When he graduated from Victoria College in 1933, Frye wanted to be a writer. He returned home to Moncton to see if he could earn his living by writing, hoping to publish short stories in magazines. During the next two years, he wrote one novel and had an outline for a second about a couple deeply in love, one of them religious, the other communist.[1] But he came to realize that fiction was not possible for him, and his reviewing, which began at this time, led him into criticism as an alternative to writing fiction. Here he achieved success. Historicizing his Canadian writings reveals a three-phase pattern or progression that characterizes his long commitment to the exploration and elucidation of his country and its cultural life.

Those who dismiss Frye's Canadian writings provide a final commentary on my theme, and their attitude only affirms the lasting significance of Frye's Canadian corpus.

In the Alexander Lectures given at the University of Toronto in 1969, W. Jackson Bate examined his sense of how the legacy of the past bears on writers in his *The Burden of the Past and the English Poet*: 'the remorseless deepening of self-consciousness, before the rich and intimidating legacy of the past, has become the greatest single problem that modern art ... has had to face' (4). While focusing on English poetry, he observed that the 'burden of the past' does not seem to cripple writers in the critical mode:

> The critic, biographer, or historian, in his consideration of the arts, has by definition a different vocation ... and in his own personal experience the situation we mention does not press home to him to the same degree or in the same way. He may have his own anxieties and competitions in the face of previous achievement, and these may certainly cripple rather than

inspire him in his own range and magnanimity as a humanist. But the accumulation of past work from which he may feel tempted or even forced to differ in order to secure identity ... is chronologically far more limited. It is primarily the product of the last fifty years. (7–8)

Since 1969, literary theory has grown in stature, significance, and volume. The literary critic too suffers, consciously or not, from 'the accumulation of past work.' Frye's detractors too suffer from this 'burden of the past,' and rather than acknowledge this anxiety, they continue to find fault with his theories, not realizing that so much of their writing uses Frye's enunciated myths as a point of departure.

In *The Burden of the Past and the English Poet*, Bate refers – and acknowledges indebtedness – to Frye's criticism. He also provides a fitting conclusion to any assessment of Frye as a Canadian critic/writer. 'The greatest single cultural problem we face, assuming that we physically survive,' Bate concludes, is 'how to use a heritage, when we know and admire so much about it, how to grow by means of it, how to acquire our own "identities," how to be ourselves' (134). And an old epigram about Plato is an all-too-fitting epigram about Frye in relation to other Canadian critics, his detractors included: in whatever direction you happen to be going, you always meet Frye on his way back.

NOTE

1 Ayre, *Northrop Frye: A Biography*, 116.

WORKS CITED

Ayre, John. *Northrop Frye: A Biography*. Toronto: Random House, 1989.
Bate, W. Jackson. *The Burden of the Past and the English Poet*. Cambridge, Mass.: Belknap, 1970.
Bowering, George. 'Why James Reaney is a Better Poet (1) than any Northrop Frye poet (2) than he used to be.' *Canadian Literature* 36 (Spring 1968): 40–9.
Brown, E.K. 'Letters in Canada 1948: Poetry.' *University of Toronto Quarterly* 18 (April 1949): 254–62.
Dudek, Louis. ' "Frye Again" (But Don't Miss Souster).' *Delta* 5 (October 1958): 26–27.
Djwa, Sandra. 'The *Canadian Forum*: Literary Catalyst.' *Studies in Canadian Literature* l (Winter 1976): 7–25.

Frye, Northrop. 'Canada and Its Poetry.' *Canadian Forum* 23 (December 1943): 207–10.

– 'Canadian and Colonial Painting.' *Canadian Forum* 20 (March 1941): 377–8.

– Canadian Art in London.' *Canadian Forum* 18 (January 1939): 304–5.

– Conclusion. In *Literary History of Canada: Canadian Literature in English*, edited by Carl F. Klinck. 1st ed. Toronto: University of Toronto Press, 1965.

– 'Letters in Canada 1959: Poetry.' *University of Toronto Quarterly* 29 (July 1960): 440–60.

– 'The Search for Acceptable Words.' *Daedalus* 102 (Spring 1973): 11–26.

Keefer, Janice Kulyk. *Under Eastern Eyes: A Critical Reading of Maritime Fiction.* Toronto: University of Toronto Press, 1987.

Mandel, Eli. 'Northrop Frye and the Canadian Literary Tradition.' In *Centre and Labyrinth: Essays in Honour of Northrop Frye*, edited by Eleanor Cook et al. Toronto: University of Toronto Press, 1983.

Mathews, Robin. *Canadian Literature: Surrender or Revolution.* Toronto: Steel Rail Educational Publishing, 1978.

Ross, Malcolm. 'Critical Theory: Some Trends.' In *Literary History of Canada: Canadian Literature in English*, Vol. 3, edited by Carl F. Klinck. 2nd ed. Toronto: University of Toronto Press, 1976.

Thomas, Clara. 'Towards Freedom: The Work of Northrop Frye.' *CEA Critic* 42 (November 1979): 7–11.

CLARA THOMAS

Celebrations:
Frye's *The Double Vision*
and Margaret Laurence's
Dance on the Earth

'And if the worst of all came upon us, if we had to fight to the last ditch for our freedom, with our brothers killed and our cities in smoking ruins, our poets would still stand over against us, and break out in hymns to the glory of God and in praise of his beautiful world' (*DG*, 124).

> I see old women dancing
> dancing on the earth
> I hear old women singing
> singing children's birth
> ...
> dance on, old women,
> dance amidst the strife,
> sing out, old women,
> sing for life
>
> I am one among them
> dancing on the earth,
> mourning, grieving, raging,
> yet jubilating birth.[1]

Ten years ago, I published an article called 'Towards Freedom: The Work of Margaret Laurence and Northrop Frye' (in *Essays on Canadian Writing*). I was impelled to do that as a debt of gratitude to the two writers who had, in my time, most strikingly and effectively liberated Canadian writers, readers, and scholars from the lingering trauma of the 'colonial cringe.' Laurence's Manawaka 'has established the authenticity of its characters and culture as part of Canada's imaginative landscape,' I wrote. It is living for her readers, densely peopled with the Curries and Shipleys, Tonnerres, MacLeods, Connors, Camerons, Logans and Gunns, with all their dilemmas, aspirations, triumphs and tragedies. Hagar, Rachel, Stacey, Vanessa, and Morag all free themselves within the limits of their situations and capabilities; the cumulative effect of the Manawaka cycle is profoundly emancipating' ('Towards Freedom,' 81). Similarly, from Frye's *Fearful Symmetry* and *Anatomy of Criticism* to his Conclusion to *Literary History of Canada*, and on through *The Bush Garden* and *Divisions on a Ground* to *The Great Code* and *Words with Power*, we have been given an unbroken line of illumination, inspiration, and the blessed assurance that we were not on the fringes but on the inside of a splendid, many-faceted, ultimately unified literary enterprise, moving finally to the goal that has been intrinsic to all of them through the years, 'a community of vision.' The final testaments of Northrop Frye and Margaret Laurence, *Dance on the Earth* and *The Double Vision*, both of them published posthumously, are in the truest sense, 'celebrations,' harvests of experience and conviction extended to us in the ways their writers knew best. Words with Power.

Margaret Laurence's convictions and affirmations first took shape in her novels and then, in her later years, in the essays she wrote and speeches she gave in aid of the many causes to which she was devoted. Her final memoir is a breakaway from both of these channels of communication; it is the testament of her own life directed as a legacy first to her daughter, her nieces, her friends, and then to all her readers. Frye's insights were embodied in his decades of lectures, as well as the books, articles, and addresses for which he was known world-wide. But his final work, *The Double Vision*, was, like Margaret's, more intimately directed, its first three chapters delivered to the alumni of Emmanuel College, his theological associates, and, in a very real sense, his lifelong, special classmates. The honorary degree, Doctor of Sacred Letters, that Margaret accepted in 1982 from Frye as Chancellor of Victoria University meant something very special to her, vindicating the thrust and intention of all her work, under threat at that time from the censors whose depredations were so hurtful to her. To me, watching the ceremony, it was a unique experience, witnessing the coming together as peers of the writer and the scholar for both of whom I felt inexpressible affection and admiration.

One from Moncton, one from Neepawa, and each of them embodying one of the powerful essences of Canadianism – Ross Woodman described *The Great Code* as providing 'a comprehensive account of the roots of the English Canadian Protestant vision' ('From the Belly of the

Whale,' 128). All of Margaret's writing, as well as all of the public responsibilities she accepted, grew from the same roots. But in each case the well-spring can be more specifically located, I believe, in that powerful religious reform movement we know as the social gospel. As Richard Allen defines the movement in *The Social Passion*, 'The social gospel rested on the premise that Christianity was a social religion, concerned, when the misunderstanding of the ages was stripped away, with the quality of human relations on this earth ... it was a call for men to find the meaning of their lives in seeking to realize the Kingdom of God in the very fabric of society' (4). On his mother's side, Frye came out of a rigorously fundamental application of Methodism. When he arrived at Victoria a few years after church union, a reforming liberalism was in the air. In a CBC interview with David Cayley, he acknowledged the Methodist roots of his thought and action: 'My religious background really *did* shape almost everything ... I've always been a bit of a pushover for anything that can be sold to me as a public service.'[2] In Allen's words again: 'It was not surprising ... that, as the social problems of a growing industrial urban society multiplied and as new currents of social thought developed, the urgency of the evangelical concern to save this man now, should have been transferred to the social sphere and social action become virtually a religious rite' (*The Social Passion*, 356).

Margaret was born the year after church union, to a formerly Presbyterian, now United Church, family, and it was taken for granted that her post-secondary education would be at the United College in Winnipeg where, as she often said, 'the social gospel aspect of the church was in the very air we breathed.' By the time she graduated she recognized herself as a political person, 'a Christian Social Democrat,' and her immediate post-college work, on two highly politicized newspapers, Winnipeg's *The Westerner* and *The Winnipeg Citizen*, further confirmed her socialist bent (*Dance on the Earth*, 106–8). She often described herself as a reformer, not a revolutionary, and her credo was repeatedly expressed in the articles and public speeches of her final decade: 'I would call myself an unorthodox Christian ... A lot of questions of faith have concerned me throughout my adult life. One thing I feel is terribly important: the social gospel. It is not enough simply to say 'my religion saves my own soul.' It is essential to go out in the world, to proclaim and to work *against* injustice.'[3] She wrote the final summary of her conviction in the last pages of *Dance on the Earth*:

We must continue in every way we can to protest non-violently against social injustice, infringement of civil liberties, cruelties, and the indifference of governments ... wherever these occur. We must continue to proclaim those things we believe in – the possibility of true communication between human individuals and between people of all cultures; the responsibility of those of us in lands rich in food and natural resources to help people in lands suffering from famine and deprivation; the sheer *necessity* – if life on earth and our earth itself are to survive – of peoples to live in peaceful co-existence with one another and with the other creatures that share our planet, and our responsibility to protect and restore the earth itself. (282)

Those strong verbs, 'protest,' 'proclaim,' 'work against,' 'protect,' 'restore,' resonate with key meanings and key calls to action throughout Margaret's work. Completely compatible with them, but less militantly stated, is Frye's perception in *The Double Vision* that today's 'real longing is not for a mass movement sweeping up individual concerns, but for an individualized movement reaching out to social concerns. Primary concerns, that is: food, shelter, the greening of the earth, and their spiritual aspects of freedom and equal rights' (*DV*, 57). Thus our two great writers, working in complete independence of each other, but out of a common body of conviction that had been 'bred in the bone,' pointed us to paths that were essentially the same path. Furthermore, and this stems from the rock-solid foundation of spiritual conviction that they held in common as well, in their public lectures neither of them felt the slightest hesitation in 'preaching their cause'; in fact both of them quite obviously felt an obligation and a mission to do so, for both of them were intensely shy people who walked into the limelight at great personal cost. As for their major works, Laurence's fiction and Frye's criticism, they were far too gifted in their art to become blatantly or clumsily didactic, though an unshakably strong undercurrent of conviction unmistakably permeated and fortified everything they produced.

In each of these final works the recognition of the power of vocation in directing the course of a life is strongly marked, admittedly inescapable and, ultimately, deeply satisfying. Years ago Naim Kattan said of Frye's work: 'The Word is both the puzzle and the solution. To gather words and to write them down is both man's work and his means of transcending work' ('A Grand Passion,' 14). Nothing is made plainer in *Dance on the Earth* than the course of Margaret's childhood recognition, and final mature and painful acceptance, of her impelling vocation to write: 'I used to cheat on my violin practice and whip up to the loft, where I kept my five-cent scribblers in which I was writing a novel entitled "The Pillars of the Nation." ... One day I confessed to Mum that I really wasn't interested in the violin; in fact I hated it, I wanted to quit.

All I was interested in was writing' (67). Some thirty years later came another and more painful confrontation: 'When I wrote the first draft of *The Stone Angel*, Jack [my husband] wanted to read it. I didn't want him to ... I allowed him to read it in the end and he didn't like it much, but for me it was the most important book I had written, a book on which I had to stake the rest of my life. Strange reason for breaking up a marriage: a novel. I had to go with the old lady, I really did, but at the same time I felt terrible about hurting him' (*Dance on the Earth*, 158). In *The Double Vision* the sense of a vocation's burden is subsumed into the recognition of its issuance in the transcendent moment of insight: 'But at a certain point the future is already here, the sense of endless plugging and slugging is less oppressive, and the goal is now an enlarged sense of the present moment. One has glimpses of the immense foreshortening of time that can take place in the world of the spirit; we may speak of "inspiration," a word that can hardly mean anything except the coming or breaking through of the spirit from a world beyond time' (*DV*, 55).

In fact, Laurence's and Frye's perception of time forges the strongest, most remarkable bond between them. Margaret's framing image of the river that flows both ways provides the pervasive structure of imagery throughout *The Diviners*, and Morag's epiphanic sighting of the Great Blue Heron, 'like a pterodactyl, like an angel, like something out of the world's dawn' (292), marks one of the crucial stages in her movement towards peace in her recognition of a cosmological design far beyond time and space as men and women can know them. In *Dance on the Earth*, where Margaret deliberately avoids the strong image patterns of her novels for the more matter-of-fact prose that seemed fitting to her for a non-fiction work, she still bases the structure of her memoirs on her central insight: 'look ahead into the past, and back into the future until the silence' (*The Diviners*, 370). She had begun the book as a chronological account of her life's adventures, but she was not happy with the work until she found a way to collapse time on the page, to move freely between then and now in her narrative, linking and mingling present concerns with past events. The structure that evolved, her forewords first, then the sections centring her mother, stepmother, Jack's mother, and finally herself, gave her the scope she needed to go back and forth at will, at the same time keeping a thematic continuity that was comprehensible to the reader. As long as I knew her, from her time of writing *The Fire-Dwellers* onwards, she had been frustrated by the illusion of time's linearity, so strongly reinforced by print, and had been constantly experimenting with ways of moving towards 'some kind of form which would convey the sense of everything happening at once, simultaneously.'[4] Frye's musings on time go back to his youth: 'The first book of philosophy that I read purely on my own and purely for pleasure was Whitehead's *Science and the Modern World*, and I can still remember the exhilaration I felt when I came to the passage: "In a certain sense everything is everywhere at all times. For every location involves an aspect of itself in every other location. Thus every spatio-temporal standpoint mirrors the world." This was my initiation into what Christianity means by spiritual vision' (*DV*, 40–1). His entire chapter on time is an expansion and application of that insight and, in fact, his entire life's work has been, he says, a writing out of a handful of insights that altogether, as we measure time, was conceived in considerably less than an hour. The essence of his meaning is profoundly optimistic, profoundly hopeful of a reformed Christianity, 'of a Father who is not a metaphor of male supremacy but the intelligible source of our being; of a Son who is not a teacher of platitudes but a Word who has overcome the world; and of a Spirit who speaks with all the tongues of men and angels and still speaks with charity' (*DV*, 58).

We who are their inheritors are moved by those words as we are shaken by the prophetic irony of the modest disclaimer of Frye's preface to *The Double Vision*: '[These] opinions should not be read as proceeding from a judgment seat of final conviction, but from a rest stop on a pilgrimage, however near the pilgrimage may now be to its close' (xvii–xviii). In Margaret's final words we read:

> I know now, as I did not know when I wrote the first draft of these memoirs, that my own dance of life has not much longer to last. It will continue in my children, and perhaps for a while in my books. It has been varied, sometimes anguished, always interesting. I rejoice in having been given it.
> May the dance go on. (*Dance on the Earth*, 222)

It is truly a miracle to me that during the years of my academic life there were two such figures in our midst, so benign in their personal examples to us, so magnificent in the work they have left us, work that has long since acted like a powerful yeast on our sense of Canadian literature and scholarship. Finally, fundamentally and always I rejoice that their two legacies are built upon religious and social conventions that are a dynamically powerful part of our Canadian heritage.

NOTES

1 Margaret Laurence, *Dance on the Earth: A Memoir* (Toronto: McClelland and Stewart, 1989), 225–8.
2 Northrop Frye, interviews by David Cayley for CBC, transcript, *Northrop Frye Newsletter* 3, no. 2 (Spring 1991): 2, 10. These CBC interviews can be found *in toto* in David Cayley, ed., *Northrop Frye in Conversation* (Toronto: Anansi, 1992).
3 Allan M. Gould, 'Margaret Laurence,' *Chatelaine*, August 1982, 40.
4 Clara Thomas, *The Manawaka World of Margaret Laurence* (Toronto: McClelland and Stewart, 1975), 124.

WORKS CITED

Allen, Richard. *The Social Passion: Religion and Social Reform in Canada 1914–28.* Toronto: University of Toronto Press, 1971.
Cayley, David. *Northrop Frye in Conversation.* Toronto: Anansi, 1992.
Frye, Northrop. 'The Ideas of Northrop Frye.' Part 2 of the 3 part CBC radio program. Written and presented by David Cayley. *Northrop Frye Newsletter* 3, no. 2 (Spring 1991): 5–16.
Gould, Allan M. 'Margaret Laurence.' *Chatelaine*, August 1982.
Kattan, Naim. 'A Grand Passion.' *Books in Canada* 2, no. 6 (June/July 1982): 13–14.
Laurence, Margaret. *Dance on the Earth: A Memoir.* Toronto: McClelland and Stewart, 1989.
– *The Diviners.* Toronto: McClelland and Stewart, 1974.
Thomas, Clara. *The Manawaka World of Margaret Laurence.* Toronto: McClelland and Stewart, 1975.
– 'Towards Freedom: The Work of Margaret Laurence and Northrop Frye.' *Essays on Canadian Writing* 30 (Fall 1984): 81–95.
Woodman, Ross. 'From the Belly of the Whale: "Frye's Personal Encounter."' *Canadian Poetry* 10 (Spring 1982): 124–31.

MARGARET ATWOOD

Norrie Banquet Ode

In a rash moment I agreed to come here and say a few words this evening. Why rash? Because this gathering swarms with literary critics, and I am a mere scribbler; and as we all know, the relation between the two is that of scientist to experimental animal, or microscope to bedbug. I'll be lucky to escape from here without getting pithed, which is what biologists do to frogs to prove that they can jump higher without their brains.

Also, I have nothing whatever to say on critical subjects at the moment. I am writing a novel, and thinking about criticism at such a delicate time spells death to the enterprise, since you start anticipating your future reviews. 'This flawed masterpiece ... this disappointing study of futility ... deconstructs itself in a semiotic *mise-en-abîme* of intertextuality,' and so forth.

However I did feel there was something I could supply that nobody else was likely to, since scribblers are notoriously less reluctant to be seen making idiots of themselves than critics are. (Critics would rather make idiots of other critics, which is a more hazardous enterprise – my way, you're never hit with a shortage of available raw material.)

But to proceed. This is the day before Hallowe'en, an important date in my yearly calendar, as those who depict me complete with black cat and broomstick already realize. On this date the souls of the dead return to earth, and the prudent offer them gifts; so I thought I would do something Norrie himself might enjoy, were he here. He was a great fan of verbal horsing around – as in the Bob Review – so it is in this spirit that I present the following ode. It was originally going to be a poem in which all the last lines rhymed with 'Northrop,' until I discovered that

the only words in the English language that actually do rhyme with
'Northrop' are 'doorstop' and 'floormop,' so I cheated. Now all the last
lines rhyme with the first syllable of 'Northrop,' or else with the less
daunting 'Norrie.' Sort of. (There are two sets of off-rhymes.)

Norrie Banquet Ode

We live in interesting times; here come deplor-
able fire and flood, hurricane, plague and war.
We and our books feel trivial, amid the uproar
and general chaos. Believe me, colleagues, there are mor-
nings when I think – hell, what's this *for*?
Maybe this writing stuff is just a verbal mor-
phine. Confess – who hasn't felt wor-
n down in the textual salt-mines, or
to use the sort of terse bad joke that Norrie used to slip in, up shit creek without an oar?

Dear Norrie, if you were here with us, at the corner, more or less, of Queen's Park and Bloor,
pacing the overheated halls and creaking floor-
boards of rambling, many-turreted Victoria, as for how many years before,
following your inner track, hunting the word quarr-
y through the jungles of the text, the distant roar
of incandescent tigers hinting at glor-
y; and in your labours, loading every rift with lore;
meanwhile, in your disguise of elderly professor,
peering at us benignly, looking somewhat like a tor-
toise with an overcoat and briefcase, what would your
opinion be, of us? You didn't suffer
fools gladly. Would you find us very boring? Too ingenious by half? Preposterous?

Well, what is done is in your honour,
so I'm sure you'd be polite. Ignore
the worst, accept the best, give us an encore –
as on so many occasions, say a few cheering words: such as: the creativity's not in the for-
m, but in the writer. Anyway, you'd think of something
to restore

our sense that what we do is wor-
th it after all – the articulation of the central core
of our real being, and the opening of the most important door.

To write, to read and think, are to be mortal, but also to build a truly human structure,
– no tyranny or bloody chamber of horrors, poisoned wasteland or for-
tress, but a city-garden, through which Nature
too could flourish.
                    Is it we who write the story
or perhaps, is it the other
way around? We know one thing, dear Norrie,
thanks to you: What keeps us going is the story.

PART III

The Visioned Poet in His Dreams: Frye, Romanticism, and the Modern

G.E. BENTLEY, JR

Blake on Frye and
Frye on Blake

Blake's Influence on Frye:
'Read Blake or Go To Hell'

For Frye, William Blake was a lifelong obsession, and Blake's works were for him a joy and a maze, an early obstacle to his professional advancement and the basis of his first book, and of archetypal criticism in general.

In 1933, when he was twenty-one, Frye took a postgraduate course on Blake at University College in the University of Toronto with the distinguished Swift scholar Herbert Davis,[1] and he plunged into Blake's works with characteristic energy. By the spring of 1934 he was describing Blake as his 'only devouring enthusiasm,'[2] and the next year he tried to persuade Helen Kemp that Blake was 'generally the greatest Englishman this side of Shakespeare.'[3]

In February 1934, Frye had to give a paper in his postgraduate course on Blake's poem called *Milton*, but he got bogged down in *The Four Zoas*, the prophecy that Blake had written just before *Milton*. It was not until the night before the seminar that he got down to writing on *Milton* itself, and then, as he later recalled: 'At about two in the morning some very curious things began happening in my mind. I began to see glimpses of something bigger and more exciting than I had ever before realized existed in the world of the mind, and when I went out for breakfast at five-thirty on a bitterly cold morning, I was committed to a book on Blake.'[4]

This was in 1934, when he was twenty-two years old, but thirteen years of struggle with Blake and with Frye's crystallizing system of archetypal criticism were to elapse before his 'book on Blake' was visible in coherent form.

Frye began writing an MA thesis on Blake under the supervision of Herbert Davis, and he soon persuaded himself that he knew 'as much about him [Blake] as any man living.'[5] His method of scholarly research on Blake, as he described it in a letter, seems to have begun rather like that of a terrier with a rat – but an intellectual terrier somewhat afflicted with adolescent hubris: 'I've spun the man around like a teetotum. I've torn him into tiny shreds and teased and anatomized him with pincers ... But what I have done is a masterpiece; finely written, well handled, and the best, clearest and most accurate exposition of Blake's thought yet written. If it's no good, I am no good. There isn't a sentence, and there won't be a sentence in the whole work that hasn't gone through purgatory.'[6]

Herbert Davis thought the draft of the thesis 'extraordinarily good,'[7] but, despite years of struggle, Frye apparently never finished his MA thesis on Blake. For that matter, he never even embarked upon a PhD, though he eventually directed more PhD dissertations at the University of Toronto than any other member of the English Department, probably more than had been written at the University of Toronto English Department in all the years before he began teaching there.[8]

Already in the 1930s Frye was preaching the gospel of Blake to a tired, strife-torn, and bewildered world as the cure for religious, political, social, and cultural catastrophes. When Helen Kemp wrote to him in 1935 about the alluring arguments of atheism, communism, and materialism, Frye replied grumpily: 'Read Blake or go to hell: that's my message to the modern world.' And in the same letter he wrote of himself in terms astonishingly like those which were to be used by critics decades later about his book on Blake, indeed about his critical work in general:

I know Blake as no man has ever known him – of that I'm quite sure. But I lack so woefully in the way of subtlety. I haven't got a subtle mind – only a pounding, driving bourgeois intellect. I don't insinuate myself between two factors of a distinction – I push them aside: if I meet a recalcitrant fact, I knock it down; which doesn't get rid of it, but puts it in a different position ... I resent criticism, because I don't know, in most cases, what the hell I mean myself, so how should anyone else pretend to do so? ... my criticisms are not, properly speaking, criticisms at all, but synthetic recreations.
Professor Davis was kind enough, or ignorant enough, to remark that what he had seen of my theoretical re-construction of Blake was a damned sight more interesting than the original, as far as the prophecies are concerned at

all events ... This is one side of me – the synthetic intellectual. I'm a critical capitalist. The English conquered India ... with a handful of soldiers. I can sail into Blake or Shakespeare or St. Augustine or the Christian religion or aesthetics with two facts and a thesis, and I can conquer it. I may be baffled and obstructed: I may get stuck in a Black Hole, as I have been more or less for a year now; but I emerge with my territory painted all in one colour, anyhow. But if you paint everything one colour you over-simplify.[9]

Frye struggled with the book on Blake, and particularly with *The Four Zoas*, while he was a student at Toronto, and then while he was a student at Oxford, and then while he was teaching in Toronto, but he could not manage to pull it together; it was ungainly, fearfully asymmetrical, without a governing synthesis.

The idea of the Orc-Urizen cycle, the struggle between rebellious energy and controlling reason, the concept which became the central thesis of the book on Blake and which gave the work its 'Fearful Symmetry,' came to him, as his biographer John Ayre recounts, in 1942 'while sitting in the bored husband's seat in a women's wear shop on Yonge Street just below Bloor' waiting for his wife Helen to finish her Saturday morning shopping (*Northrop Frye*, 177). He immediately saw that this was the synthesis for which he had been searching, the idea which would draw together all the disparate strands of the book.

However, there were still years of work before he could integrate the idea and the book. He immediately rewrote the book and submitted it in 1944 to a firm called Ambassador House, but even before he received their very belated rejection notice he had begun rewriting it.[10]

By March 1945 he had 658 pages of what he conceived of as a popular book on Blake, which he submitted to Princeton University Press, saying that it was 'complete and ready to print' except for footnotes.[11] The Press's literary editor immediately noticed that it had numerous 'side excursions into the nature of satire, the romantic poet, the historic cycle, the epic, etc.,'[12] but she thought it was sufficiently promising to send to Professor Carlos Baker, a Shelley scholar at Princeton, for a professional opinion.

Baker was both impressed and dismayed by the book; it was brilliant but disjointed, and it tried to accomplish far too much. In his reader's report he wrote:

his book is full of the most acute perceptions and insights; he has gaiety and humor, aggressive wit, and a kind of gamy truculence ... [However, I doubt that this] seemingly interminable book will materially aid the cause

of Blake after all. It requires as much of the reader as Blake's Prophetic
Books themselves do ... [It is a] diffuse epic in prose ... a treatise on the
unity of western poetry; a treatise on Blake's critical opinions; and a dictionary of Blakean symbolism.[13]

On the basis of this report, the Press replied to Frye with cautious en-
couragement, saying that the book might be more publishable if it were
reorganized and purged of what seemed to be extraneous matter.

With his usual 'pounding, driving bourgeois intellect,' Frye set to
work immediately on the revisions, cutting out chunks which totalled
170 pages, and he returned the revised version to Princeton University
Press just four months later, in August 1945.[14] This time Baker was
enthusiastic; two months later the Press wired that it would accept the
book; on 28 October 1945 Frye signed a contract; and seventeen months
later, in March 1947, *Fearful Symmetry* was finally published.[15]

Fearful Symmetry had been in gestation for thirteen years, from
February 1934, when at the age of twenty-one Frye was first 'committed
to a book on Blake,' until March 1947, when he was thirty-four and the
book was finally published. *Fearful Symmetry* was not only Frye's first
book, it was also his first significant scholarly publication. Before this he
had written reviews and very short stories, but his published credentials
were extraordinarily slight. He had no doctorate;[16] for that matter, he had
never finished his Toronto MA thesis. Before 1947, if Frye had come up
for tenure at a distinguished American university[17] without a very powerful patron, his contract almost certainly would not have been renewed.

Fearful Symmetry had an electrifying influence from the day of its
publication. Within six months it had sold 1100 copies,[18] an astonishing
number for academic books which often have a print run of no more
than 500 copies.

It was not only students of Blake who were dazzled, for *Fearful
Symmetry* appealed to readers far beyond the narrow world of Blake
enthusiasts or academic scholarship. In a review in *The Spectator*, Edith
Sitwell wrote: 'The book is of extraordinary importance, not only for the
light it throws on Blake, but also philosophically and religiously ... It is
a book of great wisdom, and every page opens fresh doors on to the
universe of reality and ... art.'[19] And when Frye wrote gratefully to her,
she replied: 'at last we have the critic we have been waiting for.'[20]

Blake's writings are the kernel from which Frye's system of archetypal
criticism sprouted and flowered. Frye's analysis of Blake and his analysis
of the nature of poetry were inextricably intertwined. He felt, obscurely

at first, that if his system of analysis would work for Blake, it would work for all poetry, indeed for all literature and for culture in general. He experienced difficulties with *Fearful Symmetry* for over a decade partly because he could not seem to disentangle his analysis of the nature of Blake's poetic myth from his revolutionary analysis of the nature of poetry. It is significant that when Frye cut 170 pages from the penultimate draft of *Fearful Symmetry*, he did not throw them away; he kept them for another ten years of bondage, and much of the material went into *Anatomy of Criticism* which was not published until 1957.[21]

In sum, Blake's writings were absolutely fundamental to Frye's development as a scholar, a critic, an academic, and a master thinker. In answer to a student's question, he once said, 'I've learned everything I know from Blake,'[22] and he believed that 'the keys to [all] poetic thought' are to be found in Blake's works.[23]

Frye's Influence on Blake Studies:
The Age of Frye, 1947–1992

Blake scholars were dazzled from the first unheralded appearance of Frye as a critic of Blake, and the publication of *Fearful Symmetry* was taken as marking a new age in Blake studies. Thirty years later, in 1977, a bibliography of Blake summarized the consensus of Blake critics and scholars:

> The critical figure who dominates, and indeed defines, this period of Blake studies is Northrop Frye, whose *Fearful Symmetry* ... is probably the most comprehensive, learned, illuminating, and profound book on Blake of this or any other era. The orientation of the work is critical ... but it makes full use of the best books and information which had preceded it. All Blake's literary achievements are synthesized into a work which has itself a gigantic and fearful symmetry. Blake's development is lucidly and wittily analysed, and the forces and influences which governed his work are displayed confidently and clearly; in particular, Frye finds that Blake was working in a tradition of archetypal symbolism, for instance in the Orc Cycle. As in any really compelling discussion of a work of art, the terms and arguments are complex in themselves, and the criticism is not unlike the original in density and profundity. The enormous merit of the book is the way in which vastly diverse details are subsumed into a directing purpose and understanding. *Fearful Symmetry* is a truly magisterial work.[24]

The influence of *Fearful Symmetry* upon Blake studies has been massive and pervasive: every serious critical book on Blake since 1947 has referred to *Fearful Symmetry*, and many have been, in effect, based upon it. The most recent book indebted to Frye, and one of the most distinguished Blake books of recent years, is *Words of Eternity: Blake and the Poetics of the Sublime* (1991) by his University of Toronto colleague Vincent De Luca, which is dedicated to Frye.

Among Blake critics, Frye has attracted a whole school of followers, a host sometimes referred to as Small Frye, though in any other pond they might seem very big fish indeed.[25] His name is writ large with honour throughout the literature concerned with Blake for the last forty-five years, from 1947 through 1992.[26]

Fearful Symmetry was by far the most influential of Frye's Blake works, and it is of course magisterial, synoptic, and comprehensive to an extraordinary degree, as if it were giving the strategic conclusions of a general surveying a whole intellectual war. However, Frye has also been a vigorous private soldier in the front lines of Blake scholarship. For twenty years after the publication of *Fearful Symmetry* in 1947, Frye was remarkably active in Blake studies, giving lectures in colleges around North America, particularly in the bicentennial year of 1957, writing essays on individual poems by Blake,[27] and reviewing all the scholarship and criticism about Blake in 1957 for the Modern Language Association of America,[28] of which he later became president. In 1953 he prepared for the Modern Library *The Selected Poetry and Prose of William Blake*, which is valuable for the introduction and notes, though the quality of the editing of Blake's text itself is negligible. In 1961 he edited his student Peter Fisher's book on Blake called *The Valley of Vision* after the author's premature death, and in 1965 he put together *Blake: A Collection of Critical Essays* by various authors, in which the most valuable original contribution was his own Introduction. He wrote reviews of books on Blake, gave radio interviews about him,[29] spoke on Blake at conferences – at least in 1983 and 1986 – and wrote an article on Blake for *The Encyclopedia of Philosophy* in 1967. For at least the twenty years after the publication of *Fearful Symmetry*, from 1947 until 1967, Frye paid his dues to Blake scholarship as if he were little more than another soldier in the trenches.

Even some of Frye's essays that seem irrelevant to Blake, such as 'Yeats and the Language of Symbolism' (1947), 'Quest and Cycle in *Finnegans Wake*' (1957), and 'The Survival of Eros in Poetry' (1986), turn largely on Blake. A surprising amount of his work is intertwined explicitly or implicitly with the ideas of William Blake.

But of course it was *Fearful Symmetry* itself which continued to dominate the field. There were over thirty reviews of it,[30] the book was reprinted in 1949, 1958, 1962, 1965, 1967, and 1969, and translated into Italian in 1976, and substantial extracts from it were printed in 1967, 1971, 1972, and 1987.

Fearful Symmetry has in many ways become so close to orthodoxy in Blake studies that it has engendered opposition merely because it represents what is now conventional wisdom on its subject. For instance, in an essay called 'Delivering *Jerusalem*,' Karl Kroeber concluded that today Blake's 'poem needs to be delivered not from oblivion but from its interpreters,' particularly Frye.[31] But a far sounder and more common judgment is that of Hazard Adams in his essay 'Blake and the Postmodern.' There he wrote: 'postmodernism ... is a criticism that seeks to answer the demands of modern art,' with its 'principle immediate source' in 'the Blakean critical theorizing of Northrop Frye' (7).

In sum, Frye's work has transformed our understanding of William lake. In Blake studies, this is the Age of Northrop Frye.

FRYE'S WRITINGS ON BLAKE[32]

Books

1947 *Fearful Symmetry: A Study of William Blake*. Reprinted in 1949, 1958, 1962, 1965, 1967, 1969. Published in Italian in 1976 (*Agghiacciante simmetria: Uno studio su William Blake*. Translated by Carla Plevano Pezzini and Francesca Valente [Milan]).[33] Excerpts were reprinted in *Toward a New Christianity: Readings in the Death of God Theology*, edited by Thomas J.J. Altizer (1967); *English Literature and British Philosophy: A Collection of Essays*, edited by S.P. Rosenbaum (1971); *Modern Literary Criticism 1900–1970*, edited by Lawrence I. Lipking and A. Walton Litz (1972); *William Blake's THE MARRIAGE OF HEAVEN AND HELL*, edited by Harold Bloom (1987).

1953 *Selected Poetry and Prose of William Blake*. Edited by Northrop Frye. Frye's Introduction and notes are excellent, but the editing of the text is negligible.[34]

1966 *Blake: A Collection of Critical Essays*. Edited by Northrop Frye. Reprinted numerous times.

Articles

1947 'Yeats and the Language of Symbolism.' *University of Toronto Quarterly* 14: 1–17. Reprinted in Frye, *Fables of Identity: Studies in Poetic Mythology* (1963). Frye distinguishes Yeats's symbolism from Blake's.

1951 'Blake's Treatment of the Archetype.' In *English Institute Essays*, edited by Alan S. Downer, 170–96. Reprinted in *Discussions of William Blake*, edited by John E. Grant (1961); *Blake's Poetry and Designs*, edited by M.L. Johnson and John E. Grant (1980); *Critical Essays on William Blake*, edited by Hazard Adams (1991). Originally given as a lecture at the English Institute.

1951 'Poetry and Design in William Blake.' *Journal of Aesthetics and Art Criticism* 10: 35–42. Reprinted in *Discussions of William Blake*, edited by John E. Grant (1961); *The Visionary Hand: Essays for the Study of William Blake's Art and Aesthetics*, edited by R.N. Essick (1973).

1957 'Blake after Two Centuries.' *University of Toronto Quarterly* 27: 10–21. Reprinted in *English Romantic Poets: Modern Essays in Criticism*, edited by M.H. Abrams (1960); Frye, *Fables of Identity: Studies in Poetic Mythology* (1963); *William Blake: Songs of Innocence and [of] Experience*, edited by Margaret Bottrall (1970). Originally given as lectures at Vassar and Wellesley (Ayre, *Northrop Frye*, 258).

1957 'Blake's Introduction to Experience.' *Huntington Library Quarterly* 21: 21–67. Reprinted in *Blake: A Collection of Critical Essays*, edited by Northrop Frye (1966); *Twentieth Century Interpretations of Songs of Innocence and of Experience: A Collection of Critical Essays*, edited by Morton D. Paley (1970); *Critics on Blake: Readings in Literary Criticism*, edited by Judith O'Neill (1970); *William Blake's Songs of Innocence and of Experience*, edited by Harold Bloom (1987).

1957 'Notes for a Commentary on *Milton*.' In *The Divine Vision: Studies in the Poetry and Art of William Blake*, edited by Vivian de Sola Pinto (1957), 99–137. This is an outgrowth in some sense of his paper on Blake's *Milton* for a postgraduate course at the University of Toronto with Herbert Davis in 1934.

1957 'Quest and Cycle in *Finnegans Wake*.' *James Joyce Review* 1: 39–47. Reprinted in Frye, *Fables of Identity: Studies in Poetic Mythology* (1963). Originally given as a paper at the MLA conference in 1956 (Ayre, *Northrop Frye*, 254). About 'the major parallels between Blake's myth of Albion and Joyce's myth of Finnegan.'

1957 'William Blake.' In *The English Romantic Poets and Essayists: A Review of Research and Criticism*, edited by Carolyn Washburn Houtchens and Lawrence Huston Houtchens, 1–31. Reprinted in 1966 (as revised by M.K. Nurmi in the rev. ed.) and 1968.[35]

1961 Peter F. Fisher. *The Valley of Vision: Blake as Prophet and Revolutionary*, edited by Northrop Frye. Reprinted in 1971.

1963 'The Road of Excess.' In *Myth and Symbol: Critical Approaches and Applications by Northrop Frye*, edited by Bernice Slote, 3–20. Reprinted in Frye, *The Stubborn Structure: Essays on Criticism and Society* (1970); *Romanticism and Consciousness: Essays in Criticism and Society*, edited by Harold Bloom (1970); *Contexts of Canadian Criticism*, edited by Eli Mandel (1971); *Modern Literary Criticism 1900–1970*, edited by Lawrence I. Lipking and A. Walton Litz (1972).

1966 Introduction. In *Blake: A Collection of Critical Essays*, edited by Northrop Frye, 1–7

1966 'The Keys to the Gates.' In *Some British Romantics: A Collection of Essays*, edited by Northrop Frye, John E. Jordan, and James V. Logan, 1–40. Reprinted in Frye, *The Stubborn Structure: Essays on Criticism and Society* (1970); *Romanticism and Consciousness: Essays in Criticism and Society*, edited by Harold Bloom (1970); *Modern Critical Views*, edited by Harold Bloom (1985).

1967 'William Blake.' *The Encyclopedia of Philosophy*, edited by Paul Edwards. 1: 319–20.

1967 'William Blake, 1757–1827.' 'Adam and Eve and the Angel Raphael,' 1808. In *Man and His World*: International Fine Arts Exhibition Expo 67. Montreal, 28 April–27 October, 1967.

1969 'Blake's Reading of the Book of Job.' In *William Blake: Essays for S. Foster Damon*, edited by Alvin H. Rosenfeld, 221–34. 'Completely rewritten' and reprinted in Frye, *Spiritus Mundi: Essays on Literature, Myth, and Society* (1976).

1986 'The Survival of Eros in Poetry.' In *Romanticism and Contemporary Criticism*, edited by Morris Eaves and Michael Fischer, 15–45.

1990 'Blake's Bible.' In Frye, *Myth and Metaphor: Selected Essays 1974–1988*, edited by Robert D. Denham, 270–86.

1990 'Blake's Biblical Illustrations.' *Northrop Frye Newsletter* 2 (Summer 1990): 1–12.

1991 Frye and Melvyn Hill (interviewer). 'The Personal Cosmos of William Blake.' In *A World in a Grain of Sand: Twenty-Two Interviews with Northrop Frye*, edited by Robert D. Denham, 109–18. (The interview was broadcast by CBC in 1971.)

NOTES

1 Herbert Davis was the examiner of my dissertation on Blake's *The Four Zoas* at Oxford in 1956, and four years later I came to University College in the University of Toronto, but I did not learn of Frye's struggles with *The Four Zoas* under Herbert Davis's supervision until many years later.

2 Northrop Frye to Helen Kemp, 19 May 1934, quoted in Ayre, *Northrop Frye: A Biography*, 103.

3 Frye to Kemp, 25 January 1935, ibid., 110.

4 Frye to Pelham Edgar, 9 August 1948, ibid., 92.

5 Frye to Kemp, 25 January 1935, ibid., 110. This judgment was (belatedly) endorsed by Professor Carlos Baker in his evaluation of the first version of *Fearful Symmetry* which Frye submitted to Princeton University Press: 'Mr. Frye appears to know more about Blake than any other living critic.' Ibid., 192.

6 Frye to Kemp, 11 March 1935, ibid., 111.

7 Ibid., 111.

8 The University of Toronto School of Graduate Studies has a very appropriate regulation which forbids those who do not hold doctorates from supervising doctoral dissertations but, clearly and appropriately, it was not enforced with respect to Frye. For that matter, the English Department regulations limiting postgraduate classes to twelve students and requiring instructors to mark all postgraduate student papers were also appropriately suspended for Frye. Several doctoral theses about Frye were written at the University of Toronto.

9 Frye to Kemp, 23 April 1935, quoted in Ayre, *Northrop Frye*, 114–15.

10 Ibid., 187.

11 Frye to Datus C. Smith (publisher of Princeton University Press), 17 March 1945, ibid., 191.

12 Jean MacLachlan to Frye, 28 March 1945, ibid., 192.

13 Carlos Baker to Frye, reader's report, 24 April 1945, ibid., 192, 193. Notice that this report was written only a few weeks after Frye had sent the book to Princeton. Such courteous press-readers are as scarce as hen's teeth.

14 Ibid., 195.

15 Ibid., 195, 196, 202.

16 No earned doctorate, that is. Of course later he had more than thirty honorary degrees from institutions such as Chicago, Columbia, Harvard, Oxford, Princeton, and Toronto. Ibid., 392.

17 Toronto, and I believe most Canadian universities, did not have a formal system of tenure until after 1963.

18 Ayre, *Northrop Frye*, 205.

19 Quoted in Ayre, *Northrop Frye*, 205.

20 Edith Sitwell to Frye, 29 April 1948, ibid., 206.

21 Ibid., 194. The 'actual connecting links between my study of Blake and my study of the theory of criticism' are given in his 'The Road of Excess,' in *Myth and Symbol*, 3.

22 Frye, 'The Survival of Eros in Poetry,' in *Romanticism and Contemporary Criticism*, 32.

23 The 'feeling that the keys to poetic thought are in' Blake is documented in 'The Keys to the Gates,' in *Some British Romantics*, 8.

24 *Blake Books*, 45 (largely repeating the section in Bentley, Jr, and Nurmi, *A Blake Bibliography* [1964]). A footnote to *Blake Books* adds: 'The only persistent criticism of the book of which I am aware is that Frye tends to see each Blake work as part of one gigantic myth, as opposed to abortive attempts at diverse myths or as quite distinct complementary myths (e.g. Blake's private myth and the public Christian myth). Frye's essays on Blake are frequently as compelling as the book itself.'

25 These followers are sometimes thought to include Hazard Adams, Harold Bloom, and E.J. Rose, whose doctoral dissertation was written at the University of Toronto (1963).

26 The names which are written small (compared to Frye's) in Blake studies of this century are chiefly those of Sir Geoffrey Keynes (for his bibliographies [1921, 1953] and his many editions of Blake [1925 ff.]); S. Foster Damon (primarily for *William Blake, His Philosophy and Symbols* [1924]); David V. Erdman (especially for his *Blake: Prophet Against Empire* [1954] and his editions of Blake's *Poetry and Prose* [1965 ff.] and his *Notebook* [1973]); Martin Butlin (particularly for his *catalogue raisonné* of Blake's art [1981]); and Robert N. Essick (chiefly for his studies of Blake as an engraver [1969 ff.]). Keynes, Erdman, and Essick have each produced over sixty works on Blake. This is an extraordinarily honourable company. I do not know any author who has been so well served as Blake by scholars and critics of this century.

27 E.g., 'Blake's Introduction to Experience,' 57–67, and 'Notes for a Commentary on *Milton*,' in *The Divine Vision*, 99–137.

28 'William Blake,' in *The English Romantic Poets and Essayists*, 1–31.

29 See Northrop Frye and Melvyn Hill (interviewer), 'The Personal Cosmos of William Blake,' in *WGS* 109–18; the interview was broadcast by the Canadian Broadcasting Corporation (CBC) in 1971 and is available on CBC Audiotapes, no. 578 (released by the Center for Cassette Studies, North Hollywood, Calif., 1975). See also his talk on Blake's works, 'Symmetry in the Arts,' broadcast on CBC, 17 November 1972 (CBC Audiotapes, no. 893). Frye gave one of the series of radio lectures for which Arnold Kettle

prepared ('for the Course Team') units 21–2 of 'A Second Level [Arts] Course' for The Open University called *William Blake (1757–1827)* (Bletchly, Bucks: The Open University 1972).

30 Denham, *Northrop Frye: An Annotated Bibliography*, 312–17

31 Kroeber, 'Delivering *Jerusalem*,' in *Blake's Sublime Allegory*, 347. One day in the turbulent 1970s (I think), when 'The Tygers of Wrath are Wiser than the Horses of Instruction' was inscribed on college walls from Berkeley to Berlin, I was walking across the University of Toronto campus and noticed an earnest young man selling copies of a pamphlet which protested, in somewhat intemperate terms, against Frye's bourgeois social preconceptions. Bemused that the revolution had reached even to Frye, I laid out fifty cents for a copy. Later, when I showed it to Professor Frye, I was astonished to discover that he seemed to be really interested in it. I therefore gave it to him – and consequently can no longer lay hands on it to cite it chapter and verse.

32 The information here is taken from *Blake Books* (1977) – generally for publications before 1976 – and *Blake Books Supplement* (1994). Both *Blake Books* and *Blake Books Supplement* omit reviews, which may be recovered from Denham, *Northrop Frye: An Annotated Bibliography*.

33 Thirty-some reviews of *Fearful Symmetry* are recorded in Denham, *Northrop Frye: An Annotated Bibliography*, 312–17.

34 *The Works of William Blake: Selected Poetry and Prose* is the identical work except that the title page has been altered; all the work by Frye is omitted; and parts 4 (Later Works) and 5 (Prose) are omitted, including all the prose (despite the title).

35 The essay is replaced by Mary Lynn Johnson, 'William Blake,' in *The English Romantic Poets: A Review of Research and Criticism*, edited by 4th ed., ed. Frank Jordan. 4th rev. ed. New York: MLA, 1985.

WORKS CITED

Adams, Hazard. 'Blake and the Postmodern.' In *William Blake: Essays for S. Foster Damon*, edited by Alvin H. Rosenfeld. Providence: Brown University Press, 1969.

Ayre, John. *Northrop Frye: A Biography*. Toronto: Random House, 1989.

Bentley, Gerald E., Jr. *Blake Books*. Oxford: Clarendon Press, 1977.

– *Blake Books Supplement*. Oxford: Clarendon Press, 1994.

Denham, Robert D. *Northrop Frye: An Annotated Bibliography of Primary and Secondary Sources*. Toronto: University of Toronto Press, 1987.

Frye, Northrop. 'The Survival of Eros in Poetry.' In *Romanticism and Contem-*

porary Criticism, edited by Morris Eaves and Michael Fischer. Ithaca: Cornell University Press, 1986.

- 'The Keys to the Gates.' In *Some British Romantics: A Collection of Essays*, edited by Northrop Frye, John E. Jordan, and James V. Logan. Columbus: Ohio State University Press, 1966.
- 'The Road of Excess.' In *Myth and Symbol: Critical Approaches and Applications*, edited by Bernice Slote. Lincoln: University of Nebraska Press, 1963.
- 'Blake's Introduction to Experience.' *Huntington Library Quarterly* 21 (November 1957): 57–67.
- 'Notes for a Commentary on *Milton*.' In *The Divine Vision: Studies in the Poetry and Art of William Blake*, edited by Vivian de Sola Pinto. London: Gollancz, 1957.
- 'William Blake.' In *The English Romantic Poets and Essayists: A Review of Research and Criticism*, edited by Carolyn Washburn Houtchens and Lawrence Huston Houtchens. New York: Modern Language Association, 1957.

Kroeber, Karl. 'Delivering *Jerusalem*.' In *Blake's Sublime Allegory: Essays on The Four Zoas, Milton, and Jerusalem*, edited by Stuart Curran and Joseph Anthony Wittreich, Jr. Madison: University of Wisconsin Press, 1973.

MONIKA LEE

Shelley's *A Defence of Poetry* and Frye: A Theory of Synchronicity

According to a Romantic theory of literary impulses, the psychological motivations behind poetic creativity are dream and desire. The subjectivity implicit in the connotations of these terms has been actively embraced by Frye as the foundation of his theory of literature. The extent to which this idea in Frye is found in William Blake has been carefully documented by Frye himself and by others.[1] The Blake-Frye nexus is well known. What is not well known is that, in certain respects, Frye exhibits even closer affinities with Percy Bysshe Shelley, particularly as a philosophical thinker and critic (these two roles were avoided by Blake, the poetic purist). Shelley and Frye are unusual in their insistence that, as Frye puts it in *The Educated Imagination*, 'literature is a human apocalypse, man's revelation to man, and criticism is not a body of adjudications, but the awareness of that revelation' (44). Shelley's *A Defence of Poetry* is a powerful articulation of the revelation that literature is a human apocalypse; in Shelley's words, 'Poetry is indeed something divine' (*Shelley's Poetry and Prose*, 503). The extent of this confluence of Frye and Shelley has remained largely unacknowledged and unexamined by critics interested in Frye.[2]

In *After the New Criticism* Frank Lentricchia draws a series of analogies between the literary theory of Frye and Shelleyan thought in a polemical denigration of both. This devaluation of Romanticism in literary commentary participates in a tradition of scepticism about Romantic poetry that extends from Thomas Love Peacock through to eminent twentieth-century thinkers such as T.S. Eliot and F.R. Leavis. More recently, Jonathan Culler has concurred with these earlier critics in finding certain Romantic lyric poems 'embarrassing,'[3] because of the conspicuous subjectivism and emotional intensity expressed in them. In line with many modernist and contemporary critics, Lentricchia devalues Romantic texts. With articulate arrogance, he charges Frye with 'pure irrationalism' (*After the New Criticism*, 12); Frye's theory is deemed 'the somnambulistic view' (12) of literary criticism; and he is said to be in possession of 'a fine and frenzied madness' (18), an epithet borrowed from Samuel Johnson. For readers who are receptive to Frye's or Shelley's theories about literature, Lentricchia's commentary is superficial and yet it represents a pervasive critical phenomenon that requires thoughtful consideration. Why do writers and theorists of a Romantic cast, such as Blake, Shelley, and Frye, make propositions about art and literature that inspire contempt in a sizeable proportion of the intellectual community, both historically, as in *The Four Ages of Man* by Thomas Love Peacock, and at present, as in Lentricchia's criticisms of Frye?

A partial response to this question involves a recognition that these literary critics themselves participate in opposing, or at least divergent, literary genres. (Here I use the term 'genre' not in Frye's sense of the word, but in the inclusive way in which recent criticism has since come to understand it, something analogous to Frye's notion of *mythoi* or narrative structures.) Critical production is not the same thing as literary production, but criticism can and does take part loosely in the generic range of fictional forms. Viewed analogically, it possesses some of the attributes of literary *mythoi* or genres. In literature, according to Frye, the *mythoi* of romance and irony are at once interrelated and opposed. Objectively speaking, neither is the correct, the more favourable or more accurate mode of imaginative expression. In a complete critical overview, recognition of the presence and validity of all the *mythoi* is necessary. It seems, moreover, that most critics have a subjective preference for one or other of the four literary *mythoi* – comedy, romance, tragedy, and irony. All of these are fundamental to generic and modal aspects of criticism itself, because criticism cannot remain entirely detached from the narrative patterns it seeks to understand, and from which it unavoidably adopts certain features. Peacock's and Lentricchia's ironic responses, then, to the idealist claims of Romantic poetry are an integral and important element in the corpus of literary criticism. Frye's responses are different; in spite of his insistence that the four literary *mythoi* or narrative structures are created equal (*AC*, Essay 3), he favours romance as the origin of all the others. Desire, and romance as the narrative of desire, are for him the foundation of myth, and therefore the basis of all literature. In constructing his own critical mythology thus, he credits the Romantic idealist perspective with a reality rarely granted it by critics.[4] Like Shelley before him, he sees in desire the infinite potential of the imagination, a world that exists powerfully insofar as it does not exist materially. Frye is not the objective critic with the aerial view of literature that many have assumed him to be;[5] after stating the broad fourfold theory of narrative structures, his writing moves generically into a kind of critical romance which is ultimately a divine comedy. This is why as a critic he frequently appeals more to poets than he does to other theorists. There are limitations to a mode of criticism that privileges only one of the four literary *mythoi*; the assumptions that such an approach inevitably betrays were inherited by Frye from the Romantic poets. The equivalent limitations of the ironic mode of critical discourse, expressed by Lentricchia with respect to Shelley and Frye, grow out of a different presupposition, one that denies reality to specific kinds of Romantic subjectivism.

Hence Lentricchia incredulously writes that 'Shelley was prepared to take literally Milton's deference to convention that the muse dictated his "unpremeditated song" ' (*After the New Criticism*, 12). Milton and Frye were also prepared to take this statement literally in ways similar to Shelley. Some force greater than the individual human will of John Milton gave rise to *Paradise Lost*. Milton would have called it God. Frye is closer than Milton to Shelley, because Shelley 'devotes himself, not merely to mythopoeic poetry but specifically to man's recovery of his own mythmaking powers' (*SR*, 89); Shelley called the impetus 'intellectual beauty' (*Shelley's Poetry and Prose*, 93) or 'the interpenetration of a diviner nature through our own' (504); Frye might have called it the literary imagination. But whatever the terms, 'the greater force' will inevitably be defined by deconstruction and other ironic perspectives as that which is absent, at least from the text. Frye approaches Romantic idealism from the direction of belief and poststructuralism does so from a position of scepticism. Both approaches are essential to understanding a poet as complex as Shelley but, as Tilottama Rajan has argued, in Shelley's own mind at least, the idealism predominates. That is, if traditional criticism has emphasized Shelley's idealism at the expense of his scepticism, it is because 'his encounter with scepticism leads him to postpone or relocate rather than revise his idealism, to respond to scepticism sentimentally rather than ironically or tragically' (*Dark Interpreter*, 59).

The feeling of divine inspiration described in Plato's *Ion* and in Shelley's *A Defence of Poetry* is a subjective and unverifiable feeling, one that comes to 'the visioned poet in his dreams, / When silvery clouds float through the wildered brain, / When every sight of lovely, wild and grand / Astonishes, enraptures, elevates' (*Queen Mab* 17, lines 68–71). Desire and dreams are treated ironically by the sceptical reader or critic. Frye radically proposes their reality and their importance with a fervour and commitment rarely heard since Shelley's *Defence*. In the essay, 'Prometheus: The Romantic Revolutionary' in *A Study of English Romanticism*, Frye divulges his sympathetic concurrence with Shelleyan subjectivity: 'If life is the dream of the Earth-Spirit, the poet is the interpreter of that dream, who creates for us a version of the world which is much closer to reality than the world we see' (103). This essay, Frye's major discussion of Shelley, reveals Frye's affinity for the narrative of *Prometheus Unbound*: a comic enactment of the drama of the human imagination releasing itself, through the twin forces of dream and desire, from various man-made forms of tyranny. The colder, objective world symbolized by Jupiter is contrasted with what Frye, in a telling phrase, refers to as 'the central authentic voice of the imagination' (110). Throughout the analysis, Frye adopts Shelley's metaphors of vision, deliverance, and resurrection of the eternal present into a critical vocabulary of his own, and the essay ends on a note that endorses Shelley's myth as potent and representative: 'Shelley has envisioned, more clearly than any other poet, the apocalyptic dilemma of modern man' (124). In *The Critical Path: An Essay on the Social Context of Literary Criticism*, Frye directly addresses Shelley's *A Defence of Poetry* and provides a synopsis of it, from which he extrapolates the role of the modern critic. In this analysis, Frye underscores a transition away from Peacock's historical argument into Shelley's psychological one 'based on intensity of emotional feeling' (*CP*, 96). Shelley's metaphor of the totality of literature, 'that great poem, which all poets, like the cooperating thoughts of one great mind, have built up since the beginning of the world' (*Shelley's Poetry and Prose*, 493), evokes in Frye an ardent response: 'the lightning flash of this image illuminates the contemporary critic's *pons asinorum*, the bridge leading over to the other shore of criticism, where the social context and reference of criticism is to be found' (*SR*, 98).

Although it would be convenient and altogether accurate to posit *A Defence of Poetry* as one of the major influences on Frye's critical theories, doing so entails a conscious dismissal of the stated intentions of both writers.[6] For them, questions of influence are largely anathema, because thought knows no ownership. The word 'synchronicity' – not altogether divested of its Jungian residue – is a more appropriate way of implying the validity of the Romantic conception of the circularity of time and the ultimate oneness of thought. But this oneness of thought, Shelley's 'One Mind' and Frye's unifying mythology, are not the static linear and monological patterns that other critics have sometimes interpreted them to be.[7] Because the oneness of thought involves a paradox of multiplicity in unity, its mystical connotations are unmistakable. Romantic oneness cannot be understood in the absence of a spiritual context. In *Hellas*, Shelley calls 'the One' 'the unborn and the undying'; in *Adonais*, oneness is a mystical identity brought about by death ('He [Keats] is made one with Nature'); in *Prometheus Unbound*, desire is the impetus behind a spiritual union of the lovers ('the desire which makes thee one with me'). Frye summarizes this unifying tendency in Shelley's *A Defence of Poetry* in the following words: 'poetry is the dialectic of love, which treats everything it encounters as another form of itself, and never attacks, only includes' (*SR*, 95). Surely, Frye's writings, marked by his disdain for evaluation and his love of inclusion, are the critical counterpart to such a poetic theory. In the study of literary and critical history, it is possible to assert the direct influence of Shelley on Frye. But in the realm of literary experiences, these writers would probably choose to see themselves as intersecting with one another in the 'order of words' and participating in the ultimate oneness of thought.

The numerous parallels between Frye and Shelley merit a more sympathetic examination than Frank Lentricchia is willing, or able, to give them. Frye takes the question of Thomas Love Peacock, which first incited Shelley to write his treatise, as a starting point for *The Educated Imagination*. It is a question that has plagued every century and that continues to vex our own: 'Is it possible that literature, especially poetry, is something that a scientific civilization like ours will eventually outgrow?' (8). Peacock's contention and the opinion of many others today is that our society already has outgrown poetry. In a moment of praise for Shelley, Frye writes, 'Shelley's essay is a wonderful piece of writing, but it's not likely to convince anyone who needs convincing' (*EI*, 8). He then grapples with the problem in his own way: 'I shall be spending a good deal of my time on this question of the relevance of literature in the world today' (*EI*, 8). But, despite Frye's more temperate and detached style, his explanation is no more likely to change the views of the unsympathetic than Shelley's. Even the essentials of their respective arguments are strikingly synchronous.

Both begin their 'apologies' with a distinction between two different classes of thinking and of language. Shelley calls these analysis and synthesis. In *The Educated Imagination* Frye uses the terms argument and imagination; in *The Great Code* he refers to the metonymic and the metaphorical phases of language, and in *Words with Power* he calls them the conceptual or dialectical and the imaginative or poetic. However, the distinction between the products of abstract reason and the creations of the imaginative faculty is the same as in Shelley. Further-more, they extend this view of the binary structure of language into a Viconian history of language from the earlier poetic age of Homer to the subsequent age of dominant reason.[8] With a Rousseauian hypoth-esis, Frye writes that 'no human society is too primitive to have some kind of literature' (*EI*, 13), and Shelley asserts that 'poetry is connate with the origin of man' (*Shelley's Poetry and Prose*, 480). In both cases, the words 'literature' and 'poetry' are used broadly and inclusively to contain more than what is generally meant by them.

Frye and Shelley take no pains to disguise their preference for imaginative linguistic forms over the solely rational. When Shelley suggests that 'the principle of synthesis has for its objects those forms which are common to universal nature and existence itself' (*Shelley's Poetry and Prose*, 480), we approach the kind of radical identification proposed by Frye as the province of the imagination. Like Shelley, Frye imagines this unity as sequentially prior to the reason that supplants it, just as they believe that romance precedes the distorting lens of irony: 'we recapture, in full consciousness, that original lost sense of identity with our surroundings, where there is nothing outside the mind of man, or something identical with the mind of man' (*EI*, 9). In *The Revolt of Islam* Shelley also envisages such an identification between the mind and what appears to be outside it: 'One mind, the type of all, the moveless wave / Whose calm reflects all moving things that are – ' (*The Complete Poetical Works*, vol. 2, canto 7, stanza 31, lines 5–6).

The feeling that mind is unifying as well as refractive, the focus on this unifying power of mind, and the subsequent implied demotion of the mind's refractive and differentiating powers are all elements of Shelley's and Frye's perspectives on the special value of literature. If we accuse either man of metaphor-making, mythologizing, or wish-fulfillment in the creation of their literary critical romances, we discover that they are conscious of these motivations and affirm their value. Paradoxical as it may seem, making metaphors is part of the critical path they choose to follow. If we strip Frye's literary theory down to the bare bones of its controlling *mythos*, we see that the myth of an original unity of consciousness, the loss or refraction of this idyllic state, and the desire for and even the re-achievement of this unity are the structure of the romance narrative behind the theory. This metaphorical approach to criticism is not so much anti-rational as it is counter-rational. If, as Shelley and Frye contend, the metaphor-making faculty of the mind is primitive and primary, and if analysis succeeds it chronologically both in the life of a child and in the history of a civilization, the elevation of metaphor as the foundation of argument is no distortion. If, however, analysis is considered as more important than metaphor-making in the critical project, Frye's theory may be attacked as 'pure irrationalism.'

However, in order to understand *A Defence of Poetry*, we might well consider it in the light of the priority that Shelley gives to imagination over reason. Let us seek a metaphor that would do justice to the predominant tone and the range of meanings in Shelley's treatise. *A Defence of Poetry* refers to many writers and ideas current in nineteenth-century England. Although the essay possesses attributes of a catalogue, the metaphors of amalgamation are not sufficient to represent it. In other words, despite the extent of Shelley's use of example, the essay does not function empirically. It is compelling and persuasive, but not as an exercise in analytical reason or logic. In fact, most readers who dismiss the treatise dislike it for reasons associated with its illogicality or the seeming randomness of its examples. Thus we can say that two of Frye's phases of language, the empirical (descriptive) and the rational (metonymic) are not the dominant kind of language used by Shelley. Here the operative mode of language is the metaphorical. In keeping with Shelley's professed belief in the imagination, *A Defence of Poetry* works much as a centrifugal prose poem does, with the metaphors tending to engulf the argument and its examples in much the way the whale might have swallowed Jonah. Once the rational argument has been transmuted by these much more powerful metaphors, as with Jonah, its mission takes on the tone and colour of conversion – in this case conversion to literature. For this reason, in contemporary theoretical debates that posit Shelley as a deconstructive poet and thinker, *A Defence of Poetry* is rarely discussed.[9] The problem for deconstruction is that the *Defence* describes a predominantly logocentric poetics; furthermore, it relies on the presence of initiates and potential converts as its readers. The initiates are all those who have ever had a powerful feeling or an ecstatic moment as a result of something they have read. Unlike the specialist élites that form schools of literary criticism, those who have had an epiphanic reading experience cross the lines of class, race, age, gender, and nation. They are the zealots of verbal art and it is to them that both Shelley and Frye address themselves.

Shelley and Frye share the same basic assumptions about the role of literature in society. Deconstruction and other sceptical and/or ironic approaches to literature teach us to recognize the metaphorical under-pinning of all assumptions. Once a metaphor is exposed, the assump-tion it cloaks may be dissolved. The metaphors of the Enlightenment, the conversion and the unification of the mind, are as subject as any to critical scrutiny. However, the metaphors underlying Frye's theories are figures readily comprehended by those who understand metaphors to be more real than the assumptions they illustrate. Furthermore, despite his zeal about literature, Frye is not dogmatic. He asserts the reality of metaphor as metaphor, in other words, as it exists in the human mind. Never does he state that literature is the means to salvation, that an educated imagination is paradise, that Shakespeare is his saviour and Blake his priest. Instead he gives validity to the desire for, and the possibility of, salvation through the literary imagination. The romance narrative has no room for moral prescrip-tions: we are not told that art or criticism must perform the following changes, only that it can be imagined thus.

In fact, Frye's and Shelley's antididactic stances are unequivocal. Shelley writes, 'A Poet therefore would do ill to embody his own conceptions of right and wrong, which are usually those of his place and time, in his poetical creations, which participate in neither' (*Shelley's Poetry and Prose*, 488). And Frye writes, 'we should trust no writer's beliefs or attitudes, but concentrate on his myth, which is infinitely wiser than he is, and is the only element that can survive when the ideology attached to it fades' (*WP*, 60). For both, the truth of a poem or a play is not to be found in its ethical dimensions, but in the underlying spiritual form, for Shelley, and in the underlying mythical structure, for Frye, both of which are understood to be prior to the poem's linguistic embodiment.

Shelley confidently asserts: 'A man cannot say, 'I will compose poetry.' The greatest poet cannot say it: for the mind in creation is a fading coal,' which 'some invisible influence, like an inconstant wind, awakens to transitory brightness' (*Shelley's Poetry and Prose*, 503–4). Frye, less dramatically, writes that the literary author is 'trying to let something take on its own form, whether it's a poem or a play or novel or whatever. That's why you can't produce literature voluntarily, in the way you'd write a letter, or a report' (*EI*, 17). Here there is a sense of numinous energy – left undefined – ambiguously referred to as 'some-thing' by Frye and as 'some invisible influence' by Shelley. The influence itself defies definition, because it transcends the verbal.

What Frye and Shelley do for literary criticism is to infuse back into it some purely literary beliefs and emotions; they thereby blur the distinctions between the literary and the critical in a way prophetic of poststructuralist textual theory. Both men assert the moral neutrality of literature, its mystical effects, the use of a metaphorical and imaginative language different from rational discourse, the importance of verbal structures that unify or synthesize, and the significance of dream and desire as sources of literary creativity. The results are two daringly ambitious attempts to defend literature according to the primary assumptions of the imagination. Works like *A Defence of Poetry* and *The Educated Imagination* are great whales with the potential to swallow a reader whole, to disrupt many empirical preconceptions, and to send the reader into the critical jungle as a zealot of art. Generically, they remain literary critical enactments of the romance *mythos* with its quest to reunify all that in the world of words has been fragmented or lost.

NOTES

1 Denham in 'Frye's Theory of Symbols,' Mitchell in 'Dangerous Blake,' Mandel in 'Toward a Theory of Cultural Revolution,' and Geoffrey Hartman in 'The Sacred Jungle 3,' are a handful of the critics who have argued the centrality of Blake to Frye's theories.
2 Deanne Bogdan is an exception; see 'Is It Relevant and Does It Work? Reconsidering Literature Taught as Rhetoric,' and 'Northrop Frye and the Defence of Literature.' Craig Stewart Walker sees 'an important link between Shelley and Frye in that both identify divine power with the imagination.' See 'Of Janus, Job and "J": A Review of *Words with Power*.'
3 Specifically, Culler objects to poetic uses of the apostrophe and the majority of his examples in *The Pursuit of Signs* are from well-known Romantic poems (135).
4 Geoffrey Hartman has written that Frye's 'great achievement is the recovery of the demon, or of the intrinsic role of Romance in the human imagination' ('Ghostlier Demarcations,' 110–11).
5 See Hartman's 'Ghostlier Demarcations' (109) for one example of this perspective. Frye's own insistence on a science of criticism is the source of misapprehensions regarding his explicit validations of subjectivity. See Denham's *Northrop Frye and Critical Method* for a clarification of Frye's use of the word 'science' to describe literary criticism (136–8).
6 Frye provides an interesting discussion of liberation and prophecy in *A Defence of Poetry* in *SR*, 120–2.

7 In his *Doing Things With Texts*, Abrams discusses what he calls the 'critical monism' (6) in Shelley's *A Defence of Poetry* and he briefly notes a similarity between Shelley's monistic treatment of literature and Frye's archetypal paradigms.

8 Frye adds to the first two ages a third, our own, which is characterized by empirical thinking and descriptive writing. This third age corresponds to Vico's 'vulgar' or demotic age (*GC*, 13). In *A Defence of Poetry* Shelley focuses only on the first two ages.

9 One noteworthy exception to this general trend is Tilottama Rajan's fine close reading and analysis of the essay's deconstructive subtext in *The Supplement of Reading*. She shows how the essay is prophetic of modern and postmodern, existential and deconstructive thought.

WORKS CITED

Abrams, M.H. *Doing Things With Texts: Essays in Criticism and Critical Theory.* New York: Norton, 1991.

Bogdan, Deanne. 'Is It Relevant and Does It Work? Reconsidering Literature Taught as Rhetoric.' *Journal of Aesthetic Education* 16 (Winter 1982): 27–38.

– 'Northrop Frye and the Defence of Literature.' *English Studies in Canada* 8 (June 1982): 203–14.

Culler, Jonathan. *The Pursuit of Signs: Semiotics, Literature, Deconstruction.* Ithaca: Cornell University Press, 1981.

Denham, Robert D. *Northrop Frye and Critical Method.* University Park: Pennsylvania State University Press, 1978.

– 'Frye's Theory of Symbols.' *Canadian Literature* 66 (Autumn 1975): 63–79.

Hartman, Geoffrey. 'The Sacred Jungle 3: Frye, Burke, and Some Conclusions.' In *Criticism in the Wilderness: The Study of Literature Today.* New Haven: Yale University Press, 1980.

– 'Ghostlier Demarcations.' In *Northrop Frye in Modern Criticism: Selected Papers from the English Institute.* New York: Columbia University Press, 1966.

Lentricchia, Frank. *After the New Criticism.* Chicago: University of Chicago Press, 1980.

Mandel, Eli. 'Toward a Theory of Cultural Revolution: The Criticism of Northrop Frye.' *Canadian Literature* 1 (Summer 1959): 58–67.

Mitchell, W.J.T. 'Dangerous Blake.' *Studies in Romanticism* 21 (Fall 1982): 410–16.

Rajan, Tilottama. *Dark Interpreter: The Discourse of Romanticism*. Ithaca: Cornell
    University Press, 1980.
– *The Supplement of Reading: Figures of Understanding in Romantic Theory and
    Practice*. Ithaca: Cornell University Press, 1990.
Shelley, Percy Bysshe. *Shelley's Poetry and Prose*. Edited by Donald Reiman and
    Sharon Powers. New York: Norton, 1977.
– *The Complete Poetical Works of Percy Bysshe Shelley*. Edited by Neville Rogers.
    4 vols. Oxford: Clarendon Press, 1975.
Walker, Craig Stewart. 'Of Janus, Job and "J": A Review of *Words with Power*.'
    Northrop Frye Newsletter 3, no. 2 (Spring 1991): 33.

HELEN VENDLER

Frye's *Endymion*: Myth, Ethics, and Literary Description

'The theme of Keats's *Endymion*,' says Frye in the introduction to his short book *A Study of English Romanticism*, 'is the bringing to birth of the imagination as the focus of society' (89). 'Really?' – a reader might object – 'I thought the theme of *Endymion* was Endymion's attempt to reconcile loving an ethereal goddess with loving a human girl.' 'No,' Frye would presumably answer, 'that is the *story* of *Endymion*.' We see at once that Frye's characteristic summary sentence about a work tends to exist at one remove from the reader's experience of the poem. It is this remove that has been most criticized in Frye; he has been justly accused, in his passion for decoding, of leaving out the details, of making works sound too much alike, of neglecting style, and so on. This is all true enough (though Frye's asides on style are more numerous, and more valuable, than his critics might allow). I am not concerned about this side of Frye: we have plenty of practical critics to talk about narrative and stylistic detail and, though it may be just to criticize Frye at that level, it is rather fruitless. He was, after all, hunting different game; and if we are to criticize him it should be done on his own plane – after first, I hope, appreciating how minimally his critical plane existed before he invented, consolidated, elaborated, and defended it.

The huge enterprise embodied in Frye's books from *Fearful Symmetry* through *Words with Power* gave many of us great, exhilarating moments through its sheer bulk and stability, as it organized a niche for everything and everything in its niche. It was, and is, a Spenserian mythological creation like the House of Alma or Merrill's Sandover, and could only have been articulated by one steeped in such structures, beginning with Noah's ark.

The niche occupied by Keats's *Endymion* in Frye's house of criticism is a minor one – a single chapter in a relatively slight book of lectures – but since Frye chose to use Keats's poem to illustrate a moment in the evolution of the imagination, it seemed to me that the commentary on *Endymion* offered a good testing-ground for Frye's theory in practice.

The chief assertion of this little book of Frye's on younger Romantics – Beddoes, Shelley, Keats – is that in Romanticism creative authority passes from God to the poet; the poet is the 'focus' through which a better vision of society is articulated. The poet, not the priest, becomes the vehicle for that 'myth of concern,' as Frye puts it, which protests the present conditions of living. The poet, says Frye, 'sees society as held together by its creative power, incarnate in himself, rather than by its leaders of action. Thus he himself steps into the role of the hero, not as personally heroic but simply as the focus of society. For him, therefore, the real event is no longer even the universal or typical historical event, but the psychological or mental event, the event in his own consciousness' (*SR*, 36). He adds, 'In Romanticism the main direction of the quest of identity tends increasingly to be downward and inward ... a hidden region, often described in images of underground caves and streams' (33). After treating the Romantic macabre in Beddoes and the Romantic revolutionary in Shelley, Frye comes to his affirmative climax, the Romantic epiphanic (as he calls it) in *Endymion*. Frye is a religious critic, and the epiphanic, or showing forth of the divine, appeals to him more than Beddoes's death-drive or Shelley's utopian atheism. We would expect then, and we ultimately find, a sympathetic reading of *Endymion* from Frye. What is Frye's method of reading? What of *Endymion* does it distil? What does it elide or omit? (I will try, to the end of my essay, to remain within Frye's own plane of discourse.)

Frye's first move, as one would expect, is to map the worlds of *Endymion*, mostly by reference to Milton, Spenser, and Blake:

Endymion has been brought up in the garden world ... but the impulse to get away from it is present in him too. We notice a feeling of *guilt* in Endymion, of a responsibility not yet assumed, which pushes him out of his world into a lower one ... Endymion's society worships Pan ... The heaven of Endymion is therefore the place of Pan ... he [Endymion] is unable to go directly into the world of Pan and Phoebe above him, and has to go in the opposite direction, through the third and fourth levels of his poetic cosmos, ... associated respectively with earth and with water ... these lower worlds are also worlds of Diana, in her full extent as the great *diva triformis*. (133–5)

This brief summation has the virtue of placing Keats's poem in a long line of mythologically structured poems from Ovid on, poems which often include underground or the underwater episodes. And yet, true as it is that Book II of *Endymion* happens under the earth, and Book III under water, it is by no means clear in the poem that these worlds exist, as Frye seems to think they do, in any clear ethical contrast to Endymion's pastoral world or Phoebe's celestial one. It might be truer to say that in *Endymion* there appear to be only two worlds, the mortal and the immortal. There is no clear analogue to the demonic in either the underground or the underwater worlds of *Endymion*; the closest thing to the demonic is the vision of Circe in Book III, which occurs on an island in the very same pastoral world where Endymion is first seen and where Glaucus has lived before his underwater punishment.

In spite of one's feeling that Frye's four worlds make a rather Procrustean bed for *Endymion*, the very fact of Frye's reminding us that a poem of an earlier century might well have fitted more easily into four worlds makes us aware of Keats's originality. What is oddest about Keats's realms is how they shift. If Pan is the god worshipped by Endymion's society, why does not the final theophany – or indeed any of the intermediate ones – display him? Keats much prefers, after the Hymn to Pan in Book I, to envisage Pan, or natural deity, under his submanifestations – here as Venus and Adonis, there as Alpheus and Arethusa, or as Glaucus and Scylla, as Neptune, as Bacchus, as Cybele, as Cynthia – perhaps even as Circe. As the god of Allness, Pan must include all aspectual epiphanies. And yet Keats is not schematic enough to say this outright. There is in Keats a deep resistance to boundaries of the sort eminently congenial to Frye. Keats cannot get along without 'worlds' or 'realms,' but they melt into each other as Endymion is insensibly translated from one to the next. The pastoral world is the roof of the ocean, and the Indian maid is now on the ground, now drawn through the air by winged horses provided by Hermes. Both death and resurrection inhabit the sea; both gems and ennui can be found under the earth. Frye himself, in his recognition of Diana as the *diva triformis*, might have suspected that the worlds in *Endymion* differ from each other only aspectually, not essentially.

As Frye retells the story of *Endymion* in brief, certain motifs oddly escape or contradict his formulations. He refers, for instance, in a baffled way, to a 'beautiful if somewhat inconclusive vision of Cybele' (*SR*, 136) in the poem; and he tries, with an inexplicable lapse into error, to make a good case for Endymion's experience with the Indian maid:

Endymion's possession of the Indian maid is for him what birth would
have been for Blake's Thel, a new life which, although it is also a form of
death, as every new life is, also gives him the roots in experience that he
lacked before:

> Now I have tasted her sweet soul to the core
> All other depths are shallow: essences,
> Once spiritual, are like muddy lees,
> Meant but to fertilize my earthly root. (137–8)

The passage that Frye here quotes from Book II as support for the
beneficence of Endymion's 'possession of the Indian maid' refers not at
all to the Indian maid (whom Endymion will not meet until Book IV) but
to Cynthia. Endymion has just 'swoon'd / Drunken from pleasure's
nipple' (II, 868–9) during his encounter with his unknown goddess, who
has made frequent references to the sky (II, 761–824). Endymion, in
consequence, reflects that the earth is now to him an inferior level:

> Now I have tasted her sweet soul to the core
> All other depths are shallow: essences,
> Once spiritual, are like muddy lees,
> Meant but to fertilize my earthly root. (II, 904–7)

What could have led Frye to ascribe these early lines about Cynthia,
denigrating the 'muddy lees' of earth, to Endymion's feeling for the
earthly Indian maid? It was perhaps Frye's premature wish for the
mythological conflation of the two love-objects. Though in the end they
become one, only Cynthia is, so to speak, indispensable; only she has the
power to show herself aspectually in the person of the Indian maid, and
to absorb, eventually, that earthly persona into her divine one. When
Endymion tries to convince himself that he can be content with the
Indian maid alone, he is acting inauthentically, as the narrator sharply
remarks. Endymion at that point has vowed bitterly to abjure his quest
for Cynthia:

> No, never more
> Shall airy voices cheat me to the shore
> Of tangled wonder, breathless and aghast. (IV, 653–5)

And in the most inauthentic lines of the poem, he addresses the Indian
maid:

> My Indian bliss!
> My river-lily bud! one human kiss!
> One sigh of real breath – one gentle squeeze –

but breaks off even in the midst of the gentle squeeze to reproach his vanished Cynthia – 'Whither didst melt?' – only to return to domestic plans with the fair Indian: 'No more of dreaming. – Now, where shall our dwelling be?' (IV, 663–70).

Endymion's temporary infidelity to Cynthia is sharply reproved by the narrator, as I have said:

> The mountaineer
> Thus strove *by fancies vain and crude* to clear
> His briar'd path to some tranquillity.
> (IV, 722–4; emphasis added)

It is important for Frye's social argument – his 'humanistic' reading of Endymion-as-Thel – to have Endymion descend into the ordinary and domestic social world. But the thrust of Keats's poem goes precisely in the opposite direction. It is a 'crude and vain fancy,' to Keats's way of thinking, to imagine that the domestic and social world can suffice. Therefore, Keats makes the Indian maid's earthly black hair and eyes metamorphose at last into the celestial golden hair and blue eyes of Cynthia:

> Her long black hair swell'd ampler, in display
> Full golden; in her eyes a brighter day
> Dawn'd blue and full of love. Aye, he beheld
> Phoebe, his passion! (IV, 984–7)

Endymion, who had 'wed [himself] to things of light from infancy' (IV, 957–8) does not find his ultimate destiny – as Frye wishes he would – in the social world of the Indian maid, but in the ethereal world of the goddess, with whom he vanishes at the end, leaving his sister to remain 'home' in the pastoral world of the 'gloomy wood' (IV, 1002–3). This is not a Thel-like descent on Endymion's part, but rather an apotheosis of the human soul into the divine. This ending does not fit Frye's program of human concern; nor, of course, does it ultimately fit Keats's own, since his final gods and goddesses – Apollo and Moneta – are far more burdened with human concern than the celestial Cynthia or Endymion in his eventual role as her consort.

It is difficult for Frye to encompass the Keatsian irresolution of realms in his account of the poem, since Frye is himself so resolute in the realm of value. Yet *Endymion* is full of perplexity and its concomitant, Negative Capability. Here is the vision of Cybele, the earth-mother, which Frye has admitted to finding 'beautiful but inconclusive':

> Forth from a rugged arch, in the dusk below,
> Came mother Cybele! alone – alone –
> In sombre chariot; dark foldings thrown
> About her majesty, and front death pale,
> With turrets crown'd. Four maned lions hale
> The sluggish wheels; solemn their toothed maws,
> Their surly eyes brow-hidden, heavy paws
> Uplifted drowsily, and nervy tails
> Cowering their tawny brushes. Silent sails
> This shadowy queen athwart, and faints away
> In another gloomy arch. (II, 639–48)

Since this passage represents Keats's first sketch for Moneta – a majestic mother with 'front death-pale' – the appearance of Cybele can hardly be dismissed as inconclusive or (Douglas Bush's words) 'not clearly relevant' (*Keats: Selected Poems*, 320). The coloration of this striking passage is sombre, sluggish, solemn, surly, heavy, drowsy, shadowy, gloomy: these are the colorations of the Mother of the Gods and her entourage. She is the Demogorgon of Keats's poem – the mystery in which the generative maternal comes charioted by the bestial. She is unclarifiable; perceived under the earth, she is also – though dimly glimpsed – the ground of being of the sky-goddess. She makes Keats's poem resist a Freudian reading in which Cybele would share attributes only with other females – since she is the mother of the male gods too. She has no consort, and therefore can make only a brief appearance in this narrative, which is so intensely centred on erotic relations. But her brief Miltonic comet-like passage ('silent sails / this shadowy queen athwart') in *Endymion* will breed the moon-Titaness Moneta presiding over that later poem, *Hyperion*, which has given up all hope of the erotic.

After Frye has summarized Book II, he states, wrongly, that Circe 'is the presiding deity of Endymion's lowest world, the hell under the sea' (*SR*, 139). But Glaucus, a sea inhabitant, says explicitly that he met Circe in the upper world, on the island of Æaea. When Scylla fled his love, Glaucus had hoped that his 'fierce agony' of desire would find help from Circe:

> ... across my grief
> It flash'd, that Circe might find some relief –
> Cruel enchantress! So above the water
> I rear'd my head, and look'd for Phoebus' daughter.
> Æaea's isle was wondering at the moon: –
> It seemed to whirl around me, and a swoon
> Left me dead-drifting to that fatal power.
>
> When I awoke, 'twas in a twilight bower;
> Just when the light of morn, with hum of bees,
> Stole through its verdurous matting of fresh trees.
>
> (III, 411–20)

It is in this bower, among the bees, that Glaucus sees Circe, who 'cradles [him] in roses' (III, 457); he finds himself in 'haunts umbrageous' (III, 467) and wanders in 'the mazy forest-house / Of squirrels, foxes shy, and antler'd deer' (III, 468–9). This is no sea scene; and Circe in fact never enters the underwater world at all. After the bower interlude, Glaucus awakes and wanders till he sees his 'arbour queen' (III, 498) surrounded by beasts (once men) whom she poisons. Glaucus flees, but Circe finds him, and condemns him to old age, immortal as he is, for a thousand years in 'the watery vast' (II, 593). As he sinks into the sea, he refers to it as 'my fresh, my native home,' whose 'tempering coolness, to my life akin, / Came salutary as I waded in' (III, 608–10).

The presider over the underwater world is not Circe, as Frye says, but Neptune. All realms in Keats are innocent. Though Circe's forest can become, through her manipulation of men, both a 'specious heaven' and a 'real hell' (III, 476) to her victims, it is, in another of its aspects, the very forest for which Pan was praised in Book I.

I have been raising objections to some of Frye's judgments. But none of my disagreements with particular judgments changes my view that Frye was right in seeking to describe Keats's ambitious construction of realms and to put them in relation to their mythological predecessors. This is necessary in order to establish how Romanticism reworks the mythology it inherited. Yet, does not Frye overschematize Keats's slippery imaginings? And overmoralize his encounter with the Indian maid to exemplify a necessary domestic 'descent'? And ascribe the ocean to Circe in order to represent one of Keats's worlds as a demonic one?

Frye says, interestingly, that 'Keats's attitude to this world is not moral, like Spenser's: it is rather, however unpoetical the word may sound, epistemological. It is the world in which the separation of the

conscious subject from everything it wants and loves is at its greatest'
(*SR*, 139). Yet immediately Frye goes on, entirely accurately, to ascribe
moral purpose to Endymion as he and Glaucus 'begin to transform a
shipwrecked society into a reintegrated one' (143). One feels that Frye
would be happier if the poem had ended with Book III at this resuscita-
tion of the drowned lovers. In a brilliant local insight, Frye sees that the
scattering of pieces of Glaucus's scroll, resurrecting the dead lovers,
substitutes for 'the traditional *sparagmos* fate of the god in the underworld' (144). Though Frye leaves the Eucharistic *sparagmos* unmentioned
here, it cannot have been far from his mind. And indeed Book III recalls
the harrowing of hell – a place which, we should remember, was not
'hell' but a place of waiting for the saved until the Redemption should
be accomplished. The Keatsian underwater world is more purgatorial
than demonic, and Circe has no place in it.

Endymion, says Frye, is, like *The Prelude*, 'a poem about the growth of
the poet's mind' (147). But for Frye it is an incomplete poem, and he
passes on, at the end of his essay on it, to *Hyperion, The Fall of Hyperion,*
and the great odes, in order to complete his conspectus of the Keatsian
program. He had earlier mentioned the hymn to Bacchus in Book IV of
Endymion as a balance to the opening hymn to Pan (144); he returns to
the hymn to Bacchus to point out that it is enclosed within the Indian
maid's song to Sorrow (153), adumbrating Keats's later entwining of
sorrow and joy in the 'Ode on Melancholy.' This is of course true; but,
because Frye's mind is on psychology, he does not notice the more
important aspect, for Keats, of the hymn to Bacchus: its 'contamination'
of Greek mythology by an incursion from Asia. The Indian maid sings
of Bacchus, and follows in his train, because he comes from her part of
the world; he rides surrounded by the fauna of Asia – the tiger, the
leopard, elephants, zebras, alligators, and crocodiles. Bacchus passes
through all lands, according to the Indian maid:

> I saw Osirian Egypt kneel adown
> Before the vine-wreath crown!
> I saw parch'd Abyssinia rouse and sing
> To the silver cymbals' ring! (IV, 257–60)

'Old Tartary,' 'the kings of Inde,' 'Great Brahma' – all make their
obeisance to Bacchus, in stanzas reminiscent of the submission of the
pagan gods to the Infant Christ in the Nativity Ode of Milton.

When Keats hybridizes 'the beautiful mythology of Greece' with a
maiden from beside the Ganges (IV, 633) and an Asian Bacchus, he

makes his poem into something wilder and less canonical than a pure adaptation of Olympus. Insofar as Cynthia needs to take on the persona of a maid from the Ganges, she needs new blood from outside the classical tradition – and so does Keats. This is a well-known historical complication of Romanticism, but it evades Frye's generalized concern with mythical worlds.

We can hear in Frye's comments his reservations about the extent to which – as he sees it – Keats's poetry distances itself from experience: 'The poetry of Keats as we have it is set against the world of experience, as something which is in that world but not of it. We see this particularly in Keats's style. The odes in particular depend on magic spells and charms, on the marking off of special holy places and the building of private temples in the mind, on escape from noise and vulgarity ... and on an intensely hieratic rather than a demotic consciousness' (154). One knows, in a large sense, what Frye means here. The odes were after all not written by Crabbe or even Byron. Frye sees the hieratic order in the odes as an élitist betrayal of Keats's ideal style, 'a style with the dramatic versatility of Shakespeare's'; and Frye accurately, and winningly, ascribes the 'uncertainties of taste' in *Endymion* to 'an attempt to develop a style without levels, which can encompass the sublime and familiar at once' (154–5). Yet Shakespeare also wrote the *Sonnets*, as hieratic a sequence as Keats's odes, and one encounters, both in Frye's critique of the 'hieratic' style, and his open approval of a style more 'demotic,' something of the Protestant colonial's distaste for a court style.

After criticizing *Endymion*'s putative arrest in a state of innocence, Frye adds that 'Keats leaves us in no doubt that he wanted to develop further in the direction of a poetry of *concern*, a poetry that would incorporate the ironic vision and the state of experience ...' (156). In view of the appearance of the Den of Quietude in Book IV of *Endymion*, which represents a negative capability of detachment truly eerie in its chill, it is difficult to see why Frye suggests that *Endymion* remains a poem of the state of innocence. However, the experience it attains at its highest point in the Den of Quietude is one of separation from the anguish of the social world; and, for Frye, there is radically insufficient ethical content to such detachment. In the Den of Quietude, it will be remembered, the soul wanders and traces its own existence. This is indeed, in Keats's own words, the 'native hell' (IV, 523) of the soul – if one is looking for a demonic passage in the poem. Yet Keats adds,

> But few have ever felt how calm and well
> Sleep may be had in that deep den of all.

> There anguish does not sting; nor pleasure pall;
> Woe-hurricanes beat ever at the gate,
> Yet all is still within and desolate
> ...
>   Enter none
> Who strive therefore: on the sudden it is won.
>   (IV, 524–32)

Ethical striving, no matter how arduous, cannot bring one to this state. 'Enter none / Who strive therefore.' It is not a place of revolutionary endeavour, nor of redemptive social imagination: it is, one might say, not Protestant. And Frye's imagination is thoroughly Protestant. Keats's den is, perhaps, Lucretian; its presiding genius is Necessity. Frye's entire critical and religious stance was antinecessitarian; I am not aware of any statement of his that embraces some version of Keats's Quietude. It is too quietist for him. It would rob him of energy.

Frye retreats from his ethical critique of Keats through a rather tortured formulation. Keats, he says, ultimately envisages a world of communion for which the 'outer court of experience would not need to exist' (159). Keats's nightingale and urn, he says, might 'seem to us, at first, images of a poetry of refuge, a dream of a lost Paradise.' He continues, 'That is a possible but shallow response: the disciplined response understands that these poems are visions on and of the battlefield itself, not the subjective fantasies of retreat' (165). Frye's battle metaphor seems misplaced: *Endymion*, and the odes, do not envisage the world as a battlefield. *Endymion* is a quest-romance, and the odes are, as Frye says, epiphanic, presenting 'icons or presences which have been at once invoked and evoked by a magical spell, and held as a focus of meditation' (159). Perhaps it is true, as Frye thinks, that all realized poetry is the result of Blakean 'mental fight' – but it would be equally true to say, with Keats, that all realized poetry is conceived in the Den of Quietude.

The most interesting thing about Frye's forty-page essay on *Endymion* is that it seems to be heading straight towards a condemnation of Keats – for escapism, for solipsism, for hierarchic consciousness, for immaturity. Yet three-quarters of the way through the essay, Frye suddenly realizes the direction of his argument, and makes a sharp 180–degree turn: 'The inference seems to be that Keats was a minor poet who would have become a major one if he had had a few more years of life and health. This seems very reasonable, except that every reader of Keats knows that it is wrong ... The mind that contemplates, the poet with his negative capability, is the focus of a universal human mind ... with which the poet identifies himself' (156–7). This formulation, which resorts to concepts like 'a universal human mind,' makes all talk of 'hierarchic' versus 'demotic' consciousness idle. It is as though Frye, by himself, has come upon the decontextualizing aesthetic of the European lyric (and *Endymion* is a prolonged lyric of 'one bare circumstance' – as Keats said – rather than a narrative poem). In lyric, the lyric speaker is not a 'character' (at either a 'hieratic' or a 'demotic' level); he is, as Emily Dickinson said to Thomas Wentworth Higginson, 'representative.' And when Frye arrives at the assertion that Keats believes in an 'interpenetrating' society (159), he seems to have forgotten his earlier strict separation of 'worlds.' ' "They interassimulate," ' says Keats, 'in an inspired portmanteau word,' Frye adds (159). This is an insight that would be worth applying to the shifting scenes of *Endymion*. Just as the bower of *The Fall of Hyperion* becomes Moneta's shrine, which then dissolves into the shady sadness of a vale, so Endymion's restless adventures are perhaps nothing but successive backdrops, 'interassimulated,' to the one philosophical mind.

Frye's essay bears some marks of haste and, as I have said, of sequential rather than planned spatial composition. But Frye had the courage to see where his conceptualizations of *Endymion* were leading him, and to rely more strongly on his readerly experience of Keats's greatness than on his mythological sense that Keats was immature. At the end of his essay, he even allows Keats's writings more moral than epistemological force – the very opposite of his initial presumption.

What does Frye leave out? Most of Book IV, with which he seems to be uneasy, remarking that 'there are signs of impatience and of a desire to begin again with the story of Apollo' (146–7). The Den of Quietude, as I have said, goes unremarked. Yet the Den lies squarely, in a Spenserian way, at the centre of Book IV, and may be said to be its climax. It follows Endymion's repeated 'perplexity' (IV, 439, 447) at his double infatuation:

> What is this soul then? Whence
> Came it? It does not seem my own, and I
> Have no self-passion or identity. (IV, 475–7)

Though Endymion flies off with his 'swan of Ganges' (IV, 465), she fades at dawn and he drops to earth, to the Den of Quietude, where he leaves identity and grief behind and comes to a centre of indifference, where he learns to remain in a state of perplexity without any irritable reaching after certitude.

Frye's poetics of literature-as-weapon on the battlefield of social concern is a very Blakean one, full of mental fight and an unsleeping sword. Frye as preacher often wins out over Frye the disinterested describer, though Frye was very good at disinterested description. Frye's values (building Jerusalem) do not really fit with either the Keatsian private epiphanic or the Keatsian necessaritarian quietude in perplexity.

The drawbacks in Frye's essay, which range from omissions (the Den of Quietude) to misrepresentations (Circe as underwater presider, lines on Cynthia applied to the Indian maid), all seem to me to stem from Frye's convictions about the place of literature in the good life. Can one continue to describe accurately after one embraces ideological convictions about the use of literature? If literature has the heartening social force that Frye ascribes to it, what purpose is served by passages like Keats's evocation of the Den of Quietude? Or by passages in which one vanishes with Cynthia into the celestial possible, as Stevens called it?

Frye's powerful social convictions drive his criticism to be an ethical criticism. For him, the good was the category in which the true and the beautiful found their ultimate meaning. For those of us who see each of the qualities of the Platonic triad as supreme, the good does not have to subsume the beautiful; the beautiful is good in itself. That latter conviction is, I think, closer to Keats's own. What I admire in Frye is that, in spite of the divergence between his own beliefs and those he intuited in Keats, he admitted to Keats's greatness and subverted his own argument, rather than let ethical concern ultimately blind him to his own deeply felt literary response.

WORK CITED

Keats, John. *Keats: Selected Poems and Letters*. Edited by Douglas Bush. Boston: Riverside Press, 1959.

JOSEPH ADAMSON

Frye's Structure of Imagery: The Case of Eros in the Poetry of William Carlos Williams

In *Words with Power*, Frye continued his lifelong exploration of what he called the order of words, extending our knowledge of the complex socio-cultural corpus of genres and conventions that structure literary works. He outlines four great variations of imagery in Western literature, designated by four central symbols: mountain, garden, cave, furnace. The second variation, the garden, concerns the imagery associated with the theme of ascent through love. As a very practical test of the potential usefulness of Frye's contribution not only to literary studies, but to a semiotics of literature, I would like to apply, in a very schematic way, this variation of a structure of imagery to the work of a single poet: William Carlos Williams. My discussion will focus on the erotic connotations of the garden imagery in Williams's poetry. The prevalence of garden symbolism in his work has certainly not been overlooked, but what to do with all these trees and flowers has been more or less up to the individual critic, and the association of such imagery with the theme of sexual desire or Eros – reflected so manifestly in titles of plays or collections such as *Many Loves, A Dream of Love, A Journey to Love* – when noted, has not been pursued in any depth. What Frye's work provides us with is the larger framework in which the imagery of an author's poetry, particular as it may be in its details, takes on the coherence of a total structure. In the case of Williams, such a framework is at least in part supplied by an understanding of the global context of erotic imagery in Western culture. While the scope of this essay prevents me from considering the many questions that arise from Williams's characteristically androcentric imagery, I would offer the following discussion as that crucial, initial step of criticism often emphasized by Frye; only when we know exactly what we are dealing with can we proceed to the necessary stage of critique.

In the Western tradition, as Frye sees it, a metaphoric structure of imagery based on the primary concern of sex is organized around the garden-body metaphor that in the Bible is found in Genesis and the Song of Songs, 'especially,' as he notes, 'in the verse "A garden enclosed is my sister, my bride; a garden enclosed, a fountain sealed" ... Here the bride's body ... is identified with the gardens and running waters of a paradise ... sexual union suggests fertility, and the bride's body is metaphorically identified with vineyards, gardens, flowers and the awakening of nature in spring' (WP, 196). An illustration of this metaphoric structure is Williams's poem 'Queen-Anne's-Lace,' which begins, 'Her body is not so white as / anemone petals nor so smooth,' and describes a field of wild flowers metaphorically as a female body that has 'blossomed' under the loving touches of a male consort (Collected Poems, vol. 1, 162). Williams often pursues the metaphor in ironic awareness of its conventional nature, as in 'Portrait of a Lady,' where the structure of a 'detailed description of the heroine's body' (MM, 49), based on the famous blazons in the Song of Songs, is self-consciously thematized and deconstructed. Another poem, 'To Mark Anthony in Heaven,' illustrates the importance of erotic love in defining the male poet's relationship to the world around him. The poet muses on the 'quiet morning light' entering his room and thinks of sexual love, metaphorically identifying 'trees and grass and clouds' – in other words, the entire natural environment – with the 'beloved body' of Cleopatra that Anthony worshipped. He hopes that Anthony saw her, 'above the battle's fury,' 'from slanting feet upward / to the roots of her hair,' for then, having won approval for his steadfast devotion to Eros, he would be 'listening in heaven' (Collected Poems, vol. 1: 124–5).

The celebration of Eros, in one way or another, is arguably the central theme in Williams. It accounts for the importance of the imagery of a renewed nature that so pervades his work. Titles of volumes such as Kora in Hell, Spring and All, and The Descent of Winter point quite explicitly to the importance of a mythological framework of seasonal imagery, and within that framework springtime is clearly associated with the theme of ascent through love. Birds, trees, and especially flowers, are everywhere. In the opening pages of the original Prologue to Kora in Hell, Williams offers an example of a truly 'fresh creation,' one which illustrates the ability to see 'the thing itself without forethought or afterthought but with great intensity of perception': it is a painting by A.E. Kerr 'that in its unearthly gaiety of flowers and sobriety of design possesses exactly that strange freshness a spring day approaches without attaining, an expansion of April' (*Imaginations*, 8–9). This is a typical matrix of imagery for Williams, and it is worth noting how he characteristically links vision with the reawakening of nature and the growing light in springtime. The ability to open one's eyes and see the world anew is by the same token linked to love, and specifically sexual love. Williams consistently associates *light* with Eros, as in the light entering the room in 'Mark Anthony in Heaven,' or the 'Holy light of love' extolled in 'The Mental Hospital Garden,' or the closing 'celebration of the light' in 'The Asphodel, That Greeny Flower.'

Not surprisingly, perhaps the single most important archetype in Williams's poetry is that of the garden. The central image of 'The Asphodel, That Greeny Flower' – the central argument of which concerns the renewal of the poet's love with his bride, whose forgiveness he seeks for his infidelities – is the transformation of the sea, associated, among other things, with the sterility of old age and the impending chaos of death, into a garden, associated with springtime and the blooming 'sexual orchid' of erotic love which restores us to what André Breton, in his own great hymn to Eros, *L'Amour fou*, calls 'la jeunesse de la sensation' (72):

> There had come to me
>   a challenge,
>   your dear self,
> mortal as I was,
>   the lily's throat
>   to the hummingbird!
> Endless wealth,
>   I thought,
>   held out its arms to me.
> A thousand tropics
>   in an apple blossom.
>   The generous earth itself
> gave us lief.
>   The whole world
>   became my garden!
> But the sea
>   which no one tends
>   is also a garden
> when the sun strikes it
>   and the waves
>   are wakened.
>   (*Collected Poems*, vol. 2: 313)

Williams, then, finds himself in a long tradition of poets who, to use Frye's words, 'preserve and emphasize the metaphorical identity of the bride's body and the garden, which enables them to associate sexual emotion with visions of a renewed nature' (*WP*, 198), and he pays homage to this tradition in the closing passage of 'The Asphodel' by evocatively quoting the refrain from Spenser's *Epithalamion*, a poem, as Frye points out, which 'paraphrases from [the Song of Songs] at some length' (198).

The imagery of rejuvenation and of a renewed nature associated with Eros is dramatized in Williams's poetry by the myth of the rising of Kora or Persephone which runs throughout his work. In this myth of springtime, as Frye summarizes it, 'the mother figure [Demeter] is linked to the old crop and the daughter [Persephone] to the new one' (*WP*, 203). The myth is so attractive to Williams because it supplies him with the kernel of the structure of imagery in his poetry. His first volume of writing was entitled *Kora in Hell*, and he explains the choice of title in *I Wanted to Write a Poem*: 'We [Williams and Pound] had talked about Kora, the Greek parallel of Persephone, the legend of Springtime captured and taken to Hades. I thought of myself as Springtime and I felt I was on my way to Hell (but I didn't go very far)' (29). In 1957, in the Prologue to the City Lights Edition, he remarks upon the myth again, and again metaphorically identifies himself with Persephone as the goddess of Springtime.

The Kora theme is succinctly developed in the opening passage of 'The Asphodel.' The significance of this flower, besides its rather ordinary appearance (a positive feature, of course, for Williams), is that, in classical mythology, it grows in hell, and, like Persephone, reappears in the spring. The garden-body metaphor is thus underlined through the identification of Kora-Flossie (Flossie is Williams's wife) with the flower of hell.

> I have invoked the flower
> in that
> frail as it is
> after winter's harshness
> it comes again
> to delect us.
> Asphodel, the ancients believed
> in hell's despite
> was such a flower.
> With daisies pied
> and violets blue,

> we say, the spring of the year
> > comes in!
> ...
>
> > Let me, for I know
> > > you take it hard,
> > with good reason,
> > > give the steps
> > > > if it may be
> > by which you shall mount,
> > > again to think well
> > > > of me.
> > > > *(Collected Poems*, vol. 2, 325–6)

Williams thus fuses the myth of the rising of Kora with that of Eurydice, led from hell by Orpheus, and joins them to the theme of the ascent through love, in which the aspiring poet-lover is drawn upwards by the 'female principle of the world,' Goethe's *Ewig-Weibliche*, evoked by Williams at the end of 'For Eleanor and Bill Monahan,' a poem written around the same time (*Collected Poems*, vol. 2, 255).

The Prologue to *Kora in Hell* is subtitled the 'Return of the Sun,' and its epigraph is three lines of verse depicting the Kora-like figure of a maiden, a clear embodiment of springtime: 'Her voice was like the rose-fragrance waltzing in the wind. / She seemed a shadow, stained with shadow colors, / Swimming through waves of sunlight' (*Imaginations*, 6). In the opening passage of the same work, the poet's mother (about whom, significantly, Williams was later to write a poem entitled 'Eve') is described as someone who, in her innocence in being taken advantage of by men, 'might be living in Eden. And indeed she is, an impoverished, ravished Eden but one indestructible as the imagination itself' (7). The use of the word 'ravished,' as well as a certain semantic ambiguity allowed by the syntax ('and indeed she is, an impoverished, ravished Eden'), suggests that the association of the woman and Eden is more like a metaphoric identity. The garden-body here, if not exactly enclosed, is at least in some sense inviolable, 'indestructible as the imagination itself.'

The image of ravishment suggests the violent abduction of Kora or Persephone and, given the subsequent description of the poet's mother in the same part of the text as 'a despoiled, molted castaway' (8), touches on that other dimension explored by Frye 'in which woman expands into a kind of proletariat, enduring, continuous, exploited humanity, awaiting emancipation in a hostile world' (*WP*, 215). In *I Wanted to Write a Poem*, Williams speaks of his mother's influence on his writing and of 'her ordeal as a woman and as a foreigner in this country. I've always held her as a mythical figure, remote from me, detached, looking down on an area in which I happened to live, a fantastic world where she was moving as a more or less pathetic figure' (16). A distinct mood of pathos surrounds those female figures in Williams who occupy what Frye describes in *Anatomy* as a suppliant position, who present 'a picture of unmitigated helplessness and destitution' and are often 'in the structurally tragic position of having lost a place of greatness' (217). The presentation of women as exiled and oppressed is a dimension particularly relevant to the theme of love in Williams's poetry. We might call it the 'Kora in hell' phase – as opposed to her rising – exemplified by 'Beautiful Thing,' the girl from the slums in Book 3 of *Paterson* who is battered in a fight between rival gangs. The imagery of flames in this section of the poem associates her with 'Hell's fire,' making the Kora theme explicit: 'Persephone / gone to hell, that hell could not keep with / the advancing season of pity' (125). The poet-lover is throughout Williams's poetry depicted as someone who identifies with women and sympathizes with them in their state of exile, subjection, or exploitation. These women range from the lonely and abandoned, as in 'The Widow's Lament in Springtime,' to the sexually exploited, such as the stripper in Juarez in 'The Desert Music,' to the working woman removing a nail from her insole in 'Proletarian Portrait.' 'I give you instead,' the poet declares at the end of *Paterson*, 'a young man / sharing the female world / in Hell's despight, graciously' (238).

The ravished Eden inhabited by the poet's mother is as 'indestructible as the imagination itself,' and she in turn seems uncannily able to retain her innocence in spite of repeated disillusionment. This capacity is related to the theme of rejuvenation, specifically to the theme of the mother who grows young and becomes a bride. In Jungian terms, as Frye points out, 'Psychologically, the rejuvenation of the mother is an internalizing and assimilating of a mother figure' (*WP*, 203). This explanation sheds considerable light on the significance of Williams's identification with his mother. 'I was personifying her' (*I Wanted*, 16), he says about her early influence on his artistic sensibilities. The presence of this theme in his writing also accounts for the importance of the figure of the crone. As a Demeter or Naomi figure – Frye's biblical equivalent of the Persephone myth being the story of Ruth – the crone stands for the end of the cycle, the 'old crop' as it were, as Ruth or the rejuvenated Persephone stands for the new. The most obvious example of such a figure is the poet's muse in 'The Wanderer,' Williams's early poem of poetic calling, which shows the influence of Whitman's great chant of vocation, 'Out of the Cradle Endlessly Rocking,' a poem framed by the image of the 'old crone rocking the cradle.' Williams's guide in 'The

Wanderer' is a 'marvellous old queen,' hovering in rags. Metaphorically married to the Passaic river, she is the symbolic mother of the poet, involved in a miraculous late birth which, like Sarah's in the Bible, suggests rejuvenation:

> Here the most secluded spaces
> For miles around, hallowed by a stench
> To be our joint solitude and temple;
> In memory of this clear marriage
> And the child I have brought you in the late years.
> *(Collected Poems*, vol. 1, 117)

Like the figure of Kora, this figure haunts Williams's poetry, and he returns to this early poem at the end of his career in the closing passages of Book 5 of *Paterson*. Evoking the image of the ouroboros, 'the serpent / its tail in its mouth' (233), which suggests a completed and self-renewing cycle, he introduces verbatim material from the closing section of 'The Wanderer.' The appearance of the poet's English grandmother at the end of *Paterson* is heralded by the cawing of crows in February, the last month of winter, recalling again the earlier poem where the crone makes her first appearance in the form of a 'young crow' (108). His grandmother

> did not want to live to be
>
> an old woman to wear a china doorknob
> in her vagina to hold her womb up – but
>
> she came to that, resourceful, what?
> He was the first to turn her up
>
> and never left her till he left her
> with child ... *(Paterson*, 238)

Bringing into focus her despoiled fertility, this graphic imagery puts her at the antipodes of that other female figure who dominates this closing section of the poem, the maidenly lady of the 'Lady and the Unicorn' tapestry, an allegorical type of the Virgin Mary. The Virgin, of course, is traditionally associated with the *hortus conclusus* or enclosed garden.

Indeed, the importance in Williams's later work of the figure of the Holy Virgin perfectly illustrates the 'theme of the ascent of love' in one of its ultimate modalities: the return, in Frye's words, to 'a childlike state of ecstatic union with the mother, or, in more traditional religious language, as a nostalgia for the lost paradise of Eden' (*WP*, 217). This can be seen clearly in the imagery based on 'a metaphorical identity between a paradisal environment and a female body' (195) that we find in a poem such as 'For Eleanor and Bill Monahan,' which is devoted to the 'Mother of God! Our Lady!' whose ecstatic union with her celebrants, her figurative children, is depicted as a return to an earthly paradise:

> that impossible springtime
>   when men
>   shall be the flowers
> spread at your feet.
>
> As far as spring is
>   from winter
>   so are we
>   from you now.
>   (*Collected Poems*, vol. 2, 253)

Section 3 of Book 5 of *Paterson* opens with an extended description of Brueghel's painting of the god of love lying 'naked on his Mother's / knees' (226). In *Pictures from Brueghel*, 'The Adoration of the Kings' repeats the scene, centred on 'the Babe in its Mother's arms' and 'the downcast eyes of the Virgin' (*Collected Poems*, vol. 2, 387–8). The poem 'The Gift' is an expression of the same complex of imagery, a celebration of the Nativity, in which the gifts proffered by the wise men, which 'stood for all that love can bring,' are miraculously transmuted as they gaze upon 'the god of love' nursing at his mother's breast: 'A miracle / had taken place, / hard gold to love, a mother's milk!' (*Collected Poems*, vol. 2: 430–1). In all cases, the depiction might just as well be that of Venus and Cupid, confirming Frye's observation that 'one consistent form of the quest of love appears to be the journey to identity with the god of love as child, whether the infant Jesus in the arms of his mother or the infant Cupid frolicking around Venus' (*WP*, 217–18).

In the same vein, a significant portion of Book 5 of *Paterson* consists of imagery inspired by the 'Lady and the Unicorn' tapestry at the Musée de Cluny, the theme of which is the allegory of 'the hunt of the unicorn and the god of love of virgin birth' (233). In the tapestry, the repeated detail of a fenced-in circular bed of trees and flowers enclosing the lady and the unicorn is an explicit icon of the enclosed garden. Williams emphasizes the garden imagery, the unicorn being seen 'against a millefleurs background,' by cataloguing the flowers that are crowded into the different scenes (231). One of the details described in this section of *Paterson* concerns a young woman whose 'rare smile' is detected 'among the thronging flowers of that field where the Unicorn is penned by a low wooden fence' (232); another, hinting at the annunciation, presents a woman demurely hid 'among the leaves, listening,' her face expressive, to 'the blowing of a hunter's horn' (237). Williams, of course, represses none of the sexual connotations of the imagery throughout this closing section of the poem.

The preceding, very schematic reading of the conventions of erotic love in Williams is far from exhaustive. I have been unable to enlarge on many points, and I have restricted myself to a minimum of illustrations. I hope, however, that I have at least gone some way towards demonstrating the value of Frye's treatment of imagery. The lack of a systematic attention to imagery continues to be a weakness in the analysis of literary works. We are enormously skilful at deconstructing texts and revealing their manifold contradictions, and we have grown remarkably adept at analysing them in the most nuanced ways as reflections of the ideological, political, and cultural limitations of their historical moment. But when it comes to the treatment of something as fundamental as imagery, too often we find ourselves working with old tools that were pretty dull in the first place, and thus our treatment remains impressionistic and speculative. Imagery speaks its own language, but as long as we tune it out as though it were a foreign one, we will remain in ignorance of one of the most significant dimensions of poetic communication. One lasting contribution of Frye's work is to have given us the ability to hear and understand this highly structured, semiotically organized language in all its complexity and detail.

WORKS CITED

Breton, André. *L'Amour fou*. Paris: Gallimard, 1937.

Williams, William Carlos. *The Collected Poems of William Carlos Williams*. Vol. 1, 1909–39. Edited by Walton Litz and Christopher MacGowan. New York: New Directions, 1986.

– *The Collected Poems of William Carlos Williams*. Vol. 2: 1939–62. Edited by Christopher MacGowan. New York: New Directions, 1988.

– *Imaginations*. Edited by Webster Schott. New York: New Directions, 1970.

– *Paterson*. New York: New Directions, 1963.

– *I Wanted to Write a Poem*. Edited by Edith Heal. Boston: Beacon Press, 1958.

MICHAEL FISCHER

Frye and the Politics
of English Romanticism

In English departments at many American universities, 'theory' has
come to be associated with opening the canon to previously excluded
texts and with respecting difference in ethnicity, class, gender, and
sexual orientation. Critics aligned with theory are said to make up what
Henry Louis Gates has called a 'Rainbow Coalition' ('The Master's
Pieces,' 95) of deconstructionists, feminists, and cultural-historical
theorists. This coalition has been fiercely attacked by Dinesh D'Souza,
Allan Bloom, and others for subverting academic standards, politicizing
appointments and reading lists, and fostering mind-numbing political
correctness. D'Souza and Bloom, in return, have been charged with
racism, ethnocentrism, and even Fascism. Each side in this dispute
accuses the other of intolerance, of repressing freedom while pretending
to uphold it.

I find it curious that Frye's work is rarely cited in this debate – curious,
because Frye not only did so much to champion theory, a key term in
this dispute, but also advocated many of the values both theorists and
antitheorists claim to be affirming: values like freedom, appreciation of
diversity, and democratic openness to other points of view. I want here
to reexamine Frye's work in light of the current quarrel over the canon
and other issues, focusing especially on the 'residual anarchism' Frye
inherits from the English Romantics (*SR*, 48). 'Residual anarchism' is
Frye's phrase for the feeling of the Romantic writers that a society
advances only 'by individualizing itself, by being sufficiently tolerant
and flexible to allow an individual to find his own identity within it,
even though in doing so he comes to repudiate most of the conventional
values of that society' (*SR*, 48). This Romantic commitment to individual-

izing society, to making it more receptive to personal difference, shows Frye's kinship with recent theorists as well as his distance from them.

At first glance, Frye would seem to be an important ally for theorists committed to diversity. Much of his writing favours an 'open mythology' over a closed one. According to Frye, a closed mythology results when a society feels that its myths of concern – its values, beliefs, and traditions – are the only right ones. Frye suspects that this seemingly arrogant assertion of superiority and correctness conceals anxiety about the form of life being defended. The very fact that a way of life needs defending, that it feels so threatened by fragmentation and discontinuity, testifies to an underlying vulnerability. Apprehensiveness, not confidence, thus prompts the nervous attempt to ward off the danger posed by difference. Frye's examples of closed mythologies include Naziism and Stalinist Marxism, each one uneasily defining itself by the brutal exclusion of purported outsiders.

Frye himself advocates an open mythology characterized by tolerance, dialogue, and change. His well-known and still controversial uneasiness with value judgments in criticism is meant to shore up respect for diversity. In a striking statement in *The Modern Century*, published in 1967, he goes so far as to say that 'an open mythology has no canon' (118). Any canon, in this view, no matter how impartial or disinterested it may appear, is élitist; it projects onto literature a hierarchy that originates in social life. Commenting on how modern critical fashions promote some writers while demoting others, Frye writes, 'we can see that every increase of appreciation has been right, and every decrease wrong': 'criticism,' he says, 'has no business to react against things, but should show a steady advance toward undiscriminating catholicity' (*AC*, 25). Instead of fleeing what he calls the infinite variety of literature, Frye thus delights in it. For Frye, as he says in *The Critical Path*, 'there are no negative visions: all poets are potentially positive contributors to man's body of vision ... Therefore ... criticism does not aim at evaluation, which always means that the critic wants to get into the concern game himself, choosing a canon out of literature and so making literature a single gigantic allegory of his own anxieties' (127).

I am quite willing to read into these comments support for current critics interested in opening the canon to works by previously excluded writers. When I think of a critic 'choosing a canon out of literature and so making literature a single gigantic allegory of his anxieties,' I think of Allan Bloom and the many fears on display in *The Closing of the American Mind*. Unlike many critics of Bloom, however, Frye does not simply ridicule these fears; he admits their power. He feels in himself the longing for security that a critic like Bloom succumbs to. An open mythology, Frye says at one point in *The Critical Path*, 'is by no means a panacea': 'Not only is there a constant pressure within society to close its mythology, from both radical and conservative wings, but the efforts to keep it open have to be strenuous, constant, delicate, unpopular, and above all largely negative' (156).

I will be explaining why even a democratic society has constantly to be kept open through strenuous opposition, but for now I want to note that Frye is making a crucial Romantic point here. I call this point 'Romantic' because it results from the 'residual anarchism' that in my view is Frye's chief inheritance from the Romantic writers who influence him, especially William Blake. According to this line of thought, all societies, even open and democratic ones, are apprehensive about perpetuating their values. They all feel tempted to close their mythology, to brook no dissent, and to claim that, finally, they have got things right. Blake expresses this scepticism towards politics when he notes in *A Vision of the Last Judgment*, 'You cannot have Liberty in this World without [what you call] Moral Virtue & you cannot have Moral Virtue without the Slavery of that half of the Human Race who hate [what you call] Moral Virtue' (554).[1] In *Anatomy of Criticism*, Frye similarly warns that 'the idea of the free society implied in culture can never be formulated, much less established as a society' (348). Drawing on how the Romantics viewed the failure of the French Revolution, Frye repeatedly cautions that political attempts to institutionalize freedom always fall short of their laudable aims. 'All forms of politics,' he concludes in *The Modern Century*, 'including the radical form, seem sooner or later to dwindle into a specialized chess game' (101).

This suspicion of political action and the possibilities of social life is intended not to discourage our quest for freedom but to unsettle our complacency.[2] Efforts to keep a mythology open have to be strenuous, unpopular, and constant because the pressure to close a mythology speaks to our deep-seated fear of change and losing control, not to mention our ever-present readiness to declare things over and done with. Taking another Romantic step, Frye makes the individual the final custodian of freedom, the force that contests a society's closure. This appeal to the individual is a Romantic step because, as Frye points out, Romanticism licenses the individual to put pressure on society: the responsiveness of society to the self takes precedence over the socialization of recalcitrant individuals. Frye shows how the Romantic writers consequently shy away from such literary genres as comedy. What Frye

calls the social emphasis of comedy makes Romantic writers feel claus-
trophobic. By 'the social emphasis of comedy,' Frye means the compro-
mise that results when individuals – obstructionist rulers, unhelpful
parents, headstrong young lovers – give up insisting too stridently on
their particular grievances, and the community in turn expands to
accommodate their differences. From a Romantic point of view, the
seemingly regenerated society affirmed by comedy is not regenerated
enough because it still blunts the full discovery and assertion of personal
difference. According to Frye, all societies do this, even ones we rightly
feel some allegiance to.

Frye accordingly pictures a never-ending tension between individuals
and the society that lays claim to them. Frye does not imagine these
individuals coming into this world with an innate, prior sense of what
is right.[3] He sees them being detached from their society – critically
distanced from it – but not separate; their efforts are largely negative
because they react against a preexistent form of life that is constantly
impinging on them. These terminally restless individuals see the
boundaries of their culture and they chafe against its limitations.

Even though Frye places the individual in society and not prior to it,
his Romantic privileging of the individual as the caretaker of freedom
still clashes with what contemporary literary theorists call the social
construction of the subject. I will be coming back to this point in a
moment, but first I need to note something else separating Frye from the
contemporary theorists I have aligned him with. For him, individuals
gain a critical perspective on society by assessing the objective truth of
its values. These individuals compose a sceptical, often unpopular
minority committed to what Frye calls the myth of freedom. They refuse
to take their culture's claims at face value; they insist on measuring their
society's concerns by the facts, reason, and evidence. According to Frye,
an open society tolerates and even encourages this appeal to objective
truth and the critical self-examination it promotes. A closed society, by
contrast, discourages intellectual honesty, distorts history, and even
falsifies the results of science, all in a desperate effort to exempt its way
of life from criticism. Put a bit differently, an open society has no fixed
canon because it welcomes exposure to the endless diversity of literature.
As Frye puts it, 'precisely because its variety is infinite, literature
suggests an encyclopaedic range of concern greater than any formulation
of concern in religious or political myth can express' (*CP*, 103). An open
society learns from the infinite variety of literature the limits of its own
concerns and the consequent value of making room for other points of

view. A closed society, however, recoils from this discovery; censorship, indoctrination, and didacticism replace the wide-ranging, objective inquiry Frye favours.

I mentioned earlier that Frye's respect for the individual as a guarantor of freedom places him at odds with tendencies in recent literary theory. So does his esteem for what he often calls the autonomy of scholarship, or this recourse to objective truth, reason, and evidence that I have been describing. Much as current critics emphasize the social construction of the individual subject, they equate 'truth' with what a particular society or interpretive community happens to count as truth. According to this argument, a culture's myths of concerns shape what it calls objective knowledge; the latter disappears as a free-standing, culturally transcendent yardstick.[4] What Frye wants to distance from society – independent individuals and the objective criteria they call on – thus get reinscribed within society.

Frye anticipates this argument and tries to answer it. In *The Critical Path*, he puts the problem of achieving objectivity this way:

> There is also a philosophical issue involved which concerns the degree to which anything in words can tell the truth at all, in terms of the truth as correspondence. In truth of correspondence a verbal structure is aligned with the phenomena it describes, but every verbal structure contains mythical and fictional features simply because it is a verbal structure. Even the subject-predicate-object relationship is a verbal fiction, and arises from the conditions of grammar, not from those of the subject being studied. Then again, anything presented in words has a narrative shape (*mythos*) and is partly conditioned by the demands of narrative. (119)

From this point of view, every verbal structure may have mythical and fictional features shaping its representation of things as they are and thus blocking its crucial access to extralinguistic truth. Access to objective truth is again crucial for Frye because it provides individuals with a vantage point for criticizing their culture's myths of concern.

Frye tries to salvage objectivity by conceding that the standards of logic, truth, and evidence are 'approximations' and 'analogies' of a world that admittedly may not exist. In other words, while not the unimpeachable guides a positivist might want them to be, these standards for Frye work well enough as 'ideals of procedure, however impossible it may be to realize them completely' (*CP*, 119). This pragmatic recuperation of objectivity has many analogues in contemporary criticism. Jacques

Derrida, for example, speaks of Claude Lévi-Strauss's 'double intention' with respect to metaphysical concepts like origin and centre: Lévi-Strauss wants 'to preserve as an instrument something whose truth value he criticizes' ('Structure, Sign, and Play,' 1120). Frye takes a similar approach to the truth of correspondence but, like Lévi-Strauss in Derrida's analysis, he ends up needing to treat this truth *as truth*, as something much more than a possible approximation or mere analogue. For Frye, the truth of correspondence is indispensable to personal freedom; it gives the individual leverage against the myths of concern anxiously demanding his or her assent. Frye's problem is that politically he cannot do without truth, evidence, and so on (lest he undermine his case for freedom), but philosophically he cannot support these ideals in the cognitive terms that alone give them real authority. Dissent needs to have truth on its side: as Frye puts it in *The Critical Path*, 'the socially critical attitudes, which perceive hypocrisy, corruption, failure to meet standards, gaps between the real and the ideal, and the like, are anti-ritualistic, and cannot attract much social notice without the support of their one powerful ally, the truth of correspondence revealed through reason and evidence' (45). By attenuating access to things as they are, Frye's epistemology creates difficulties for his politics.

Although Frye's argument is strained, his intent is clear and I think admirable. He means 'to show by example that beliefs may be held and examined at the same time' (*CP*, 109). At one point Frye observes parenthetically that 'in times of stress the inadequacy or impossibility of objective truth ... is much insisted on' (*CP*, 119). I would argue that today is one such time of stress and that, lacking confidence in objective truth, we have difficulty seeing how beliefs can be held and examined at the same time. Theorists like Stanley Fish, for example, argue that having beliefs precludes our examining them, at least from some nonavailable objective vantage point, whereas neoconservatives fear that critically analysing beliefs impairs our confidence in them. In his writing Frye steers between these two extremes. He achieves in practice the dialogue between commitment and self-criticism that he cannot quite account for in theory. As any reader of Frye knows, he has beliefs, takes stands, and makes assertions. But even as he insists 'this is so,' he respects the voice that urges 'but suppose *this* is so' – the sceptical voice that prolongs committee meetings, complicates decision making, and tugs at resolution.[5] Frye shows why this tension between belief and doubt has to continue, lest belief degenerate into fanaticism and doubt end up excusing inaction.

NOTES

1 In 'The Keys to the Gates,' Frye explains that, although Blake hoped for a considerable social response to his art, he felt that no society could actualize the values art keeps alive: 'even if everybody responded completely and at once, the City of God would not become immediately visible: if it did, it would simply be one more objective environment' (253) – one more society in need of imaginative critique.

2 Frye's scepticism towards political action leads Frank Lentricchia to conclude that Frye has 'a thoroughly despairing and alienated understanding of the possibilities of historical life. For Frye actual history can be nothing but a theatre of dehumanization, a place of bondage and torture' (*After the New Criticism*, 26). In my view, instead of destroying our confidence in political action, Frye tempers it.

3 Here is one place where Frye dissents from Romanticism, specifically from what he regards as the Romantic tendency 'to think of the individual as ideally prior to his society.' He prefers seeing the new baby as 'his own society appearing once again as a unit of individuality' (*AC*, 97).

4 For further discussion of this tendency in contemporary criticism, see my 'Perspectivism and Literary Theory Today.'

5 I allude here to a comment in *Anatomy of Criticism*: 'Between religion's "this is" and poetry's "but suppose *this* is," there must always be some kind of tension, until the possible and the actual meet at infinity. Nobody wants a poet in the perfect human state, and, as even the poets tell us, nobody but God himself can tolerate a poltergeist in the City of God' (127–8). Nobody wants a poet in the perfect human state because poetry inveterately speculates about other, perhaps better possibilities. I think Frye similarly taxes the patience of conservative and radical activists when he insists on keeping all concerns open to critical inspection. This may help explain why both sides in the canon wars overlook him. Along similar lines, Frye hints that we resist Romanticism because it says something we do not want to hear: 'the residual anarchism at the heart of the Romantic movement is still with us, and will be until society stops trying to suppress it' (*SR*, 48).

WORKS CITED

Blake, William. *The Poetry and Prose of William Blake*. Edited by David V. Erdman. Garden City: Doubleday, 1970.

Bloom, Allan. *The Closing of the American Mind*. New York: Simon and Schuster, 1987.

Derrida, Jacques. 'Structure, Sign, and Play in the Discourse of the Human Sciences.' In *Critical Theory Since Plato*, edited by Hazard Adams. Rev. ed. New York: Harcourt Brace Jovanovich, 1992.

D'Souza, Dinesh. *Illiberal Education*. New York: Free Press, 1991.

Fischer, Michael. 'Perspectivism and Literary Theory Today.' *American Literary History* (Fall 1990): 528–49.

Frye, Northrop. 'The Keys to the Gates.' In *Romanticism and Consciousness*, edited by Harold Bloom. New York: W.W. Norton, 1970.

Gates, Henry Louis, Jr. 'The Master's Pieces: On Canon Formation and the African-American Tradition.' In *The Politics of Liberal Education*, edited by Darryl J. Gless and Barbara Herrnstein Smith. Durham: Duke University Press, 1992.

Lentricchia, Frank. *After the New Criticism*. Chicago: University of Chicago Press, 1980.

J. EDWARD CHAMBERLIN

Mathematics and Modernism

Poetry and mathematics have a lot in common. Other than sex, they seem to cause more anxiety among high school and university students than almost anything else. Which is curious, since most children love words and numbers. Something has gone wrong.

Something else has gone wrong about our attitude towards poetry and mathematics. This time it has to do with Frye. None of us – or maybe I had better say few of us – who teach literature would advise students to skip the end of a book. In fact, for the past fifty years or so, many of us have been paying a lot of attention to endings, and to the ways in which authors achieve or eschew closure. And yet hardly anybody has paid any attention to the ending of Frye's *Anatomy of Criticism*.

The last five pages of the book consist of a sustained meditation on the relationships between literature and mathematics. It is not a sudden turn, for we are well prepared by a succession of comments throughout the book. There is no closure, but instead a series of questions. Questions about the relationships between the imagination and reality, or the links between what Frye calls 'creation and knowledge, art and science, myth and concept' (*AC*, 354). It is a catechism that recalls the centre of his work, and the crux of modernism. And it leads to mathematics.

Let me briefly recall the key points of his narrative. Early in the *Anatomy* during the course of a discussion on one of his favourite topics, the truth of poetry, Frye comments: 'the poet, like the pure mathematician, depends not on descriptive truth, but on conformity to his hypothetical postulates. The appearance of a ghost in *Hamlet* presents the hypothesis "let there be a ghost in *Hamlet*." It has nothing to do with whether ghosts exist or not, or whether Shakespeare or his audience thought they did. A reader who quarrels with postulates, who dislikes *Hamlet* because he does not believe that there are ghosts or that people speak in pentameters, clearly has no business in literature' (76). Or, by implication, in mathematics. A little later, Frye repeats this tenet: 'Mathematics, like literature, proceeds hypothetically and by internal consistency, not descriptively and by outward fidelity to nature. When it is applied to external facts, it is not its truth but its applicability that is being verified' (93).

This is essential modernism, and quintessential Frye. On the final page of *Anatomy*, he repeats the same point: 'Literature, like mathematics, is a language; and a language in itself represents no truth, though it may provide the means for expressing any number of them' (354). Bertrand Russell, another modernist and a mathematician as well, put it more bluntly: 'Mathematics is a science in which we never know what we are talking about nor whether what we say is true.'[1] As Frye would say, that is what makes mathematics so similar to literature. The association of literature and mathematics, or more generally of art and science, may at first seem merely a superficial product of the idealism that informed a great deal of modernist intellectual inquiry. But in fact it was the result of a much more complex, and much less certain, attitude towards reality and the imagination, an attitude that – to be mischievous – I would suggest gets routinely misunderstood by the totalizing discourses of postmodernism. This attitude was grounded in a recognition that the perceiving self not only discovers, but in some sense invents, phenomena, and conditions both our understanding of the truths of the real world and our sense of its beauties. Reality mirrors the essential workings of our mind. Both scientists and artists believed that. This is what Gerard Manley Hopkins was talking about when he wrote, 'Hope holds to Christ the mind's own mirror out' ('Hope Holds to Christ,' 186) – the humility of the priest closely approximating that of the physicist.

Possibly the greatest advocate of these intellectual trends in the latter part of the nineteenth and the early twentieth century was Ernst Mach (1838–1916).[2] There is a lot of attention given to the natural sciences during this period, and to its great imaginative achievements. But the physical sciences and mathematics also generated speculation which was extraordinarily influential, and which closely paralleled developments in aesthetic thought and artistic practice, reinforcing tendencies in the general tenor of early modernist intellectual life. (Indeed, even Hopkins, to take just one unlikely example, proposed to write what he referred to as 'a sort of popular account of Light and the Ether' [*Correspondence*, 139], in order to counter the materialist tendencies of the time by demonstrating the essentially spiritual character of the discourses of the physical sciences.)

Ernst Mach was at the forefront of scientific inquiry by the 1880s. He was also one of the most influential figures in fin de siècle Vienna (though he is seldom mentioned by its popular chroniclers). He was a kind of godfather to the Vienna Circle, a group of philosophers and scientists who gave wide currency to the principles of logical positivism, and which included local figures such as Rudolf Carnap, Kurt Gödel, Karl Menger, and Hans Hahn, as well as colleagues elsewhere like Ludwig Wittgenstein. Mach was also sufficiently important – and with his focus on the way in which sensations generate ideas through the act of observation, was deemed sufficiently subversive – that Lenin devoted almost a year of his busy life in 1908 to researching and writing a book attacking Mach and some of his colleagues. It was titled *Materialism and Empirio-Criticism*, and it held out against the antimaterialism that was such a constant refrain during this period, not only with scientists such as Mach and Ernst Haeckel, but also with the artists and critics of impressionism and symbolism. Lenin's book reminds us how influential scientific inquiry was during this period, with radical notions just as likely to emanate from mathematics and physics as from the biological and social sciences.

Mach certainly had radical notions, coming up with startling proposals such as his idea that the perception of colour could be separated from the perception of space. He applied the positivism of Auguste Comte to explain the necessary and sufficient convenience of scientific theory, aids to understanding, as it were, and to communication, with a powerful shaping influence, but with only limited and contingent authority. In this he paved the way for the linguistic speculations of Edward Sapir and Benjamin Whorf, who argued that the significant structural and conventional differences between languages – exemplified in their syntactic and lexical forms and phonetic symbolisms – determine not only contingencies of meaning, but also fundamentally different ways of understanding reality and of behaving towards it. That is, assumptions embedded in language generate culturally specific epistemologies and ontologies. This principle of linguistic relativity, as Whorf called it, was closely related to Ernst Mach's earlier speculations.

Mach had challenged some of the conventions of mechanics which, in his view, had assumed unjustified authority since Newton, insisting that science begins not with definitions but with assumptions. Hypotheses. Like *Hamlet*. A similar understanding of the conceptual significance of hypothetical – that is, structurally contingent – axioms in geometry by the German mathematician David Hilbert in 1899 led the way both to the 'new' (non-Euclidean) geometries and to fundamental changes in many other areas of scientific inquiry.

Mach took greater risks than many of his contemporaries, especially in his persistent association of the physical and psychical. But in other respects he was simply (and very consciously) working in the tradition of philosophers such as David Hume, insisting that it was improper to assign many apparently material relationships, such as cause and effect, anything more than psychological authority. Mach was breaking down the accepted relationships between events in much the same way that Freud was doing. And, after all, they were living in the same town, at the same time.

Mach formulated the thesis that the state of any system is a consequence of the interaction of that system and everything else, no matter how different or distant. It was this notion, more than any other, that prompted Einstein – who specifically acknowledged his great debt to both Hume and Mach – to insist on the role of the observer in the measurement of phenomena, so that even the simultaneity of two events is not an intrinsic property of those events but depends as well on the motion of the observer who is recording them. This, of course, is at the heart of both the general and the special theory of relativity. It is also at the heart of modern science.

This line of thought was developed in a somewhat different direction by scientists such as Karl Pearson, whose influential *Grammar of Science* appeared in 1892 with a sustained attack on metaphysics and an exposé of popular illusions about space and time and the relationship between mind and matter. Insisting on the unknowability of things-in-themselves, Pearson proposed a new image of human consciousness. He insisted that

we are like the clerk in the [new] central telephone exchange [in London] who cannot get nearer to his customers than his end of the ... wires. We are indeed worse off than the clerk, for to carry out the analogy properly we must suppose him never to have been outside the telephone exchange, never to have seen a customer or anyone like a customer – in short, never, except through the telephone wire, to have come in contact with the outside universe ... The real universe for him would be the aggregate of his constructs from the messages which were brought by the telephone wires in his office ... We are cribbed and confined in this world of sense impressions like the exchange clerk in his world of sounds, and not a step beyond can we get. (61–3)

For many of Pearson's readers in the 1890s, these remarks would have recalled Walter Pater's grim description of our 'whole scope of observation [being] dwarfed to the narrow chamber of the individual mind ... Every one of those impressions is the impression of the individual in his isolation, each mind keeping as a solitary prisoner its own dream of a world' (*Selected Writings*, 59–60). This dream, of course, takes one of its forms in the literature – and the mathematics – that Frye celebrates. In the final footnote in *Anatomy*, he adds that 'it is difficult to see how aesthetic theory can get much further without recognizing the creative element in mathematics' (364). He then goes on to suggest a place for it in a circle of the arts. Oscar Wilde had turned around Matthew Arnold's popular dictum about seeing the object as in itself as it really is, and spoke instead about seeing it as it really is not.[3] For Wilde, as for Frye (who always acknowledged his debt to Wilde), that also described the motive of art.

In all of his comments on mathematics and literature, Frye draws us close to the central concerns of modernism: the autonomy of art; its self-reflexive language and self-contained logic; its disinterested irrationalism, which gives it its unreasonable power not just to change the way we see the world, but to change the world itself. All good criticism begins with this irrationality, said the great modernist critic Ernst Robert Curtius (*Essays*, passim). According to Frye, it ends there too, hovering like Plato's ultimate act of apprehension somewhere between the mathematical and the mythical (*AC*, 354).

The irrational is, in fact, a good place to enter the discussion about mathematics. That is what Frye did, for it is in reference to what were called irrationals that he makes his only mention of a specific development in modernist mathematics. 'Irrational numbers in mathematics may be compared to prepositions in verbal structures,' notes Frye, adding that they share what he calls a 'centripetal character,' directed inwards towards the structure of the discourse rather than outwards towards some ostensible referent in the real world (*AC*, 351).

Frye did not know much about mathematics. But in rhetorical terms, he knew what he was doing. In mentioning irrationals, Frye was locating himself at the centre of a major mathematical controversy, in many ways much more far-reaching than the preoccupation with the irrational in psychology and the other social sciences. Irrational numbers – numbers (such as the square root of 2) which cannot be expressed as fractions – had a long history in mathematics. They were discovered by the Pythagoreans, one of whom, a scholar named Hippasus, showed that the side of a square and its diagonal are not commensurable – that is, there is no line segment, no matter how small, that will divide evenly into both. If the sides of the square are of length 1, for example, then the length of the diagonal is the square root of 2. This was very upsetting to the Pythagoreans, the idolizers of numbers that match. The story goes that they were so upset that they took Hippasus out to sea and threw him overboard.[4]

Hippasus may have been out of the way, but irrationals continued to plague everybody. Another troublemaker named Hippocrates – the mathematical, not the medical, one – brought irrationals into the spotlight again with his attempt to construct a square of equal area to a given circle: that is, to square the circle. For over 2000 years, mathematicians tried to finish what he had started. They failed. And then finally, in 1882, in the springtime of modernism, a German mathematician named Ferdinand Lindemann proved that it was impossible.

Let us be clear about what this means, because it bears directly on Frye's view of the relationship between literature and mathematics. It does not mean that there cannot exist a square of the same area as a given circle. It's easy to show that there can. But it will be an *imaginary* existence, not a real one. Imagine a square of light projected on the page beside a given circle. Let us move the projector so that the square has an area smaller than the circle. Then we move the projector back, away from the page, and soon we get a square larger than the circle. We must assume that at some instant the area was the same. But we cannot construct such a square, at least not with the limited means that classical geometry puts at our disposal – the compass and the straight edge, the only begetters of real squares and circles. When Lindemann demonstrated the existence of imaginary numbers such as irrationals, he was illustrating what the new mathematics was all about – relationships between the real and the imagined. And this is why Frye called upon mathematics to illuminate his new sense of what literature was all about.

'Imaginaries in mathematics are a form of the impossible,' grumbled the Larousse dictionary in 1873. 'Why study such problems, since irrational numbers do not exist?' rejoined Leopold Kronecker, probably the most powerful mathematician in the most powerful mathematics institution of the time, the University of Berlin. 'What good is your beautiful investigation?'[5] And his was a fairly generous remark. Most comments sounded like the familiar denunciations of decadent art and of aestheticism. Full of fear and loathing.

Given the fin de siècle preoccupation with irrational behaviour, it is what mathematicians might call an elegant coincidence that the term 'irrational' was used – in German, French, and Russian, incidentally, as well as in English – to refer to these numbers which so completely defied the logic of mathematical realism. And there was another class of numbers brought into the foreground around the same time, to further confound this logic. They were called 'transcendentals'; and unlike irrationals, they were not even algebraic (that is, they were not the solution of any algebraic equation with rational coefficients, as the square root of 2, for example, is a solution of the equation $x^2 - 2 = 0$). The number pi, the ratio of a circle's circumference to its diameter, is a transcendental. So is the number e, the basis of the system of logarithms (or, more precisely, the limit of $[1+1/n]$ to the nth power as n increases without limit). And transcendentals too were proven to 'exist'; or more precisely, to exist in the realm of mathematics. But not without some consternation. 'I turn aside in horror from this lamentable plague,'[6] remarked Charles Hermite, the French mathematician who devised the proof of the imaginary existence of transcendentals in 1873.

It was disturbing stuff. But it was on the fringes of an even more disturbing idea – the mathematical idea of infinity. From the Greek philosophers to the greatest nineteenth-century mathematician, Karl Friedrich Gauss, there had been a universal horror of infinite quantities. 'Infinity is by its very nature incomprehensible to us,' Galileo had said. 'The mathematical idea of infinity is a disease from which one hopes to recover,'[7] said Henri Poincare, a modernist mathematician of no small talent himself. In 1874, the year Claude Monet exhibited his celebrated paintings of the Rouen cathedral and the year after Hermite confirmed the existence of transcendentals, a Russian-born, German-educated genius named Georg Ferdinand Ludwig Philip Cantor made a breakthrough, developing a completely new mathematical theory called the theory of sets. It laid the foundation for a new way of looking at infinity.

Cantor had a brilliant and courageous instinct for mathematics as a system essentially independent of the reality to which it refers, but at the same time offering our readiest access to it. He began with the simple, but very significant, insight that comparisons, or equivalents, are essential for the measurement of things, things such as sets of objects or numbers. He assumed that if we establish a one-to-one correspondence between *finite* sets, then they have the same number of objects in them – that is, they are equivalent. (This is an assumption we all make every time we count on our fingers.) Cantor then proposed that the same was true of sets with an *infinite* number of objects in them. And he proved it, after figuring out a way – this was his remarkable accomplishment – of putting such sets into one-to-one correspondence.[8]

Some awkward paradoxes emerged, to which Cantor responded by underwriting the theory with certain axioms. These in turn produced other questions, questions which preoccupied the next two generations of mathematicians and finally drove Bertrand Russell to give up the great encyclopaedic enterprise that he had undertaken with Alfred North Whitehead, *Principia Mathematica*. One of the most problematic issues had to do with what was called the class of all classes not members of themselves. Is such a class a member of itself or not? If it is, it should not be; and if it is not, it should be. As one contemporary, Henri Lebesgue, said, 'we called them paradoxes (rather than contradictions) – which sounds ever so much less disturbing.'[9]

Cantor's theory had other extraordinary implications, which were not paradoxical in this sense, but which were certainly very disconcerting. They also formed the basis of twentieth-century mathematical science, including the ideas of incompleteness and indeterminacy that the postmodernists routinely take as their own. Among the consequences of Cantor's mathematics was the startling conclusion that any two line segments, regardless of their length, possess the same number of points, and that the number of whole numbers and the number of even whole numbers (or the set of odd whole numbers – take your pick) is exactly the same. The part *is* the same as the whole, a kind of mathematical confirmation of the chief tenet of symbolism. This is the connection that Frye picked up, and then took a step further. 'Both [literature and mathematics] drive a wedge between the antithesis of being and non-being that is so important for discursive thought,' he suggested.

> The symbol neither is nor is not the reality which it manifests. The child beginning geometry is presented with a dot and is told, first, that that is a point, and second, that it is not a point. He cannot advance until he accepts both statements at once. It is absurd that that which is no number can also be a number, but the result of accepting the absurdity was the discovery of zero. The same kind of hypothesis exists in literature, where Hamlet and Falstaff neither exist nor do not exist, and where an airy nothing is confidently located and named. (*AC*, 351)

Many others, of course, were aware of these kinds of inspired contradictions. The artists and architects at the Bauhaus – Paul Klee and Wassily Kandinsky, in particular – had a long-standing interest in modernist mathematical developments, and mathematicians were regularly invited to speak there. Klee developed an elaborate theory for his class on form that drew upon mathematical thought, laced with Pythagorean mysticism. And science writers such as Arthur Eddington and James Jeans, whom Frye mentions in the final pages of *Anatomy*, were making clear to everyone what had been common knowledge for at least fifty years, that the objects of perception are constructed by our imaginations, where all the serious business of life takes place. Frye relates Jeans's speculations about mathematics to his own about literature: 'pure mathematics exists in a mathematical universe which is no longer a commentary on an outside world, but contains that world within itself. [It] is at first a form of understanding an objective world regarded as its content, but in the end it conceives of the content as being itself mathematical in form, and when a conception of a mathematical universe is reached, form and content become the same thing' (AC, 352).

Frye also suggests another analogy, between what he calls 'the units of literature and of mathematics, the metaphor and the equation' (AC, 352). In making this association, he was drawing on a quite different modernist tradition that brought literature and mathematics together. And it was at the heart of one of the most significant innovations of the time, one affecting Frye's other abiding interest – education. In 1929, the American philosopher Scott Buchanan published a book called *Poetry and Mathematics*. At the time, Buchanan was Assistant Director of the People's Institute in New York, organizing lectures at the Cooper Union. His colleagues included Mortimer Adler, Robert Hutchins, Mark Van Doren, Stringfellow Barr, and Richard McKeon; and they carried on a remarkable program of popular adult education, which had been initiated by Charles Sprague Smith, a professor of Comparative Literature at Columbia thirty years earlier. Adler had already introduced the Columbia Honors Course in Great Books to seminars in the New York Public Library system. They were intended, not as canonical expressions of certain universal truths, by the way, but as pedagogical tools, exemplifying the very principles about literature specifically – and about verbal structures generally – which Frye discusses in *Anatomy*. They were selected, that is, for their usefulness in transforming students into their own teachers.

The list had originally come from Sir John Lubbock in London, who had edited a series of texts (Sir John Lubbock's Hundred Books, published by George Routledge) for use (among other purposes) in the Workers and Mechanics Institutes in the 1880s and 1890s. The practice of the liberal arts which this program embodied – and the principles of continuing education sustained by the formal habits of learning induced by the texts themselves – were soon incorporated into the teaching at the People's Institute. Buchanan was convinced that the study of mathematics belonged in this arena – a modern reconstruction of the seven classical liberal arts, consisting of the trivium (grammar, rhetoric, and logic) and the quadrivium (arithmetic, geometry, music, and astronomy); and he developed a set of analogies between literature and mathematics that were very like those that Frye proposed. In due course, Buchanan went to join Stringfellow Barr at Virginia, while Adler and McKeon were brought by Hutchins to Chicago – and the most radical reform in American higher education this century began. Eventually, Buchanan and Barr went to revive and restructure St John's College in Annapolis, which eventually extended a campus to Santa Fe; and it remains one of the most challenging educational experiments on the continent, so unlike the authoritarian models developed elsewhere and so consistent with the ideals that Frye espoused. He knew a great deal about all this; and Buchanan's book, which represents its spirit, is informed by the same delight in the connections between literature and mathematics that Frye celebrates at the end of his *Anatomy*.

NOTES

1 Russell, quoted in Lucienne Felix, *The Modern Aspect of Mathematics*, 53.

2 Mach's writings include *The Science of Mechanics* (1883) and *The Analysis of Sensations and the Relationship of the Physical to the Psychical* (1886). There is a useful brief commentary on Mach in Newman's *The World of Mathematics*, vol. 3, 1784ff. Some of my comments on Mach (and on Georg Cantor, below) are included, in an expanded form, in my essay ' "Whose Spirit is This?" ' in *Fin de Siècle/Fin du Globe*, 217–24.

3 Matthew Arnold's comment was made at the beginning of his essay 'The Function of Criticism at the Present Time,' in *Essays in Criticism: First Series*, 1; Wilde's, in his essay 'The Critic as Artist,' in *Oscar Wilde*, 29.

4 Dunham, *Journey Through Genius*, a book to which I am indebted for my account of the irrationals (see pp. 10, 22–3) and of Georg Cantor (see pp. 245–83).

5 Quoted in Felix, *Modern Aspect of Mathematics*, 37, 10.

6 Quoted in Felix, *Modern Aspect of Mathematics*, 10, 43.

7 Quoted in Kline, *Mathematics in Western Culture*, 395–7.

8 For Cantor's own account, see *Contributions to the Founding of the Theory of Transfinite Numbers*. See also Hans Hahn's lecture 'Infinity,' delivered under the auspices of the Vienna Circle and published in Newman, *The World of Mathematics*, vol. 3, 1593–1611; Kline, *Mathematics in Modern Culture*, 395–409; and Maor, *To Infinity and Beyond*.

9 Quoted in Felix, *Modern Aspect of Mathematics*, 49.

WORKS CITED

Arnold, Matthew. *Essays in Criticism: First Series*. In *The Works of Matthew Arnold*, vol. 3. New York: AMS, 1970.

Buchanan, Scott. *Poetry and Mathematics*. 1929. Reprint. Chicago: University of Chicago Press, 1962.

Cantor, Georg. *Contributions to the Founding of the Theory of Transfinite Numbers*. Translated with introduction by Philip E.B. Jourdain. Reprint. New York: Dover, 1915.

Chamberlin, Edward. ' "Whose Spirit is This?" Some Questions about Beginnings and Endings.' In *Fin de Siècle / Fin du Globe*, edited by John Stokes. London: Macmillan, 1992.

Curtius, Ernst Robert. *Essays on European Literature*. Translated by Michael Kowal. Princeton: Princeton University Press, 1973.

Dunham, William. *Journey through Genius: The Great Theorems of Mathematics*. New York: John Wiley, 1990.

Felix, Lucienne. *The Modern Aspect of Mathematics*. Translated by Julius H. Hlavaty and Francille H. Hlavaty. New York: Basic Books, 1960.

Hopkins, Gerald Manley. *Poems of Gerard Manley Hopkins*. Edited by W.H. Gardner and N.H. MacKenzie. 4th ed. Oxford: Oxford University Press, 1970.

– *Correspondence of Gerard Manley Hopkins and Richard Watson Dixon*. Edited by C.C. Abbott. 2nd rev. ed. London: Oxford University Press, 1955.

Kline, Morris. *Mathematics in Western Culture*. New York: Oxford University Press, 1953.

Maor, Eli. *To Infinity and Beyond: A Cultural History of the Infinite*. Princeton: Princeton University Press, 1991.

Newman, James R. *The World of Mathematics*. Vol. 3. New York: Simon & Schuster, 1956.

Pater, Walter. *Selected Writings of Walter Pater*. Edited by Harold Bloom. New York: Columbia University Press, 1974.

Wilde, Oscar. 'The Critic as Artist.' In *Oscar Wilde: Plays, Prose Writings and Poems*, edited by Isobel Murray. New York: Dutton, 1975.

PAUL CORNEA

The Modern Century:
An East-European Reading

While visiting Canada for a congress on comparative literature at the beginning of the 1970s, I read a copy of Frye's *The Modern Century*, which I found in the McGill University bookshop. It was not so much a book about Canada as it was about the great problems of contemporaneity, recalled not systematically but in a simple and colloquial style that avoided any rhetorical, sentimental, or militant temptation.

In those years, when Romanian national communism displayed its so-called successes arrogantly, and the West unfortunately encouraged our dictator, Frye's book impressed me enormously. It did not contest totalitarianism directly, as did Jean François Revel or Raymond Aron, but instead strengthened the reader's belief in values, aptitude for assessing things in moderation, and confidence in hope. In times of confusion, when the ground under one's feet is no longer secure, it is a great comfort to realize that the fundamental landmarks of free thinking go on subsisting; that, just like the compass hand which invariably points to the north, Europe is still there, America is still there, and freedom is alive.

Reread today, the basic statements of *The Modern Century* continue to be topical. The extraordinary upsets of these past years, which led to the collapse of communism, did not extinguish the book's ideas. Even if some statements ought to be differentiated into shades of meaning, as a whole I would contend that the great historical changes recently undergone increase its diagnostic force.

Let us start with an essential question: What is the modern epoch characterized by? Frye's answer has been given by many others, from

Spengler to Foucault: discontinuity. From this point of view, the year 1867 (when the Canadian Confederation came into being) offers a symbolic coincidence: Baudelaire dies, and *Das Kapital* of Marx is published. On the one hand, art rids itself of romantic rhetoric and begins its intellectual, nonconformist adventure; on the other hand, economy turns from manufactured production to large-scale industry, from a provincial status to a planetary one.

The modern world is the first civilization in history to focus on the study of itself (*MC*, 18–20). It made an attempt (and still does) to find out the presuppositions that direct its behaviours, and continues to try and understand its past, and thereby – if only to a relative extent – control its future. This self-awareness, Frye believes, provoked the emergence, and then the deepening, of an antagonism between two attitudes: one of involvement, a critical examination of events and phenomena, an effort to struggle forward to a new acceptable way of life; the other, of indulging oneself in passivity, of living at random, without asking questions or seeking solutions.

We find this separation between those who accept the world as it is and those who want to change it, or at least to know it, in the mythologies governing our representations and faiths. According to Frye, since the nineteenth century Christian mythology has been replaced by one that rejects theology, as well as teleology. This modern mythology removes God from his position as the creator and legislator of the universe; thus human beings become the product of natural evolution and the authors of civilization and knowledge.

Nevertheless, the modern mythology works, either in its closed or open version. The former is based on clichés and standard answers acquired in school and reinforced by the mass media. It is illustrated by communist practices, but it occurs, as well, in less coherent patterns, as in liberal societies, religious ritual, or in the famous American Way of Life. Therefore, the widely circulated texts comprise vestiges of Christian mythology in evasive or transgressive forms (the myths of Paradise, the Fall, Exodus, Apocalypse, etc.).

The open mythologies, characteristic of democratic societies, are loose structures – so much so that even the term 'structure,' a metaphor of solidity, seems to be inadequate. They continue to enrich through the creations of some of our great minds, from Rousseau, Marx, Freud, up to the existential philosophers. Frye also mentions the so-called idea books, which hover over the intellectual world – or wide fields of it – helping us to coordinate and make sense of numberless striking and contradictory aspects of human existence. Among the authors he mentions in this connection are Spengler, Toynbee, Hannah Arendt, Whitehead, Fiedler, Eddington, Marcuse, Martin Buber, and Harold Rosenberg (*The Tradition of the New*), among others. The common feature of these historians, scholars, critics, and philosophers is that they deal with human situations from an essential perspective, beyond the particular case of each field activity. Focusing on human beings as biological, social, and metaphysical entities, they assess knowledge and technique in relation to them ('myth of concern').

The active-passive distinction mentioned above separates the artistic creation – in the proper meaning of the word – from communication techniques and mass culture based on stereotypes and recurrent formulas. Creation requires the reader's imagination and involves his or her active collaboration. Communication addresses automatic comprehension; it implies preexisting answers and a passive response. This approach is well known in the modern theory of reader-response criticism. Frye's contribution (*MC*, 26ff.) seems to me relevant here, particularly in the discussion of advertisements and propaganda, two communicative techniques widely used in contemporary society. The way in which these techniques utilize shock and extreme and unexpected and sometimes absurd statements puzzles or discourages the critical conscience. Ads and propaganda insinuate themselves into timorous, credulous, or childish minds – unfortunately these represent a majority – where they gain ground and finally settle their slogans, defeating any kind of resistance. They do not cause adherence necessarily, but, as happens with drugs, they bring about an unmediated dependence on the versions of reality they provide.

Frye's idea can be applied in an interesting way, assuming that ads and propaganda represent activities specific to the two systems. Thus I find ads relevant for liberal societies, since they imply a separation between economic and political structures. In the former socialist countries, where the political used to govern all powerfully, the products offered were the same in terms of range and quality; throughout the home trade, ads were mere simulacruma, as were the parliamentary institution and the liberties written down in the constitution. In Ceaucescu's Romania there were notices on display in visible places which stated: 'Buy goods from the state shops,' in spite of there being only state shops. In contrast, propaganda was an effective weapon because of the generalized, obsessive nature of its impact. The simplistic slogans were uttered time after time by all the means available to the mass media, from the parliamentary rostrum, the elementary school, and the academy. As Huxley, Orwell, and many others have revealed in their negative utopias, what was intended was the ideological vaccination of the population, the replacement of education with training.

In this perspective, Frye's following statement is a surprise: 'Even propaganda based on the big lie, as when an American or Chinese politician tries to get rid of a rival by calling him a communist or a bourgeois counter-revolutionary, can establish itself and command assent if it makes more noise than the denial of the charge' (*MC*, 27). The situation described is only theoretically possible. In fact, the lie of the American politician can be denied at any time, whereas the lie of the Chinese politician can be denied only if the state is interested in having it denied. In a totalitarian country there is only the monologue of power. The alternative sources of information are forbidden. The logic of the system does not tolerate dissidence, opposition, or heresy. Nobody is allowed publicly to oppose the official allegations. The truth is only what the tyrant reckons as such.

One of the most characteristic features of the modern epoch, and one that Frye gives much prominence to, is the rapid pace of change. As a consequence of the acceleration of technological progress, a new perception of time has appeared. The steady motion, the fact that every day, every hour changes the daily landscape, dramatizes the individual's sense of existence. A lot of people feel a genuine panic about change, so much so that they become incapable of putting up with the ceaseless mutations and metamorphoses in social life. They are not able to meet the presuppositions of progress: the dynamic is preferred to the static, the process to the result, the organic to the mechanical. Alienation insinuates itself into human minds: the faster we travel, the more dependent we are on vehicles, yet the more we give up driving these vehicles, the bigger our apprehension becomes. Nevertheless, within all the mechanisms of progress, we are merely passengers travelling with an unknown driver.

A typical example (*MC*, 32) of 'a progressive machine' is, according to Karl Polanyi, the self-regulating market of laissez-faire. The market's independent functioning for more than a century, with indisputable successes as well as contradictions and failures, suggested a noncritical dependence on what Polanyi called 'the alleged self-healing virtues of the unconscious growth' (*MC*, 32). This implies that the fulfillment of social progress has been transferred from human will to autonomous social forces. A similar example (*MC*, 32) is provided by 'communist theology' within which the historical process is granted the part of the Holy Spirit in the Christian faith, that of omnipotent force cooperating with human will without depending on it.

Frye wonders (*MC*, 34–5): How can we know that we made for the right direction, and ensure that tomorrow will be superior to today? Is it worth sacrificing the present to the future (as communist leaders have always required)? Were not, and are not, the most awful aspects of contemporaneity likely to be accounted for by the desire to achieve 'the better'? The massacre of civil populations 'helps' to win wars and to settle peace; the racial crimes 'solve' the Jewish problem or the problems of other persecuted minorities; starvation of millions of people 'keeps up' the farmers' living standard.

Technology does not represent in itself a means of improving life. It can change the world without altering people's souls. Furthermore, it works within a mechanism that swings between advantages and disadvantages. Any improvement in a field gives birth to a lack of balance which stimulates strains, followed by further disturbances. If, for instance, there is produced a superior sports car, we seem to get more freedom, but the gain is more theoretical than real because the police quickly respond by establishing new restrictions to control traffic. Neither does science, abandoned to itself, develop automatically towards excellence. It does not exist outside society, and society, either openly or secretly, directs the course of science. When the direction is open, there is competition between relatively autonomous factors. When it is secret, as in totalitarian countries, there is little competition. In both cases, society, deliberately or unawares, directs the development. In this perspective Frye rejects McLuhan's speculations (*MC*, 39–40), in whose rigid determinism he finds an oversimplified form of rhetoric. Thus, the famous identification between medium and message has to be interpreted according to the active or passive response of the receiver. Television's 'coolness' and radio's 'hot' character are not intrinsic: 'All forms of communication, from transistors to atom bombs, are equally hot when someone else's finger is on the button' (*MC*, 40). The quality of the medium results from the way it is used.

Another disadvantage of progress is the oppressive tendency towards standardization (*MC*, 36). The hideous outskirts of the huge metropolises all look alike, irrespective of the country to which they belong, as do the standardized products of big industry. The everyday speech clichés sound the same. Everything seems to symbolize an alarming tendency towards spiritual conformity, a proliferation of the passive response.

Displaying a view which reminds one of *A Brave New World*, Frye warns us that, if some tendencies inherent in our civilization are not put to an end, they could lead rapidly to a society 'which, like that of a prison, would be both completely introverted and completely without privacy' (*MC*, 38). The new electronic media could penetrate the ultimate fortresses of the inner mind, making a short circuit in its associative structures and replacing them with the prefabricated ones of the media. A society wholly controlled by slogans and clichés would become completely introverted, because people would no longer have anything to say: 'there would only be echo, and Echo was the mistress of Narcissus.'

While true, this viewpoint does not seem to me sufficiently clear in its subtle shades of meaning. In the former Eastern socialist countries, the dictators tried manipulating the media in order to control education and make existence ritualistic: to make everyone think alike. In spite of the huge effort expended, they failed. At night, behind locked doors, a whole people were listening to Free Europe, the BBC, or the Voice of America; many authors had become used to transgressing the rigours of censorship by using an Aesopic language, and wide masses of readers had acquired the ability to read between the lines. Everybody, from the young to the old, realized that the dictator lied. That is why, in the last years preceding 1989, the genuine problem was not one of conditioning (from the insidious reiteration of the same silly slogans), but one of schizophrenia (having to live a double life: at work people had to keep silent or lie, but at home they could 'speak').

The myth of progress received a nasty blow with the stock market crash and financial bankruptcy of 1929 (*MC*, 42–3). Since then many other dramatic events have occurred, helping to open the eyes of the naive. Frye mentions H.G. Wells who had bet for a long time on the self-developing capacity of science. Wells's last book, *The Mind at the End of Its Tether* (1940), is permeated with the bitterness and fury of a disappointed idealism. But he is still far from the nightmare recalled by Orwell, and by so many other authors of distopias who describe culture, technology, science, and language operating in demonic or perverted forms.

The optimism about progress cherished by the eighteenth century seems completely out of date today. After the catastrophic collapse of communism, who can ever believe now that a pure and reasonable society could be reborn and cleansed from an accumulation of injustice and absurdities by means of a purifying revolution? Is not Swift more realistic when he holds that slavery is at least as natural for human beings as freedom (*MC*, 43)? At present, we understand that progress means progression to a target that may be closer to disaster than to perfection. If once a sense of alienation and anxiety were contemplated as a fear of Hell, nowadays this fear is attached not to the world of the dead, but to the future of our own world. The collapse of belief in progress intensifies the sense of anxiety originating in the consciousness of death.

Finally, I shall make one more point, not only because it is tragically current, but also because it paradoxically suggests to us a less sceptical Frye. I am referring to his idea that the nation is an out-of-date category: 'It seems to me ... quite clear that we are moving towards a post-national world. What is important about the last century, in this country, is not that we have been a nation for a hundred years, but that we have had a hundred years in which to make the transition from a pre-national to a post-national consciousness' (*MC*, 17).

It is true that in 1967 there were plenty of people who thought that, in a world of interplanetary communications and economic interdependence on a world scale, the nation was an anachronistic reality. However, when Frye was writing his book, nationalism in Eastern Europe was in full swing. It was cultivated by the leading bureaucracy to create a diversion; it was meant to distract people's attention from economic hardships and isolate dissident movements. In these efforts, Ceaucescu proved to be an expert. Examples abound in the mid 1980s: Romania exported food while its citizens starved; the villages were 'systematized'; the old urban centres were destroyed; the women were required to submit to periodic gynaecological examinations. In exchange, under colour of the so-called policy of independence from Moscow, the dictator promoted an aggressive, primitive, megalomaniacal nationalism with Manichean connotations, which became very popular at home and misleading for Western leaders. Other Eastern leaders kept pace with him: the Bulgarian Jivkov put into practice the plan of denationalizing the Turks, and the German Honecker invented the existence of a socialist German nation, different from the bourgeois German one. At present, in Romania, we witness the disastrous effects of a policy meant to homogenize peoples by force and rouse intolerance towards minorities.

While Western Europe develops toward economic and political unity – not smoothly, of course – flabbergasted humankind witnesses the outburst of violence and cruelty in Yugoslavia. At present it is obvious that, while central authority is broken up, while poverty and insecurity are more manifest than ever, the old national frustrations and antagonisms burst out with a new terrible and devastating force.

The idea that nation is an out-of-date category may not be wrong, but the problem is that humankind develops differently from what the experts predict. Under the circumstances, when hazard is disguised retrospectively by some people as necessity, history sometimes preserves the ridiculous on its stage, rehabilitating what is marginal and generally having fun refuting our expectations.

But even if, in the perspective of the 1960s, Frye seemed to ignore the negative potential of nationalism in Europe and also, like all the others at the time, could not notice yet the seriousness of the ecological planetary disaster, his conclusions are devoid of any triumphal spirit. They stress the sense of moral responsibility. Since the world we live in is abandoned to itself, as heavens are void and God is absent, the problem of values becomes the core of it. On what basis can they be legitimized? Who authorizes the authority of law? How is God to be replaced without creating idols? Frye writes: 'If we can no longer feel that this world was once created for us by a divine parent, we still must feel, more intensely than ever, that it is the world we ought to be creating and that whatever may be divine in our destiny or nature is connected with its creation' (*MC*, 121). The loss of faith is, of course a religious problem, yet it has a political dimension as well. Frye expresses this in the question: To whom do we owe our loyalty in society? In fact, this is a transposition of Dostoyevsky's and Nietzsche's terrible question: If God does not exist, is anything permitted?

To clear up these points, Frye quotes an apologue of William Blake (*MC*, 120–1). In the poem 'The Lamb,' from the cycle *Songs of Innocence*, a child asks the first question of the catechism: 'Who made you?' The answer is reassuring: Jesus Christ made the lamb because he himself is both a child and a lamb, joining the human and the subhuman world within the divine personality. But in the poem 'The Tyger,' from the cycle *Songs of Experience*, the question 'Did he who made the lamb make thee?' is left without an answer. The vision has disappeared of a world created by a reasonable, beneficent power, in which there live only lambs, or where there are allowed both lions and tigers provided they become harmless. The world we live in is that of the tiger, the trivial one of the blind instincts, of alienation, and the rush to power; it is not the one of reason, tolerance, and reliability. In it, men and women are the only creative beings, but, as with the iceberg, the good part floats over unfathomable depths, populated by the forces of evil and destruction.

Nevertheless, in trying hard to imagine or create a better world beyond everyday troubles and trivialities, there seems to survive something of the child's innocence. We feel obscurely that the dream of the impossible creation, which gives sense to human action, is not altogether lost. The ideal exits but something of it is still there, hidden under the slime of reality. The hidden side of America emerging from Thoreau's or Whitman's works, as well as from Lincoln's personality, is at the height of the iceberg's tip. 'All nations have such a buried or uncreated ideal, the last world of the lamb and the child' (*MC*, 122). Only the poets reveal to us what is hidden. Only they find what has not been found and hear what the noise of the world prevents us from hearing. In this respect, Frye concludes: 'The Canada to which we really do owe loyalty is the Canada that we have failed to create' (*MC*, 122–3). And further on: 'I should like to suggest that our identity like the real identity of all nations is the one that we have failed to achieve. It is expressed in our culture but not attained in our life' (*MC*, 123).

Frye's idea can be applied to a larger area. Since democracy is a self-referential system and its exercise is not guaranteed by any transcendence, there is only one legitimate alternative: to save freedom without falling into anarchy, we have to develop an autonomy based on consensual solidarity. If, as Castoriadis said, 'nous sommes ceux qui ont pour loi de faire leurs propres lois,' the only reasonable behaviour would be to hope to fulfill that identity of democracy we know from books, but which we have failed to achieve so far in practice.

WLADIMIR KRYSINSKI

Frye and the Problems
of Modern(ity)

Let me make the following initial statement in celebration of Northop Frye: if, in the history of modern criticism and of modern theory, there have ever been critics who never relinquished wisdom in acquiring knowledge, they were probably Bakhtin and Frye. We can call Frye an ironic Canadian who continually conveyed the same global message, with consequences unrivalled in their significance. And one can define that message as follows: the stuff of Western literature has some basic informing structures and they are myth, archetype, and the Bible. Frye's irony and wisdom were probably the weapons that protected him against any kind of avant-garde instances of modernity, such as the famous slogan of Ezra Pound, 'Make it new!' Being a holistic, systematic, and systemic critic, Frye repeats himself throughout his books and his essays. He continually underlines the same obsessively strong meaning of literature: whatever literary forms and discourses may be, they are reducible to a few elementary structures that inform literature. Myth, archetype, and the Bible are therefore both the structural and the spiritual food of Western literature. In a way, it is impossible to go beyond them insofar as they underlie and overdetermine literary discourse. Needless to say, such wisdom as Frye's relativizes any possible extension of the knowledge of literature. It relativizes it as a critical metanarrative that constantly seeks to discover the same things, not to say the sameness of literature. Reading Frye, rereading him today, one discovers a brilliant and ironical mind at work, a mind which is looking precisely for the core of literary discourse: the repetition and re-affirmation of myth, of archetypes, and of the Bible. I would say, how-ever, that the greatness of Frye lies somewhere between wisdom and knowledge. To quote T.S. Eliot, one can assume that Frye was never trapped 'between futile speculation and unconsidered action' (*The Rock*, 29). He has not 'lost the wisdom in knowledge,' but also he has not 'lost the knowledge in information' (7).

I believe that Frye's greatness as a critic resides in the way his incisive and perspicacious sentences follow closely on and support each other in thoroughly integrated syntax. This is the greatness of a perfect, critical intuition which cannot be wrong. It cannot be wrong because it possesses wisdom, that is to say, a deep understanding of literature based on the conviction that the substance of literature is repetitiously the same. Possessing wisdom thus defined means, however, being monotonously right. Monotony once conveyed through repetition may be an everlasting boredom. Frye, of course, spares the reader boredom. Between his wisdom and his knowledge, between the critic's information and the informing of the critic, the reader has at least one possible escape. And the escape route lies in what Frye communicates to the reader as a reader. He communicates his sensitive and insightful understanding of the discourse under discussion, the discourse of the other person.

In epistemological terms, the dilemma for the reader of Frye consists in choosing between the critic's knowledge and his wisdom. Wisdom communicates the monotony of *sapientia*. Knowledge offers a changing but still sustained series of penetrating observations, of surprising formulas and of keen affirmations. Knowledge thus defined leads the reader to the regained paradise of intelligence. He or she suddenly discovers that literature is not just an affair of snobs, of sellers and buyers of books. It is an ethical reality. The realm of literature is passionately built up by such people as Blake, Milton, Shakespeare, Yeats, Joyce, T.S. Eliot, and Wallace Stevens. By choosing them for his exercise of ethical and of aesthetic judgment, Frye conducts his inquiry into fearful symmetry, educated imagination, and fables of identity.

Now I would like to propose my inquiry into Frye's writings as a critic and theoretician of modernity. If what I called the wisdom of the critic is the recognition of the regular repetition of the *corso* and *ricorso* of myths and of archetypes, the understanding of modernity can, or rather should, basically rely on the acknowledgment of the fact that modernity is nothing more than a discourse which offers nothing other than the illusion of the new. As a matter of fact, for Frye there is no such thing as real novelty. The new is nothing other than an accident of inventiveness which, at any rate, will be relativized. Modernity is therefore the 'modern age' which in fact is another age added to the previous ages. It may differ in its forms and in its specific themes but its substance is fundamentally the same. It is the return of myths and of archetypes. Hence Frye's scepticism as far as fashion is concerned. As Frye states: 'Thus if there appears a vogue for white lipstick among certain groups of young women, that may represent a new impersonality in sexual relationship, a parody of white supremacy, the dramatization of a death-wish, or the social projection of the clown archetype' (MC, 21).

What strikes me in this statement is the progressive reduction of the new: 'a new impersonality in sexual relationship' to a series of critical items and topoï the function of which is returning to that which is permanent and stable behind any fashion. In fact, fashion is merely disguised archetypical behaviour. And Frye punctuates serially: a 'parody of white supremacy,' the 'dramatization of a death-wish,' 'social projection of the clown archetype.' I have therefore to concede that the new is not new. It is rather an extravaganza that disguises something serious.

How can an archetypically oriented critic foster a proper theory or conception of modernity? He probably cannot. Yet Frye tried to do it and he did not completely fail. Let us try to grasp Frye's vision and understanding of modernity. To start with, we have to note that there is no systematic research into modernity in Frye's critical writings. And the term itself is rather unpopular in Frye's criticism. Frye deals with modernity deprived of the suffix '-ity.' That is to say, he deals with some visions and some epiphenomena of the modern limited to one hundred years in human history. Instead of dealing with modernity, the ironic Canadian deals with the modern and more specifically with the modern century. And the word 'modern' acquires a truly specific meaning in The Modern Century. It is a book in which Frye parasystematically explores social, literary, and philosophical aspects of what is being called the modern century, that is to say, the period of time which according to Frye's view stretches from 1867 to 1967 – the year Frye delivered his Whidden Lectures at McMaster University.

Frye does not deal with modernity as a transcultural and transhistorical concept, as a system, or as a philosophical or aesthetic project, but I concede that The Modern Century is a book on some manifestations of the modern, taken in the sense either of the Hegelian Zeitgeist or of certain dominant features of the immediate social, political, or literary history. What Frye tells us about the modern concerns mainly arts and literature, but his extensive view also encompasses some critique of what I would call the 'stately reasons' and the 'social consequences' of the disintegration of the faith in progress. Frye's formula 'alienation of progress' defines a specific state of human affairs in which neither the individual nor the community can rely on the future as a promise and as the realization of a better spiritual, social, cultural, and, last but not least, the ecological environment. Frye is an implacable critic of the overall failure of humanity which is unable to create a human world free from alienation and from anxiety. I have just linked Frye's greatness with the thoroughly integrated syntax of his incisive and perspicacious statements. In the first chapter of *The Modern Century*, entitled 'City of the end of things,' Frye is great throughout almost all the pages. I would like to quote extensively from this chapter but I will only choose some pivotal statements:

> Taking thought for the morrow, we are told on good authority, is a dangerous practice. In proportion as the confidence in progress has declined, its relation to individual experience has become clearer. That is, progress is a social projection of the individual's sense of the passing of time. But the individual, as such, is not progressing to anything except his own death. Hence the collapse of belief in progress reinforces the sense of anxiety which is rooted in the consciousness of death. (35)

Since mass media and communication are among Frye's topics in *The Modern Century*, I would like to recall his ironic treatment of McLuhan's prophecies:

> The role of communications media in the modern world is a subject that Professor Marshall McLuhan has made so much his own that it would be almost a discourtesy not to refer to him in a lecture which covers many of his themes. The McLuhan cult, or more accurately the McLuhan rumour, is the latest of the illusions of progress: it tells us that a number of new media are about to bring in a new form of civilization all by themselves, merely by existing. (38–9)

Frye also provides this cruel and yet so precise and adequate synthesis of our present political and social condition:

> All the social nightmares of our day seem to focus on some unending and inescapable form of mob rule. The most permanent kind of mob rule is not anarchy, nor is it the dictatorship that regularizes anarchy, nor even the imposed police state depicted by Orwell. It is rather the self-policing state, the society incapable of formulating an articulate criticism of itself and of developing a will to act in its light. This is a condition that we are closer to, on this continent, than we are to dictatorship. In such a society the conception of progress would reappear as a donkey's carrot, as the new freedom

we shall have as soon as some regrettable temporary necessity is out of the
way. No one would notice that the necessities never come to an end,
because the comunications media would have destroyed the memory. (45)

As pessimistic as Frye's vision may be, it is nevertheless implicitly
underpinned by an ethical vision of humanity. Hence the principle of
hope which pervades Frye's discourse: 'The picture itself reflects anxiety,
and as long as man is capable of anxiety he is capable of passing through
it to a genuine human destiny' (49).

The Modern Century is a doubly circumstantial book. It celebrates the
centenary of Canada and it refers to the year 1867 which forms the starting point of the modern in culture, literature, and society, according to
Frye. Incidentally, 1867 coincides with the year of Baudelaire's death.
This fact is underlined by Frye when he states: ' "Modern,' so used, describes certain aspects of an international style in the arts which began,
mainly in Paris, about a hundred years ago. Out of compliment to our
centenary, I shall date it from 1867, the year of the death of Baudelaire'
(51).

What may strike the average, educated, reader of literature is the fact
that no attempt is made here to rethink Baudelaire's idea of modernity.
Keep in mind that in 1863 Baudelaire published in *Figaro* a series of
articles entitled *Constantin Guys: The Painter of Modern Life (Constantin
Guys: Le peintre de la vie moderne)*. These articles are extremely important
for the understanding of literary and cultural life. Baudelaire proposes
to study both the manners of the present and the beauty of the present.
In his article entitled 'La Modernité,' Baudelaire gives probably the first
coherent and challenging definition of modernity. He defines it as 'the
transitory, the fugitive, the contingent, one half of art, the second half of
which is the eternal and immutable' (19). Baudelaire's definition of the
modern relies strongly on the copresence and coexistence in modernity
of a double temporality: that of the immediate present and that of the
permanent and eternal past. For Frye the 'modern' is primarily an
'international' style (*MC*, 51). It does not seem to rely on the 'tradition of
the new.' It encompasses a number of writers whom Frye enumerates:
Rimbaud, Flaubert, Dostoyevsky, and Nietzsche, and it is characterized
by a number of phenomena which Frye mentions without any hierarchical or systematic development. However, his observations are always
relevant, keen, and subtle. Let me provide a series of examples:

In fact the modern is often popularly supposed to be primarily a matter of
'streamlining,' of suggesting in furniture and building, as well as in the

formal arts themselves, the clean, spare, economical, functional lines of a swiftly moving vehicle. (65)

Modern poetry tends to be discontinuous, to break the hypnotic continuity of a settled metre, an organizing narrative, or a line of thought, all of which, it is felt, are apt to move too far in the direction of passive response. (66)

The anti-rhetorical tendency in modern literature is part of a general tendency in modern culture to plant a series of anti- tank traps, so to speak, in the way of the rumbling and creaking invaders of our minds. (67)

Modern art, especially in such developments as action-painting, is concerned to give the impression of process rather than product, of something emerging out of the heat of struggle and still showing the strain of its passing from conception to birth. (70)

I have chosen these particular excerpts from *The Modern Century* in order to stress the fact that Frye makes a series of observations which, if they were systematically put together, would constitute a real treatise on modern art and literature. What strikes me in Frye's discourse, however, is his unwillingness to deal exhaustively or systematically with the subject of modernity. The anatomist of criticism prefers rather to describe the modern century quite randomly, with emphasis on a few specific facts, phenomena, and processes relevant to Canadian history. Frye treats this history itself in a fragmentary and general way in terms of ethical formulas and synthetic visions. It is important to remember that for Frye 'modern,' like romantic or baroque, is a historical term but its meaning is primarily cultural. His book is therefore about modern culture understood as an extended social landscape examined from the perspective of cultural practices in literature, in painting, in communication, in media, in film, and so on. At the same time this extended social landscape is examined from the perspective of modern mythology in which the central myth is defined by Frye as the 'myth of concern' (114–17). And the function of this myth is to judge 'the effects of science on human life' (115).

In this sense, *The Modern Century* is the best possible title the critic could have chosen for this book, which is mainly a demonstration of what the modern century is, seen from the cultural perspective. And the modern century is many things; it does not necessarily have a dominant structure. From the jumble of things and contradictions Frye chooses, some significant elements serve his description, insofar as it is an attempt to understand the changes that took place in the world and in Western society (particularly in Canada) between 1867 and 1967. If Frye inscribes the problem of Canada in his book, this is because the historical development of the modern age (taken in the sense of the German *Neuzeit*, as employed in Hans Blumenberg's seminal book *The Legitimacy of the Modern Age*) is linked with the constitution of national identity and of the nation-state. This is true for Germany and for Italy in the nineteenth century. According to Frye, The Confederation Act of 1867 should also be considered as marking the progress of modernity onto Canadian soil.

The description of changes with its emphasis on certain specific differences, which define not just modern art and literature but also modern history and modern society, allows Frye to accomplish his ethical and critical discourse. In that sense, *The Modern Century* is a highly political and critical book. It is a critique of the state, of society, and of what Jean-François Lyotard was to call in 1979 'grand metanarratives.' It is important to bear in mind that Lyotard explicitly links metanarrative and metadiscourse to his definition of the modern. This definition is as follows: 'I will use the term modern to designate any science that legitimates itself with reference to a metadiscourse of this kind making an explicit appeal to some grand narrative, such as the dialectics of Spirit, the hermeneutics of meaning, the emancipation of the rational or working subject, or the creation of wealth' (*The Postmodern Condition*, xxiii). Lyotard defines the postmodern as an 'incredulity toward metanarratives' (xxiv).

In fact, Frye's *The Modern Century*, published in 1967 exactly twelve years before *The Postmodern Condition*, deals with at least one of those metanarratives, that is to say, with progress. By showing its failure, Frye is of course expressing his incredulity toward it. It does not mean that he proposes to replace the modern by the postmodern. Instead he argues for a utopia which paradoxically enables him provisionally to resolve the problem of Canada. Frye recalls the Portuguese etymology of Canada, 'nobody here' or rather 'nothing here,' and he goes on to say: 'The Canada to which we really do owe loyalty is the Canada that we have failed to create' (122–3). This is not necessarily a bad thing, according to Frye: 'But, as we enter a second century contemplating a world where power and success express themselves so much in stentorian lying, hypnotized leadership, and panic-stricken suppression of freedom and criticism, the uncreated identity of Canada may be after all not so bad a heritage to take with us' (123).

Is this the voice of hope, or is it the voice of naiveté? Does Frye offer us an ideal or a prediction here? Perhaps the case of Canada is for Frye a pretext for demonstrating the fact that the modern Canadian century has not been as modern as certain developments in the arts and literature elsewhere in the world. The basic implication of Frye's argument is that in terms of politics and history, and in terms of the so-called just society, Canada has not lived up to the expectations of modernity understood as the project of *Aufklärung*. Canada possesses the modern institution of state and of federation, but it has not achieved the modern emancipation of identity, of authenticity and of recognition, at least as far as its ethnic and cultural minorities are concerned. As Charles Taylor puts it in *The Malaise of Modernity*: 'But the importance of recognition has been modified and intensified by the understanding of identity emerging with the ideal of authenticity. This was also in part an offshoot of the decline of hierarchical society' (47). And further: 'The importance of recognition is now universally acknowledged in one form or another; ... On the social plane, we have a continuing politics of equal recognition' (49).

Frye's *The Modern Century* is a discourse which paradoxically announces both the crisis of modernity and the coming of postmodernism. Even though in 1967 Frye did not develop a systematic theory of modernity, he came quite close to the way in which Jürgen Habermas in 1980 was to qualify the malaise of modernity as an 'incomplete project.' Frye also came quite close to the idea of the failure of the metanarratives that underlie the establishment of the consensus essential to modernity. In other words, Frye's understanding of the modern century has a strong postmodern intuition, in the sense that the 'alienation of progress' is nothing else than a failure to legitimize modernity by means of metanarrative called 'progress.' If we cannot call Frye a postmodern thinker it is because for him the idea of 'genuine human life' is a predominant value. The postmodernists have correctly understood the fact that after Auschwitz and after some other inhuman episodes in so-called human history the ideal of 'genuine human life' cannot be realized. I would venture to say that Frye's discourse is based on a sort of double bind in the sense that his critique of the alienation of progress does not prevent him from believing in the existence of genuine human life. And, in fact, since such a utopia has also become wishful thinking, the only thing that really might remain to be practised is an ironic discourse. However, the seriousness of the subject prevents Frye from ironizing the alienation of progress. Consequently, *The Modern Century* is also a book about the failure of hope. Hope cannot provide a principle of intelligibility for an increasingly complex world. Between the crisis of the modern and the resurrection of myths and archetypes, such as that of the tiger, there is no solution other than that of describing moments of negation. The salvation for Canada as a premodern, and yet quite postmodern, country lies in the real and pragmatic recognition of the multiplicity of its identities, and Frye seems to recognize this fact while situating these Canadian differences among the family of nations. 'Like Switzerland in nineteenth-century Europe, Canada must now preserve its identity by having many identities' (131). The preservation of this multiple identity has failed somewhat. Politically and ethically, the modern Canadian century has prevented Canada from becoming a truly modern nation.

Frye is a critic of illusion and of confusion. But he is also an advocate of fusion. If the pandora's box opened by the Meech Lake controversy were now to be closed on the basis of an agreement about recognition, identity, and authenticity, the Canadian malaise of modernity would be resolved. But the malaise seems to be so significantly prey to the alienation of progress that Frye's negative vision may be an adequate and objective assessment of a situation which has so many stumbling blocks.

'The world we are in,' says Frye, 'is the world of the tiger, and that world was never created or seen to be good. It is the subhuman world of nature, a world of law and of power but not of intelligence or design' (121).

Since the Canadian crisis is also a crisis of modernity, we are perhaps doomed to remain in Blake's bestiary as long as recognition, authenticity, and identity do not find their peaceful solution.

WORKS CITED

Baudelaire, Charles. *Constantin Guys: La peintre de la vie moderne*. Geneva: Éditions la Palatine, 1943.

Eliot, T.S. *The Rock*. London: Faber and Faber, 1934.

Lyotard, Jean-François. *The Postmodern Condition: A Report on Knowledge*. Translated by G. Bennington and B. Massumi. Minneapolis: University of Minnesota Press, 1984.

Taylor, Charles. *The Malaise of Modernity*. Concord, Ont.: Anansi, 1992.

PART IV

Dunsinane, Birnam Wood, and Beyond:
Frye's Theoria *of Language*
and Literature

'In the Middle of Ordinary Noise ...': An Auditory Masque

text by James Reaney
music by John Beckwith

———

narrator, Jerry Franken
singers, Monica Whicher, Erik Oland
clarinet, Robert W. Stevenson
keyboard 1, John Beckwith
tape and keyboard 2, Omar Daniel

———

N: Narrator
S: Soprano
B: Baritone

'In the Middle of Ordinary Noise ...':
A Note from the Librettist

When we decided to create a musical piece that would be a portrait of Frye, I started looking up all and everything he had ever said about music and sound.

You run across hilarious things such as a comment on Milton's *At a Solemn Musick*: 'This conception of "perfect diapason" is all very well as a literary metaphor, but when translated into music it opens up the discouraging prospect of spending the whole of eternity screaming the chord of C major.'

Our portrait starts with an illustration of another great quote: 'A musical sound, in the middle of ordinary noise, reminds us ... of music itself and the whole range of its possibilities.' Hold tight while our narrator and singers play upon coffee grinders and blenders until a musical phrase brings order out of disorder.

We then go back to Frye's boyhood in Moncton, New Brunswick (bicycle wheel, piano lessons, hymns, Purcell, early radio, and – prophetic of things to come – typing classes).

The piano lessons and his teacher George Ross are notable because, apparently, from the grammar and conventions of classical music he first saw the possibilities of describing literature in terms of wheels and mandalas.

The train whistles and the sounds of a typing contest transfer him to Toronto (bells, streetcars) and eventually Victoria College (sermons, hymns), where he developed the critical theories that our performers show in action by playing a mandala of all the possible dramatic forms as a game. Watch for 'Celia ... crucified near an anthill' (*The Cocktail Party*), after which the narrator and singers progress through Spring (Comedy), Summer (Romance), Fall (Tragedy), and Winter (Irony), and so back to 'Celia' again. Then, we do a second wheel, repeating the pattern through lyric, ending with W.B. Yeats's *There*.

I've always felt that Frye's ideas could make a very enjoyable board game, and that's what you'll find our performers doing – at play with the work of a great thinker who gave us such new perspectives on the whole range of literature itself.

'IN THE MIDDLE OF ORDINARY NOISE' ...:
AN AUDITORY MASQUE

RADIO plays (loud). PERFORMERS enter, turn down radio, turn on assorted noisemakers: blender, coffee grinder, drill ... TAPE: crowd sounds, traffic, swelling up & down. MUSIC: overture, up & fade for dialogue.

N: When we hear a musical sound in the middle of ordinary noise, we hear something ...

N, S, B: ... that that reminds us, not of any specific piece of music, but of music itself – and the whole range of its possibilities.

TRAIN WHISTLE. BICYCLE SPOKES: soft tinkling.

RADIO resumes.

S, B: Moncton, New Brunswick.

N: Radio? In the twenties it was mostly scratching and screaming for a very long time.

ANCIENT VOCAL RECORDING (John McCormack) battling with static, scratches; live singers imitate this. Fade for dialogue.

N: We never had a radio in our house, just a heavy supply of static. Canadian radio was then very largely a matter of all the kids building crystal sets and tuning in on all the squeals and groans that got produced.

TAPE: Squeals & groans ... MUSIC: *Golden Sonata* (Purcell): fading to b.g.

N: I remember one group of
Welsh singers came purely by
accident to Moncton, and I
myself realized that I actually
wanted to hear them. In the
course of it they played Purcell's *Golden Sonata*, and it hit
me like a cold shower ... I was
nine or ten, I think.

MUSIC: Purcell fragment dissolves
into baritone solo from *The Voice of
the Wind* (Ross), fading to b.g.

N: George Ross, the organist at
St John's Presbyterian
Church, Moncton, was my
music teacher.
S: Hubert Parry was your musical grandfather.
N: He was George Ross's teacher
... I wish someone would dig
out his doctoral exercise,
submitted some time around
1931. Unfortunately it was
based on a text by Mrs He-
mans, but the fugue at the end
was very interesting ... I just
saw the score: I have never
heard it performed, nor did
he.

MUSIC: piano & clarinet practice; a
collage of music-lesson exercises.
Continue under.

N: The symmetrical grammar of
classical music, with its circle
of fifths, its twelve-tone chromatic and seven-tone diatonic
scales, its duple and triple
rhythms, its concords and
cadences and formulaic progressions, make it something
of a mandala for the ear.

MUSIC: scales & arpeggios blend into fragments from *Song without words* op. 38, no. 2 (Mendelssohn); fade to b.g.

N: At fourteen, one of Mendelssohn's *Songs without words* was about my speed.

Mendelssohn continues, interrupted by sounds of typing (TAPE & actual). Continue under.

B: There were, in fact, two keyboards that figured prominently in your life.

N: The two forms of touch don't seem to have clashed a great deal.

S: He plays the piano as though it were a typewriter.

B: Well, he plays the typewriter as if it were a piano.

S: Oh! but Oh! the accuracy.

MUSIC & TAPE end. A Brief silence.

N: If only composers would stop trying to express themselves with grunts and squeaks and squeals, and choose a convention.

MUSIC & TAPE: a 'kitchen symphony' faintly recalling the opening 'ordinary noise' sequence, continuing under, getting louder ...

N: When perspective was discovered in painting, music might well have gone in a similar direction ... external sounds imitated in music ...

Machine noises up, then fading ...

S: Taps dripping, fridges humming ...

B: The juicer, the electric fan ...

N: ... but music did not take this turn, and the result is that the

structural principles of music
are clearly understood, and
can be taught even to
children.

N: The system of twenty-four
 interlocking keys ...
S,B: ... music shapes itself ...
N: a mandala for the ear ...
B: 'All tears are wiped away ...
S,B: ... and so are dominant
 sevenths' ...
N: ... twelve-tone chromatic and
 seven-tone diatonic scales ...
B: concords and cadences ...
N: ... formulaic progressions ...
S: ... a circle of fifths ...
S,B: ... an octave ...

S: I remember seeing him riding
 down Pine Street in Moncton
 here on his bicycle. I was just
 taking a Mozart piece from
 my music teacher, so I asked
 him what he knew about
 Mozart. He stopped and told
 me more about Mozart in five
 minutes than I have ever
 learned since that day.

N: I came up to Toronto to
 operate an Underwood typewriter for a contest that the
 company was running. I got
 my way paid to Toronto, and

Kitchen symph. swells up, spoken &
sung lines rising above the fireworks
...

Kitchen symph. subsides. MUSIC:
piano vamping; continuing under.
BICYCLE SPOKES: a few bursts.

BICYCLE: one more spurt. MUSIC:
piano merges with minuet from
Clarinet Trio K.498 (Mozart). Up &
then fade. TAPE: typing sounds,
very fast.

that was how I managed to
get to the University of
Toronto ... I won the second
prize.

TAPE: train whistle. City
Hall clock chime, church bells,
harbour bell. A streetcar approaching and fading. RADIO
sounds: an evangelist, news report,
hockey game. This collage fades for
MUSIC: *St Gertrude* (Sullivan).

N,S,B: Toronto!

N: Take the symbol of the Christian church in a well-known
hymn ...

S,B: (sung) We are not divided /
All one body we: / One in
hope and doctrine, / One in
charity.

Continue wordlessly under the
dialogue.

N: Anyone who has been, let us
say, on an ecumenical action
committee might well wonder
how even a hymn-writer
could bring himself to write
this appalling blither.

Briefly up & out. Silence.

B: (clerical collar?) My friends, I
recommend religion on the
ground that ...

N: I once heard a preacher
advocate religion on the
ground that ...

B: ... Science is too cold and dry
to serve as a guide to life.
Politics? (Pause.) Does not the
heat of its revolutionary zeal
leave one thirsting for something more?

N: He was basing his sermon on
the four principles of

substance: hot, cold, moist
...

B: Religion is all wet ...

N: Hot, cold, moist, and dry.

B: ... and so religion, being wet, exudes a fertilizing moisture that will warm the scientists and ...

N: Fire, Air, Water, Earth

B: ... warm the scientists and cool
...

N: Spring, Summer, Fall, Winter.

B: ... and cool the radicals.

N: Comedy, Tragedy, Satire, Romance.

N,S,B: LAUGHTER SEQUENCE (score)

                                 MUSIC accompanying.

N,S,B: SCALE SEQUENCE (score)

                                 MUSIC accompanying. TAPE: baby sounds ...

N: Envision an innocent baby gurgling away to itself ...

S,B: Demonic modulation!

                                 The gurgles become ogre roars.

N: In a Russian fairy tale, this same baby suddenly becomes a giant baby thirty feet tall.

S: And also a dragon ...

N: ... Sometimes modulates into 'the friendly dragon.' / In 1632 Milton composed *At a Solemn Musick*.

                                 MUSIC: intro to Milton sequence.

S,B: MILTON SEQUENCE (score)

                                 MUSIC: Sustain C-Major ff

N: This conception of 'perfect diapason' is all very well as a literary metaphor, but when

translated into music it opens
up the discouraging prospect
of spending the whole of
eternity screaming the chord
of C major.

MUSIC: Up to ff again, then x-fade
to *The Lost Chord* (Sullivan), sung
with narration.

N: 'The Lost Chord' depicts an
organist discovering and then
losing a wonderful chord
which ...
N,B: 'seemed the harmonious
echo / To our discordant life,'
...
N: ... yet which musically
speaking must have been a
highly complicated discord,
otherwise the sufferer could
have found it again easily
enough. A musical discord is
not an unpleasant sound, it is
a sign of musical energy.
(Pause.) In poetry, think of
Browning:

MUSIC: intro to Browning sequence;
continue accompanying ...

N,S: (singing + recitation)
I could favour you with
sundry \ touches
Of the paint-smutches with
which \ the Duchess
Heightened the mellowness of
her \ cheek's yellowness
(To get on faster) until at last
her \
Cheek grew to be one master-
\ plaster
Of mucus and fucus from
mere use of \ ceruse:

In short, she grew from scalp
  to udder
Just the object to make you
  shudder.

MUSIC: intro to Mandala sequence
no. 1

N,S,B: Very late winter, very
  early spring.
S: 'It would seem that she must
  have been crucified / Very
  near an anthill. / But Celia! ...
  of all people!'

MUSIC: Mandala sequence no.1
(Dramatic). TAPE: ironic party
babble, laughter. Fades. Mand. 1
continues ...

S: Comedy?
N: Well – *The Cocktail Party*.
  'Neurotic society unchanged.'
B: (sung) 'Cosi fan tutte.'
N: 'I am a woodland fellow.'
S: *All's Well that Ends Well*.
B: 'There we are.'
S: The last words of *The
  Ambassadors*.
N: 'Where is much love, all
   discord ends.
  What says my mad lord
   mayor to all this love?'
B: *The Shoemaker's Holiday*.
S: Cheerier:
B: 'So, this is the forest of
  Arden.'
S: Even cheerier:
N: 'One face, one voice,
   one habit,
  and two persons,
  A Natural Perspective,
   that is, and is not.'
S: *Twelfth Night*.
N,S,B: Romantic comedy:
S: 'Once there was a man who
  had a house by a churchyard.'

N: *The Winter's Tale.*

MUSIC: spring variations giving
way to dreamier 'summer'
variations ...

N,S,B: Summer!
B: 'Moses in the bullrushers ...'
N: Huckleberry Finn on re-birth.
S: '... on to their morning's rural
work they haste,

MUSIC: phrases from *Die Lotosblume*
(Heine/Schumann) ...

Among sweet dews and
flowers, where any row of
fruit trees, over-woody,
reached too far
Their pampered boughs ...'
N: Adam and Eve before the
Fall.
B: 'A gentle knight was pricking
on the plain.'
S: *The Faerie Queene.*
N: 'Whanne that Aprille with her
shoures soote ...
folk langen to goon on
pilgrimage.'

MUSIC: 'Epiphany of Heaven'

N,B: Romance; tragedy ...

MUSIC: *Three Shakespeare Songs*, no.
2 (Stravinsky)

S: (sung) 'Full fadom five thy
father lies.'
N: *The Tempest.*
B: 'Or, if the air will not permit,
Some still removèd place will
fit,
Where glowing embers
through the room
Teach light to counterfeit a
gloom,
Far from all resort of mirth,
Save the cricket on the
hearth.'
N,S: *Il Penseroso.*

TAPE: static interruptions.
MUSIC: becoming more jagged,
spasmodic ...

N,S,B: Autumn.

N: (Pause.) 'Thunder and
   lightning. Enter three
   witches.'

B: (A Scottish play.)

S: 'I am Duchess of Malfi still.'

B: 'Henceforth I learn that to
   obey is best.'

MUSIC: brief ref. to *Lucia di
Lammermoor* (Donizetti) ...

N: Adam, *after* the Fall. (Pause.)
   'I had lost my name.'

B: Edgar in *Lear.* 'Eyeless at Gaza
   at the mill with slaves.'
   (Pause.) 'Get your staring
   over with.'

N: *Prometheus.*

N,S,B: Winter.

B: 'The midwife laid her hand on
   his thick skull / With this
   prophetic blessing, *Be thou
   dull.'*

S: *Absalom and Achitophel.*

N: 'That man was hired to
   depress art.'

B: William Blake said that.

N: 'To think how we stood
   sweatin, shakin, / And pissed
   wi' dread, / While he, wi'
   lungen lip and snaken, / Held
   up to his head.'

S: Robert Burns.

B: 'Her stature tall – I hate a
   dumpy woman.'

N,S: Lord Byron!

N: 'The most pernicious race of
   odious little vermin.'

MUSIC: dark, black ('Epiphany of Hell'); then brighter ...

B: Jonathan Swift.
S: Irony.
N: 'In the destructive element –
    immerse.'
S: Joseph Conrad?
B: 'We give birth astride a
    grave.'
N: Samuel Beckett. (Pause.)
    'There may be heaven, there
    must be hell.'
S: (Browning.)
N,S,B: Cacophony.
S,B: (staggered entries) 'Light
    dies before thy uncreating
    word!'

MUSIC: *Pigeons in the grass, alas*
(Stein/Thomson) ...

N: Alexander Pope.
S: '...crucified very near an
    anthill ... Celia! of all people.'

MUSIC: Brief reprise of Mand. no. 1;
intro to Mandala no. 2, continuing ...

N,S,B: Spin it again!
B: This time *lyric* instead of
    dramatic.
N,S,B: Summer!
N: 'I caught this morning
    morning's minion, kingdom
    of daylight's dauphin,
    dapple-dawn-drawn Falcon,
    in his riding of the rolling
    level underneath him steady
    air, and ...'
S: Hopkins.

MUSIC: *Dundee* (Scottish Psalter)
...

S,B: (sung) How lovely are thy
    dwellings fair!
    O Lord of hoasts, how dear
    Thy pleasant tabernacles are!

Where thou do's dwell so
   near.'

N: (Psalm 84.)

N,S: 'Thunder, thunder,
   thunderation \ We're the
   Leamington delegation ...'

B: A school yell.

N,S,B: 'When we fight with
   determination
   We create a sensation!'
   (Pause.) Autumn

S: 'No motion has she now, no
      force;
   She neither hears nor sees;
   Roll'd round in earth's
      diurnal course,
   With rocks, and stones, and
      trees.'

B: Lucy.

N: 'The earth goeth on the earth
   Glistening like gold; ...'

B: 'The earth goeth *to* the earth
   Sooner than it wold; ...'

S: An Anglo-Saxon tombstone.

N: 'The earth *builds* on the earth
   Castles and towers; ...

N,S,B: Winter!

N,B: 'The earth says to the earth:
   All shall be ours.'

B: (sung) 'Tweed said to Till ...'

N: A Berwickshire rhyme.

B: 'Tweed said to Till
   What gars ye rin sae still?' ...

S: 'Till said to Tweed,
   Tho' ye rin wi speed,
      And I rin slaw,
   Where ye drown one man,
      I drown twa.'

N: 'Thou shalt not kill; but
      needst not strive
   Officiously to keep alive;

Do not adultery commit;
   Advantage rarely comes of it.'
B: (Arthur Clough.)
S: (rapid) 'A Route of
   Evanescence
   With a revolving
   Wheel – ' ...
N,S,B: Spring!
S: '... A resonance of Emerald
   A Rush of Cochineal –
   And every Blossom on the
     Bush
   Adjusts its tumbled Head –
   The Mail from Tunis,
     probably, ...'
N,B: Emily Dickinson.
S: '... An Easy Morning's Ride – '
N: (Pause.) 'There all the barrel-
   hoops are knit, ...'
N,S,B: Midsummer.
N,B: 'There all the serpent-tails
   are bit, ...'
N,S,B: 'There all the gyres
     converge in one,
   There all the planets drop in
     the Sun.'
N: Yeats.

N: A musical sound in the
middle of ordinary noise ...

TAPE: recapping 'ordinary noise'
elements, crowds, train whistle ...
BICYCLE: a couple of spins, slowing
to a stop ... MUSIC: piano &
clar. practice sounds ...

... subsiding to real & taped
typewriter and some fragments of
K.498, dying away to nothing ...

N,S,B: ... reminds us of music
   itself ... the whole range of its
   possibilities

... (typewriter is the last audible
sound)

ANGUS FLETCHER

Frye and the Forms of Literary Theory

Northrop Frye gave to a generation of critics new ways of thinking about the vitality of literature. By bringing all of the genres into relations with each other, by establishing – however indefinitely – a literary universe, *Anatomy* discovered in literature the seemingly endless sources of symbolic energy. Two central processes of myth and metaphor deliver this energy, which otherwise remains bound up and unreleased, stockpiled in the inert language of the dictionary. Myth and metaphor, a physicist might say, make the energies of language available. *Anatomy* and the essays treat literature as a kind of nature, a living system, a vital nexus. I remember experiencing this powerful sense of vitality, not merely of the critic's personal style and perception, but of literature itself, the life within the symbolic universe. The interinanimation of words that I.A. Richards discerned in rhetoric now found a cosmic structure – literature – in which to act, upon the poem, and upon the reader.

The task of theory became to isolate the myriad ways in which literature aptly expresses the vicissitudes of desire, individual yearning, communal wish, across the whole social range. It was a nobly ample enterprise, and its pursuit gave to Frye his well-deserved renown. Yet if literature was alive in and for social humanity – if Frye's myths of freedom and concern defined the poles of universal aspiration, the world over – it is no wonder that it is difficult to analyse the theory of theory that would correctly describe such a vast enterprise. I can make only the merest suggestions.

If Frye's general theory expresses itself, as we shall see, through a specific literary genre, it nevertheless presents a continuous problem of orientation. From *Fearful Symmetry* to *Words with Power*, Frye remained centred on a biblical world-view. He neutralized Christian dogma by arguing that the Bible is radically mythic and metaphorical. This focus upon the ever-changing Word is at heart Blakean and free from particular dogmas, but it still leaves a question: Is not literature in a significant Western sense always fundamentally pagan? From Homer to the moderns, literature (and all other arts) develop in opposition to the Hebraic-Christian tradition of iconoclasm, with its persistent antipathy to the image. At the very least, we would need to explore the ways Frye approaches the inherent hospitality of paganism toward the aesthetic continuum. A biblical focus would seem necessarily to require downgrading to what used to be called humanism, with promotion of that problematic hybrid, Christian humanism. Is the conflict truly resolved in Frye?

A second orientation raises the question of postmodernism: How is current criticism to view *Anatomy of Criticism* and *The Great Code* in relation to those master narratives – *grands récits* – which Lyotard has claimed we cannot continue to believe? There is no law dictating that Frye, or anyone else, must hew to this Lyotardian line, and yet one cannot help wondering if Frye, in his preference for mythic structures, was not inventing, or reinventing, the modernist's master narrative of 'the old story turned self-reflexive.' The biblical centre is itself the source of Frye's story, a master narrative that begins with Alpha (the Book of Genesis) and ends with Omega (the Book of Revelation). This Hebraic-Christian story suggests that, despite all his protean inventiveness, Frye remains dedicated to ideas of ideological fusion such as were taught in his university years, as epitomized not so much by his immediate friends and mentors (say Pratt or Edgar) as by Renaissance scholars like Woodhouse.

Frye's whole enterprise, of course, expresses his fusion of Blakean revolutionary thinking and the modernist sense that myth, while under attack from irony, is the only lasting source of literary power.

Genealogically, one might say, Frye's critical theory grows out of two essays, 'The Critic as Artist' and 'The Decay of Lying,' by Oscar Wilde, in which, for the twentieth-century modern period, there was developed a renovated theory of Romantic imagination. Frye's work is a defence of the myth-making imagination.

Because every myth seeks its most comfortable form or genre, and because Frye's theory is itself projected as a conceptual myth, we have to ask how, besides his use of essay and lecture, Frye ordered his thoughts into a larger story. Here the most inclusive form in which Frye expressed his conceptual interests, the anatomy, is all important. Self-reflexively, with *Anatomy of Criticism*, he defined for his theorizing the limits of its manner and genre of organization. What holds for this celebrated book holds for the separate essays, and for the final two books on the Bible. The anatomy, in its satiric Menippean form, 'deals less with people as such than with mental attitudes' (309). The genre has the power to 'handle abstract ideas and theories ... and presents people as the mouthpieces of the ideas they represent' (Menippean satires, say Swift in *Gulliver's Travels* and Lucian in his *Dialogues*, rely 'on the free play of intellectual fancy and the kind of humorous observation that produces caricature') (310). As compared with the normalizing flow of novelistic narrative, with these Menippean works 'the intellectual structure built up from the story makes for violent dislocations in the customary logic of narrative.' This literature of 'a conflict of ideas' leads, then, to caricatural, even at times farcical, intellectual play. Another aspect of the genre is equally critical to Frye's master narrative: the move toward the encyclopaedic array. He observes that, while novelists excel in analysing human relationships and social phenomena, 'The Menippean satirist, dealing with intellectual themes and attitudes, shows his exuberance in intellectual ways, by piling up an enormous mass of erudition about his theme or in overwhelming his pedantic targets with an avalanche of their own jargon' (311). Athenaeus, Rabelais, Flaubert (in *Bouvard et Pécuchet*) are well-known cases, while 'This creative treatment of exhaustive erudition is the organizing principle of the greatest Menippean satire in English before Swift, Burton's *Anatomy of Melancholy*.' For Burton the word 'anatomy' means 'a dissection or analysis, and expresses very accurately the intellectualized approach of this form' (311).

A paperback reprint of *Anatomy of Criticism* – the title indicates an interest in method and process – is adorned with quotes from reviews, one of which calls it 'a brilliantly suggestive and encyclopedically erudite book,' while another characterizes it as a 'brilliant but bristling book.' Frye bristles because he insists upon encyclopaedic scope, raising always the question as to how this range and Blakean exuberance affect the task of theorizing.

Anatomy-theory requires the isolation of contoured features in literature, such as the typical rhythmic gestures accompanying a given kind of poem or narrative. Frye's criticism is featural. This in turn requires constant scanning of the larger literary horizon, under any given broad heading. Frye rarely gives us a continuous close reading of a text, but instead moves back to a middle distance so that whatever detail or feature he is noting will be visible also in relation to other possible features of a scope larger than the one he is momentarily adopting. He not only watches the forest as well as the individual trees; he watches to see what lies beyond the forest.

The consequence of reading in a middle distance is that Frye gains an abstraction, while affirming the vitality of the work as inhering in its Blakean details, its features. The organizing strategy becomes one of shifting by analogy, by means of featural parallels. Every literary category noted in *Anatomy* is noted as being like or unlike some other category; all parallels have their contrary motions, their parodies. The quickest way to grasp what occurs in Frye is to recall his lifelong musical involvement, particularly with the works of Bach, his favourite composer. Frye does critical theory on a strictly canonical plan, in a musical sense, so that whatever he says, here and now, is counterpointed against what he has been saying, there and then. This musical, polyphonic analogizing governs all Frye's work. (One cannot help wondering at the fact of two supreme geniuses of *musica speculativa* and *musica practiva* living at the same time, in the same culture, same nation, same town – Frye and Glenn Gould – both of them addicted to Bach, although Frye played Clementi sonatas, while Gould played Sibelius. The congruence of Gould and Frye is worth pondering in some depth, especially with a view to understanding their reserved ideas about the excessive ways in which so-called artistic and aesthetic experience is valued by our commodified culture.) To return from this Menippean digression, the point about polyphonic music as a model is that it allows Frye to find places and planes for literary features, within the work, within the larger scheme, just as the composer must find places and give the correct movements to his or her musical ideas, motifs, or harmonies. Music is a motion that contains. Again, by analogy, the free play of polyphony is controlled play, and yet often enough a canonical or contrapuntal development of themes will lead to clutters of overgrown thematic profusion. Frye was aware of this and more than once defends himself, in *Anatomy*, against what he calls 'apparent inconsistency.' The contrapuntal effect in Frye requires perhaps more of a musician's memory for where we have been than most of us have – at the passage in question, for example, Frye makes the following remark in parentheses: '(for the apparent inconsistency of this with the revolutionary nature of the form just mentioned, see the introductory comment on the *mythos* of romance in the previous essay)' (306). To indicate how easily such memory lapses might occur, let me quote a methodological passage (not atypical) from a few pages further on: 'To sum up then: when we examine fiction from the point of view of form, we can see four chief strands binding it together, novel, confession, anatomy, and romance. The six possible combinations of these forms exist, and we have shown how the novel has combined with each of the other three' (312). This 'inexcusable Pythagorisme,' as Sir Thomas Browne might have called it, is as nothing compared to what we need to keep straight, musically, contrapuntally, in 'Theory of Myths' (Essay 3).

Polyphonic complexity reveals at once the strength and, some have said, the weakness of the whole approach. At the very least, the stretto-like complexity of certain theoretical moments in Frye needs to be positioned, as we shall discover, in the Blakean light of his purposes, which are visionary.

Critics, from various directions, have questioned the strong analogy between the two domains of literature and music. As a character in Gide's *Counterfeiters* remarks, music seems considerably more mathematical than literature, especially the novel, with its real-world concerns. On the other hand, Frye adopts a motivic as well as featural approach, and he constructs the argument of *Anatomy* on an assumption that literature displays large and complex coherences, as nature displays lawful interactions. The method of the anatomizing is to move through systems of fourfold order – in this case the four strata of coherences denoted by the four essays of *Anatomy*. *Mode*, then, gives the level at which literature articulates power relations – heroes at different modal levels displaying different degrees and kinds of power (most obviously the gods of myth proper are superpowerful as compared with the enfeebled Gullivers and Gregor Samsas of satire and ironic modality). *Symbol*, the subject of Essay 2, is similarly analysed into different existential groups, here corresponding with some alteration to the medieval fourfold symbolic levels of literal, allegorical, moral, and anagogical. These four ancient categories Frye subsumes under Dante's governing term, the polysemous, but he analytically preserves a fourfold: motif (sign), image, archetype, and monad. Essay 3, on *myth*, which most would call the centre of the whole theoretical map, permutates the same fourfold arrangement into a general theory of archetypal meaning, where the degrees and kinds of individual and social empowerment are displayed in their most rooted ancient shapes. Comedy, romance, tragedy, and irony characterize the *mythos* of spring, summer, autumn, and winter – and this, it turns out, has nothing much to do with actual weather conditions. Then, finally, moving to Essay 4, on *genre*, we find yet another set of four different fundamental rhythms (here music shows perhaps most clearly through the surface of the literary argument), and epos, prose, drama, and lyric display the rhythms of recurrence, continuity, decorum, and association.

Frye's *Anatomy* is composed according to a contrapuntal, four-part, fugato system. Frye emphasizes that *mythos* is what Aristotle early called a soul of literature, but then Frye analyses seemingly myriad stories into four basic archetypal shapes of action. As long as one recalls that he was consciously on guard against misplaced concreteness, the fourfold analysis will remain theoretically neutral – in short, Frye's anatomizing is conceived as a schematic, featural description of literature. It is not, he hoped, an allegory of literature. Were a phenomenological critic to object that it is an allegory, one tenet of such a critique would hold that nothing as humanly variable, as this-worldly, as actual literary practice could ever issue in a fugally restricted account like the system of repeated fourfolds Frye devised for his schematic descriptive purposes. An argument ensues, between the phenomenalist and the structuralist (or, as Frye is often called, the formalist). One party to the argument would certainly want to say that literature is far less pure and mathematical than the verbal order Frye's *Anatomy* and other essays and treatises would seem always to promote. The counterargument would perhaps start from the notion that the mathematics are in principle unavoidable, that all conceptual schemes (even those denying the fact) are related not so much to the world of literature as it is, as they are to our ways of looking at things and framing intelligible accounts. Hence, all arguments for and against the speculative musicality of Frye's theorizing will concern the very nature of theorizing, every bit as much as the nature of literature.

Here we approach what seems a critical aspect of Frye's thought, taken in the large. To clarify, let me return again to one consequence of his chosen form, anatomy. In a word, this consequence is vision, the visionary – yet vision and the visionary in an unusual, even monstrous sense.

Without any a priori definition for vision in a literary context, one can yet say that it involves seeing beyond, seeing through superficial appearances, seeing the hidden interconnections between ideas, images, and reality, seeing in truth. In a biblical context, vision means either prophecy or apocalypse. In a political or public sphere, it would imply a capacity to see through the tangle of conflicting ideas, ideologues, hypocrisies, interests, passions, hopes, fears, and present realities, with a clarity not born of slavish calculation, but permitted rather, to the visionary, to the see-er, the seer, by virtue of a higher order of summation, what often looks more like an inspired guess. As Richard Feynman said in his Messenger Lectures on the nature of natural laws, the theoretical scientist has often to guess, looking for an emergent order.

Anatomy and the other essays and treatises are all studies in emergent order, an order emerging as it does in any complex musical composition.

Yet there is another critical analogy at work here, based on the thought that the contrapuntal lines and overlays of Frygean analysis furthermore resemble a library, the ideal or utopian library Borges invents. 'The Library of Babel,' one of the *Ficciones*, begins: 'The universe (which others call the Library) is composed of an indefinite and perhaps infinite number of hexagonal galleries, with vast air shafts between, surrounded by very low railings. From any of the hexagons one can see, interminably, the upper and lower floors. The distribution of the galleries is invariable. Twenty shelves, five long shelves per side, cover all the sides except two; their height, which is the distance from ...' (51), and so on. Then: 'In the hallway there is a mirror which faithfully duplicates all appearances. Men usually infer from this mirror that the Library is not infinite (if it really were, why this illusory duplication?); I prefer to dream that its polished surfaces represent and promise the infinite' (51). There follows one of Borges's riddling Gnostic puzzles, about the unreal Library, about the finite and infinite possibilities of books held on its shelves, about the origins of time and time's relation to what is written. Are there unique copies of books? Is there a Man of the Book? Is there somewhere among the hexagons 'a book which is the formula and perfect compendium *of all the rest*'? Do some books keep changing into others? 'In truth,' the narrator observes, 'the Library includes all verbal structures, all variations permitted by the twenty-five orthographical symbols, but not a single example of absolute nonsense' (57). To resolve his uncertainties as to the possible infinity of the Library, the narrator eventually proposes that '*The Library is unlimited and cyclical*. If an eternal traveler were to cross it in any direction, after centuries he would see that the same volumes were repeated in the same disorder (which, thus repeated, would be an order: the Order). My solitude is gladdened by this elegant hope' (58).

So ends this elegant fable. But not quite. One final touch adds a footnote to the last line, according to which 'Letizia Álvarez de Toledo has observed that this vast Library is useless: rigorously speaking, *a single volume* would be sufficient, a volume of ordinary format, printed in nine or ten point type, containing an infinite number of infinitely thin leaves. (In the early seventeenth century, Cavalieri said that all solid bodies are the superimposition of an infinite number of planes.) The handling of this silky *vade mecum* would not be convenient: each apparent page would unfold into other analogous ones; the inconceivable middle page would have no reverse' (58).

Students of Bach's more speculative works, such as the *Art of the Fugue*, will at once perceive parallels between such ideal constructions (and deconstructions) and the Borgesian collision of finite and infinite. Borges, like Bach, invents fables and myths of our mental capacity to perceive linkages between widely and even wildly remote parts of a symbolic or actual world. In 1971, Didier Anzieu, the French psychoanalyst, observed that Borges's Library of Babel 'has all the characteristics of the unconscious, not only according to Freud, but also according to Lacan: it is universal, eternal and, moreover, it is structured like a language.'[1] The analogy is drawn between two systems by which individual features and 'contours of the body' are musically developed into seemingly infinite numbers of recombinations, as if a simple master-code of displacement and condensation could achieve unrestricted multiplicity, according to rules that remain unconscious. On such a plan, literary theory would give a virtually monstrous visionary place to the idea of the book.

The Borges story gives the correct parabolic impression of this somewhat monstrous character of visionary perception in Frye. *Anatomy of Criticism* moves inexorably towards anagogy, as it moves towards the eminent positioning of *Finnegans Wake*, a kind of infinite book, a book seemingly both 'unlimited and cyclical,' to use the Borgesian narrator's phrase. The *Wake* is shown to share in the encyclopaedic vitality of the anatomy form itself. Referring to Joyce's 'ideal reader suffering from an ideal insomnia,' Frye links the anatomy-like totality (or is it infinity?) of the *Wake* with his own aim of 'reforging the broken links between creation and knowledge, art and science, myth and concept,' a reuniting which will 'appear to be, with increasing obviousness, the social and practical result' of the critic's labours (354).

Of course there exists, for the West, a kind of 'single volume,' to use the phrase of Letizia Álvarez de Toledo – the Bible. This work can scarcely be called a work, and even its customary name, the Book, is troublesome to the critic accustomed to volumes of more limited scope. It was to the elucidation of the place, the role, the dynamism, the vitality of the Bible that Frye gave most of his energy in later years. Frye called, in *Anatomy*, for a 'genuine higher criticism' of the Bible, what he called 'a synthetizing process which would start with the assumption that the Bible is a definitive myth, a single archetypal structure extending from creation to apocalypse' (315). On this view, the Bible is a typological unity, where, for the two Testaments (for the Christian reader like Frye), the principle of interconnection is not that one allegorizes the other, but that each is a 'metaphorical identification' of the other (315). One might suppose that *The Great Code* and its glossing companion, *Words with Power*, belong simply to the Christian theorizing of typological shadows.

But the most cursory examination of the two treatises, *The Great Code* especially, shows that Frye was taking the Bible to be, not solely the believing Christian's book, but rather the ultimate book of all books for that mysterious 'Man of the Book' in Borges's story. To understand the Bible in its literary force and form, then, would be to understand literature itself, for literature then becomes, as an infinite library, identified metaphorically with the book of all books, the book within the book, the book as mystical body.

It will be asked: Was it not Frye's quest, at long last, to go beyond the secular scriptures of romance and to secularize even the sacred text? Would this not mean consigning the sacred text to serving the authority of a higher theory of myth and metaphor? There seems to be an Emersonian question hidden within this question about the nature of the sacred text: How may society and its purposes intersect with literature? Perhaps Frye thinks of the Bible and *Finnegans Wake* as speaking the infinite, Viconian, cyclical voices of human craving for an emergent order in the vision of social development.

The question for theory arises out of the seemingly inexorable movement of Frye's vision, as I have called it, from its initial stage in the analysis of myth and metaphor towards its final opening out onto an idea of the infinite book, be it the *Wake* or the Bible. A striking openness in late Frye is his evident hospitality toward the Derrida who owes so much to the *Wake*. This must have been a *rapprochement* based on Derrida's Mallarméan concern with the paradox of closure: the book is a unity which is always opening out into a disbounded space, through its being centred on the *decentring* device of metaphor.

We need then to ask what kind of unity the ultimate volume is regarded as possessing. What is the meaning of the mandala this volume constructs? For the typical shape of an argument in Frye will have this circular or cyclical shape although, whereas the Tibetan mandala serves a ritual meditative purpose, here the instrumentality serves a critical analytic purpose. That is, with Frye we are typically led to consider a topic, to see its main dimensions, its main contours, its chief features, its differences, its primary dynamic. Yet this is to note only the featural readings typical of a Frye essay. There remains the continuing drive towards the anagogic, towards the Book.

As Christian thinker, Frye would emphasize the possibility of a Blakean incarnation of the infinite human being divinized through vision. As mere critic, however, as raw theorist, he found in the notion of the final book a model for the sort of totality he believed the critic should seek to elucidate. Not Marxists only, but virtually all students of literary and cultural theory need, as Fredric Jameson insists with regard to postmodernism, to discover some way of mapping a sufficiently large totality of human actions. Otherwise theory will produce only short-term, essentially vicious profits, based on shrivelled horizons. Instead theory needs a vision of literature wide enough to approach a sufficient totality. This is the criterion met by Frye's constant tendency toward considerations of final causes. At the same time a passion for literature as totality leads, with Frye, to a persistent accounting of featural detail. What seems to me original in his criticism, his philosophy I would prefer to call it, is the way he attempts to articulate the idea of imbricated purposes beyond immediate persuasion, beyond representation, and beyond self-centredness. Frye was an odd throwback – he was interested in truth as well as peace. He was, at heart, a peacemaker, albeit a polemical peacemaker.

NOTE

1 Anzieu, 'Le Corps et le Code dans les contes de Jorge Luis Borges,' 195: 'Notons au passage que la Bibliothèque possède toutes les caractéristiques de l'inconscient non seulement selon Freud, mais aussi selon Lacan: elle est universelle, éternelle et, de plus, structurée comme un langage.'

WORKS CITED

Anzieu, Didier. 'Le Corps et le Code dans les contes de Jorge Luis Borges.' *Nouvelle de Psychoanalyse* 3 (1971): 177–210.
Borges, Jorge Luis. *Ficciones*. Edited by Anthony Kerrigan. New York: Grove Press, 1962.

NELLA COTRUPI

Verum Factum:
Viconian Markers along Frye's Path

I suppose it is inevitable that commentators on the Viconian refrain in
Frye should hang their rhetorical hats on the topos of the spiralling curve
or pathway.[1] As my title indicates, I do not intend to betray this tradition
which was suggested, after all, by Frye himself when he wrote in *The
Critical Path*: 'The conventions, genres and archetypes of literature do not
simply appear: they must develop historically from origins, or perhaps
from a common origin. In pursuing this line of thought, I have turned
repeatedly to Vico, one of the very few thinkers to understand anything
of the historical role of the poetic impulse in civilization as a whole'
(34).

   This passage is only one of the many acknowledgments that Frye gives
us of his debt to Vico, whose influence was first felt indirectly through
the work of Cassirer, Spengler, and Joyce at a time when Frye was preoccupied primarily with Blake's poetic and philosophical symmetries.[2]
Yet, despite these many avowals of indebtedness, there is a curious
inconsistency about these statements that calls for some scrutiny. We see,
for example, that in *The Great Code* Frye notes that, although Vico's
theory of linguistic modes was his point of departure, there was very
little left of Vico in what finally emerged (5). He goes on to state that the
influence of Vico was more pronounced in *Anatomy of Criticism*, a text,
it should be remembered, that does not include the name Giambattista
Vico in its index, but does have it in the body of the text in a reference to
Joyce's 'Viconian theory of history' (62). More recently, in the introductory chapter to *Words with Power*, Frye states without equivocation that
'*The Great Code* owed a good deal to Vico' (xii). Even concluding, as
Domenico Pietropaolo has done in 'Frye, Vico and the Grounding of

Literature and Criticism,' that Frye was not a Vico scholar, and that his turning to Vico was motivated solely by the necessity 'to pursue the implications that Vico's line of thinking has for his own' (96), the jarring contradictions that arise in comparing many of Frye's references to Vico seem to warrant further inquiry.

This is not to deny that Frye attended to the markers that Vico set out in tracing the trajectory of the critical path, as my ensuing arguments will underscore. Indeed, it is the very proximity and intensity of this affinity that adds a note of irony to Frye's more puzzling reflections on Vico. In *Words with Power* Frye states, for example, 'Vico had a limited interest in the continuous social function of literature, and he paid little attention to the principle that makes it insistent' (xii–xiii). The incongruousness of this remark is highlighted when Frye observes in the same text: 'The discoverer of the principle that all verbal structures descend from mythological origins was Vico, and Vico's axiom was *verum factum*: what is true for us is what we have made' (82). Furthermore, this key Viconian tenet is explicitly stated to be the 'essential axiom of criticism' (135). To add yet another turn to the screw, we note that some years earlier, in an essay entitled 'The Responsibilities of the Critic' (1976), in which Vico is prominently discussed, Frye describes Vico as having entertained 'a great vision of the development of social institutions out of what he calls "poetic wisdom," or an original mythology' (129).

Setting aside for a time Frye's puzzling contradictoriness, we may note the increasing numbers of explicit references to Vico in texts published after *Anatomy* and suggest that these references are in keeping with the tendency in Frye's thought to move away from formalistic preoccupations and towards expanding perspectives on questions of broad cultural concern, including meditations on the place of the critic and of criticism in the social order.[3] This movement, together with its powerful Viconian impetus, may well be seen as Frye's attempt to negotiate his way along the critical agenda he had proposed in concluding *Anatomy*, his way of 'reforging the broken links between creation and knowledge, art and science, myth and concept' (354).

In moving beyond purely taxonomical questions within the realm of poetics in order to interrogate the social and epistemological implications of the *verum factum* principle, Frye embarked on a line of thought that has prompted skittish objectivists like Gerald Graff to describe him as one of those 'well-intentioned humanists' engaged in aiding and abetting the 'literary vanguard's revisionary assaults on realism' by focusing not on knowable reality but on ideology and myth.[4] Frye, like Vico, would probably have responded that, on the basis of the *verum factum* principle, the only reality that we can know is the one that we make and, yes, mythological structures do shape all such makings.

Although the roots of the *verum factum* principle have been traced to scholastic meditations on the divine creative logos, it was Vico who ingeniously combined this concept with the impulses of Renaissance humanism in order to redress the misplaced confidence of Descartes in the logical, deductive method and in the psychologism of the *cogito*.[5] Preliminary formulations of this axiom may be extracted from some of Vico's earlier compositions, but it is in *The New Science* that it is given full expression, and its implications for human history submitted to close and thorough scrutiny.[6] As translated by Bergin and Fisch from the third edition of 1744, the key section reads: 'the world of civil society has certainly been made by men, and ... its principles are therefore to be found within the modifications of our own human mind. Whoever reflects on this cannot but marvel that the philosophers should have bent all their energies to the study of the world of nature, which, since God made it, He alone knows; and that they should have neglected the study of the world of nations, or civil world, which, since men had made it, men could come to know' (par. 331).

What underlies Vico's epistemology is the problematic distinction between nature and culture which has been at the heart of critical considerations since at least the time of Aristotle. Vico insisted that human knowledge of nature is limited to the 'certain' in that it consists only of outward or sensory data; it is not genetive knowledge, that knowledge from causes that manifests itself in the act of making. This type of knowledge *per causas*, knowledge of the 'true,' is operative not in the realm of nonhuman nature, but in the mind, in the artistic constructs, intellectual paradigms, and scientific projections that represent the substance of humanity's truth(s).

Frye has his eye firmly fixed on this distinction when he insists that humanity operates within a cultural envelope, insulated from nature by its very descriptions of nature (*GC*, 50–1). In making such a claim, Frye is not attempting to 'transcend history, the natural and the all-too-human world,' as Daniel O'Hara, among others, has suggested (*The Romance of Interpretation*, 176). Rather, like Vico before him, Frye is attempting to come to terms with human nature and its distinctive relationship to the rest of the given cosmos. What is implicit here is the belief that humanity operates within a radically contingent universe, with the sentient centre of that universe, the individual human thinking and feeling apparatus, being not least among the sources of this contingency.

Vico and Frye focus on the products of human creative activity, that is, on culture, not for what it may disclose about the world as distinct from the mind, but rather for what such products reflect about that aspect of human nature which most blatantly seems to distinguish it from the rest of the perceptible existential order. In doing so, neither Vico nor Frye leaves himself open to charges of epistemological asymmetry or hypocrisy; they do not claim a perspective outside, and thus objective to, the spiralling turns of human cultural production. Vico insists that his work is a *'scientia,'* an ordered, ideational structure of general propositions. This is the same conception of science that underlies Frye's appeals for a disciplined literary criticism, one that is causal rather than casual, systematic rather than random (*AC*, 7–8). Furthermore, Vico described his history of human cultural modalities as 'ideal,' that is, as a mental construct or system. Frye, in turn, describes his own metacritical review of literary criticism as an 'anatomy.' In view of the definitions of the genre provided in the glossary and body of the text, in phrases such as 'creative treatment of exhaustive erudition' (311) and 'a vision of the world in terms of a single intellectual pattern' (310), the irony of this title is telling.

In Vico as in Frye, there is a privileging of verbal as opposed to other cultural products. This rests on what has come to be known as the 'relativity hypothesis,' the notion that thought and language are inextricably intertwined and seem to evolve *pari passu*.[7] Vico expended a good deal of intellectual energy debunking the notion – or, as he called it, the 'conceit' – that reason is veiled in the mythological and metaphorical constructs of poetic language. On the contrary, he insists, the disclosure of the 'real' in rational, logical, or analogical discourse is, insofar as it is a verbal construct, of the same order as poetry. The 'real' that is disclosed is always and already a human fabrication. Regardless of the formal domain of human conceptual activity, all such operations are conducted through mental analogues that we create for ourselves whether in the form of poetic images or as scientific hypotheses.[8]

Frye summarizes this proposition neatly when he states that 'nothing built out of words can transcend the nature and condition of words ... the nature and conditions of *ratio*, so far as *ratio* is verbal, are contained by *oratio*' (*AC*, 337). Vico's precocious hypothesis, to which Frye subscribes, is that language, like thought, is fundamentally tropological and represents the common, if always changing, epistemological place or space of humanity: 'figures of speech are not the ornaments of language, but the elements of both language and thought' (*StS*, 94). In critical discourse as in art, it is inevitably a formal, hypothetical statement that is made, and it is by way of these statements that we make sense or non-sense of the here, the now, and the has-been. The conceptual paradigms of scientific inquiry and of analytical logic, and their respective semiotic codes and

linguistic conventions, represent a different, not a truer, way of con-
figuring a universe. The belief in scientific or logical truth is just as
tenuous and contingent as was the belief in the truth of Jove. The shift
from image or figure to abstract concept represents a change in
psycholinguistic idiom, yet the essentially psycholinguistic mode of
being remains constant. Whichever pycholinguistic variant is operative,
the object of language is always a contingent mental construct and not
an independent reality.[9]

Frye describes culture as 'a total vision of possibilities,' as 'the total
body of imaginative hypothesis in a society' (AC, 127). Frye's utilization
of the body metaphor, which may be traced back to Blake, carries special
significance for Frye and will be discussed in due course. What is to be
noted at this juncture is that, on the basis of this definition, such a body
may be at least provisionally dissected or anatomized in order to disclose
just what the range of discretely operating organs might be. This, of
course, is the operation that was undertaken by Vico and Frye. For both
of them three crucial cultural nodes emerged, together with their respective identifying primary linguistic modes. For Vico, as for Frye, the
range appears to be a limited, recurring one, and, whether the critical
scalpel is applied diachronically or synchronically, the crux of the matter
situates itself at that juncture where the ouroboros begins to swallow its
tail and the corso becomes a ricorso. For Frye, this transition is identifiable, in the literary domain, at the point of maximum displacement along
the vector of mimesis where irony appears as an oscillating bridge between verisimilitude and a radically mythopoetic mind-set. Where, in
other words, the tendency of language to be externally focused, centrifugal, is reversed and the centripetal self-absorption of language emerges
again as the dominant literary and cultural modality (AC, 140).

Timothy Bahti has suggested that for Frye the great challenge of
critical thinking was to effect an exponential leap outside of the linear,
dialectical alternations of tropological phases in order to effect a
synchronic, intellectually neutral reanalysis of all phases of the human
cycle ('Vico and Frye,' 128). Is this not a description of the very metacritical, metahistorical, metatextual activity that both Vico and Frye – and
those others identified by Bhati as Vico's real successors, the 'Hegel of
the Encyclopedia, Nietzsche, Heidegger, and Walter Benjamin' (129) – had
embarked upon? And, in view of the verum factum principle, is not the
discursive mode which most appropriately identifies this realm of activity not that very threshold area where irony and metaphor, deconstruction and recreation grapple for dominion? Indeed, the spiral configura-
tion is most apt, for what we face is a mise en abîme, an infinite regress of

unending centres and circumferences, framings and reframings, where it is conceded, at last, that mental paradigms constitute both the form and the content of the body of human culture. Regardless of the epistemological distance that we may try to inject between our eye and the chosen object, including culture itself, the eye is inevitably and already a part of that configured object (*GC*, 14). The words 'metacritical,' 'metahistorical', and 'metatextual' are ironic precisely for this reason; they represent a contradiction in terms. To the extent that criticism, history, and texts are intellectual constructs, there is no way to scramble to a higher level. All we can ever do is unfurl a little more the coil of culture.

There is in Vico and Frye a concentration on metaphorical language that is profoundly connected to the *verum factum*. Vico perceived in the operation of metaphor the originary process which allowed humanity not to discover or uncover the world, but to call it into being, to make or invent it for human consumption from the raw data of sensory perception. In radical or 'anagogic' metaphor, to use Frye's term, the paradoxical element, the semantic impertinence, is not discarded as being logically problematic. Rather, its dialectical energy is harnessed and emerges as the source of metaphor's epistemological power and emotional intensity. This intensity ensues when the mind experiences its own inventive capacities, its power to launch out, to improvise connectors or common ontological places where the tidy fixities of logical discrimination and distanciation are undermined, and there is instead the vertigo of feeling simultaneously part of a larger design and of containing the larger design (*WP*, 85). In literature that is radically metaphorical, readers may be led to the powerful experience or awareness of the lightness of being, of its ungroundedness, and this occurs 'through an interchange of illusion and reality. Illusion, something created by human imagination, is what becomes real; reality, most of which in our experience is a fossilized human creation from the past, becomes illusory' (*WP*, 85). In ecstatic or anagogic metaphor the *verum factum* principle is given its most economical and intense expression and the power that such words convey is, precisely, the generative power of language and thought.

In the radically ironic language and thought that is the basis of so much of the twentieth-century literature which we call metafiction and postmodern fiction, a negative axiological veil is often cast on this conviction that we exist in a 'prison house of language.' As Hayden White has noted, there is a sense of 'a fatal asymmetry between the processes of reality and *any* verbal characterization of those processes' (*Metahistory*, 232). This focus on incommensurability is accompanied by a feeling of despair, by the fear of being doomed to a life of delusion

(231). Frye writes of ironic literature that it 'begins with realism and tends towards myth, its mythical patterns being as a rule more suggestive of the demonic than of the apocalyptic' (AC, 140). In defining demonic symbolism, Frye underscores the aura of futility and sterility that is intrinsic to it, and thus to the extreme ironic mode as well (AC, 147); furthermore, Frye discerns in ironic literature the complete disappearance of the heroic element (AC, 228). For Frye, what is mirrored in these and other traits of late ironic literature is that utter 'failure of nerve' that marks the beginning of the ricorso (MM, 134).[10]

This kind of cynicism and defeatism was unequivocally rejected by both Vico and Frye. Instead of wallowing in delusion, they prefer to tinker with the constructive possibilities of illusion, to dwell on the social responsibilities that must be shouldered once it is recognized that human existence, by definition, entails acts of recreation. In the pedagogical preoccupations and activities of both thinkers, we may witness the translation of this belief into praxis, into acts aimed at breaking the pattern of the ricorso through the education of the imagination.

I turn now to an aspect of Frye's critical undertakings that was scrupulously avoided by Vico, the area where critical thought merges with religious faith. It is here that we may look, perhaps, for the source of Frye's ambivalence towards Vico and his implicit shortcomings. Vico was adamant that the biblical tradition was excluded from the purview of his ideal eternal history. This bracketing of Hebrew history and the biblical narrative arose not only for reasons of personal expedience, although, given the lively activities of the Inquisition in the Naples of his day, this would certainly be understandable. It may be ascribed as well to the fact that Vico never did satisfactorily resolve the tension between his 'Theism and his humanistic historicism, between his conception of the cunning of Providence, and his constant emphasis on the creative and self-transforming labours of men.'[11] Vico was incapable of postulating, as his explicitly archetypal figure of a thundering Jove surely suggests, a Judaeo-Christian deity that was another variant of the severe, anthropomorphic, trauma-induced projection of a prohibitionist sky-father. This was a step that Frye, considerably assisted by Blake, was quite prepared to entertain.[12] In Frye's description of the Bible as a work closer to literature than to history or doctrine (CP, 116), and in his critical analysis of the Bible in The Great Code and Words with Power, the determination to explore the Bible as a product of human culture is apparent.

Perhaps the most problematic and enigmatic aspect of Frye's study is the description of kerygma, the prophetic or oracular sphere within the Bible's verbal operations. This linguistic idiom, says Frye, has affinities to the figured language of rhetoric and poetry but has a further, special function which is to induce in the reader or listener an ecstatic sense of language's own creative power (*GC*, 29–30; *WP*, 114–19). Although Bhati quickly dismisses kerygma as being irrelevant to a study of the Viconian strain in Frye's thought ('Vico and Frye,' 121), it would appear instead that here we encounter the *verum factum* translated into theological terminology. This conclusion is supported by the repeated tendency in Frye's later writings to converge Vico's key epistemological axiom with Blake's theology of the imagination. In the essay 'Blake's Bible' published in 1987 Frye reiterates Vico's *verum factum* and then proceeds to give it a Blakean twist: 'in Blake ... God and creative man being the same thing, his apocalypse is neither a humanistic vision of a better future or a show of fireworks put on by God ... It is the attaining of a divine and human identity whose creative powers are entirely without limits' (*MM*, 286). More recently, in a 1990 broadcast, Frye and his interviewer discuss Blake's 'vision' in unmistakably Viconian terms: 'Reality is something that we make in perceiving it, and we can't understand what we haven't made. Our capacity to do this is what Blake called "vision."'[13]

This tendency emerges also, though less explicitly, in *Words with Power* where Vico's axiom introduces a description of the Bible as pointing towards a reality that stretches from the mystery of creation at the beginning of time to the same reality manifested in the new apocalyptic creation in which humanity participates (135). In the merging of these creative activities into the single enterprise or form of the Incarnation, we are provided with the theological ground for Frye's earlier description of culture based on the Blakean image of the universal human body. This is the same image that underlies Frye's discussion of the 'royal metaphor' (*GC*, 87), in which is implicit a containment of the entire chain of being, not as a hierarchy but as a 'vision of plenitude, in which everything is equal because identical with everything else' (165).

Although a detailed examination of Frye's understanding of kerygma is beyond the scope of this inquiry, what is relevant for our purposes is that there seems to be a focus on the experience of creative freedom that ensues when we, as readers and listeners, are confronted with words of sufficient power to eradicate the anxiety structures erected by the divisive secondary concerns of ideology. Through the rhetorical impetus of kerygma we are compelled into a recognition of our freedom to make and thus to know the world and, it is hoped, to accept the discipline and responsibility that accompany such recognitions (*GC*, 231–2). Frye describes this liberated state in words that once again look back to Vico: 'when in the age of the people the gods become names for human powers that belong to us, and that we can in part recover' (*MM*, 140).

It would appear, then, that this liberated state, finally, represents for Frye the beginning and the end of the critical path. He reiterates the message of the thunderclap that first brought Vico to the *verum factum* principle, to the realization that 'man has created his gods, his rulers, his institutions, his machines, and it is only when he enters the created world, through a door that someone's imagination has opened, that he can participate in this and feel that the word *subject*, in all its contexts, no longer applies (*MM*, 139).

NOTES

1 See, for example, Balfour, *Northrop Frye*, 69, and Pietropaolo, 'Frye, Vico, and the Grounding of Literature and Criticism,' in *Ritratto di Northrop Frye*, 95–6.

2 Although I have not been able to determine the time of Frye's first encounter with Vico, we are given some general indicators in 'Cycle and Apocalypse in *Finnegans Wake*,' *MM*, 357–8, and in 'Expanding Eyes,' *SM*, 113. For an early reference to Vico, see 'The Rhythm of Growth and Decay,' *NFCL*, 141, 145.

3 I am responding here to Pietropaolo's comments in 'Frye, Vico, and the Grounding of Literature and Criticism' (89), where he describes the phenomenological status of the literary work as the principal focus of Frye's long career.

4 Graff, *Literature against Itself*, 26; see especially chap. 1.

5 For a comprehensive discussion of the *verum factum* principle in Vico, see Berlin's *Vico and Herder*; Pompa's *Vico: A Study of the 'New Science'*; and Cantelli's *Mente, corpo linguaggio*.

6 See especially 'Il metodo degli studi del tempo nostro' and 'Dell'antichissima sapienza italica,' in *Giambattista Vico Opere*.

7 Neussel, 'Metaphor and Cognition: A Review Essay,' in *Metaphor, Communication & Cognition*, 15. See also *GC*, chap. 1; and Books 1 and 2 of *The New Science of Giambattista Vico*.

8 Cantelli, *Mente, corpo linguaggio: saggio sull'interpretazione vichiana del mito*, 289.

9 Ibid., 288.

10 For a more detailed discussion of irony and the *ricorso*, see White, *Metahistory*, 230–3.

11 Berlin, *Vico and Herder*, 82.

12 For Frye's comments on Vico's bracketing of the Bible, see 'The Responsibilities of the Critic,' *MM*, 133.

13 Taken from a transcript of 'The Ideas of Northrop Frye,' CBC radio documentary, reproduced in *Northrop Frye Newsletter* 4, no. 1 (Winter 1991–92): 7–18.

WORKS CITED

Bahti, Timothy. 'Vico and Frye: A Note.' *New Vico Studies*, no. 3 (1985): 119–29.

Balfour, Ian. *Northrop Frye*. Boston: Twayne, 1988.

Berlin, Isaiah. *Vico and Herder: Two Studies in the History of Ideas*. London: Hogarth, 1976.

Cantelli, Gianfranco. *Mente, corpo linguaggio: saggio sull'interpretazione vichiana del mito*. Firenze: Sansone, 1986.

Cayley, David. 'The Ideas of Northrop Frye.' CBC radio documentary, March 5, 1990. Reproduced in *Northrop Frye Newsletter* 4, no. 1 (Winter 1991–2): 7–18.

Graff, Gerald. *Literature against Itself: Literary Ideas in Modern Society*. Chicago: University of Chicago Press, 1979.

Neussel, Frank. 'Metaphor and Cognition: A Review Essay.' In *Metaphor, Communication & Cognition*, edited by Marcel Danesi. Toronto: Toronto Semiotic Circle, 1988.

O'Hara, Daniel. *The Romance of Interpretation: Visionary Criticism from Pater to de Man*. New York: Columbia University Press, 1985.

Pietropaolo, Domenico. 'Frye, Vico and the Grounding of Literature and Criticism.' In *Ritratto di Northrop Frye*, edited by Agostino Lombardo. Rome: Bulzoni, 1990.

Pompa, Leon. *Vico: A Study of the 'New Science'*. London: Cambridge University Press, 1975.

Vico, Giambattista. *Giambattista Vico Opere*, edited by Fausto Nicolini. Milan: Ricciardi, 1980.

– *The New Science of Giambattista Vico*. Rev. ed. Translated from 3rd ed. of 1744 by Thomas G. Bergin and Max H. Fisch. Ithaca: Cornell University Press, 1970.

White, Hayden. *Metahistory: The Historical Imagination in Nineteenth-Century Europe*. Baltimore: Johns Hopkins University Press, 1973.

EVA KUSHNER

Frye and the Historicity of Literature

Pondering the legacy of Northrop Frye necessarily leads to the recognition of its scope, which goes far beyond the study of the literary system alone; this in turn entails recognizing the philosophical status of his thoughts. In *Anatomy of Criticism*, once he had established the specificity of the critical activity among intellectual disciplines, Frye showed little interest in the labels others would apply to his own sphere of activity: critic, or historian, or theorist, or philosopher. In practice, however, he always dealt, explicitly or by implication, with the whole universe of human culture, emphasizing the role of works of imagination within it. The philosophical dimension of Frye's concept of literary historicity will also lead us to discover what implications his transformation of historicity harbours for overcoming the perpetual hesitancy of literary studies between the more and the less historical, and how these implications extend to the conceptualizing and writing of literary histories of the present and of the future. Histories are stories; histories of literature, it should not be forgotten, are the stories of stories (like myth, fable, or romance), and as such they will continue to be written because nations, and sometimes even the international community, aspire to have their cultural icons enshrined in continuous narratives.

In our own time, the emphasis on identity and otherness has refocused attention upon the individual, the unique, that which is most difficult to reduce to system. Does Frye's thought respond to this need? The answer to this question lies, in part, within his concept of historicity and the manner in which it is able to capture the time-bound and the unique within the coherence of a total history.

The structure of Frye's literary system manages to incorporate time without isolating any part of the system in a temporal ghetto in which it could no longer relate to, and be compared with, any other part of the system. On many occasions he calls forth phenomena from immensely distant temporal and spatial, as well as cultural, horizons in order to emphasize their relatedness; but he does so without negating these distances, without eradicating the historical character of each element.

If we consider, as an example, Frye's ordering of the phases of satire, we see that it defies rigid periodizations, and in that sense it may appear separate from chronology; yet in itself it tells of a concatenation of changes which tells a continuous story of relations that can be either sequential or paradigmatic at a given time, or both. The sixth phase of satire, which 'presents human life in terms of largely unrelieved bondage' (*AC*, 238) and may feature prisons, madhouses, lynching mobs, and places of execution, as well as forms of social tyranny, goes back a very long way to Dante's *Inferno*, manifesting itself as well in Baudelaire's *Les fleurs du mal*, Kafka's *Penal Colony*, and Faulkner's *The Sound and the Fury*. Granted, the archetypal framework of these groupings is designed for transhistorical comparability of narratives severed from their mythical backgrounds; but even as they intersect and communicate they create a time of their own – call it mythical or literary – which relates metonymically to human states.

Specific literary histories, often based on preset periodizations, tend to colour literary phenomena in terms of those periodizations. Frye, on the other hand, demonstrates commonalities of phenomena that may be either distant or close in time as well as space; and, whether close or distant, history is what their relations engender. In short, his universals work synchronically as well as diachronically. Obvious examples of this process are shown in *The Secular Scripture*, where the hierarchy of four verbal structures – highly mythical ones such as the biblical or the Platonic; nonliterary, serious verbal structures; 'relatively serious' ones in agreeable, popular forms; and 'literature designed only to entertain or amuse, which is out of sight of truth' (21) – is shown to operate for centuries, indeed millennia, as is the even more radical opposition of the mythical and the fabulous. The past tense Frye uses in these universalizing, broad-brush statements indicates that they are meant historically. For example, the severely Platonic distinction between truth-oriented and enjoyment-oriented verbal structures became eroded, partly on account of 'Aristotle's more liberal conception of mimesis,' so that in the subsequent tradition 'literature did succeed in gaining a real place in the Christian social order. As its place was essentially secular, the imaginative standards came to be set by the fabulous writers, and the mythical ones had to meet those standards' (21). That these should be statements about the past made in the past tense is only natural, since they are meant to summarize and organize immense corpora of the past in such a way as to orient the analysis of story-telling in modern times; as well, they do not contradict detailed intellectual and aesthetic histories dealing with the relationship between truth-claim and form in various temporal layers of the Western past. The point here is that these glimpses over the past from the stratosphere of a certain present have become materials for the construction of a system that aspires to universality and stresses recurrence rather than temporal distance.

For Frye, the periods of cultural history are elementary facts of life which can be taken for granted: 'The history of literature seems to break down into a series of cultural periods of varying length, each dominated by certain conventions' (28). In contradistinction to the kind of literary history from which Frye distances himself, these cultural periods are not containers of dead storage: at all times any part of the system can gain renewed life if a critical reading lifts it from the past into a new transhistorical relationship; and that critical reading itself enters literary history. It is this ongoing conversion of the 'merely' historical into the live contemporaneity of the literary system which distinguishes Frye among all critical thinkers. It explains his own practice and also paves the way for new work capable of overcoming the handicaps of literary history – which Frye, René Wellek, and many others have identified – by incorporating a renewed historicity into the system itself. By the same token it helps to overcome the opposition, which had long divided the entire field of literary studies, between the historical and the theoretical attitude, one situating the truth about texts in various aspects of their genesis, the other in a timeless continuum or, more recently, in the discontinuities of individual reading experiences, which no system can reunite.

To read Frye is to encounter, at every step, statements that provocatively describe the vast historical landscapes resulting from this vision; invariably, the reader is challenged to probe the universality of their scope. At the intersection of the 'everywhere and always' of literary symbolization as it appears in times and cultures very distant from one another, and of the irreducible and irreplaceable 'here and now' of each work, Frye calls attention to this encounter of the universal and the particular. The first thing that *Anatomy of Criticism* creates is precisely this radical transformation of historicity, rather than a denial of it. We should heed A.C. Hamilton's warning: 'For those who had not read Frye's earlier articles, it must have been surprising that he should base his poetics on a new literary history that reveals the specific historicity of all literary works – so surprising that the essay was misunderstood then and remains so now' (*Northrop Frye*, 45).

From this perspective, the system introduced by *Anatomy* constructs, indeed is, a new literary history. By and large, early readers and critics emphasized the new history less than Frye's demolition of traditional literary history. *Anatomy* initially seemed to coincide most easily with the various forms of New Criticism and with literary structuralism. Yet the literary historical dimension should have been emphasized because – in whatever way a thinker decides to deal with works of the imagination in relation to history – literary works cannot be severed from the cultural processes linked to their birth. These cultural processes are internal to literature; they are 'history within literature' (*CP*, 24), rather than what the French call *histoire événementielle* with its presumed causative effects upon literature.

To sum up, the internal order of literature invoked by Frye excludes neither history nor literary history nor, most importantly, historicity itself; it includes them, however, within its own articulation. Its specific temporality has to do, in Proustian terms, with the 'time regained' of the literary system rather than with the 'time lost' of past occurrences. One of the first consequences of this is that chronology will not be the ordering principle of literary history reborn. According to A.C. Hamilton, the new discipline will 'go beyond a chronological survey of literature to an awareness of its total order' (*Northrop Frye*, 55), incorporating the diachronic within the synchronic.

The fictional modes which form the core of the chapter on historical criticism in *Anatomy* constitute an overarching example of such a total order, with a temporal succession broadly applicable to literatures anywhere, since all have sacred beginnings and portray gods and heroes before descending from romance to high mimetic, low mimetic, and finally ironic modes. As with any evolutionary theory – and one must remember that Frye's Spenglerian antecedents predispose him to think in evolutionary terms – there is danger in claiming universal validity for such broad schemata. Though it might be tempting to portray it so, history cannot be predetermined. Metahistory, as Hayden White calls it, is not a system of insuperable rules but a place of reflection, of watching for the crises and creations of human consciousness, of possibilities for interpretation. This is particularly important in the case of literatures that have not been fully inventoried and codified, such as emerging literatures, minority literatures, literatures written in exile. Undeniably, however, and regardless of the degree of necessity we may attribute to his own conception of it, Frye introduces among literary phenomena an order of succession.

Throughout his work, Frye has left countless indications of the way in which literary works (or aspects of works, or groupings of works) enter this order and, by the same token, adumbrate directions for future literary historiography. To show the continuity of Frye's attitudes, let us examine *The Great Code* to see if, in this respect, it coherently echoes the much earlier *Anatomy*. In defining the relationship of the poetic and the historical, the essential movement consists in purifying the former from all circumstantial history, which at any rate is not there. In biblical stories such as the Exodus, 'when we move into what looks like actual history, to which we can attach some dates and supporting evidence,' Frye writes in *The Great Code*, 'we find that it is didactic and manipulated history' (40). Or again: 'The priority is given to the mythical structure or outline of the story, not to the historical content' (41). The Bible is composed of 'mythical accretions' rather than identifiable 'facts': 'It is the bits of credible history that are expendable, however many of them there may be' (42). And finally: 'Homer's sense of history does not mean that he is writing history. Similarly with the Bible' (42). Granted, these statements deal with myth in the Bible and are grounded in what Frye calls the metaphorical phase of language. But this is precisely what makes them so seminal: it is the very prototype of literature, the model of models, that derives its literary nature from being mythical and not depending on historical evidence in the factual sense.

Thus, not unlike many formalists and structuralists, Frye assigned secondary importance to the genesis of literary phenomena, and primary importance to the understanding of their relations and structures. However, his opposition to older concepts of literary history did not stem from any diffidence towards historical change as if it were an intellectual impurity. Rather, in his eyes, the potential for intellectual impurity lay in failing to understand the necessary severance of literary works from their origins. In the history of Russian formalism, which at first excluded temporality, the return of temporality by dint of, for example, the concept of evolution as expounded by Tynianov was hailed as a breakthrough; and as a postwar structuralist Lévi-Strauss, in *Tristes tropiques*, proudly reinstated the very diachrony that he had banished both for instrumental and for epistemological reasons. For Frye, the relevance of literary temporality is obvious; but he does not stress it when bringing together comparable elements within the system, which might originate in widely separate times and places. The distinction French scholars have long made between *histoire littéraire* (the history of writers and institutions) and *histoire de la littérature* (the temporal unfolding of literature itself) receives in Frye's theory, as well as in his practice, its fullest embodiment ever.

An example drawn from one of Frye's unpublished notebooks might serve to illustrate the manner in which his mind transmuted phenomena into the history that was to become *Anatomy*. Notebook 39 contains materials concerning English poetry of the sixteenth and beginning of the seventeenth century.[1] Frye, as a very young teacher, structured the outline of his presentation of Renaissance English poetry up until Donne. It is by no means devoid of background information about social life in the Renaissance, – such as descriptions of class tensions between the aristocracy and new oligarchy, the rise of capitalism, the geographical explorations – or about the state of the English language, inasmuch as it conditions the evolution of poetry. In discussing Sidney, Frye included plans to deal not only with his poetry and poetics, but also with his personality as a 'complete man' and his position among the writers of his time.

However, such contextual elements are scarce in the outline, which privileges the description of each writer's poetry, though not solely its formal characteristics; the 'mental outlook' of Spenser in *The Faerie Queene*; and genre groupings, with names of poets attached to them: the lyric, the pastoral, sonnet cycles, the didactic, etc. It is also interesting to note that this minimal, compulsory list of topics is followed by a menu of two subjects, between which Frye intended to choose 'if there is more time.' Either he would dwell longer on the formal and thematic study of Donne's poetry or he would develop, first, the intellectual presuppositions of sixteenth-century thought through Plato, Augustine, Calvin, Machiavelli, Montaigne, and even cynical and pessimistic tendencies, and, second, Renaissance ideals, including medieval and Gothic ones still held in Elizabethan England. Thus, while helping undergraduate students begin to understand how Renaissance poetry was born, Frye structured his course according to the requirements of the poetic system itself; and if this were to be called history, it would be strictly that of the unfolding of the genre, with very few biographical or contextual elements intervening.

Notebook 39 was to serve two purposes: right-hand pages were to be used as lecture notes and left-hand pages, as material for 'the book.' Clearly that book, which was to have been a sequential, chronologically ordered history of English Renaissance poetry, was never written as such; this exemplifies Frye's gradual but energetic departure from a merely chronological ordering towards a multidimensional vision of English poetry within English literature as a whole, and within the literature of the world, as unveiled in *Anatomy of Criticism*.

All concepts basic to Frye's critical theory deal, in one way or another, with temporal becoming. The case of the five fictional modes with their respective types of protagonists is perhaps the most obvious: 'Looking over this table, we can see that European fiction during the last fifteen centuries, has steadily moved its center of gravity down the list' (AC, 34). Other sequences are of course possible in a world perspective; but, given Frye's premises, it is difficult to imagine a situation in which the mythical would not have anteriority over the literary. In fact, the identification of the mythical and of the literary on Frye's terms rests upon that anteriority, and seems irreversible. Anteriority, it is true, can be logical rather than temporal; but the process of displacement whereby myth is transformed into literature necessarily occurs in time.

Drawing its structural unity from its mythical origins, the infinite diversification of literature in the world develops as a history: 'The conventions, genres and archetypes of literature do not simply appear: they must develop historically from origins or perhaps a common origin' (CP, 34). It is, furthermore, a historicity specific to literature itself: 'I wanted a historical approach to literature, but an approach that would be or include a genuine history of literature, and not simply the assimilating of literature to some other kinds of history' (CP, 23). It is this specific literary historicity that forms part of the framework of critical activity: 'Instead of fitting literature into a prefabricated scheme of history, the critic should see literature as a coherent structure, historically conditioned but shaping its own history ... This total body of literature can be studied through its larger structural principles' (CP, 24). Clearly, this vision encompasses existing historical studies that respect the specificity of literature, as well as a variety of possible future historical studies written in a similar spirit. In other words, the historical aspect of Frye's thought does not disqualify or destroy literary history as a mode of intellectual discourse, but sets out for it certain theoretical standards governing inclusions and exclusions. And, above all, it demands coherence of inquiry.

The coherence of the inquiry presupposes coherence of the literary system itself; that is, the kind of spatio-temporal interrelatedness that Frye devises for it. Literary works are studied independently from their origins and their original settings. 'Nearly every work of art in the past had a social function in its own time ... It may have been originally made for use rather than pleasure, and so fall outside the general Aristotelian conception of art, but if it now exists for our pleasure it is what *we* call art' (AC, 344–5). Like Todorov in Les genres du discours, Frye sees genres initially identified with the speech acts that gave them birth. Moving away from these original contexts and functions, literary works enter into their own history, in which their functions relate only to the functions of other literary works, in the time of their reception: 'One of the tasks of criticism is that of the recovery of function, not of course the restoration of an original function, but the recreation of a new function in a new context' (*AC*, 345). We might remember, for example, that post-colonial readings of *The Tempest* are now themselves part of our cultural history. Similarly, every new appropriation makes cultural history in its own time and place; the life of the literary work continues to *make* history. 'The culture of the past is not only the memory of mankind, but our own buried life, and the study of it leads to a recognition scene, a discovery in which we see, not our past lives, but the total cultural form of our present life. It is not only the poet but his reader who is subject to the obligation to "make it new." Without this sense of "repetition" [in the Kierkegaardian sense] historical criticism tends to remove the products of culture from our own sphere of interest' (*AC*, 346).

Our understanding of Frye's concept of historicity would be distorted were we to neglect the underlying link between literature as history and the manner in which the present responds to history. By definition, the literary system moves forward in time to receive new creations. But to say this is still to describe it in mechanical terms which would totally betray Frye's sense of the role of literature in society and of the role of the reader in giving life to the literary work. It would not be an exaggeration to say that literature enters history precisely inasmuch as it becomes literature; the process of its creative severance from its original circumstantial history strangely resembles its creative severance from truth claims and ideologies, a severance without which it could not add new dimensions, new visions, new riches to the history of humankind.

NOTE

1 Robert Denham kindly drew my attention to the importance of the note-book.

WORKS CITED

Hamilton, A.C. *Northrop Frye: Anatomy of His Criticism.* Toronto: University of Toronto Press, 1990.
Lévi-Strauss, Claude. *Tristes topiques.* Paris: Librairie Plon, 1955.
Todorov, Tzvetan. *Les genres du discours.* Paris: Editions du Seuil, 1978.

JAN GORAK

Frye and the Legacy
of Communication

1

What do we understand by the legacy of communication? In a world swaddled in messages, saturated with symbols, glutted with images, twentieth-century literary intellectuals have often imagined communication as a dystopian surplus of threatening subhuman antitypes. When Frye commemorated Canada's centenary year of confederation, he chose to deliver some admonitory words on the disintegrative tendencies of what he called 'the modern century.' Among the most disintegrative forces in modern culture, he identified 'communications media, especially the newer electronic ones' as the most destructive, since they promoted subjective expectation while enforcing centralized control. For Frye, 'A society entirely controlled by their slogans and exhortations would be introverted, because nobody would be saying anything: there would only be echo, and Echo was the mistress of Narcissus ... The triumph of communication is the death of communication: where communication forms a total environment, there is nothing to be communicated' (*MC*, 38).

In a world of total communication dominated by predominantly electronic media, Frye sees a tacit declaration of war on the human communicating potential of what he calls 'the inner mind.' Because communication has such life and death significance for Frye, it is too important to be left to mechanical communicators. Its proper custodians are the poets, especially the visionary poets, whose creations Frye habitually views as the antithesis of mechanical communication and whom he calls the sole vessels for 'real' communication.

Frye's views on communication provide the basis for his powerful dissident testimony against the coercive forces masked as seductive attractions during the modern century. Yet they also exemplify some of the key divergences in method that have separated literary critics from their opposite numbers in the social sciences. The latter see communication in terms of an ongoing rule-bound symbolic interaction, a continuous process in which social actors define and interpret actions, gestures, and words according to publicly accessible intersubjective norms. Until very recently, students of literary criticism, inspired by the powerful example of testimony like Frye's, saw literary communication as a supreme fiction, a Lyotardian grand narrative that saw the life and death significance of some messages as in some way compensating for the triviality of all others. This effectively meant that the legacy of communication was transmitted across two completely separate channels. The first enjoyed the framing, protecting context of art and in this way conducted its visionary mission of human liberation under the aegis of an independent consciousness. The second was rule-bound and predictable, the staple idiom of habitual social transactions in legal, commercial, religious, and political institutions. Here were two legacies of communication, one invested with a redemptive vocation, the other entrusted with the daily processing of social transactions. Literary studies rejected the premises of the human or social sciences, becoming in effect a superhuman antisocial science that mapped its territory by articulating the sovereign acts of communication invested in a creative consciousness.

2

Are there any areas of common ground between students of communication in literary studies and the social sciences? If one interprets their joint legacy in a broad sense, tracing it back to the early years of the twentieth century, then I think some important common concerns and characteristics emerge. First, the legacy of both fields can best be written under the trope of reversal or peripeteia. So many of the disciplinary formations designed to consolidate and even to expand the authority of progressive, rational, scientific, bourgeois European civilization repeatedly uncovered evidence that chipped away at the legitimacy such disciplines initially aimed to serve. At the start of the century, students of classical civilization saw the canonical masterpieces of Greek antiquity as seamlessly joined to our own world, a cultural legacy of unquestioned authority and untroubled succession. Yet within a few years, the research of F.M. Cornford, Jane Harrison, and A.W. Verrall showed that a whole range of canonical cultural categories – history, tragedy, science – did not mean to the

Greeks what they meant to us. By history, Thucydides referred to our modern category myth;[1] by religion, the Greeks meant what we would classify as magic. Such discoveries emphasized that communication – what a Greek playwright meant when he transmitted a message that he was about to write tragedy – was culture-specific, not universal. Classical knowledge provided no longer a lingua franca for an educated group, but a highly particular language to be reconstructed by specialist knowledge. History itself, as historians like Benedetto Croce, Lucien Febvre, and later R.G. Collingwood acknowledged, must be reconstructed in new ways, must be imagined as a matrix of new problems and not as a legacy of authoritative precedents.

The emerging discipline of social anthropology enforced similar lessons. Anthropological fieldwork did not substantiate established claims about the superiority of a single entity designated as European civilization, but rather led to discoveries about the differential status of the multiple systems of communication we designate as a culture. The idea of a 'primitive mind' or an 'underdeveloped culture' that aimed at European standards but repeatedly fell short of them could not withstand the battery of empirical evidence brought forth by Malinowski, Evans-Pritchard, and their successors. The sum of this evidence, Lévi-Strauss was to argue, effectively reversed dominant assumptions about European superiority, since their allegedly primitive counterparts displayed parity and even superiority in key processes of classification, communication, and tool production. At the end of *La Pensée Sauvage*, Lévi-Strauss notes: 'The idea that the universe of primitives (or supposedly such) consists principally in messages is not new. But until recently a negative value was attributed to what was wrongly taken to be a distinctive characteristic, as though this difference between the universe of the primitives and our own contained the explanation of their mental and technological inferiority, when what it does is rather to put them on a par with modern theorists of documentation' (267).

Lévi-Strauss urges his audience not to assume the transparency of messages or the natural superiority of any one model of culture, but to think in terms of a perpetual interaction between different systems of communication, each operating by its own coherent logic, tacit principles, and limited permutations. He sees law, kinship, economics, trade, and religion as communication systems, not natural facts, and he emphasizes that in each of these systems the production, consumption, and exchange of symbols forms the basis of all meaningful social action and interpretation.

But what is the relationship between the different kinds of logic that operate in given communication systems and given cultures? When

Tzvetan Todorov shifted the study of communication from a synchronic to a diachronic axis, he cleared the path for understanding communication in terms of conflict as well as diversity. For if not all cultures think alike, then there is no reason why they should agree. The epochal encounter between Europeans and American Indians, as Todorov represents it, becomes a battle between systems of communication. He notes: 'Would it be forcing the meaning of "communication" to say, starting from this point, that there exist two major forms of communication: one between man and man, the other between man and world, and then to observe that the Indians cultivate the former and the Spaniards the latter?' (*The Conquest of America*, 69).

What happens to messages in the conditions Todorov describes? They become screened out, distorted, and mistranslated. Most important of all, they will be subordinated to what Harold Innis called 'the bias of communication,' the inbuilt but culture-specific incorporation of images into regulated channels. Innis noted that some communication systems were better 'suited to the dissemination of knowledge over time than over space,' while others were better suited 'to the dissemination of knowledge over space than over time' (*The Bias of Communication*, 33). Since, by what we can term 'Innis's law,' communication systems habitually aspire to conditions of monopoly, then situations of conflict, situations like those described by Todorov, constitute the rule and not the exception. Consequently, Braudel's 'third level' for historical transactions, the cultural level of symbolic communication, can escape none of the great public conflicts that rage across world history.[2] Todorov reverses the legacy of communication from one of assumed universality into one of historical struggle, opening the way for a historiography that acknowledges the explosive force unleashed by clashing communication systems at key points of political tension – the Reformation, the French Revolution, the Soweto uprising.

For Michel Foucault, however, the coercive force of dominant communication systems lies in their power to render such conflicts invisible.[3] Foucault reverses Lévi-Strauss's expectation that the interpretation of culture as a set of interlocking codes will create a new respect for diversity. For Foucault, rather, the interlocking codes inside a given culture converge on the common purpose of defining, regulating, and controlling acceptable images of human identity, while simultaneously presenting such limitations as natural and not coercive. In *I, Pierre Rivière*, Foucault supplies a parable about the annexation of communication systems by centralized power. The eponymous hero, a provincial adolescent whose speculative frame of mind conflicts with orthodox belief and whose sudden violence habitually embroils him in village gossip, rejects social norms by slaughtering most of his immediate family. From then on, a systematic ensemble of translations returns the horror that Pierre unleashes to conformity inside an acceptable framework. Pierre must be mad, atheistic, or condemned by bad blood. The whispers and gossip that circulated before his crime must be processed into evidence that settles his public responsibility. Any testimony that Pierre offers on his own behalf – his disturbing and unconventional autobiography, for example – must be trimmed to the needs of a case that now controls any interpretation of his identity. Pierre cannot be allowed the unmediated access to the public mind enjoyed by his fictional contemporary, Balzac's Vautrin, a criminal hero who exists in the protected sanctuary called culture. Vautrin constitutes, as the local newspaper the *Pilote* repeatedly insists, a threat to public safety. It is only in the cultural realm that what Foucault calls 'the monstrous' can enjoy the liberty of autonomous communication. In the public realm, the legacy of communication, as Foucault understands it, is a legacy of domination and isolation, a legacy that endlessly enriches centralized power at the expense of human liberty, a counter-Enlightenment by which all forms of knowledge – medical science, law, penology – are deployed as canons of regulation.

The human sciences in this century have greatly enlarged the range of activities subsumed under communication. They have reversed time-honoured assumptions of privilege, drawing our attention to the fact of diversity. They have also characterized the conflicting logics underlying the various systems of communication and shown that these logics co-exist only by virtue of the supreme illusion of 'the natural.' They have drawn our attention to the coercive function of notions of 'the real' inside a culture, challenging us to rethink these notions more imaginatively. They have challenged their practitioners to renegotiate history by investigating channels previous generations thought beneath notice. Each reversal in the human sciences leaves the official narrative of European civilization on less secure foundations, forcing students of accepted culture into a widening uncertainty about their instruments and their subject matter. The testimony of the human sciences above all else reverses any easy assumption that the legacy of communication transmits itself in a universal language grafted painlessly and ineradicably into our consciousness.

Of all literary critics and theorists in the twentieth century, Frye appears to be one of the most fervent apologists for such a universal language. Not only does he strenuously assert the autonomy of poetic language, but he also argues that traces of such language linger in our universal human consciousness. Frye also emphasizes the difference between literary communication and its nonliterary counterparts, although his emphasis on this difference altered during the course of his career. In a review of Paul Valéry's *The Art of Poetry*, he meditates on the words 'shut up your doors' from *King Lear*. Viewed in isolation, do they seem any different in the Globe Shakespeare from the way they appear in the Toronto *Globe*? The poet, Frye laments, 'has to use the same dissolving words that we use for ordinary speech where we are attending not to them but to what they point to' (*NFCL*, 191). Poetic raw materials, words, bear the same relation to the ultimate cultural product, literary communication, as marble in a quarry does to Michelangelo's *David*.

Frye first poses this antithesis in terms of the difference between nature and culture. At this stage, literature, like religion, science, or law, tries to order a world that, in the state we inhabit it, is a world of loss and random disorder. In a review of Suzanne Langer's *Feeling and Form*, he notes: 'All the arts show us, architecture most vividly, that there are two orders of reality: the world that nature presents to us, and the world that human society constructs out of it, the world of art, science, religion, culture, and civilization ... the difference between neurosis and art is the difference between a private and a public world. If we think of such words as *culture* or *civilization*, we can see that we do in fact live in the world created as an artistic image' (*NFCL*, 116).

Art, science, religion, and poetry – in short, culture – conform to a common logic and combine in the common goal of making the world human. Their various messages accumulate into a world constructed through the beneficence of the visionary imagination.

Frye moves away from this track, however, suggesting that there are significant differences even inside the unified world of civilization. Like F.M. Cornford, he begins to think that poetry mysteriously reverses realistic assumptions or ratiocinative activity. 'Thinking is one of many things that man does,' he concedes in an essay called 'Myth as Information,' adding that 'it is not the only thing he does. Hence ... to put logical thought in its place as one of a number of human operations is more realistic than to consult it as an oracle which reveals to man the existence of a systematic and rational order in an objective world' (*NFCL*, 68). For all his objections to rational oracles, Frye will now emphasize the structural differential of poetic communication, foregrounding its family likeness to the logic of myth and religion rather than the logic of philosophical or political discourse: 'poetry, as distinct from discursive language, uses the language of identification ... which is a relation of identity ... There is thus a strong natural alliance between the language of poetry ... and the aim of the religious impulse, which in the long run can find no other speech than that of the poetic symbol' (*NFCL*, 98–9).

How will Frye avoid the complaint that to raise allegory and myth to a new centrality is to make poetry a source of messages and not an autonomous art? Frye answers by emphasizing the structure of the poetic message. In *A Natural Perspective*, his study of Shakespearean comedy, he stresses that a comedy is not only a play that ends happily but also one that begins miserably. Reversal, one of the key items in Frye's critical inventory and in twentieth-century thought as a whole, promotes 'a kind of ultimate confrontation of a human community with itself' (30). It no longer seems so bad to Frye that literature embeds itself in words, since literary communication uses words to entangle us further and further in the fallen world of nature but then shapes these same words into visionary structures that deliver us from it. As he notes in *The Critical Path*, 'Literature is unique ... in being able to reflect the world escaped from, in its conventions of tragedy and irony and satire, along with the world escaped to, in its conventions of pastoral and romance and comedy' (169). Frye's parenthesis reverses the direction of genre theory by making it less a matter of taxonomy than of cognitive mapping. As Frye understands them, genres do not so much classify literary messages as they provisionally position them in a world of gradual ascent from the subhuman to the transcendent.

Frye returns again and again to the trope of reversal, seeing in it both the individuating feature of literary communication and the collective hope of cultural renewal. Geographically, Greece and Israel refer only to 'two tiny chopped-up countries'; culturally, their writings 'have imposed themselves on our consciousness until they have become part of the map of our own imaginative world' (*GC*, 218). Historically, Shakespeare represents for Frye a virtual case study in negation; he has 'no opinions, no values, no philosophy, no principles of anything except about dramatic structure' (*NP*, 38). Yet the bold reversals that take *The Tempest* from Renaissance statecraft to the visionary world of Cockaigne enable a provincial 'incompetent thinker' to rival Plato in his political imagination. Like Christ's, Shakespeare's kingdom does not conform to earthly canons. Competence in thinking according to the world's terms belongs to some of Shakespeare's most unpleasant creations – Edmund, Iago, Antonio. Like Christ, Shakespeare chooses the implausible and the folly-ridden as vehicles for his visionary wisdom: Bottom, Gonzalo, Falstaff. Similarly, Shakespeare's appropriate reception becomes a process of stripping away layers of cultural habit.

One begins by reading or seeing a play like other plays, subject to the conditions and limitations of its own age and to our corresponding limitations in receiving it. One ends with the sense of an exploding force in the mind that keeps destroying all the barriers of cultural prejudice that limit the response to it. In other words, we begin within a notion of what the play might reasonably be assumed to mean, and end with realizing that what the play actually does mean is so far beyond this as to be in a different world of understanding altogether. (*MD*, vii–viii)

At this point, Frye's systematic reversal of the priorities governing nonliterary communication accumulates into a veritable counterhistory of modern civilization. Like Frances Yates, with whom he shares many affinities, Frye constructs an alternative map of European cultural history, a map that reverses the disappointments of actual history to engage with what Yates calls its 'hopes.' Frye and Yates both think 'Hopes ... are as much a part of history as the terrible events which falsify them,'[4] and they both map out alternative social futures that conform to civilization's better self.

3

Like all contributors to this volume, I acknowledge a responsibility not just to evaluate the legacy of Northrop Frye, but to hypothesize about what we can do with that legacy. I have argued that Frye ultimately conceives of literary communication as a visionary legacy tuned to the reversal of our culturally restricted structure of expectations about what constitutes plausible action, critical thinking, cultural authority, and political wisdom. Frye thinks that at best such expectations, about time, sequence, political organization, can only run into impasses of the sort embodied in the play he imaginatively locates at 'the normal beginning of secular history in Shakespeare's day' (*MD* 62), *Troilus and Cressida*. Literary communication, like religious communication, embodies a kind of desperate endgame, a hope for a final order that can liberate us from the imposing monoliths dedicated to coercive order all around us. Such monoliths appear solid enough, Frye acknowledges. But the messages of literary communication unmask them as airy nothings, vehicles for vested interests and secondary concerns. To the degree that Frye sees the actual world as an imperfect replica of the visionary world, he is no liberal, no exponent of the *via media*, but a thinker whose interests, like those of Kierkegaard, occupy 'the dangerous edge of things.' Today, Frye appears not just the 'residual anarchist' identified by Michael Fischer elsewhere in this volume, but a writer whose anarchy infects his entire understanding of literary communication and its function in society.

Frye does not conceive of the legacy of communication in ways that someone working in the human sciences would recognize. He argues for the suspension of the rules that govern nonliterary communication inside the autonomous world of literary representations. Outside *The Tempest*, Prospero would exemplify the authoritarian personality; inside it, he can participate in 'the great code' of utopian liberation. Such a code has driving force for many other inner minds than Frye's, but by turning literary communication into a *utinam* rather than an *as if* (a 'we wish it were' rather than 'what would it be like if it were like this'), he makes it hard to conceive of literary communication as a representation of a social action or an essay in symbolic interaction.

Does Frye's legacy still speak to a generation that conceives of its goals as materialist and worldly? On the face of it, Frye appears to offer little to such a group. Two of Frye's late works, the oddly neglected study of Shakespeare's problem comedies *The Myth of Deliverance* (1983) and his 'second study of "the Bible and literature"' *Words with Power* (1990), force us to reconsider this verdict. In the latter, Frye announces the intellectual benefits of 'reversing one's direction, going upstream to one's source' (xxiv) before moving into an extended consideration of the relationship between literary and nonliterary communication. In the former, Frye turns once more to investigate 'comedy and its relation to human experience.' Although the course of Frye's apparent argument follows a pattern set down in 'The Argument of Comedy,' *A Natural Perspective*, and *The Secular Scripture*, the detailed working out of that argument proves very different. Frye reaffirms his belief that literary communication represents the world in which we want to live, not the world that encloses it. Even so, what might surprise a reader of his earlier work is his sensitivity to the ideological shape of the societies represented in the problem comedies. In *All's Well That Ends Well* Frye describes a society of ruthless individualism, a society where war in effect provides a logical outcome to the tacit conventions of aggression that govern every deed and every message. In this world, communication follows the rules of individual self-assertion so closely that it becomes anarchy, the anarchy of Parolles's obscure self-fashioning or Bertrand's bottomless devotion to his own self-appraisal. Without any admixture of realism, Shakespeare still manages to represent a kind of ideological archive of Renaissance individualism and to dramatize its apparently endless systems of ideological exchange. Shakespeare shows a society where, in Philip Larkin's words, 'self's the man,' but where the self can never know stability but must perpetually expand and transform itself in ever more elaborate artifice.

Paradoxically, Frye's focus on these plays, now viewed as manifesting a 'myth of deliverance,' forces him to scrutinize the social structures from which the plays seek visionary release. Instead of opposing literary communication to its nonliterary opposite, Frye sees literary and nonliterary communication in relationship, as two sides of the image of human beings in society. In *Measure for Measure*, he sees a celebration of delivery from the bondage and deadlock imposed by law and ecclesiastical authority. But if Frye's notion of delivery is subtracted from his analysis, then he leaves us with an interpretation of the play that shows a new sensitivity to the structures of ideology that legitimate Renaissance authority. He begins his analysis by emphasizing the importance of social mobility in shaping the play's dramatic action. When Duke Vincentio relinquishes his authority and invests it in Angelo, he clears a space for a source of power that Shakespeare subjects to intense scrutiny. In Angelo, the new governor and new man, Shakespeare gives his audience an image of power imagined freshly. Streaked with 'the fault and glimpse of newness,' Angelo represents 'the body public' as subordinate to his own disciplined power, conceiving it as

A horse on whom the governor doth ride,
Who, newly in the seat, that it may know,
He can command, lets it feel the spur. (1.2.164–6)

In the first half of the play, image after image dramatizes the channelling of diverse message systems – law, government, sexuality, and religion – to accommodate the demands of surveillance and nearly universal policing. The second half of the play metamorphoses into a celebration of perpetual improvisation that also serves the purpose of social control. Where Frye sees a shift in genre and world-view – a movement from a dramatization of the way things are to a celebration of the way we all desire them to be – we can see a movement from a representation of the prison-like structures that enclose the world outside the play to a self-referring celebration of that world restructured as a play. On the one hand, the play anatomizes a communication system that perfects the instruments of surveillance, a system G.R. Elton considers the cope-stone of Tudor hegemony. On the other hand, it investigates communication as the perpetually shifting self-creation that Jacob Burckhardt sees as the foundation of the Renaissance state.[5] By interpreting the play's central concerns in this culture-specific way, we can see it as 'of an age' and not 'for all time.' In this way, we bring the history of literary communication closer to the history of communication in general. Like René Wellek, who published the first part of his *History of Literary Criticism* two years before *Anatomy of Criticism* appeared, Frye belonged to a critical generation eager to establish the autonomy of literary communication. In his last works, however, he reverses these priorities to focus on the relationship between literary and nonliterary communication, acknowledging that 'a subordination of poetic and metaphorical to dialectical language' (*WP*, 33) characterizes the world we actually inhabit, if not the world we desire to inhabit. Literary critics earlier in this century frequently conducted their affairs as if the dominance of rhetorical and dialectical communication – the world of science, philosophy, advertising, and politics – amounted to an unfortunate mistake. But it is only by exploring the relationship between the world of visionary desire and the cycle of rhetorical exchange that critics can return a just verdict on the legacy of communication. The later Frye seemed eager to reexamine this legacy, although his death prevented him from doing so very fully. By emulating his willingness to reverse his earlier priorities in order to explore these issues, we can expand the legacy he has bequeathed to us. It is paradoxical but not contradictory to say that the reversal of his legacy might prove the fulfillment of that legacy.

NOTES

1 See Cornford's *Thucydides Mythhistoricus: From Religion to Philosophy*; and *Before and After Socrates*.
2 For a discussion of 'third level' history, see Darnton, 'The Symbolic Element in History,' 218–34.
3 *I, Pierre Rivière*. Also see *The Archaeology of Knowledge*.
4 See Gombrich, *Tributes*, 213.
5 See Elton, *Reformation Europe: England under the Tudors*; *Policy and Police*; Burckhardt, *The Civilisation of the Renaissance in Italy*.

WORKS CITED

Burckhardt, Jacob. *The Civilisation of the Renaissance in Italy*. London: Phaidon, 1965.

Cornford, F.M. *Thucydides Mythhistoricus.* Philadelphia: University of Pennsylvania Press, 1971.

– *Before and After Socrates.* Cambridge: Cambridge University Press, 1960.

– *From Religion to Philosophy.* New York: Harper Torchbooks, 1957.

Darnton, Robert. 'The Symbolic Element in History.' *Journal of Modern History* 58 (1986): 218–34.

Elton, G.R. *Reformation Europe: England under the Tudors.* London: Methuen, 1955.

– *Policy and Police.* Cambridge: Cambridge University Press, 1942.

Foucault, Michel. *I, Pierre Rivière.* Lincoln: University of Nebraska Press, 1982.

– *The Archaeology of Knowledge.* New York: Pantheon Books, 1972

Gombrich, E.H. *Tributes.* Oxford: Phaidon, 1984.

Innis, Harold. *The Bias of Communication.* Toronto: University of Toronto Press, 1951.

Lévi-Strauss, Claude. *La Pensée Sauvage.* Chicago: University of Chicago Press, 1966.

Todorov, Tzvetan. *The Conquest of America.* New York: Harper Torchbooks, 1987.

ROSS WOODMAN

Frye, Psychoanalysis, and Deconstruction

One radical difference (which for Frye is not to say opposition) between Frye and the deconstructionists lies in their contrary working assumptions about the origins of literary language. For Frye literary language, which is to say, the language of myth and metaphor, has its origins in the Logos, or Word, understood as kerygma (*DV*, 18), a word which he borrows from Rudolph Bultman and which means (or carries as meaning) voice, proclamation, revelation, divine breath, apocalypse. For many deconstructionists – and here I think particularly of Derrida, Lacan, Kristeva, and de Man, though ignoring their differences and stressing their Freudian bias – literary language has its origins not in spirit but in flesh, more specifically, as in the case of Kristeva, in the biological mother's tactile intercourse with her infant, an intercourse which, beginning orally at the breast, spreads erotically throughout the infant's body in a manner which Freud described as polymorphous perverse. Frye, on the other hand, focuses on what he calls 'a conception of language in which words were words of power, conveying primarily the sense of forces and energies *rather than analogues of physical bodies*' (*GC*, 17; emphasis added).

Frye's theory is father-oriented, patriarchal, in the archetypal, rather than biological, sense. Language at its archetypal source is God speaking, proclaiming, revealing, unveiling, and finally incarnating himself as the 'I am that I am,' or, as Frye prefers, ' "I will be what I will be" ' (*GC*, 17), which is to say, 'what I will become.' God being what he will become is, Frye argues, God becoming human, humanity being the supreme instrument of his becoming. Though for Frye God becomes what he is in Christ, the Christ whom he becomes is potentially present in all of us.

This potential presence finds its metaphorical and mythical embodiment in literature, most especially, or quintessentially, in romance which assembles unto itself Frye's four *mythoi* of literature. Literature thus becomes what Frye calls the secular scripture. If Christ is in the spiritual sense the incarnate or literal body of God, literature is his metaphorical body. Metaphor and myth, that is, bind literature fictionally to the Logos, or Word, in a state of suspended disbelief which Coleridge calls 'poetic faith' (*Biographia Literaria*, chap. 2, 6). Christ, on the other hand, binds us actually to God in a state of active belief or religious faith.

For Frye, as for Coleridge, poetic faith is the secular displacement of religious faith. It 'does everything that can be done for people except transform them,' Frye writes in *The Double Vision*. 'It creates a world that the spirit can live in, but it does not make us spiritual beings' (16). Literature, that is, provides in the world of the flesh a home for the spirit. To inhabit that home, to take up here and now a temporal residence in it, we must first become spiritual beings. The process of becoming spirit so as to inhabit 'a world the spirit can live in' requires religious, rather than poetic, faith. Suspended disbelief depends for its suspension upon a mental act of displacement in which what is demanded by belief relaxes into play. 'It is,' Frye writes of poetic faith, 'at once a world of relaxation, where even the most terrible tragedies are still called plays, and a world of far greater intensity than ordinary life affords' (*DV*, 16).

And because it is a world of relaxation and play ('Me —— to play,' declares Beckett's God about to ham it up in *Endgame* [2]), 'it would be absurd,' declares Frye, 'to see the New Testament as only a work of literature' (*DV*, 16). Literature subordinates its moral and spiritual demands to the operations of the pleasure principle. 'I have even compared the literary universe to Blake's Beulah, where no dispute can come,' Frye told the members of the English Institute, 'where everything is equally an element of a liberal education, where Bunyan and Rochester are met together and Jane Austen and the Marquis de Sade have kissed each other.'[1]

Beulah is Blake's threefold *imago* of the married land in which the absence of dispute resides in the pre-Oedipal incestuous bonding of the madonna and child, a bonding which in its undisturbed state renders the father *imago* a shadowy figure which has, like the mythical Joseph in relation to Mary and Jesus, no obvious or explicit biological role to play.

Though Frye focuses as a literary theorist upon the secular scripture as the mythical and metaphorical displacement of the Logos, or Word, at the same time he renders it answerable to the Word. More than that, he identifies the secular scripture archetypally with the mother *imago* even as he identifies the Bible archetypally with the father *imago*. Beulah as at once the married land and 'the literary universe where no dispute can come' contains an ideal vision of the union of the Bible and literature in and through their shared language of metaphor and myth. Frye, in his Christian commitment to literature, casts himself as the offspring of this marriage. As a pleasurable world of relaxation and play, literature gratifies at an adult level certain abiding infant desires constellated in a maternal myth of the madonna and child in which the father *imago* assumes no active role.

As a literary theorist, however, Frye renders the pleasure principle operative in his aesthetic response to literature answerable finally to the Logos in which the father *imago* assumes the dominant role. Though engaging on one essential level in the erotic play between the mother *imago* and her offspring in a Beulah where Bunyan and Rochester are met together and Jane Austen and the Marquis de Sade kiss, Frye's ultimate goal is at-one-ment with the Father. Frye, like Milton before him, understood the 'uncessant care' which rendered 'sport with Amaryllis in the shade' answerable to 'all-judging Jove' (*Lycidas*, 64–82).

Deconstruction, on the other hand, operating within language itself, disrupts the harmonious relations between the parental *imagos* which govern Frye's verbal universe. Identifying metaphysics with the Logos, or Word, Derrida, in 'Structure, Sign and Play,' argues that 'there is no sense in doing without the concepts of metaphysics in order to shake metaphysics.' 'We have,' he explains, 'no language – no syntax and no lexicon – which is foreign to this history; we can pronounce not a single destructive proposition which has not already had to slip into the form, the logic, and the implicit postulations of precisely what it seeks to contest' (*Writing and Difference*, 280–1). To deconstruct the Logos as a metaphysics of presence, to contest its authority as the authority of what Lacan calls the symbolic or the name-of-the-Father, an order which, he argues in *Speech and Language in Psychoanalysis*, envelops as culture and civilization the life of human beings from the instant of their conception to the moment of their death and even beyond their death (42), is not to slay the Father, destroy the law, overthrow culture. It is, rather, to recognize that the symbolic is, in Shelley's phrase, 'pavilioned upon chaos' (*Hellas*, 772).

Dismemberment for the deconstructionist is not death. For Paul de Man the decaying corpse of Shelley inscribed on the last manuscript page of his unfinished *The Triumph of Life* is itself the paradigm of all texts which necessarily suffer the mutilation that is language. 'It may seem a freak of chance,' he writes in 'Shelley Disfigured,' 'to have a text thus molded by an actual occurrence [the drowning of Shelley in the Bay of Lerici], yet the reading of *The Triumph of Life* establishes that this mutilated textual model exposes the wound of a fracture that lies hidden in all texts. If anything, this text is more rather than less typical than texts that have not been thus truncated' (*Rhetoric of Romanticism*, 120–1).

For the deconstructionist a literary text is not, as Frye argues, an organic unity mirroring the unity of the Word; it is always already fractured or dismembered. Deconstruction is not an action performed upon the text; it is, at least for the deconstructionist, an action which literary language by its very nature performs upon itself. Thus the Freudian deconstructionist, Julia Kristeva, like Lacan, a psychoanalyst, describes the dismemberment within poetic language as the traces of the mother's body which she calls the 'semiotic' (*Desire in Language*, 40–2). Prosody, she argues in *Revolution in Poetic Language*, derives from the infant's pre-Oedipal, incestuous bonding with the mother's body, a bonding which she describes as a flow of relatively unorganized '"energy" charges' or drives as well as '"psychical" marks' which articulate what she, borrowing from Plato's *Timaeus*, calls a '*chora*: a nonexpressive totality formed by drives and their stases in a motility that is as full of movement as it is regulated' (25). For Kristeva, therefore, the madonna and child as an icon of what Frye, following Blake, calls Beulah is not a place of peace and harmony; it is the subversion of the Logos, the Lacanian symbolic, the place of revolution and overthrow.

Analysing in *Desire in Language* a series of madonnas and child by Giovanni Bellini, Kristeva shows the way in which Bellini's madonna, as the aggressive phallic mother who ravishes her child, threatens it with castration (237–70). The role of the mother image is perpetually to challenge the authority of the Logos, Lacan's symbolic or name-of-the-Father. It is perpetually to diffuse the power of the father archetype which, according to Derrida, has from Plato to Hegel enshrined the authority of language itself as the custodian of meaning with its power to make present the will of the divine. Beulah, far from being passive, is the aggressive arena for the overthrow of the Logos understood as patriarchal power.

The chief literary figure to which many deconstructionists, including Derrida and de Man, naturally gravitate is Rousseau, whose *Essay on*

The Origin of Languages fully articulates the myth of a maternal source which is gradually usurped by the Logos, or Word. 'To the degree that needs multiply,' Rousseau writes, 'that affairs become complicated, that light is shed [knowledge is increased], language changes its character. It becomes more regular and less passionate. It *substitutes* ideas for feelings. It no longer speaks to the heart but to reason. For that very reason, accent diminishes, articulation increases. Language becomes more exact and clearer, but more prolix, duller, and colder' (quoted in Derrida's *On Grammatology*, 244). In his deconstruction of Rousseau's essay in *Of Grammatology*, Derrida argues that Rousseau uses the maternal myth of the origin of languages, a myth which renders 'voice' as *'pulsion,'* infant cry, or what Derrida calls 'animal language,' not only prior to writing but even superior to writing (142). Writing, Rousseau suggests, is the silencing of the mother, the repression of the infant's bodily contact with her by the Logos, by the logocentric increase of knowledge.[2] What Derrida sees in Rousseau is the coming into consciousness of what, from Plato onwards, remained a hidden struggle of writing with itself, a struggle in which words as signifiers enacted the absence of what they signified, an absence which, he writes, no metaphysical or ontological concept can comprehend (246).

Confronting the living, speaking corpse of Rousseau in *The Triumph of Life*, Shelley enacts, as de Man suggests, the struggle with the mother *imago* who, as a dancing 'shape all light' (352), blots out with her feet 'the thoughts of him who gazed on them' (384). The 'figure all light' is deconstructing language, which is, as language, language deconstructing itself. 'Figures ever new,' declares the Shelleyan narrator who acts as the poet's other confronting him less as poet than as writing,

> 'Rise on the bubble, paint them how you may;
> We have but thrown, as those before us threw,

> 'Our shadows on it as it past away.' (249–51)

Shelley reading Rousseau is deconstructing a text which neither he nor Rousseau, but writing itself, is writing. De Man describes the process as 'the endless prosopopoeia by which the dead are made to have a face and a voice which tells the allegory of their demise and allows us to apostrophize them in our turn. No degree of knowledge can ever stop this madness, for it is the madness of words' (*Rhetoric of Romanticism*, 122). For the deconstructionist, 'the madness of words' resides in the absence of the signified. It lies, as Lacan argues, in desire denied its object because the symbolic, the name-of-the-Father, has, like the Freudian super-ego, repressed it. For Frye, the Logos, far from repressing desire, fulfills it by carrying it, as Plato's dialectic carries it, to its metaphysical object.

To write, Derrida argues, deconstructing the logocentricism of Plato, is to deface, to forget, to erase. A Derridean text, Tilottama Rajan suggests, is 'a perpetual contesting and cancelling of its own meaning, and hence a projection of its own nothingness' (*Dark Interpreter*, 17n). This is too severe. Nothingness for Derrida signifies the absence of the thing to which it conventionally points; it is not in this literal sense a sign, a view with which Frye himself would in part agree in arguing for the autonomy of the Word. The contesting of meaning does not cancel meaning. Rather, it locates meaning in the perpetual contesting of it, even as in Blake meaning is located in ceaseless 'Mental Fight' (Preface to *Milton*, plate 1). Resolution into meaning would, in this sense, be the defeat of meaning, reducing it to closure, to a corpse, which is for deconstruction what every text threatens to become. The task for the poet writing is to keep the corpse speaking, as Shelley keeps Rousseau speaking. His task as poet is to keep writing writing, the meaning of a text being another text even as the meaning of *Paradise Lost* is for the Romantics their ceaseless (re)writing of it.

In a cover story for *Maclean's*, Frye told Mark Czarnecki that the Bible, as his mother taught it to him at home until he first entered school in the fourth grade, was 'a load of crap' ('The Gospel,' 42). His lifelong effort to make logocentric sense of the Bible was his attempt to release it from the literalist reading his mother insisted on, a reading which he more and more experienced as a Jonah being swallowed by a whale. Frye's struggle to break free of this literalist reading through, among other things, an understanding of myth and metaphor, which bound literature to the Bible without endowing it with the authority of the Bible, was a liberating experience which he described as the liberal knowledge available to the educated imagination.

'It is the schematic thinker, not the introspective thinker,' Frye told the members of the English Institute assembled in 1965 to assess his work, 'who most fully reveals his mind in process, and so most clearly illustrates how he arrives at his conclusions.'[3] This paper has made no attempt to show how as a 'schematic' thinker – a word he preferred to 'systematic'[4] – Frye arrived at his conclusions. My concern is, rather, to catch a glimpse of the 'introspective thinker' whom Frye for obvious reasons kept not hidden, but well in the background. Particularly because of its Freudian bias, deconstruction opens up, especially in its maternal myth of language origin, a contesting of Frye's logocentric criticism, a contesting which, far from cancelling its meaning, serves to further complicate it by bringing into focus a mental struggle hidden within the system itself. Deconstruction enacts the unconscious operative within Frye's system which the system as system fails as struggle to engage. That struggle, I suggest, is between the fathering of the word as the operations of the Logos and the mothering of the word as relaxation and play. From an introspective point of view, which invites a nonschematic approach to what Frye calls 'his mind in process,' Frye's scheme enacts the struggle of the Logos to transform the mother *imago*, who is the subversive phallic mother presiding over deconstruction.

While Frye said he learned more about Christianity from Blake than from any other poet, the left-wing Protestant Milton remained his favourite. 'Jesus returns to his mother's house at the end of the temptation,' Frye writes in 'The Revelation of Eve,' commenting upon the concluding lines of *Paradise Regained*, 'but leaves it again to be about his father's business when he starts on his ministry, or work in the world proper.'[5] Like Jesus at the conclusion of Milton's brief epic, Frye, it may be argued, also returns to 'his mother's house' in his experience of literature as the relaxed play-world of Beulah. Like Milton's Jesus, however, 'he leaves it again to be about his father's business when he starts on his ministry, or work in the world proper.'

Frye remarked that, though ordained, he had never really been a minister except for a few months as a student circuit preacher in Saskatchewan. 'The Puritans,' he said to David Cayley, 'distinguished between a congregation and a church and I feel that I am a fully active member of the congregation although my field of activity has been the university and my writing' (*NFC*, 185–6).

Frye goes on in 'The Revelation of Eve' to explain Milton's Puritan understanding of the return of Jesus to his mother's house. The mother, he points out, must be understood archetypally as 'the female principle complementing Jesus' (43), which is not the mother in the literal or biological sense, but the redeemed mother of the imagination when the imagination is understood as the secular or human counterpart of divine grace. Understood in this sense, the redeemed mother becomes what Frye interpreting Milton calls 'the redeemed Bride or Church.' 'Christians,' the Puritan Frye continues, 'should think of their Church as a bride, a young virgin, still under tutelage' (43–4). The mother as 'redeemed Bride' is for Frye the transformation rather than the repression of Kristeva's semiotic by the Lacanian symbolic. Through the metaphor-making power of the imagination that transcends the incest taboo of the reductive or restrictive Freudian libido, the traces of the mother's body become Frye's verbal universe, one metaphor of which is Blake's Jerusalem, at once a city and a bride.

In the context of Frye's ministry or field of activity as a literary theorist, literature becomes metaphorically his church, which is to say, his bride. His relation as literary theorist to literature itself thus becomes a secular version of Christ's relation to his church and Adam's unfallen relation to Eve. In its severest formulation, which Frye in 'The Revelation of Eve' identifies with his own left-wing Protestant reading of Paul, this means that 'the Word, the male principle, should have "absolute rule"; the Church, has only to murmur "unargued I obey"' (44). 'Absolute rule' and 'unargued I obey,' I hasten to add, are Milton's words, not Frye's. Frye's employment of them, however, makes his essential and reiterated point abundantly clear: literature like nature is dumb; she cannot explain herself. She therefore remains dependent upon the Logos, 'the male principle,' critical theory, to release her meaning from the silence she otherwise maintains, like Keats's 'still unravished bride' in 'Ode on a Grecian Urn.'

When the notion of an autonomous literature, which claims the authority to teach the Word, is identified with the Puritan notion of an autonomous church as an unfaithful bride or harlot, Frye's implicit critique of deconstruction (which has nothing to do with rejection) begins to surface. Divorcing language from the operations of the Logos, the deconstructionist views literature as the perpetual subversion of what Frye calls 'the male principle' by a phallic mother who forever remains by her very nature a harlot or unfaithful bride. Deconstruction, that is, fully inhabits a fallen world which language always already unredeemably enacts. The mother's house to which Jesus returns is not for the deconstructionist the house of 'the redeemed Bride' over which the Logos presides. It is, rather, far closer to the Freudian scene of the warring parents-in-coitus which renders forever absent the fantasized object of tantalized desire. Frye's attempt as a literary theorist to transform in the name of the Logos the mother *imago* is, for the deconstructionist, always already subverted by the recalcitrance of matter or *mater*, which is the recalcitrance of language itself.

Far from cancelling Frye's logocentric system, deconstruction, I suggest, both complicates its dynamic and, more importantly, releases it from the closure which otherwise as system continues to threaten its ongoing life. Radically opposed to the tyranny of closure – 'no writer who is not completely paranoid wants his house to be either a fortress or a prison'[6] – Frye, rather than opposing deconstruction, viewed it as a contrary necessary to critical progression. 'I think criticism becomes more sensible when it realizes that it has nothing to do with rejection, only with recognition,'[7] Frye told the members of the English Institute in 1965, years before most deconstructionist texts were written and read.

Continuing all his life to work out his own views of literature, Frye welcomed the fact that, side by side with his own, there were also a great number of other views, actual and possible, with which his were 'neither reconcilable nor irreconcilable.' He then added: 'They interpenetrate with him, and he with them, each a monad as full of windows as a Park Avenue building.'[8] Years later in 1985, following a lecture he had given, and in answer to a question from the floor, Frye implicitly drew a contrast between himself and Derrida. The specific reference was to Derrida's treatment of Rousseau: 'I don't think that in the long run deconstruction will seem different in its view of literature. It may seem to be different for a while, but wherever you have deconstruction, you also have construction. Wherever you have somebody analyzing the metaphorical structure of Rousseau, you will have somebody else wondering what the metaphorical structure in itself means by being there. The two methods of approach, it seems to me, are complementary rather than antithetical' (*WGS*, 9) .

NOTES

1 Krieger, ed., *Northrop Frye in Modern Criticism*, 143.
2 'The sadness of young children just prior to their acquisition of language,' Kristeva writes in *In the Beginning Was Love*, 'has often been observed; this is when they must renounce forever the maternal paradise in which every demand is immediately gratified. The child must abandon its mother and be abandoned by her in order to be accepted by the father and begin talking' (40–1).
3 Krieger, ed., *Northrop Frye in Modern Criticism*, 28.
4 Ibid., 136.
5 'The Revelation of Eve,' in *Paradise Lost: A Tercentenary Tribute*, 43.
6 Krieger, ed., *Northrop Frye in Modern Criticism*, 27.
7 Ibid., 29.
8 Ibid., 29.

WORKS CITED

Beckett, Samuel. *Endgame*. New York: Grove Press, 1958.

Blake, William. *The Complete Poetry and Prose of William Blake*. Edited by David Erdman. Berkeley: University of California Press, 1982.

Coleridge, Samuel T. *Biographia Literaria*. Edited by James Engell and W.J. Bate. Princeton: Princeton University Press, 1983.

Czarnecki, Mark. 'The Gospel According to Frye.' *Maclean's* 5 April 1982.

De Man, Paul. *The Rhetoric of Romanticism*. New York: Columbia University Press, 1984.

Derrida, Jacques. *Of Grammatology*. Translated by Gaytri Spivak. Baltimore: Johns Hopkins University Press, 1976.

– *Writing and Difference*. Translated by Alan Bass. Chicago: University of Chicago Press, 1978.

Frye, Northrop. 'The Revelation of Eve.' In *Paradise Lost: A Tercentary Tribute*, edited by Balachandra Rajan. Toronto: University of Toronto Press, 1969.

Keats, John. *The Poems of John Keats*. Edited by Jack Stillinger. Cambridge: Harvard University Press, 1976.

Krieger, Murray, ed. *Northrop Frye in Modern Criticism*. New York: Columbia University Press, 1966.

Kristeva, Julia. *In the Beginning Was Love: Psychoanalysis and Faith*. Translated by Arthur Goldhammer. New York: Columbia University Press, 1987.

– *Revolution in Poetic Language*. Translated by Margaret Waller. New York: Columbia University Press, 1984.

– *Desire in Language: A Semiotic Approach to Literature and Art*. Edited by Leon Roudiez and translated by Thomas Gora, Alice Jardine, and Leon S. Roudiez. New York: Columbia University Press, 1980.

Lacan, Jacques. *Speech and Language in Psychoanalysis*. Translated by Anthony Wilden. Baltimore: Johns Hopkins University Press, 1981.

Milton, John. *The Oxford Authors: John Milton*. Edited by Stephen Orgel and Jonathan Goldby. Oxford: Oxford University Press, 1991.

Rajan, Tilottama. *Dark Interpreter: The Discourse of Romanticism*. Ithaca: Cornell University Press, 1980.

Shelley, Percy B. *Shelley's Poetry and Prose*. Edited by Donald H. Reiman and Sharon B. Powers. New York: W.W. Norton, 1977.

ELEANOR COOK

The Function of Riddles
at the Present Time

This paper owes its existence to Northrop Frye and to Wallace Stevens: to Frye's essay, 'Charms and Riddles,' and to a passage from a 1943 essay by Stevens together with his late poem, 'The Sail of Ulysses.' It owes its impetus to an oddity I observed some ten years ago, as follows. Although deconstructionists deeply mistrust most rhetorical figures, there is one figure they do not mistrust. On the contrary, they adore her, they desire her, they remain faithful to her. She is their blue flower always pursued though never possessed. She alone is not deconstructed. Her name is enigma, traditionally, the riddle.

Paul de Man speaks of lyric poetry as 'an enigma which never stops asking for the unreachable answer to its own riddle' (*Blindness and Insight*, 186). Other examples abound. 'Deconstruction,' to follow Geoffrey Galt Harpham, 'seems to have sprung from a passage in Nietzsche's *Beyond Good and Evil* which describes a "new species of philosopher" who "*want* to remain a riddle"' (*The Ascetic Imperative*, 264). Enigma is to deconstruction what metaphor is to so-called logocentrism.

In this, deconstruction is part of a larger movement. For enigma has undergone a dramatic reversal of fortune from her nineteenth-century woes. Ruskin was irritated that Goethe spoke darkly in enigmas about those moral precepts which he, Ruskin, saw so clearly in the work (*The Works of John Ruskin*, 284). 'Riddle redundant' served to describe Browning in an 1883 parody.[1] Fontanier omits the figure of *énigme* altogether from his *Les Figures du Discours*, but then for Fontanier an allegory must first of all be *transparente* (114), which leaves no room for obscure allegory, a common definition of enigma from Quintillian onward.

In the late nineteenth and twentieth centuries, enigma has come into her own. As Frye put it: 'Charm poetry ... dominated taste until about 1915, after which a mental attitude more closely related to the riddle began to supersede it' (*SM*, 142). Mallarmé's remark is well known: 'Il doit y avoir toujours énigme en poésie, et c'est le but de la littérature.' Not revelation but enigma, though for Valéry the enigmas of Mallarmé were precisely a revelation.

But, of course, I should be asking, *what* riddle, what enigma? For, obviously, they differ in kind. The deconstructionists who adore enigma do not have in mind that most famous of biblical enigmas, St Paul's in I Corinthians 13:12, 'For now we see through a glass darkly' (ἐν αἰνίγματι).

In what follows, I would like to outline a proposed anatomy of the enigma or riddle, considered as masterplot. (The word 'masterplot' is taken from Terence Cave, in his book, *Recognitions*, which he in turn takes from Peter Brooks's *Reading for the Plot*.) I am speaking of the literary riddle rather than the folk riddle. And I am putting together two senses of riddle from *The Oxford English Dictionary*: '(1) A question or statement intentionally worded in a dark or puzzling manner, and propounded in order that it might be guessed or answered, esp. as a form of pastime; an enigma; a dark saying'; '(2) Something which puzzles or perplexes; a dark or insoluble problem; a mystery.' We tend to separate these two meanings, though Sophocles did not, nor did W.S. Gilbert: 'Life's perhaps the only riddle / That we shrink from giving up' ('The Gondoliers'). The *OED*'s quotations make clear that riddles tend to be either very small in duration and apparent use, or else very large – sometimes so large as to constitute everything, the enigma, the mystery of the universe. Riddles seems to dislike the middle ground of familiar mimetic writing. They simplify and condense, as do those other two primitive genres, the charm and the proverb.

In pulling together the two meanings of riddle, I am not thinking so much of neck-riddles, where your life depends on answering a conundrum, as in *Pericles* or *Monty Python's Holy Grail*. I am thinking more of two master riddles, what I want to call Pauline riddling and Oedipal riddling. These constitute my first two types of enigma. By Pauline riddling I mean riddle as in 'For now we see through a glass darkly; but then face to face' (1611, drawing on the Geneva Bible). Tyndale, 1534: 'Now we see in a glass even in a dark speaking.' Luther, 1522: 'Wir sehen jetzt durch einen Spiegel in einem dunkeln Wort.' Latin Bibles repeat the original Greek word, *aenigma*: 'Videmus nunc per speculum in aenigmate' (Vulgate). The text is so familiar I hardly need observe that this is the kind of riddle that will end in revelation, in light, in the dispersal of cloud, in the clarifying of the obscure, in the answering of the inexplicable, in the straightening of the labyrinthine, and so on through many a well-known trope for enigma. Light comes with our death, in God. (I am reading synchronically here, and setting aside differences in context as well as historical problems.)

Such lexis of the riddle is standard, though not always noted as such. Donne offers a compendium: 'Poor intricated soul! Riddling, perplexed, labyrinthical soul!' (Sermon XLVIII, 1628–9). Tennyson knows the lexis well: 'dawn's creeping beams ... dissolved the mystery / Of folded sleep' ('Dream of Fair Women,' 261–3) – 'folded' as in the Latinate 'intricate'; 'dissolved' not a firm 'resolve,' as in Eliot's 'Resolving the enigma of the fever chart' (*East Coker*).

Pauline riddling provided an authoritative masterplot in Christendom for centuries, and not only for the verbal disciplines. Newton's work on the enigmas of the Book of Revelation was not inimical to his work in physics but consistent with it. As John Maynard Keynes put it, 'he looked on the whole universe and all that is in it *as a riddle* [sic] ... He regarded the universe as a cryptogram set by the Almighty – just as he himself wrapt the discovery of the calculus in a cryptogram when he communicated with Leibnitz' (*Collected Writings*, 10:366). Riddles remain today, but that once-authoritative masterplot has radically altered, if not largely vanished.

Oedipal riddling moves downward to darkness: it is Pauline riddling turned upside down. Not the Epistle to the Corinthians but the man from Corinth, Oedipus. I have asked myself whether Paul had in mind the connection of Corinth with famous enigmas when he used the word *aenigma* (αἴνιγμα) in his letter to the church at Corinth. There are good reasons this might be so, and Paul's engima does reverse Oedipal riddling. Oedipus begins by answering the famous neck-riddle of the Theban Sphinx. If you do not answer her riddle, she eats you, a graphic rendering of the inside-outside logic of the figure of enigma. But Oedipus has more than one riddle to answer, and his story ends in blinding and darkness. Paul reverses the inside-outside logic. We already see as *in aenigmate*, within an enigma, but then face to face. Sight not blindness; the riddle solved by God, not by us; light eventually though not in this life. Greeks like Plato and Aristotle distrusted what was obscure and riddling, to follow W.B. Stanford, because such things were 'relics of the dark days when the utterances of Sphinx or Oracle or Seer were too often things to be dreaded' (*Greek Metaphor*, 24). Paul, I assume, is designing a Christian enigma as against an Oedipal enigma.

It is, I think, precisely because the Sphinx's riddle and biblical riddling constitute two contrary types that Dante juxtaposes them in the closing books of the *Purgatorio*: 'My prophecy, obscure as / Themis and Sphinx ... the hard enigma' (XXXIII. 46–50, translated by Singleton from 'buia ... attuia ... enigma forte'). A fuller version of this paper would want to spend a little time on the end of the *Purgatorio*, showing how Dante works specifically with the figure of enigma, and suggesting his aesthetic and doctrinal reasons for doing so.

So also Milton contrasts the Sphinx's riddle and biblical riddling in *Paradise Regained*, where Satan, having vainly tempted Christ, falls 'as that Theban monster that proposed / Her riddle, and him who solved it not, devoured, / So strook with dread and anguish fell the Fiend' (IV. 572–6). Milton does not point out that Oedipus himself will also fall – rather as Samson does, I suppose. My type 2 enigma, Oedipal riddling, is not so much Oedipal as Sphinxine in the work of Dante and Milton. I make the distinction because the dominant form of Oedipal engima in our day is Freud's masterplot. If it also follows the pattern of a fall, of light versus darkness, of outside versus inside, the context is very different from that of the Sphinxine riddle as conceived by Milton, Dante, and, I think, St Paul. For Oedipus is partly a wisdom figure, a master interpreter of riddles, a figure for psychoanalysis itself insofar as it reads enigmas rather than being read by them.

Here I want to make a leap towards criticism, in accordance with my allusive title, which follows Frye's own alluding in his 1949 essay, 'The Function of Criticism at the Present Time.'[2] Frye's criticism is sometimes said, and justly so, to follow a romance or a quest pattern. The masterplot it follows is that of the Pauline riddle. For criticism following the pattern of Oedipal riddling, we should turn to Freudian critics: to the work of Peter Brooks, who calls Freud's patternings a masterplot for our fictions, and, preeminently, to the work of Harold Bloom, his work being dialectically related to that of Frye.

The desire of deconstruction, I take it, is to remove itself altogether from logocentrism, including criticism along what might be called the Frye-Bloom axis. If we look for a type of enigma for deconstruction, we should look for the unanswerable riddle. Not the riddle whose answer we do not know or even whose answer we shall never know, but the riddle that has no answer, the self-mirroring riddle, the self-enclosed riddle. This constitutes my type 3 enigma. In the latter part of the nineteenth century through much of the twentieth century, the alternative to Pauline enigma is often seen as this type of unanswerable and hence threatening enigma. We are, I think, still working through the sense of such a threat, as witness our sometime bafflement or nostalgia. Even Frank Kermode allows the word 'disappointment' in the last sentence of *The Genesis of Secrecy* (145). And Paul Ricoeur, in the conclusions to *Temps et récit*, returns to the ancient topos of contemplating '*[le] mouvement souverain des astres*' (391) – the word 'souverain' linking him with the Psalmist as with Kant, though distancing him from Stevens, who revises this topos more than once.

Historicist criticism, as far as I know, pays little attention to enigma, apart from the special case of esoteric riddles and their use by slaves for purposes of disguise (see Hegel). But enigma as masterplot does not appear to interest new historicists; it is a question how far any end-directed plot interests them, and whether they read all end-directed plots as essentially *Heilgeschichten*.

As for feminist criticism, my riddle-types map readily, in familiar figures: (1) enigma as resolved in the Madonna or a Beatrice figure; (2) enigma as propounded by the Grecian Sphinx; (3) the unanswerable riddle that all women are (as we know).

It is time to come to Stevens on enigma. For some years, I read Stevens's kind of enigma in his late work as a variation on my type 3. But I think it constitutes a fourth type, rather harder to define. Consider this speech from Stevens's essay, 'The Figure of the Youth as Virile Poet': 'No longer do I believe that there is a mystic muse, sister of the Minotaur. This is another of the monsters I had for nurse, whom I have wasted. I am myself a part of what is real, and it is my own speech and the strength of it, this only, that I hear or ever shall' (*The Necessary Angel*, 60, 67). The last sentence sounds very like deconstruction and is so read. The first part gets ignored. Stevens revised this speech at the end of his essay. You might suppose he would sweep away Minotaurs and muses, together with the whole *le-pli* family of riddling, folded, implicated, inextricable, labyrinthine words. Not so. Here is the revision, now spoken by the young poet himself: 'Inexplicable sister of the Minotaur, enigma and mask, although I am part of what is real, hear me and recognize me as part of the unreal.' And so on.

Stevens has reinvented, even invoked, this mysterious female – not mystic, not a monster, but still – note – sister of the Minotaur, and now 'inexplicable,' an 'enigma,' a 'mask.' The familiar sister of the Minotaur is, of course, Ariadne, 'la tua sorella,' as Dante calls her (*Inferno*, xii. 20). She is the rescuer from labyrinthine riddle and the standard rescue plot. But his alternative is not the unanswerable enigma, my type 3. Nor does he turn his back on end-directed plots. A sister of the Minotaur returns as mask and enigma, and explicitly as 'guide.' 'Mask' (*persona*) is easy enough. But enigma? That is also easy enough in one sense: the mystery of creation, etc.

Yet Stevens's own figurings of enigma are so intelligent and precise that I doubt he wants to end his essay on so ready and general a thought. To trace the development of the figure of engima through Stevens's work is not possible here. Let me simply move to the 1954 poem, 'The Sail of Ulysses,' which ends thus:

> The great sail of Ulysses seemed,
> In the breathings of this soliloquy,
> Alive with a enigma's flittering ... [sic]
> As if another sail went on
> Straight forwardly through another night
> And clumped stars dangled all the way. (131)

The very short version of this poem (24 lines as against 172) includes all six lines just quoted. (Five of the six lines have their words slightly altered, the exception being the line on enigma; see 'Presence of an External Master of Knowledge' [131].) I want to call this type of enigma Sibylline because of the Sibyl figure in the Stevens poem. The ancient Sibyls were riddlers, of course, first classical riddlers, then Christian prophetesses. Stevens's late Sibyl is descended from these but different in kind; she descends more immediately from his 1943 inexplicable enigma and mask. She is an everyday Sibyl; she is like the commonplace or plain sublime of the 1949 poem, 'An Ordinary Evening in New Haven.' Here she is:

> 'What is the shape of the sibyl? Not,
> For a change, the englistered woman ...
> ...
> It is the sibyl of the self
> ... the sibyl's shape
> Is a blind thing fumbling for its form,
> A form that is lame, a hand, a back,
> A dream too poor, too destitute
> To be remembered, the old shape
> Worn and leaning to nothingness,
> A woman looking down the road,
> A child asleep in its own life.
> As these depend, so must they use.' (130)

Stevens writes this sibyl against the famous twentieth-century sibyl who lives in the antechamber to *The Waste Land* – writing, as he put it elsewhere, of plain reality not grim reality (*Letters*, 636).

'Alive with an enigma's flittering': what criticism would this enigma be like? The enigma of that flittering sail, the sail of Ulysses, voyaging. Not sailing towards the Mount of Purgatory in an angel-winged boat, eventually to come to the *di bianco in bianco* in the *Paradiso* (xxxi. 16) – 'tiers and tiers of immaculate reflections,' to adapt Elizabeth Bishop ('Seascape'). For Stevens says at the start that Ulysses is sailing under the 'middle stars.' Not sailing past the Pillars of Hercules on a *thanatos* voyage, nor (it appears) on a perpetually curving, dualistic course, whether *eros-thanatos* or challenge-response. Not sailing randomly or round and round: 'Straight forwardly,' says Stevens. The female figure for this type 4 riddle would be a Wisdom figure, but of this earth, and so neither Athena (who is the patron of Odysseus) nor the eternal Sophia. She would be the woman who corresponds to Ulysses, a many-wiled woman – perhaps, as in Stevens, a Penelope or an ordinary Sibyl.

What I have proposed as Sibylline enigma is Stevens's late type of riddle and not Frye's. Or is this too simple? Aphorisms, like riddles, belong in wisdom literature, and Frye spoke of his own work as aphoristic. He also said: 'Holism is not only not the end of the critical enterprise; it is an axiom pursued for its own rewards, which at a certain point may turn inside out ...'[3] Turn inside out, and move back to aphorism, just as Pauline riddle turns inside out at the end of Frye's essay 'Charms and Riddles,' when we refuse the riddle gambit and search instead for better questions.

In a recent review, Denis Donoghue argued that Frye's work went into 'eclipse' 'when readers lost interest in "first and last things" and set about a political program of one kind or another.'[4] He did not point out that Frye attended all his life to practical, social, even political matters in what I have called elsewhere the confessional aspect of his criticism. Nor that stories, including some biblical stories, can be morally empowering – a point made by Charles Taylor, who cites Frye (*Sources of the Self*, 96).[5] But what matters most is the fact that Donoghue seems to allow what Frye never would: a divorce between immediate contemporary concerns and the visionary – whether first and last things or (as Stevens might say) long-term things – those things which the figure of enigma holds before us.

It seems to me that we still have a problem with end-directed reading in that we desire it, and yet find it difficult to imagine alternatives to the dominant ones we have known. The deconstructionist questioning of ends can itself become an end. The historicist questioning of ends, valuable as a test, is hazardous if it isolates short-term from long-term goals. Living as we do on this planet where knowledge about means increasingly outstrips wisdom about ends, we literary critics might think again about masterplots or end-directed plots. No body of work would help us more in this task than that of Frye.

NOTES

1 'Browning is ——— what? / Riddle redundant, / Baldness abundant, / Sense, who can spot?' Anonymous, *Punch* (21 April 1883). The parody is of Browning's 'Wanting is ——— What?'
2 Frye, 'The Function of Criticism at the Present,' 1–16.
3 Quoted in *Eighteenth Century Studies: Special Issue on Northrop Frye*, edited by Howard Weinbrot, 249.
4 Donoghue, 'Mister Myth,' *New York Review of Books* 39 (9 April 1992): 28.
5 Further on the question of whether 'the good can empower,' see 504–5.

WORKS CITED

Brooks, Peter. *Reading for the Plot: Design and Intention in Narrative*. New York: Knopf, 1984.

Cave, Terence. *Recognitions: A Study of Poetics*. Oxford: Clarendon, 1988.

de Man, Paul. *Blindness and Insight: Essays in the Rhetoric of Contemporary Criticism*. 2nd ed. Minneapolis: University of Minneapolis Press, 1983.

Donoghue, Denis. 'Mister Myth.' *New York Review of Books* 39 (9 April 1992): 25–8.

Fontanier, Pierre. *Les Figures du Discours*. 1827, 1830 Paris: Flammarion, 1977.

Frye, Northrop. 'The Function of Criticism at the Present.' *University of Toronto Quarterly* 19 (1949): 1–16.

Harpham, Geoffrey Galt. *The Ascetic Imperative in Culture and Criticism*. Chicago: University of Chicago Press.

Kermode, Frank. *The Genesis of Secrecy: On the Interpretation of Narrative*. Cambridge: Harvard University Press, 1979.

Keynes, John Maynard. *Collected Writings of John Maynard Keynes*. Vol. 10, *Essays in Biography*. Edited by D.E. Moggridge. Cambridge: Cambridge University Press, 1971.

Ricoeur, Paul. *Temps et récit*. Vol. 3, *Le temps raconté*. Paris: Éditions du Seuil, 1985.

Ruskin, John. *The Works of John Ruskin*. Vol. 17. Edited by E.T. Cook and
  Alexander Wedderburn. London: George Allan, 1912.

Stanford, W.B. *Greek Metaphor: Studies in Theory and Practice*. Oxford: Blackwell, 1936.

Stevens, Holly, ed. *Letters of Wallace Stevens*. New York: Knopf, 1966.

Stevens, Wallace. 'The Figure of the Youth as Virile Poet.' In his *The Necessary
  Angel: Essays on Reality and the Imagination*. New York: Knopf, 1951.

– 'The Sail of Ulysses' and 'Presence of an External Master of Knowledge.' In
  Opus Posthumous. Rev. ed. Edited by Milton Bates. New York: Knopf, 1989.

Taylor, Charles. *Sources of the Self: The Making of the Modern Identity*. Cambridge: Harvard University Press, 1989.

Weinbrot, Howard D., ed. *Eighteenth Century Studies: Special Issue on Northrop
  Frye* 24 (1990–1).

JULIA KRISTEVA

The Importance of Frye

Everything separates me from Frye – my age, my social and political experience, my gender, my interest in the materiality of language and its unconscious logic. Nevertheless I underwent – as many of us did – the revelation that was his masterful book on William Blake. *Fearful Symmetry* (1947), which I read long after its publication, at the end of the 1960s when I was attempting to go beyond formalism and structuralism, struck me by the way it inserted the poetic text in the English tradition (Spenser, Milton) and, beyond, in the tradition of Scripture which sustains Western literature from the King James Bible to James Joyce. In Frye's exposition of symbolic derivations and models, I found, in counterpoint, the confirmation of what I proposed at that time under the notion of 'intertextuality.' The myths of Creation, of the Fall, of redemption through sacrifice, by the duality of Apocalypse and Resurrection, are not, of course, in my mind, untouchable myths – I will come back to this point. I saw here nevertheless, in the rediscovery that Frye made for me at the heart of Blake's text, a radical proof of this dialogism, this polyphony, which, as I see it, characterizes the Western imagination.

Anatomy of Criticism (1957), for its part, highly informed by Aristotelian terminology, opens up the field of literary criticism to an ambition which may appear excessive but which, only in this way, can ever hope to approach the extraordinary polysemy of literary art and take up the challenge it permanently poses. The modalities of criticism, designated or hoped for by Frye – historical, ethical or symbolic, archetypal, and rhetorical or classificatory – are well known. They can be disputed; others can be added. But it is undeniable that these types of critical approaches allow us, once they are linked, to decompartmentalize the technical enclosures in which contemporary literary theory habitually delights and to aspire to a capable interdisciplinarity. The particular emphasis that Frye puts on the archetype as a symbol which links one poem to another and thus allows us to unify and integrate our literary experience seems to me indeed an ethical requirement – not to lose sight of the content conveyed by rhetorical play, and to anchor this content in the Western metaphysical tradition, to view literature as an inseparable counterpoint of religion but also of Western philosophy. *The Great Code: The Bible and Literature* (1982) confirms Frye's spiritual aspiration to preserve, through the literary variants of the centuries and the wealth of Western literature, the biblical and evangelical message, as well as that of the Greek and Roman tradition. In a world increasingly deprived of values, this valorization of memory seems to me the primordial task of literary criticism. When we find ourselves faced with a nihilism which, after having rightly denounced the dead ends and horrors of the West, wears itself out in attacks that reject the complexity of tradition in the name of who knows what political correctness, it falls to humanists and most particularly to literary theory and criticism to defend, by elaborating, that tradition. I have tried, for my part, to pursue this task as it pertains to the contribution of Greek, Jewish, and Christian thought in the conception of the other, of the foreigner, but also in the conception of love, as well as of themes which engulf us today, such as abjection or depression. From this point of view, I can only side entirely with the suggestion of Frye, in *The Critical Path* (1971), that we centre the educational program in this communal mythology that we have inherited from the Bible, from the Greeks and Romans.

It is no less true that, while considering this fundamental religious and metaphysical legacy in order to rethink the unity of the West at the very moment when it must open itself to the grafts of immigrant cultures, I do not think that the symbol – the archetype – is the final level of analysis. Heir of the Enlightenment and Freud, I am among those who maintain that God can be analysed because he is the unconscious itself. Semiology conceived as semanalysis unfolds symbolism, illuminates its moral, as well as its constraining, force, and uncovers the underlying logic of the sacred, without ever exhausting it. This 'navel of dreams' to which Freud refers always remains an unknown in the most daring of interpretations. But, ultimately, is not the sacred that our tradition transmits to us – beyond any symbol – quite simply the desire for meaning and the infinite power of interpretations? This desire and these interpretations do not destroy the symbol. Quite the contrary. In analysing it, they constantly enrich it, revitalize it. This trans-symbolic lucidity, which I propose, could not even begin to be carried out without an immense erudition and a deep regard, as serious as it is playful, for our memory, for the roots of this civilization. In this respect, Frye bestows on us an exceptional experience, rich in erudition and wisdom, which not one of us has yet equalled. I join very sincerely in the homage being paid him.

Translated by Joseph Adamson

Appendix:
Northrop Frye's Books

This list contains the editions of all of Northrop Frye's books, including edited volumes, that I have been able to identify. While I was preparing this list, I learned that the following books, copies of which I have not yet seen, have been published in Korea: *The Bush Garden* (trans. Sang Ran Lee), *The Educated Imagination* (trans. Sang Il Kim), *Anatomy of Criticism* (trans. San Woo Lee), *The Developing Imagination* (trans. In Hwan Kim), and *The Critical Path* (trans. Bu Eung Koh). In the catalogue that follows, I have not listed a number of the books that have been reprinted with covers different from their originals or other slight variations. Page sizes are to the nearest centimetre. (I have not seen copies of 2d and 19h.)

Robert D. Denham

BOOKS

1. Fearful Symmetry (1947)

1 *Fearful Symmetry: A Study of William Blake.* Princeton: Princeton University Press, 1947. 462 pp. 23.5 x 15.5 cm. Illustrations follow pp. 3, 74, 140, 208, 300, and 386. Casebound.

1a *Fearful Symmetry: A Study of William Blake.* Princeton: Princeton University Press, 1958. 462 pp. 23.5 x 15.5 cm. Illustrations follow p. 54. Paperback.

1b *Fearful Symmetry: A Study of William Blake.* Boston: Beacon Press, 1962. 462 pp. 20.5 x 13.5 cm. Incorporates several minor changes and contains a preface written for this edition. Illustrations follow pp. 3, 74, 140, 208, 300, and 386. Paperback.

1c *Fearful Symmetry: A Study of William Blake*. Princeton: Princeton University Press, 1969. 462 pp. 21.5 x 13.5 cm. Same text as 1b, but with a preface written for this edition. Illustrations follow p. 54. Casebound.

1d *Fearful Symmetry: A Study of William Blake*. Princeton: Princeton University Press, 1969. 462 pp. 21.5 x 13.5 cm. Paperback.

1e *Agghiacciante simmetria: Uno studio su William Blake*. Translated by Carla Plevano Pezzini and Francesca Valente, with the assistance of Amleto Lorenzini. Milan: Longanesi, 1976. 492 pp. 21.5 x 14.5 cm. Contains, in addition to the preface of 1c, another preface written in 1975 for this translation. Illustrations follow p. 64. Stiff paper wrappers.

2. Anatomy of Criticism (1957)

2 *Anatomy of Criticism: Four Essays*. Princeton: Princeton University Press, 1957. x + 383 pp. 23.3 x 15.3 cm. Casebound.

2a *Analyse der Literaturkritik*. Translated by Edgar Lohner and Henning Clewing. Foreword by Edgar Lohner. Stuttgart: W. Kohlhammer Verlag, 1964. 380 pp. 21 x 13 cm. Paperback.

2b *Anatomy of Criticism: Four Essays*. New York: Atheneum, 1965. 383 pp. 21 x 13.3 cm. Paperback.

2c *Anatomie de la critique*. Translated by Guy Durand. Paris: Gallimard, 1969. 454 pp. 22.5 x 13.7 cm. Stiff paper wrappers.

2d *Anatomia della critica: Quattro saggi*. Translated by Paola Rosa-Clot and Sandro Stratta. Turin: Einaudi, 1969. 484 pp. No index in this translation. Paperback.

2e *Anatomy of Criticism: Four Essays*. Princeton: Princeton University Press, 1971. x + 383 pp. 21.6 x 13.8 cm. Paperback.

2f *Anatomia della critica: Quattro saggi*. Translated by Paola Rosa-Clot and Sandro Stratta. 2nd ed. Revised with the help of Amleto Lorenzini. Turin: Einaudi, [1972]. 484 pp. 18.1 x 10.7 cm. No index in this translation. Paperback.

2g *Anatomia criticii*. Translated by Domnica Sterian and Mihai Spariosu. Bucharest: Editura Univers, 1972. 473 pp. 19.9 x 12.9 cm. Includes a preface by Vera Calin. Paperback.

2h *Anatomia da crítica*. Translated by Péricles Eugênio and Silva Ramos. Sao Paulo: Editora Cultrix, [1973]. 362 pp. 19.3 x 12.9 cm. Stiff paper wrappers.

2i *Anatomia de la critica: Cuatro ensayos*. Translated by Edison Simons. Caracas: Monte Avila Editores, 1977. 500 pp. 17.4 x 11.9 cm. Paperback.

2j *Anatomija kritike: Cetiri eseja*. Translated by Giga Garcan. Zagreb: Naprijed, 1979. 407 pp. 19.9 x 12.3 cm. Casebound.

2k *Hihyo no kaibo*. Translated by Hiroshi Ebine et al. Tokyo: Hosei University Press, 1980. viii + 529 + 34 pp. 18.7 x 12.5 cm. Includes a sketch of Frye's career by Hisaaki Yamanouchi, a bibliography of books by and about Frye, and translator's notes and acknowledgments. Casebound.

2l *Anatomy of Criticism: Four Essays*. Korean Student Edition. N.p.: United Publishing and Promotion Co., 1984. x + 383. 22.6 x 14.9 cm. 'The Korean Student Edition is exclusively authorized by Princeton University Press for manufacture and distribution in the Republic of Korea.' Paperback.

2m *Anatomy of Criticism: Four Essays*. Markham, Ont.: Penguin, 1990. x + 383 pp. 19.8 x 12.8 cm. Paperback.

2n *Anatomy of Criticism: Four Essays*. Taipei: Bookman Books, n. d. x + 383 pp. 20.7 x 14.7 cm. 'This is an authorized Taiwan edition published under special arrangement with the proprietor for sale in Taiwan only.' Paperback.

3. The Educated Imagination (1963)

3 *The Educated Imagination*. Toronto: Canadian Broadcasting Corporation, 1963. 68 pp. 20.3 x 12.4 cm. Casebound.

3a *The Educated Imagination*. Toronto: Canadian Broadcasting Corporation, 1963. 68 pp. 20.3 x 12.7 cm. Paperback.

3b *The Educated Imagination*. Bloomington: Indiana University Press, 1964. 156 pp. 20.2 x 13.3 cm. Casebound.

3c *The Educated Imagination*. Bloomington: Indiana University Press, [1966]. 156 pp. 19.9 x 12.9 cm. Paperback.

3d *The Educated Imagination*. Edited by Hisaaki Yamanouchi. Tokyo: Tsurumi shoten, 1967. viii + 135 pp. 18.2 x 12.7 cm. Paperback.

3e *Kyôyô no tame no sôzôryoko*. Translated by Toro Egawa and Masahiko Maeda. Tokyo: Taiyosha, 1969. 188 pp. 18.5 x 12.7 cm. Casebound.

3f *Pouvoirs de l'imagination: essai*. Translated by Jean Simard. Montreal: Editions HMH, 1969. 168 pp. 20.5 x 14 cm. Stiff paper wrappers.

3g *L'imaginazione coltivata*. Translated by Amleto Lorenzini and Mario

Manzari. Milan: Longanesi, 1974. 125 pp. 18.4 x 11.8 cm. Stiff paper wrappers.

4. Fables of Identity (1963)

4 *Fables of Identity: Studies in Poetic Mythology.* New York: Harcourt, Brace & World, 1963. 265 pp. 20.2 x 13.5 cm. Paperback.

4a *Favole d'identità: Studi di mitologia poetica.* Translated by Ciro Monti. Turin: Einaudi, 1973. ix + 346 pp. 18 x 10.5 cm. Paperback.

4b *Doitsusei no guwa.* Translated by Tetso Maruko et al. Tokyo: Hosei University Press, 1983. iv + 469 + 9 pp. 18.7 x 12.5 cm. Includes translator's notes and epilogue. Casebound.

5. T.S. Eliot (1963)

5 *T.S. Eliot.* Edinburgh: Oliver and Boyd, 1963. 106 pp. Paperback.

5a *T.S. Eliot.* New York: Grove, 1963. 106 pp. Paperback.

5b *T.S. Eliot.* New York: Barnes & Noble, 1966. 106 pp. Paperback.

5c *T.S. Eliot.* Rev. ed. Edinburgh: Oliver and Boyd, 1968. 106 pp. 18.2 x 11.4 cm. Paperback.

5d *Eliot.* Translated by Jesús Diaz. Madrid: Ediciones y Publicaciones Españolas, 1969. 173 pp. 17 x 11 cm. Paperback.

5e *T.S. Eliot.* New York: Capricorn Books, 1972. 106 pp. 18.4 x 10.9 cm. Paperback.

5f *T.S. Eliot: An Introduction.* Chicago: University of Chicago Press, 1981. 109 pp. 20.3 x 13.1 cm. Includes updated bibliography of secondary sources. Paperback.

5g *T.S. Eriotto.* Translated by Hikaru Endo. Tokyo: Shimizukobun-do, 1981. xvi + 150 + 71 pp. 20.8 x 14.6 cm. Casebound in slipcase.

5h *Eliot.* Translated by Gino Scatasta. Bologna: Il Mulino, 1989. 126 pp. 20.4 x 12.3 cm. Paperback.

6. The Well-Tempered Critic (1963)

6 *The Well-Tempered Critic.* Bloomington: Indiana University Press, 1963. 160 pp. 20.3 x 13.3 cm. Casebound.

6a *The Well-Tempered Critic.* Bloomington: Indiana University Press, 1965. 160 pp. 19.9 x 13 cm. Paperback.

6b *Il critico ben temperato.* Translated by Amleto Lorenzini and Mario Manzari. Milan: Longanesi, 1974. 141 pp. 18.4 x 11.7 cm. Stiff paper wrappers.

6c *Yoi hihyoka.* Translated by Michiko Watanabe. Tokyo: Yashio shuppansha, 1980. 151 pp. 18 x 12.7 cm. Casebound in slipcase.

6d *The Well-Tempered Critic.* Markham, Ont.: Fitzhenry & Whiteside, [1983]. 160 pp. 18.4 x 12.4 cm. Paperback.

6e *The Well-Tempered Critic.* Bloomington: Indiana University Press, [1983]. 160 pp. 18.4 x 12.4 cm. Paperback.

7. A Natural Perspective (1965)

7 *A Natural Perspective: The Development of Shakespearean Comedy and Romance.* New York: Columbia University Press, 1965. ix + 159 pp. 20.2 x 13.5 cm. Casebound.

7a *Shakespeares Vollendung: Eine Einführung in die Welt seiner Komödien.* Translated by Hellmut Haug. Munich: Nymphenburger Verlagshandlung, 1966. 195 pp. 20.6 x 13 cm. Paperback.

7b *A Natural Perspective: The Development of Shakespearean Comedy and Romance.* New York: Harcourt, Brace & World, [1969]. ix + 159 pp. 20.3 x 13.3 cm. Paperback.

7c *Shakespia kikeki to romance no hatten.* Translated by Konsai Ishihara and Hitoshi Ichikawa. Tokyo: Sansyusya, 1987. 241 pp. 18.7 x 12.5 cm. Casebound.

8. The Return of Eden (1965)

8 *The Return of Eden: Five Essays on Milton's Epics.* Toronto: University of Toronto Press, 1965. viii + 145 pp. 20.2 x 13.7 cm. Casebound.

8a *Five Essays on Milton's Epics.* London: Routledge & Kegan Paul, 1966. vii + 158 pp. 18.4 x 12 cm. Casebound.

8b *The Return of Eden: Five Essays on Milton's Epics.* Toronto: University of Toronto Press, 1965. viii + 145 pp. 20.2 x 13.5 cm. Paperback.

9. Fools of Time (1967)

9 *Fools of Time: Studies in Shakespearean Tragedy.* Toronto: University of Toronto Press, 1967. vii + 121 pp. 20.2 x 13.5 cm. Casebound.

9a *Fools of Time: Studies in Shakespearean Tragedy.* Toronto: University of Toronto Press, 1973. vii + 121 pp. 20.2 x 13.5 cm. Paperback.

9b *Tempo che opprime, tempo che redime: Riflessioni sul teatro di Shakespeare.* Translated by Valentina Poggi and Maria Pia De Angelis. Bologna: Il Mulino, 1986. 197 pp. 21.2 x 13.3 cm. Part 1 (pp. 13–113) is a translation by Valentina Poggi of *Fools of Time.* Part 2 (pp. 115–97) is a translation by Maria Pia De Angelis of *The Myth of Deliverance.* Paperback.

10. The Modern Century (1967)

10 *The Modern Century.* Toronto: Oxford University Press, 1967. 123 pp. 18.4 x 11.7 cm. Casebound.

10a *Le siècle de l'innovation: essai.* Translated by François Rinfret. Montreal: Editions HMH, 1968. 162 pp. 19.7 x 12.5 cm. Paperback.

10b *La culture face aux media: essai.* Translated by François Rinfret. Tours: Maison Mame, 1969. 115 pp. 21 x 10.9 cm. Paperback.

10c *The Modern Century.* London: Oxford University Press, 1969. 123 pp. 20.3 x 13.3 cm. Paperback.

10d *Cultura e miti del nostro tempo.* Translated by Vittorio Di Giuro. Milan: Rizzoli, 1969. 120 pp. 20.6 x 14.8 cm. Stiff paper wrappers.

10e *Gendai bunka no hyaku nen.* Translated by Hiroshi Ebine. Tokyo: Otowa shobo, 1971. 152 pp. 18.6 x 12.5 cm. Casebound.

10f *The Modern Century.* Edited by Toshihiko Shibata. Tokyo: Tsurumi shoten, 1971. ii + 138 pp. 18.1 x 12.7 cm. Paperback.

10g *The Modern Century.* New ed. Includes Frye's 1990 address, 'The Cultural Development of Canada.' Toronto: Oxford University Press, 1991. 135 pp. 18.5 x 11.5 cm. Paperback.

11. A Study of English Romanticism (1968)

11 *A Study of English Romanticism.* New York: Random House, 1968. vi + 180 pp. 18.3 x 10.7 cm. Paperback.

11a *A Study of English Romanticism.* Chicago: University of Chicago Press, 1982. vi + 180 pp. 20.2 x 13 cm. Paperback.

11b *A Study of English Romanticism.* Brighton, Sussex: Harvester Press, 1983. vi + 180 pp. 20.2 x 13 cm. Paperback.

11c *Igirisu Romanshyugi no Shinwa.* Translated by Michiko Watanabe. Tokyo: Yashio shuppansha, 1985. 245 pp. 18 x 12.7 cm. Casebound in slipcase.

12. The Stubborn Structure (1970)

12 *The Stubborn Structure: Essays on Criticism and Society.* Ithaca: Cornell University Press, 1970. xii + 316 pp. 21.1 x 13.9 cm. Casebound.

12a *The Stubborn Structure: Essays on Criticism and Society.* London: Methuen, 1970. xii + 316 pp. 21.1 x 13.9 cm. Casebound.

12b *The Stubborn Structure: Essays on Criticism and Society.* Ithaca: Cornell University Press, [1971]. xii + 316 pp. 21.1 x 13.7 cm. Paperback.

12c *La estructura inflexible de la obra literaria: Ensayos sobre crítica y sociedad.* Translated by Raphael Durbán Sánchez. Madrid: Taurus, 1973. 411 pp. 21 x 13.2 cm. Paperback.

12d *The Stubborn Structure: Essays on Criticism and Society.* London: Methuen, 1974. xii + 316 pp. 21.1 x 13.7 cm. Paperback.

12e *L'ostinata struttura: saggi su critica e società.* Translated by Leonardo Terzo and Anna Paschetto. Revised by Amleto Lorenzini. Milan: Rizzoli, 1975. 267 pp. 21.7 x 13.9 cm. Paperback.

12f *The Stubborn Structure: Essays on Criticism and Society.* London: Methuen, 1980. xii + 316 pp. 21.5 x 13.4 cm. Issued as Methuen Library Reprint. Casebound.

13. The Bush Garden (1971)

13 *The Bush Garden: Essays on the Canadian Imagination.* Toronto: House of Anansi, 1971. x + 256 pp. 21.5 x 13.7 cm. Casebound.

13a *The Bush Garden: Essays on the Canadian Imagination.* Toronto: House of Anansi, 1971. x + 256 pp. 21.5 x 13.5 cm. Paperback.

13b *The Bush Garden.* Translated by Sang Ran Lee. 1990. 312 pp. 22.3 x 14 cm.

14. The Critical Path (1971)

14 *The Critical Path: An Essay on the Social Context of Literary Criticism.* Bloomington: Indiana University Press, 1971. 174 pp. 20.1 x 13.5 cm. Casebound.

14a *The Critical Path: An Essay on the Social Context of Literary Criticism.* Bloomington: Indiana University Press, 1971. 174 pp. 19.8 x 13 cm. Paperback.

14b *O caminho crítico: Um ensaio sobre o contexto social da crítica literária.* Translated by Antônio Arnoni Prado. Sao Paulo: Editora Perspectiva, 1973. 169 pp. 20.5 x 11.3 cm. Paperback.

14c *Hihyo no michi.* Translated by Hiroichiro Doke. Tokyo: Kenkyu-sha, 1974. 212 pp. 18.7 x 12.8 cm. Casebound.

14d *The Critical Path: An Essay on the Social Context of Literary Criticism.* Brighton, Sussex: Harvester Press, 1983. 174 pp. 21.5 x 13.7 cm. Paperback.

14e *El camino crítico: Ensayo sobre contexto social de la crítica literaria.* Translated by Miguel Mac-Veigh. Madrid: Taurus, 1986. 21 x 13.4 cm. 149 pp. Paperback.

15. The Secular Scripture (1976)

15 *The Secular Scripture: A Study of the Structure of Romance.* Cambridge: Harvard University Press, 1976. vii + 199 pp. 20.5 x 14 cm. Casebound.

15a *The Secular Scripture: A Study of the Structure of Romance.* Cambridge: Harvard University Press, 1976. vii + 199 pp. 20.4 x 13.8 cm. Paperback.

15b *La scrittura secolare: Studio sulla struttura 'romance.'* Translated by Amleto Lorenzini. Bologna: Il Mulino, 1978. 191 pp. 21.3 x 13.1 cm. Paperback.

15c *Le escritura profana: Un studio sobre la estructura del romance.* Translated by Edison Simons. Barcelona: Monte Avila, 1980. 235 pp. 17.4 x 11.9 cm. Paperback.

15d *Le escritura profana: Un studio sobre la estructura del romance.* Translated by Edison Simons. Barcelona and Caracas: Monte Avila, 1992. 234 pp.

16. Spiritus Mundi (1976)

16 *Spiritus Mundi: Essays on Literature, Myth, and Society.* Bloomington: Indiana University Press, 1976. xvi + 296 pp. 20.8 x 13.8 cm. Casebound.

16a *Spiritus Mundi: Essays on Literature, Myth, and Society.* Bloomington: Indiana University Press, 1976. xvi + 296 pp. 21.5 x 13.4 cm. Paperback.

16b *Spiritus Mundi: Essays on Literature, Myth, and Society.* [Markham, Ont.]: Fitzhenry & Whiteside, [1983]. xvi + 296 pp. 21.5 x 13.4 cm. Paperback.

16c *Spiritus Mundi: Essays on Literature, Myth, and Society.* [Richmond Hill, Ont.]: Fitzhenry & Whiteside, [1991]. xvi + 296 pp. 21.5 x 14 cm. Paperback.

17. Northrop Frye on Culture and Literature (1978)

17 *Northrop Frye on Culture and Literature: A Collection of Review Essays.* Edited by Robert D. Denham. Chicago: University of Chicago Press, 1978. viii + 264 pp. 20.1 x 13 cm. Casebound.

17a *Northrop Frye on Culture and Literature: A Collection of Review Essays.* Edited by Robert D. Denham. Chicago: University of Chicago Press, 1978. viii + 264 pp. 20.4 x 13 cm. Paperback.

18. Creation and Recreation (1980)

18 *Creation and Recreation.* Toronto: University of Toronto Press, 1980. 76 pp. 21.5 x 13.7 cm. Paperback.

19. The Great Code (1982)

19 *The Great Code: The Bible and Literature.* New York: Harcourt Brace Jovanovich, 1982. xxiii + 261 pp. 23.2 x 15.2 cm. Casebound.

19a *The Great Code: The Bible and Literature.* Toronto: Academic Press, 1982. xxiii + 261 pp. 23.2 x 15.2 cm. Casebound.

19b *The Great Code: The Bible and Literature.* London: Routledge & Kegan Paul, 1982. xxiii + 261 pp. 23.2 x 15.2 cm. Casebound.

19c *The Great Code: The Bible and Literature.* San Diego: Harcourt Brace Jovanovich, 1983. xxiii + 261 pp. 20.3 x 13.3 cm. Paperback.

19d *The Great Code: The Bible and Literature.* Toronto: Academic Press, 1983. xxiii + 261 pp. 20.3 x 13.3 cm. Paperback.

19e *The Great Code: The Bible and Literature.* San Diego: Harcourt Brace Jovanovich, 1983. xxiii + 261 pp. 20.3 x 13.3 cm. Type has been slightly reduced for this edition, the book is printed on lighter stock, and the frontispiece has been reproduced on the inside front cover. Paperback.

19f *The Great Code: The Bible and Literature.* London: Ark Paperbacks, 1983. xxi + 261. 19.7 x 12.8 cm. Paperback.

19g *Le Grand Code: La Bible et la littérature.* Translated by Catherine Mala-moud. Preface by Tzvetan Todorov. Paris: Editions du Seuil, 1984. 339 pp. 20.4 x 13.8 cm. Paperback.

19h *Veliki kod(eks): Biblija i knjizevnost.* Translated by Novica Milic and Dragan Kujundzic. Belgrade: Prosveta, 1985. 283 pp.

19i *Il grande codice: la Bibbia e la letteratura.* Translated by Giovanni Rizzoni. Turin: Einaudi, 1986. 306 pp. 20.4 x 12.3 cm. Paperback.

19j *De Grote Code: De Bijbel en de literatuur.* Translated by Léon Stapper. Introduction by W. Bronzwaer. Nijmegen: SUN, 1986. 351 pp. 22 x 13.8 cm. Paperback.

19k *El gran código: una lectura mitológica y literaria de la Biblia.* Translated by Elizabeth Casals. Barcelona: Editoria Gedisa, 1988. 281 pp. 22.5 x 15.3 cm. Paperback.

19l *The Great Code: The Bible and Literature.* Markham, Ont.: Penguin, 1990. xxiii + 261 pp. 21 x 13.8 cm. Paperback.

19m *Den store kode: Bibelen & lityeraturen.* Translated by Ole Lindegård Henriksen. Introduction by Jan Ulrik Dyrkjoeb. Århus, Denmark: Aros, 1991. 351 pp. 13 x 20 cm. Stiff paper wrappers.

20. Divisions on a Ground (1982)

20 *Divisions on a Ground: Essays on Canadian Culture.* Edited by James Polk. Toronto: House of Anansi, 1982. 199 pp. 21.5 x 13.5 cm. Casebound.

21. The Myth of Deliverance (1983)

21 *The Myth of Deliverance: Reflections on Shakespeare's Problem Comedies.* Toronto: University of Toronto Press, 1983. viii + 90 pp. 21.4 x 13.8 cm. Paperback.

21a *The Myth of Deliverance: Reflections on Shakespeare's Problem Comedies.* Brighton, Sussex: Harvester Press, 1983. viii + 90 pp. 21.5 x 13.6 cm. Casebound.

21b *The Myth of Deliverance: Reflections on Shakespeare's Problem Comedies.* Brighton, Sussex: Harvester Press, 1983. viii + 90 pp. 21.4 x 13.9 cm. Paperback.

21c *Tempo che opprime, tempo che redime: Riflessioni sul teatro di Shakespeare.*

Translated by Valentina Poggi and Maria Pia De Angelis. Bologna: Il Mulino, 1986. 197 pp. 21.2 x 13.3 cm. Part 1 (pp. 13–113) is a translation by Valentina Poggi of *Fools of Time*. Part 2 (pp. 115–97) is a trans. by Maria Pia De Angelis of *The Myth of Deliverance*. Paperback.

21d *The Myth of Deliverance: Reflections on Shakespeare's Problem Comedies.* Introduction by A.C. Hamilton. Toronto: University of Toronto Press, 1992. 21.4 x 13.8 cm. Paperback.

22. Harper Handbook to Literature (1985)

22 [With Sheridan Baker and George W. Perkins]. *Harper Handbook to Literature.* New York: Harper & Row, 1985. ix + 563 pp. 20.9 x 13.9 cm. Paperback.

23. Northrop Frye on Shakespeare (1986)

23 *Northrop Frye on Shakespeare.* Edited by Robert Sandler. Markham, Ont.: Fitzhenry & Whiteside, 1986. vi + 186. 22.7 x 15 cm. Casebound.

23a *Northrop Frye on Shakespeare.* Edited by Robert Sandler. New Haven: Yale University Press, 1986. vi + 186 pp. 22.7 x 15 cm. Casebound.

23b *Northrop Frye on Shakespeare.* Edited by Robert Sandler. Markham, Ont.: Fitzhenry & Whiteside, 1986. vi + 186. 22.8 x 15.1 cm. Paperback.

23c *Northrop Frye on Shakespeare.* Edited by Robert Sandler. New Haven: Yale University Press, 1986. vi + 186 pp. 22.6 x 15 cm. Paperback.

23d *Shakespeare et son théâtre.* Translated by Charlotte Melançon. Paris: Boréal-Express, 1988. 272 pp. 21.4 x 13.7 cm. Paperback.

23e *Shakespeare: Nove lezioni.* Translated by Andrea Carosso. Turin: Einaudi, 1990. x + 201 pp. 25 x 12.3 cm. Paperback.

24. Northrop Frye on Education (1988)

24 *Northrop Frye on Education.* Markham, Ont.: Fitzhenry & Whiteside, 1988. 211 pp. 22.7 x 15 cm. Casebound.

24a *Northrop Frye on Education.* Ann Arbor: University of Michigan Press, 1988. 211 pp. 22.7 x 15 cm. Casebound.

24b *Northrop Frye on Education.* Markham, Ont.: Fitzhenry & Whiteside, 1990. 211 pp. 22.7 x 15 cm. Paperback.

25. Mito metaphora simbolo (1989)

25 *Mito metaphora simbolo*. Translated by Carla Plevano Pezzini and Francesca Valente Gorjup. Rome: Editori Riuniti, 1989. 218 pp. 21.5 x 14.4 cm. Paperback.

26. Myth and Metaphor (1990)

26 *Myth and Metaphor: Selected Essays, 1974–1988*. Edited by Robert D. Denham. Charlottesville: University Press of Virginia, 1990. xviii + 386 pp. 23.5 x 15.3 cm. Casebound.

26 *Myth and Metaphor: Selected Essays, 1974–1988*. Edited by Robert D. Denham. Charlottesville: University Press of Virginia, 1991. xviii + 386 pp. 23.4 x 15.1 cm. Paperback.

27. Words with Power (1990)

27 *Words with Power: Being a Second Study of 'The Bible and Literature.'* New York: Harcourt Brace Jovanovich, 1990. xxiv + 342 pp. 22.5 x 15 cm. Casebound.

27a *Words with Power: Being a Second Study of 'The Bible and Literature.'* Toronto: Viking, 1990. xxiv + 342 pp. 22.5 x 15 cm. Casebound.

27b *Words with Power: Being a Second Study of 'The Bible and Literature.'* Toronto: Penguin, 1992. xxiv + 342 pp. 21 x 14 cm. Paperback.

27c *Words with Power: Being a Second Study of 'The Bible and Literature.'* New York: Harcourt Brace Jovanovich, 1992. xxiv + 342 pp. 21 x 14 cm. Paperback.

28. Reading the World (1990)

28 *Reading the World: Selected Writings, 1935–1976*. Edited by Robert D. Denham. New York: Peter Lang, 1990. xvi + 416 pp. 22.7 x 15 cm. Casebound.

29. The Double Vision (1991)

29 *The Double Vision: Language and Meaning in Religion*. Toronto: United Church Publishing House, 1991. xviii + 85 pp. 22.4 x 15.1 cm. Paperback.

29a *The Double Vision: Language and Meaning in Religion*. Toronto: University of Toronto Press, 1991. xviii + 85 pp. 22.7 x 15 cm. Casebound.

29b *The Double Vision: Language and Meaning in Religion.* Toronto: University of Toronto Press, 1991. xviii + 85 pp. 22.4 x 15.1 cm. Paperback.

29c *La duplice visione.* Translated by Francesca Valente Gorjup and Carla Plevano Pezzini. Venice: Marsilo, 1992.

30. A World in a Grain of Sand (1991)

30 *A World in a Grain of Sand: Twenty-Two Interviews with Northrop Frye.* Edited by Robert D. Denham. New York: Peter Lang, 1991. 351 pp. 22.7 x 15 cm. Casebound.

31. Reflections on the Canadian Literary Imagination (1992)

31 *Reflections on the Canadian Literary Imagination: A Selection of Essays by Northrop Frye.* Edited and introduced by Branko Gorjup. Afterword by Agostino Lombardo. Rome: Bulzoni Editore, 1992. 196 pp. 15 x 21 cm. Stiff paper wrappers.

32. Northrop Frye in Conversation (1992)

32 *Northrop Frye in Conversation.* Interview with David Cayley. Concord, Ont.: House of Anansi, 1992. x + 228 pp. Paperback.

33. The Eternal Act of Creation (1993)

33 *The Eternal Act of Creation: Essays, 1979–90.* Edited by Robert D. Denham. Bloomington: Indiana University Press, 1993. xix + 188 pp. 15.2 x 23.5 cm. Casebound.

34 *Letteratura e arti visive e altri saggi.* Translated by Francesca Valente Gorjup. Catanzano: Abramo. Forthcoming.

BOOKS EDITED

35 John Milton. *'Paradise Lost' and Selected Poetry and Prose.* New York: Holt, Rinehart and Winston, 1951. xxxviii + 601 pp. 18.7 x 12 cm. Paperback.

36 Pelham Edgar. *Across My Path.* Toronto: Ryerson, 1952. xiv + 167 pp. 21.1 x 13.7 cm. Casebound.

37 William Blake. *Selected Poetry and Prose of William Blake.* New York: Modern Library, 1953. xxx + 475 pp. 17.7 x 11.8 cm. Casebound.

37a William Blake. *Selected Poetry and Prose of William Blake*. Modern Library College Editions. New York: Modern Library, 1953. xxx + 475 pp. 18.2 x 10.8 cm. Paperback.

38 Charles Trick Currelly. *I Brought the Ages Home*. Toronto: Ryerson, 1956. xx + 312 pp. 22.4 x 14.8 cm. Casebound.

38a Charles Trick Currelly. *I Brought the Ages Home*. Toronto: Ryerson, 1967. xx + 312 pp. 20.2 x 13.2 cm. Paperback.

39 *Sound and Poetry: English Institute Essays, 1956*. New York: Columbia University Press, 1957. xxvii + 156 pp. 19.6 x 13.5 cm. Casebound.

40 E.J. Pratt. *The Collected Poems of E.J. Pratt*. 2nd ed. Toronto: Macmillan, 1958. xxviii + 395. 22.7 x 13.7 cm. Casebound.

41 William Shakespeare. *The Tempest*. Pelican Shakespeare. Gen. ed. Alfred Harbage. Baltimore: Penguin, 1959. 112 pp. Paperback.

41a William Shakespeare. *The Tempest*. Rev. ed. Pelican Shakespeare. Gen. ed. Alfred Harbage. Baltimore: Penguin, 1970. 112 pp. 18 x 11 cm. Paperback.

42 Peter F. Fisher. *The Valley of Vision: Blake as Prophet and Revolutionary*. Toronto: University of Toronto Press, 1961. xi + 261 pp. 22.7 x 15 cm. Casebound.

43 *Design for Learning: Reports Submitted to the Joint Committee of the Toronto Board of Education and the University of Toronto*. Toronto: University of Toronto Press, 1962. x + 148 pp. 23 x 14.7 cm. Casebound.

44 *Romanticism Reconsidered: Selected Papers of the English Institute*. New York: Columbia University Press, 1963. ix + 144 pp. 19.6 x 13.5 cm. Casebound.

45 *Blake: A Collection of Critical Essays*. Englewood Cliffs, NJ: Prentice-Hall, 1966. 183 pp. 20.2 x 14.2 cm. Casebound.

45a *Blake: A Collection of Critical Essays*. Englewood Cliffs, NJ: Prentice-Hall, 1966. 183 pp. 20.2 x 14.2 cm. Paperback.

46 [With James V. Logan and John E. Jordan]. *Some British Romantics: A Collection of Essays*. Columbus: Ohio State University Press, 1966. 343 pp. 20.9 x 13.8 cm. Casebound.

47 [General editor]. *Shakespeare Series. I: King Lear, Twelfth Night, Antony and Cleopatra*. New York: Odyssey Press, 1968. Paperback.

47a [General editor]. *Shakespeare Series. II: Hamlet, The Tempest, Henry IV, Part I*. New York: Odyssey Press, 1969. xx + 519. Paperback.

[**47** and **47a** were part of the College Classics in English series, also published in Toronto by Macmillan. Frye was general editor for twelve other volumes in the series, although his General Editor's Introduction appears only in the two volumes of the *Shakespeare Series*.]

48 [Supervisory editor]. *Literature: Uses of the Imagination*. 12 vols. New York: Harcourt Brace Jovanovich, 1972–4. 23.2 x 17.7 Paperbacks.

49 [With Sheridan Baker and George Perkins]. *The Practical Imagination: Stories, Poems, Plays*. New York: Harper & Row, 1980. xxi + 1448 pp. 23.3 x 14.8 cm. Casebound.

49a [With Sheridan Baker, George Perkins, and Barbara Perkins]. *The Practical Imagination: Stories, Poems, Plays*. Revised, compact edition. New York: Harper & Row, 1987. xix + 1445 pp. 23.5 x 15.4 cm. Paperback.

49b [Edited with Sheridan Baker and George Perkins]. *The Practical Imagination: An Introduction to Poetry*. New York: Harper & Row, 1983. xx + 499 pp. 23.4 x 15.4 cm. Paperback.